GEARY AND KANSAS.

GOVERNOR GEARY'S ADMINISTRATION

IN

KANSAS:

WITH A COMPLETE

HISTORY OF THE TERRITORY

UNTIL JULY **1857**:

EMBRACING A FULL ACCOUNT OF

ITS DISCOVERY, GEOGRAPHY, SOIL, RIVERS, CLIMATE, PRODUCTS; ITS ORGANIZATION AS A TERRITORY, TRANSACTIONS AND EVENTS UNDER GOVERNORS REEDER AND SHANNON, POLITICAL DISSENSIONS, PERSONAL RENCOUNTRES, ELECTION FRAUDS, BATTLES AND OUTRAGES.

ALL FULLY AUTHENTICATED.

BY

JOHN H. GIHON, M.D.,
PRIVATE SECRETARY OF GOVERNOR GEARY.

PHILADELPHIA:
CHAS. C. RHODES.
1857.

PREFACE.

In giving this work to the public, the author has been actuated solely by a sense of duty. Unbiassed by any partisan or personal considerations, he has related, in as plain and comprehensive a manner as possible, the facts, as they came under his own observation, were communicated to him by individuals immediately connected with the events described, or have been gleaned from other reliable sources.

The writer is alone responsible for the contents of the book. During his official connection with Governor Geary, he availed himself of his opportunities for information, and has substantiated many of his statements, by the official documents, now on file in the Department of State at Washington, and which passed through his hands in the executive office in Kansas. These are public property, and there has been no impropriety or breach of trust in their employment.

Many important incidents have been omitted for want of sufficient corroboration; the writer having determined to tell the truth, and nothing but the truth. The *whole* truth can only be brought to light in that great day when all human secrets and mysteries will be revealed.

The author cannot be accused of any undue prejudices in

favor of the free-soil party. When he went to Kansas, all his proclivities were on the opposite side, which he did not hesitate to make known on all proper occasions, and among all classes of people. The free-soilers regarded him as their enemy, and the pro-slavery leaders received him with marked favor as a new accession to their forces. With the latter he constantly associated, and his impressions were strengthened by their representations of territorial affairs. Hence his letters to the eastern papers, with which he corresponded, were severely condemnatory of the free-state party of Kansas. He resisted as long as possible the daily accumulating evidences of his error; but with many others like himself, was at length forced, though unwillingly, to acknowledge the truth of the statements contained in this volume.

Governor Geary, during his administration in Kansas, observed a strict neutrality in regard to the question of slavery, and invariably pursued that impartial line of policy which his official documents indicate. He was, however, a firm and unwavering Democrat, and for aught that has appeared to the contrary, still adheres closely to the party with which he has always been associated. The writer is also an advocate of the true principles of Democracy; but he repudiates that new plank which has been surreptitiously inserted into the Democratic platform, that gives to the single idea of slavery extension an ascendancy over every other consideration.

CONTENTS.

CHAPTER VI.

CHAPTER VII.

CHAPTER VIII.

CHAPTER IX.

CHAPTER X.

CHAPTER XI.

CHAPTER XII.

CHAPTER XIII.

CHAPTER XIV.

CHAPTER XV.

CHAPTER XVI.

CHAPTER XVII.

CHAPTER XVIII.

CHAPTER XIX.

CHAPTER XX.

CHAPTER XXI.

CHAPTER XXII.

CHAPTER XXIII.

CHAPTER XXIV.

CHAPTER XXV.

CHAPTER XXVI.

CHAPTER XXVII.

CHAPTER XXVIII.

CHAPTER XXIX.

CHAPTER XXX.

CHAPTER XXXI.

CHAPTER XXXII.

CHAPTER XXXIII.

CHAPTER XXXIV.

CHAPTER XXXV.

CHAPTER XXXVI.

CHAPTER XXXVII.

CHAPTER XXXVIII.

CHAPTER XXXIX.

CHAPTER XL.

CHAPTER XLI.

CHAPTER XLII.

CHAPTER XLIII.

CHAPTER XLIV.

CHAPTER XLV.

APPENDIX.

HISTORY OF KANSAS.

CHAPTER I.

Description of the Territory,—Its boundaries—rivers—prairies—woodlands—soil—climate—appearance—and general characteristics.

THE territory of Kansas is a strip of land over two hundred miles in width, extending from the western boundary of Missouri to the highest ridge of the Rocky Mountains. It is bounded on the north by the territory of Nebraska; on the east by the state of Missouri; on the south by the Indian Territory and New Mexico; and on the west by the territory of Utah.

Its principal river is the Kaw or Kansas, which empties into the Missouri in latitude 39°, and longitude 94°, at the southern point, where that river separates the territory from the state of Missouri. It flows eastward to this point, receiving in its course many tributaries, some of which, the Republican and the Smoky Hill Forks, take their rise in the Rocky Mountains.

The north-western portion of the territory is watered by the tributaries of the Platte, which flows through Nebraska; and the eastern and southern districts by the Osage and Upper Arkansas and their branches.

None of these streams are navigable. A light-draught steamboat has passed up the Kansas more than one hundred miles, to Fort Riley; but very few attempts have been made to repeat the experiment. They might be successful, with a boat drawing from twelve to twenty inches of water, two or three months in the year. The bed of this river is wide, and the bottom a quicksand, which is constantly shifting with the current, forming bars and changing the course of the channel. Its water is always muddy, like that of the Missouri, whilst some of the streams that empty into it are remarkable for their clearness and purity. A number of these branches which, during the seasons of freshets, swell to streams of considerable magnitude, are perfectly dry the greater portion of the year, although in many places pure water can be obtained a short distance below the dry surface.

The only portion of the territory that possesses any peculiar value for agricultural purposes, is the eastern district, extending from the northern to the southern boundary, and varying from one hundred to two hundred miles westward from the Missouri line. This district is remarkable for the exquisite beauty of its scenery, and the unrivalled fertility of its soil. It is a high rolling prairie, covered in the summer months with tall grass, sprinkled with an immense variety of beautiful flowers, and over which the eye has an unbroken prospect for many miles in extent.

The soil is a rich black loam, several feet deep, with a porous clay subsoil, resting upon a limestone basis, and is capable of producing hemp, maize, wheat, and all the grains, vegetables and fruits common to temperate regions, in vast abundance and in great perfection.

Timber is confined exclusively to the margins of the numerous rivers and creeks, along the smaller of which it consists chiefly of stunted oaks, cotton-wood, &c., insignificant in quantity and of but little value. But the banks of the Kansas, Osage, Arkansas, Wakarusa, and other of the more important streams, are lined with wide strips of forest, embracing large quantities of heavy and valuable timber, among which are found white and black oak, walnut, hickory, elm, ash, sycamore, maple, cotton-wood, and other useful varieties.

There is an abundance of excellent stone for building purposes in all this region, and good coal is said to be plentiful.

The only game worth naming is the prairie-fowl or grouse, and this is not so abundant as in Illinois. But few fish are found in the streams, the varieties being chiefly the buffalo and catfish, the latter attaining an enormous size, and, like those of the Mississippi River, scarcely fit for food.

The country west of this district, for a number of miles, is well described in a letter dated December 27th, 1856, addressed to Governor Geary by Lieutenant Francis T. Bryan, of the United States corps of Engineers, and furnishing an account of a journey he had just completed.

"My route," he says, "can easily be followed on the map accompanying Stansbury's report, or, indeed, any other reliable map of the Territory. Leaving Fort Riley, I went up the Republican River for one hundred and five miles. This valley is fertile, and is cut by many creeks, with wooded banks. Out of the valley, or bottom of the river, the country is high and covered with short buffalo grass. The stone of the country is limestone.

"Leaving the Republican, the route led over the high prairie thirty-five miles to the Little Blue River, crossing several small creeks, with wooded banks. This country, I think, would be too dry for agricultural purposes. Crossing the Little Blue, the route lies along its banks for about fifteen miles, and then leaving the river, goes to the Platte, touching several water holes. From the point where the road first touches the Platte to Fort Kearney, is about fifteen miles, and along the valley of the Platte. The distance from Fort Riley to Fort Kearney we made one hundred and ninety-three miles.

"From Fort Kearney the route lay along the valley of the Platte for about two hundred miles. This valley is too well known to need any description. There is little or no wood, and the soil is sandy. Any attempt at agriculture, I think, would prove a failure.

"Crossing the South Platte below the mouth of Pole Creek, we followed the creek to its head in the Black Hills. The country is generally high, grass mostly short, and no wood for most of the distance. Buffalo chips are used for fuel. Pole Creek breaks through two ranges of hills, which we called Pine Bluffs and Cedar Bluffs. These are the only points where wood can be obtained along the creek until the Black Hills are reached. Grass can be found in spots.

"The route then crossed the Black Hills, where was plenty of fuel and water, but very little grass. Leaving these hills, we found ourselves in the Plains of Laramie, and crossed the east branch of the Laramie River at about five miles from the foot of the hills. About four miles further appears the first fork of Laramie River. Both of these streams have good water and good grass, but little fuel.

"We then struck the emigrant road near the Medicine Bow Mountains, and followed it to the crossing of the South Platte, having wood, water and grass at convenient distances. The road is over a gravelly soil, and is generally very good and hard. Hard stone, such as granites, &c., is found in these parts.

"Crossing the South Platte, we struck for the head of Sage Creek, over a most barren and desolate-looking country. Very little fuel or grass. Water was in abundance, and small patches of grass and clumps of trees were found in the hills. Coal was found on the South Platte, a few miles from where we crossed it, and in a situation where it could easily be worked.

"Buffaloes were seen in large numbers, from the Republican over to the Platte, and for some days up the Platte. Then the game consisted almost entirely of deer. In the Black Hills, and through the Plains of Laramie, antelopes, wolves, and elks were seen and killed, besides prairie dogs, hares, sage chickens, &c.

"The country through which we had passed on the outward route, was, with little exception, sterile, being too high, dry and stony to possess much value in an agricultural point of view. Along the creeks were some small strips of wood land.

"The return route was over the same country as the outward route until we reached the east fork of the Laramie River. Then turning to the south we followed the *Cache-la-Paudre* to its mouth in the South Platte, passing over several very pretty valleys, and having plenty of wood and grass. Following down the South Platte for several days, we came to where the river turns to go north. The country is the same as elsewhere on the Platte. Then sixty miles across a barren region of land and hills, with little water or grass, to a creek emptying into the Republican. For the first one hundred miles down the Republican the country is barren and sandy, with little wood. It then improves. The soil is better, and there are numerous creeks with wooded banks. The river bottom is of good soil, and furnishes excellent grass in large quantity, which affords pasturage to immense numbers of buffaloes. This kind of country continues on to Fort Riley.

"Along the main streams of the Platte, Republican, and Solomon's Fork, the wood is almost entirely cotton-wood. On the creeks which empty into them, it is generally hard wood, such as ash, elm, walnut, &c. On the Solomon's Fork, the soil of the bottom land appears even better than that on the Republican, and the wooded creeks quite as numerous. These bottoms are very wide in places, and covered with excellent grass. Buffaloes and elk are found in this region also, and in great numbers.

"I have thus given you a hasty view of the country over which we have passed. That along the lower part of the Republican and Solomon's Fork appears to be by far the best that we saw, though there are some very pretty spots on the creeks in the mountains; but there is no good land in large bodies in that region."

The section beyond that travelled by Lieut. Bryan, embracing the space between the Black Hills and the main chain of the Rocky Mountains, is thus described by another writer:—

"Here nature has presented us with every variety and aspect of soil. There are stupendous mountains, the grandeur and sublimity of which create mingled emotions of awe and terror. There are beautiful valleys, embosomed by amphitheatres of hills, where Calypso and her nymphs might have delighted to ramble, variegated by hill and dale, traversed by sparkling rivulets, and adorned with placid lakes. Fruits and flowers spangle the green sward; vines hang in festoons from tree to tree; cascades spring in rainbow hues from the cliffs; pines and cedars, the growth of ages, spread their sombre shade upon the mountain sides, and the stupendous peaks, shooting up into the skies, are crowned with a glittering coronet of snow.

"A few hours' travel leads us out of this scene of primeval beauty into one in intense contrast with it. Here we find a sterile expanse of many miles in extent, covered with waving lines of sand, producing only stunted artemesia and a few other miserable plants. The rivulets are lost as they descend from the bare ridges around; their hollow murmurs may be heard beneath the feet; and the surrounding peaks are immense piles of bare granite, which seem to have been thrown by some great convulsion into inextricable confusion."

The climate is not so agreeable as in the same latitudes nearer the Atlantic sea-board. It is dry and variable. The changes of weather are frequent, sudden, and severe, the thermometer not unfrequently rising and falling thirty or forty degrees in a few hours. This is specially the case during the winter season. High winds are very prevalent, sweeping fiercely and almost daily over the unbroken prairies.

Along the banks of the rivers and smaller streams, the only places where settlements to any extent have yet been made, bilious and intermittent fevers are as common as in more southern latitudes on the Mississippi River. The progress of agriculture will not improve the condition of the country in this regard, as an unhealthy miasma must necessarily arise from turning under to any great extent the heavy sod, and exposing the rich soil to the atmosphere and the rays of the sun. This will in a measure be counterbalanced by the erection of more substantial and suitable habitations for the people, the supply of a greater variety of wholesome food, and other sources and means of health and comfort. To the want of these, as well as to the unsteady habits of a large portion of the population, may justly be attributed much of the sickness that has heretofore prevailed.

CHAPTER II.

Discovery and early exploration of Kansas.—The Indians of the Territory.—Their reserves.—The Shawnee Mission.

THE discovery of the valley of the Missouri is said to have been made by Father Marquette, a French missionary, about the year 1673; and that portion of the country now embraced in the Territory of Kansas, appears to have first been explored by M. Dutisne, a French officer, sent by his government for that purpose, in 1719. At that time it was claimed as part of the empire of Louis XIV. In 1762, it was ceded by France to Spain, and thus passed under the dominion of the Spanish crown; but subsequently, (in 1800,) it was ceded back to France. In 1801 it came into the possession of the United States, through the negotiation of Thomas Jefferson, by which, for fifteen millions of dollars, he purchased all the western territory belonging to the French government.

When first discovered to the civilized world, and until within a very few years, the Territory of Kansas was occupied solely by a few roving tribes of Indians, whose subsistence was obtained by hunting. There were no civilized residents, in fact, until about the time of its organization, except the few Christian missionaries who went there to convert the Indians; the soldiers by whom the forts were garrisoned; the fur traders; and such of the Indians who had mingled with the white people in other districts, or were connected with the missions.

No use was made of this country by the government, until, it becoming necessary to remove the Indian tribes occupying districts where the progress of civilization rendered it inexpedient for them to remain, some of its best lands were granted to them by treaty, upon which they settled, and have since possessed. These tribes are the Shawnees, Delawares, Potawattomies, Wyandots, Kickapoos, Ottowas, Chippewas, Sacks and Foxes, Peorias and Kaskaskias, Weas and Piankshaws.

The immense tracts of land appropriated to the use of these Indians, were, at the time the treaties were severally made, considered of little importance; but the great flood of civilized emigration that has steadily been pouring westward, has so increased their value as to render their owners the wealthiest, though the most miserable population in the world.

The reservation of the Wyandots, but few in number, was purchased from the Delawares, and is, perhaps, the most eligible and valuable in the Territory. It is the fork at the confluence of the Kansas and Missouri Rivers. It extends six miles from the mouth of the Kansas, and embraces twenty-three thousand, nine hundred and sixty acres. The towns of Wyandot and Quindaro, both of which promise to be of some importance, are upon this reserve. The shares in these towns have recently attracted the attention of speculators, and have reached and obtained almost fabulous prices. A Wyandot Indian, (half breed,) named Walker, is at the head of this speculative movement, and was a member of the late Legislative Assembly of Kansas. He is a shrewd and intelligent man, and will make the most of his opportunities to acquire a princely fortune.

Immediately above the Wyandot begins the Delaware reserve. It stretches along the north side of the Kansas River westward forty miles, and to an equal or greater distance northward on the Missouri. It is a beautiful tract of prairie and woodland, and lies in a position to give it eminent advantages and make it especially valuable. Leavenworth City is built upon this reservation, the entire northern portion of which has for some time been covered with squatters, in violation of the Indian treaty, and in despite of a protest issued by the chiefs of the tribe. The whole of this large reserve, however, was sold in November, 1856, agreeably to a treaty made with the Delawares on the 6th of May, 1854, except a strip on the north side of the Kansas River, forty miles long and ten miles wide. According to the Proclamation of the President, the lots were to have been sold at public auction to the highest bidder, after having been appraised by appointed commissioners, none of them to be disposed of, however, at prices lower than were fixed by the appraisement. But at a meeting of the squatters, it was resolved that no competition should be permitted at the sales; that each man should be allowed to purchase his own claim at the appraised value; and to commit violence upon those who should attempt to bid against him. This arrangement was mutually agreed to by the auctioneer, the Indian agent, the settlers, and the speculators, many of whom had assembled from distant parts, at Fort Leavenworth, where the sales were conducted. It was argued that the settlers having improved the lands and thus enhanced their value, the government would do them injustice by allowing others to purchase, and thus deprive them of the money and labor they had bestowed upon their claims. The proper reply was, that they had violated a treaty of the government with the Indians, in making those settlements and improvements, and instead of being rewarded were deserving of punishment for that act. But then, again, the government had neglected its duty in not driving these squatters from their settlements before the improvements were made. In allowing them to remain their right was virtually acknowledged. At all events, the lands were sold; squatter sovereignty prevailed; and the Indians received more money for their possessions than they had any reason to expect, quite as much as they deserved, and too much for their own best interests. The balance of this reserve is now covered with squatters, some of them having staked out and laid claims to entire sections, and the same policy is being pursued toward it as that which governed the trust lands that were sold.

The half-breed Kaws, of whom there are but several, own a tract of heavy woodland, equal in value to any in the territory, directly west of the Delaware reserve on the north side of the Kansas River. This is the tract, for speculating in which, Governor Reeder and Judges Elmore and Johnson were ostensibly removed from office; though it is alleged in some quarters, that there were stronger reasons than his desire to purchase a few acres of Indian lands, that actuated the powers at Washington in this measure, so far as the governor was concerned. This reserve, like every other in the territory, is now covered with squatters who are making fortunes by cutting the fine timber for the neighboring saw-mills, and are unmolested by the Indian agents.

The Potawattomie reserve is a spacious tract west of the Kaws, and lying on both sides of the Kansas River. This reserve is also taken up by settlers, who, without being disturbed by the government agents, are making the best of their time by cutting the timber for fuel and building purposes.

Just south of the northern line of Kansas, on the Missouri River, there is a reservation for the Iowas, another for the Sacks and Foxes from Missouri, and a colony of half-breeds. The Sacks and Foxes from the Upper Mississippi are located on the Osage River. These reserves are small, and the tribes number but few families.

The land assigned to the Kickapoos is a fine tract of prairie country, of about twelve hundred square miles, westward and northward of the Delaware reservation and south of the small tribes above named.

The Shawnees is the most important tribe in the territory. They are more numerous and farther advanced than any others in civilization. Their reserve is one of the most fertile tracts of land, chiefly prairie, in Kansas. It is well watered with several considerable streams and has an abundance of excellent timber. It lies on the Missouri border south of the Kansas River, and covers a space of country equal in extent to about fifty miles square. While the late legislature were making arrangements for the passage of a law to take the census of Kansas preparatory to an election for delegates to form a State Constitution, about three thousand citizens of Missouri, partly to seize upon the Indian lands, and partly to be registered as voters to carry out the object of the contemplated act, were rushing across the border and staking out claims upon this reservation. On every quarter section they laid what they call a "foundation." This is done by placing four poles upon the ground in the form of a square. In order to conform as they supposed, more fully to the letter, if not the spirit of the pre-emption laws, some of these ingenious squatters, also "roofed in" their "foundations." This was accomplished by standing a pole upright in the centre of the square and nailing to the top of it a half-dozen shingles to represent a roof. In looking at these singular creations, it is difficult to determine which most to admire, the ingenuity or the dishonesty which could prompt men to resort to such miserable pretexts to avail themselves unjustly of the benefit of a law, the true meaning and intent of which is too clearly and definitely expressed to be misunderstood. Having laid their foundations and shingled their houses, and thus established their claims, agreeably, as they pretend, to the requirements of the pre-emption laws, to lands granted by solemn treaty to the Indians, and having registered their names as citizens and legal voters, these worthy squatters returned to their Missouri homes, to await the election day, and then come back to exercise the freeman's right of suffrage and stultify the votes of actual and honest settlers. Should the lands be opened for pre-emption and settlement by treaty with the Shawnees, as is anticipated, the claims made upon these shallow pretexts, will be maintained with pistol and bowie-knife, against any who may dare to question their legality. Such is squatter sovereignty as understood and practised on the western borders of Missouri.

On this reservation, near Westport, Mo., stands the "Shawnee Mission" of the Methodist Church South. Three sections of their best lands were granted by the Shawnees to this mission, which are handsomely fenced in, partly with stone, and upon which are erected several substantial and capacious brick buildings, all of which has been accomplished by government funds and per centages on Indian annuities. Two sections of the three comprising this elegant farm, which is better improved and more profitably cultivated than any in the territory, has, by skilful management on his part, become the property of Rev. Thomas Johnson, the head of the church, and late President of the Council of the Legislative Assembly.

Although there are shades of difference in the moral condition and industrial habits of the Indians in Kansas, there are very few of them, who are likely to profit materially by the arts of civilization. It is an exception to the general rule when a full blooded Indian is found to possess any admirable traits of character. Neither education nor Christianity seems to make any marked improvement in his habits or deportment. He is improvident, inhospitable and treacherous, with just industry and energy enough to keep himself from starvation, but not enough to pay any proper regard to personal cleanliness. Yet it is no uncommon thing to hear white men boast of the possession of Indian blood. What peculiar enviable quality it is supposed to impart it would be difficult to determine. An anecdote is told of a certain judge, the head of one of the "first families in Virginia," who was exceedingly proud of his Indian origin. He was haughty, vain, tyrannical and somewhat celebrated for his ill manners. In conversation with a gentleman, who happened to make a remark that displeased him, the judge insolently replied: "I suppose, sir, you do not know that I have Indian blood in my veins?" "No sir," was the answer, "I did not *know* it, but I would *judge* so from your behaviour!"

The destiny of the Indian races, is so plainly written that it can easily be read. The idea that they can live among and mingle with white people, acquire their habits and adopt their customs, is not entertained by any who understand their character. They will readily learn and imitate all the evil practices of civilized life, but they generally fail to profit by those which are good.

The recent treaties with the different tribes, are intended to give to each individual of each tribe his own quota of land, and not again to attempt their removal to a distant locality. The land thus acquired, they are too indolent to cultivate. It will soon pass into the hands of the crafty and grasping white man, and the proceeds be squandered in the purchase of bad whiskey. If sloth, and filth, and drunkenness fail to kill them, they must leave the white man's settlements, and wander, (who can tell where?) fugitives and vagabonds upon the face of the earth. Another century will not have passed, when the Indians of America will have an existence only on the pages of history.

CHAPTER III.

Application of Missouri for admission into the Union.—The restriction and compromise bills of 1818-19-20.—Debates on the Kansas-Nebraska Bill.—The Organic Act of Kansas Territory.

THE inhabitants of Missouri being desirous of admission into the Union, a bill for that purpose was introduced into Congress in the session of 1818–19. In consequence of Mr. Taylor, of New York, having introduced into it what was then called "the Restriction," providing that involuntary slavery should not exist in the proposed new State, the bill, after having passed in the House of Representatives, was lost in the Senate.

After the adjournment of Congress, the "restriction" became a question of very general public interest. It was liberally discussed in the leading journals, and speeches in relation to it were delivered to large assemblies by some of the most prominent men of the country.

It was revived in Congress at its next session, which met on the 7th December, 1819, and debated in both Houses for a great length of time with a bitterness of feeling on both sides which exceeded anything that had ever been known in the national councils.

At length a "compromise" was proposed by Mr. Thomas, of Illinois, fixing the line of 36° 30′ as the future boundary between free and slave States. This, at first, met with little better favor in certain quarters than the absolute "restriction," and was discussed with quite as much spirit and rancor. It finally, however, passed both Houses, and after being submitted by President Monroe to all the members of his Cabinet to ascertain their opinions in regard to its constitutionality, it received his signature and became a law on the 6th of March, 1820.

The distinguishing feature of this bill is embraced in the following section:

"SECT. 8. *And be it further enacted*, That in all that territory ceded by France to the United States, under the name of Louisiana, which lies north of 36° 30′ north, not within the limits of the state contemplated by this act, slavery and involuntary servitude, otherwise than in the punishment of crime, whereof the parties shall have been duly convicted, shall be and hereby is, forever prohibited."

It was generally supposed that by the passage of this act the question of slavery extension in the United States was forever set at rest. But on the 7th of June, 1836, a bill was passed, without opposition, ceding to Missouri a triangular piece of land between the Missouri River and the west line of the State. By the "compromise," this tract, lying north of 36° 30′, was, with all other portions of the Territories, to be forever free from slavery; but from the period of its cession to Missouri until the present time, slaves have been introduced and held therein.

At the session of Congress for 1853–'4, a bill was introduced which provided that all that part of the territory of the United States included between the summit of the Rocky Mountains on the west, the States of Missouri and Iowa on the east, the 43° 30′ north latitude on the north, and the Territory of New Mexico and the parallel of 36° 30′ north latitude on the south, should be organized into a temporary government by the name of the Territory of Nebraska.

This bill was introduced to the Senate by Mr. Dodge, of Iowa, on the 14th of December, 1853, and referred to the Committee on Territories, and on the 4th of January following was reported back by Mr. Douglas, of Illinois, chairman of the committee, with sundry important amendments; and subsequently the same gentleman introduced a substitute for the original bill, which provided for the creation of two territories—Kansas and Nebraska—and repealed or abrogated the compromise of 1820 respecting the extension of slavery.

The debates upon this bill were even more strong, if possible, than those which resulted in the passage of the compromise act. Nor was the interest excited confined to Washington. The whole country was awakened to the importance of the measure proposed, and public meetings were held in various localities either for its approval or condemnation. Speeches especially characterized by the violence of their denunciations were delivered; the press teemed with partisan maledictions; and addresses and petitions were forwarded to Congress to influence its action. In both Houses the discussion was carried on with a vehemence and passion rarely exhibited in a deliberative body.

Several amendments were made to the substitute of Mr. Douglas before its final passage on the 25th of May, 1854. It received the signature of President Pierce on the 30th of the same month. The most important part of this act, so far as it relates to the Territory of Kansas, is as follows:

"SECT. 19. *And be it further enacted*, That all that part of the territory of the United States included within the following limits, except such portions thereof as are hereinafter expressly exempted from the operations of this act, to wit, beginning at a point on the western boundary of the state of Missouri, where the thirty-seventh parallel of north latitude crosses the same; thence west on said parallel to the eastern boundary of New Mexico; thence north on said boundary to latitude thirty-eight; thence following said boundary westward to the east boundary of the Territory of Utah, on the summit of the Rocky Mountains; thence northward on said summit to the fortieth parallel of latitude; thence east on said parallel to the western boundary of the state of Missouri; thence south with the western boundary of said state to the place of beginning, be, and the same is, hereby created into a temporary government by the name of the Territory of Kansas; and when admitted as a state or states, the said territory, or any portion of the same, shall be received into the Union with or without slavery, as their constitution may prescribe at the time of their admission: *Provided*, That nothing in this act contained shall be construed to inhibit the government of the United States from dividing said territory into two or more territories, in such manner and at such times as Congress shall deem convenient and proper, or from attaching any portion of said territory to any other state or territory of the United States: *Provided further*, That nothing in this act contained shall be construed to impair the rights of persons or property now pertaining to the Indians in said territory, so long as such rights shall remain unextinguished by treaty between the United States and such Indians, or to include any territory which, by treaty with any Indian tribe, is not, without the consent of said tribe, to be included within the territorial limits or jurisdiction of any state or territory; but all such territory shall be excepted out of the boundaries, and constitute no part of the Territory of Kansas, until said tribe shall signify their assent to the President of the United States to be included within the said Territory of Kansas, or to affect the authority of the government of the United States to make any regulation respecting such Indians, their lands, property, or other rights, by treaty, law, or otherwise, which it would have been competent to the government to make if this act had never passed."

"SECT. 32. *And be it further enacted*, That a delegate to the House of Representatives of the United States, to serve for the term of two years, who shall be a citizen of the United States, may be elected by the voters qualified to elect members of the legislative assembly, who shall be entitled to the same rights and privileges as are exercised and enjoyed by the delegates from the several other territories of the United States to the said House of Representatives, but the delegate first elected shall hold his seat only during the term of the Congress to which he shall be elected. The first election shall be held at such time and places, and be conducted in such manner as the governor shall appoint and direct; and at all subsequent elections the times, places, and manner of holding the elections, shall be prescribed by law. The person having the greatest number of votes shall be declared by the governor to be duly elected; and a certificate thereof shall be given accordingly. That the constitution and all laws of the United States which are not locally inapplicable, shall have the same force and effect within the said Territory of Kansas as elsewhere within the United States, except the eighth section of the act preparatory to the admission of Missouri into the Union, approved March sixth, eighteen hundred and twenty, which being inconsistent with the principles of non-intervention by Congress with slavery in the states and territories, as recognised by the legislation of eighteen hundred and fifty, commonly called the compromise measures, is hereby declared inoperative and void; it being the true intent and meaning of this act not to legislate slavery into any territory or state, nor to exclude it therefrom, but to leave the people thereof perfectly free to form and regulate their domestic institutions in their own way, subject only to the Constitution of the United States: *Provided*, That nothing herein contained shall be construed to revive or put in force any law or regulation which may have existed prior to the act of sixth March, eighteen hundred and twenty, either protecting, establishing, prohibiting or abolishing slavery."

CHAPTER IV.

The organic act a compromise measure.—Kansas intended for a slave state.—Conduct of the pro-slavery party.—Persecutions of free-state people.—New England Emigrant Aid Societies.—Public meetings.—Blue Lodges.—Invasion from Westport.—Arrival of Governor Reeder.—Judges of the Supreme Court.

THE repeal of the compromise bill of 1820 by the passage of the Kansas-Nebraska act of 1854, was, of itself, though not so specified or implied, a sort of compromise measure. The original act as has been stated, provided for the organization of a single territory, to be called Nebraska, which was to embrace all that section of country which now constitutes the Territory of Kansas. The locality of the greater portion of Nebraska as thus designed; its ready access to immigration from the north; and its peculiar adaptation as respects both climate and soil, to free labor, rendered it certain of being received into the Union at an early day as a free State. The southern politicians could not wisely and openly object to its organization upon this ground. Hence a more judicious policy, as it was less likely to meet with determined opposition and condemnation, was adopted. The substitute of Mr. Douglas, though it could not prevent the erection of a new free state, would at least so far keep up the equality as also to create another state, into which slavery would be introduced. By the proposition to erect two new territories instead of one, as at first proposed, and to allow the inhabitants of each to determine for themselves whether slavery should or should not be admitted, it was intended and so understood, that Nebraska should become a free and Kansas a slave state. This was, beyond all question, the object and meaning of the Kansas-Nebraska bill of Mr. Douglas, and it was so regarded, as all its acts show, by the late administration. This, in fact, is the only excuse, although by no means a sufficient one, that can be offered in extenuation of the outrages that have subsequently been committed against free-state settlers. Many members of the pro-slavery party, believing it to have been a matter understood and fixed by certain contracting powers and the heads of the general government, that Kansas was to become a slave state, in order to keep up an equilibrium of northern and southern sectional and political interests, conscientiously supposed that instead of its being a criminal offence, it was not only justifiable, but a virtue, to persecute, even to death, all northern people who should enter the territory with a disposition to defeat or thwart that object. All such were regarded as intruders, whom it was proper to remove at all hazards and by whatever means, however cruel or oppressive, that could be employed. This sentiment was not confined to Kansas and the adjoining State of Missouri, but was entertained by persons high in authority elsewhere, and especially at the seat of the federal government. By many it was freely acknowledged and boldly advocated. On the other hand, there were many northern men who regarded the Kansas-Nebraska act as an infamous scheme to violate a sacred compact, and to perpetuate and extend, in opposition to every honorable principle, an institution which they view with horror and detestation.

No sooner was the passage of the Kansas-Nebraska act made known than great numbers of the residents of Missouri crossed into the new territory, seized upon its best lands, not respecting the rights of the Indians to their reservations, and availing themselves of the squatter sovereignty clause of the act, commenced laying foundations for the permanent establishment of slavery.

The reputed value of the lands and salubrity of the climate, also directed the attention of many eastern and northern people towards Kansas, and a large emigration from those regions commenced at an early day. To facilitate this, "Emigrant Aid Societies" were established, and under their auspices companies were formed, the first of which numbering about thirty persons, arrived in the territory on the first of August, 1854, and settled at what is now the town of Lawrence. Other parties arrived soon after, and located themselves in that and other neighborhoods.

The pro-slavery party fancied it saw in the immigration of these large northern companies serious cause to apprehend the defeat of a measure that had occasioned great anxiety; been attended with many difficulties; which was of such momentous importance; and until now gave promise of certain and ultimate success. It therefore resolved, as a matter of safety and interest, not only to disperse those who had already entered the territory, but to prevent if possible, the admission of all others of similar character. To this end meetings were held in various parts of the territory and in the border towns of Missouri, at which speeches were made and resolutions adopted of the most incendiary and inflammatory description. Some of these were so exceedingly violent and disgustingly profane, as to be unfit for publication. The tenor and spirit of them all was, that Kansas must be a slave state; that abolitionists, and this meant all northern men not pledged to favor slavery extension, had no right to come there, and that all such should be driven from the territory or destroyed.

At one of these meetings, held at Westport, Mo., in July, 1854, an association was formed, which adopted the following resolutions :—

"*Resolved,* That this association will, whenever called upon by any of the citizens of Kansas Territory, hold itself in readiness together to assist to remove any and all emigrants who go there under the auspices of the northern emigrant aid societies.

"*Resolved,* That we recommend to the citizens of other counties, particularly those bordering on Kansas Territory, to adopt regulations similar to those of this association, and to indicate their readiness to operate in the objects of this first resolution."

Not content with holding public meetings, to carry out the objects specified in these resolutions, secret organizations were formed, and signs, grips and passwords were adopted, and the members bound together by secret oaths and dreadful penalties, for that special purpose. In the report of a committee of Congress, appointed to investigate the Kansas difficulties growing out of the elections, the following description is given of these secret institutions:—

"It was known by different names, such as 'Social Band,' 'Friends' Society,' 'Blue Lodge,' 'The Sons of the South.' Its members were bound together by secret oaths, and they had passwords, signs and grips, by which they were known to each other. Penalties were imposed for violating the rules and secrets of the order. Written minutes were kept of the proceedings of the lodges, and the different lodges were connected together by an effective organization. It embraced great numbers of the citizens of Missouri, and was extended into other slave states and into the territory. Its avowed purpose was not only to extend slavery into Kansas, but also into other territory of the United States, and to form a union of all the friends of that institution. Its plan of operating was to organize and send men to vote at the elections in the territory, to collect money to pay their expenses, and, if necessary, to protect them in voting. It also proposed to induce pro-slavery men to emigrate into the territory, to aid and sustain them while there, and to elect none to office but those friendly to their views. This dangerous society was controlled by men who avowed their purpose to extend slavery into the territory at all hazards, and was altogether the most effective instrument in organizing the subsequent armed invasions and forays. In its lodges in Missouri the affairs of Kansas were discussed, the force necessary to control the election was divided into bands, and leaders selected, means were collected, and signs and badges were agreed upon. While the great body of the actual settlers of the territory were relying upon the rights secured to them by the organic law, and had formed no organization or combination whatever, even of a party character, this conspiracy against their rights was gathering strength in a neighboring state, and would have been sufficient at their first election to have overpowered them, if they had been united to a man."

The pro-slavery newspapers also took up the subject, and denounced the northern immigrants in the most violent terms the English language affords, and called upon Missourians and others friendly to the institution of slavery, to drive them from the territory, or utterly exterminate them, in case of their refusal to leave.

On the 6th of October, a large body of armed men, in wagons and on horseback, with grotesque banners and other strange devices, came from Westport to Lawrence, to disperse the settlers at that place. They demanded that the abolitionists should take away their tents and be off at short notice, or otherwise they would be "wiped out." The immigrants refused to obey this mandate, but prepared themselves in martial array, to protect their property and lives. This was entirely unexpected on the part of the invaders. They never imagined the possibility of the abolitionists showing fight. So, after considerable swaggering, they started back for Missouri, threatening, with huge oaths, that they would return in a week, with a force sufficiently large to compel submission to their requirements. These threats were unheeded; the settlers continued to build up their town; and the invaders did not return at the appointed time.

Bands of armed men were also organized to intercept the passage of the Missouri River. These parties entered the upward-bound steamboats at Lexington and other Missouri landings, and upon finding companies of northern emigrants, deprived them of their arms, and, in many instances, compelled them to go back. These outrages became so frequent and intolerant, that the river was virtually closed to all free-state travellers, who could only reach Kansas by taking the northern land route through Iowa and Nebraska.

Andrew H. Reeder, Esq., of Pennsylvania, having been appointed Governor of Kansas, arrived at Fort Leavenworth on the 6th of October, at which time the difficulties between the pro-slavery and free-state parties had not yet assumed a very serious or dangerous aspect. The governor was immediately surrounded by voluntary and patriotic advisers. Kansas has always been blessed with a number of this class of persons. By directing and controlling his policy, they were determined to be the governors of the governor. If he was too independent to submit to their insolent dictation, then all the machinery at their command was set in motion to thwart and embarrass his laudable undertakings. Reeder was a gentleman of talent and education, of unquestioned intelligence and integrity, and a lawyer by profession. He had been a life-long Democrat, and had done some service for his party. He, however, declined becoming the pliant tool of the faction that presumed to dictate his course, preferring to discharge the duties he had conscientiously assumed with justice and impartiality. This failed, of course, to give satisfaction where nothing could satisfy but adherence to the principles and an unscrupulous disposition to promote the interests of the slavery party, whose influence was not confined to Kansas and Missouri, but constituted a "power behind the throne" at Washington, even "more powerful than the throne itself;" and the consequence was a very brief duration of the governor's official existence.

At the time Reeder was appointed governor, Samuel Dexter Lecompte was chosen Chief Justice, and Rush Elmore and Sanders N. Johnson Associate Justices of the Supreme Court of the Territory. Judge Lecompte immediately affiliated with the most ultra of the pro-slavery men; declared himself warmly attached to their "peculiar institution;" received their unqualified approbation; applauded their acts; addressed their meetings; and went quite as far as the most exacting could possibly expect or desire. Judge Elmore was a slaveholder, and brought his slaves with him into the territory. But he was a just and conservative man, disposed to act fairly and honorably toward all classes of citizens, and disapproved of many of the outrages that were being so wantonly committed against the "abolitionists." His conduct was conciliatory, and he sought rather to preserve peace among the citizens than aid in promoting contention and strife. Judge Johnson took no part whatever in the prevailing disturbances.

The two latter named gentlemen were removed from office at the same time and upon the same pretence as Governor Reeder. They were charged with having speculated in the half-breed Kaw lands; the charge being founded upon the fact that they had stipulated for the purchase of those lands on condition of being able to obtain the consent of the government.

Chief Justice Lecompte is still retained, though he was one of the early squatters upon the Delaware Trust Lands, in which he now owns a valuable estate near Leavenworth City, and has acquired considerable property in sundry pro-slavery towns. Lecompton, the capital, received his name as an acknowledgment of his fidelity, zeal, and devotion to the party by which it was founded.

The places of Judges Elmore and Johnson were filled by the appointment of Sterling G. Cato, Esq., of Alabama, and J. M. Burrell, Esq., of Pennsylvania. Judge Cato has followed closely in the footsteps of Lecompte. Judge Burrell, after remaining a short time in the territory, and becoming disgusted with the outrages and official malfeasance, it is supposed, to which he was compelled to be a witness, without having the power to remedy, returned to his home at Greensburg, where he died in October, 1856. Judge Thomas Cunningham, of Beaver county, Pennsylvania, was appointed his successor; but he, too, after visiting the territory, resigned without ever entering upon the duties of his office.

CHAPTER V.

Elections.—Gen. Whitfield's politics.—Meetings in Misssouri to control the Kansas elections.—The Missouri press.—The Lynching of William Phillips.—Outrages upon the free-state citizens approved.—Destruction of the "Parkeville Luminary."

THE first election in the territory was held on the 29th November, 1854, and was for a delegate to Congress. There were three candidates, viz: a Mr. Flenniken, who came to Kansas with Governor Reeder; Judge J. A. Wakefield, an acknowledged free-state man; and General John W. Whitfield, an Indian agent, and one of the most ultra of the pro-slavery party.

That no mistake could be made in regard to Whitfield's sentiments on the slavery question, he very clearly expressed them in a speech made subsequent to the election. It is alleged, however, that previous thereto he was less positive. He then advocated the doctrine of popular sovereignty, and declared his intention to aid the actual settlers to form their own domestic institutions in their own way. His sentiments seem to have undergone a material change when he uttered the following:

"We can recognize but two parties in the territory—the pro-slavery and the anti-slavery parties. If the citizens of Kansas want to live in this community at peace and feel at home, they *must* become pro-slavery men; but if they want to live with gangs of thieves and robbers, they must go with the abolition party. There can be no third party—no more than two issues—slavery and no slavery, in Kansas Territory."

At the November election, large parties from Missouri, who had entered the territory for that purpose, insisted upon voting, and having done so, returned on the same day to their homes. Of 2871 votes polled, 1729 were ascertained to be illegal, all of which were cast for Whitfield, who was elected. The following extract in regard to this election, is from the report of the Congressional Committee:

"Thus your committee find that in this, the first election in the territory, a very large majority of the votes were cast by citizens of the State of Missouri, in violation of the organic law of the territory. Of the legal votes cast, Gen. Whitfield received a plurality. The settlers took but little interest in the election, not one-half of them voting. This may be accounted for from the fact that the settlements were scattered over a great extent, that the term of the delegate to be elected was short, and that the question of free and slave institutions was not generally regarded by them as distinctly at issue. Under these circumstances, a systematic invasion, from an adjoining state, by which large numbers of illegal votes were cast in remote and sparse settlements for the avowed purpose of extending slavery into the territory, even though it did not change the result of the election, was a crime of great magnitude. Its immediate effect was to further excite the people of the northern states, induce acts of retaliation, and exasperate the actual settlers against their neighbors in Missouri."

Several weeks previous to this election Gen. B. F. Stringfellow, Ex-Vice-President David R. Atchison, and other prominent citizens of that state, addressed large meetings in Missouri, urging the people "to enter every election district in Kansas, in defiance of Reeder and his vile myrmidons, and vote at the point of the bowie-knife and revolver." The cause, it was urged, demanded it, and "it was enough that the slave-holding interest wills it, from which there is no appeal," and if the pro-slavery party should be "defeated, then Missouri and the other southern states will have shown themselves recreant to their interests, and will deserve their fate."

These aggressions upon the rights of the settlers soon led to difficulties of a serious character. A retaliatory disposition was aroused and scenes of violence and bloodshed became quite common. The feelings evinced in certain quarters in regard to such disturbances are fully avowed in the following paragraph from the *Squatter Sovereign*, published at Atchison, by Dr. John H. Stringfellow.

"Monday of last week a fight came off at Doniphan, K. T., in which bowie-knives were used freely. The difficulty arose out of a political discussion; the combatants being a pro-slavery man and a free-soiler. Both parties were badly cut, and *we are happy to state* that the free-soiler is in a fair way to peg out, while the pro-slavery man is out and ready for another tilt. Kansas is a hard road for free-soilers to travel."

In regard to certain strictures upon Kansas outrages published in New York, the same paper discoursed as follows:—

"We can tell the impertinent scoundrels of the *Tribune* that they may exhaust an ocean of ink, their Emigrant Aid Societies spend their millions and billions, their representatives in Congress spout their heretical theories till doomsday, and His Excellency Franklin Pierce appoint abolitionist after free-soiler as our Governor, *yet we will continue to lynch and hang*, to tar and feather, and drown every white-livered abolitionist who dares to pollute our soil."

Governor Reeder called an election for the Legislative Assembly, to be held on the 20th of March, following. At this election outrages were committed exceeding in atrocity anything that had ever transpired in the history of the country Many protests were entered against the returns, which resulted in the call of an especial election, to be held on the 22d of May, for several districts, against the evidently fraudulent returns of which, affidavits and petitions had been filed.

In consequence of this order of the governor, a public meeting was held on the 30th of April, at Leavenworth City, which was "ably and eloquently addressed by Chief Justice Lecompte, Col. J. N. Burns of Weston, Missouri, and others." At this meeting it was

"*Resolved*, That the institution of slavery is known and recognised in this territory; that we repel the doctrine that it is a moral and political evil, and we turn back with scorn upon its slanderous authors the charge of inhumanity; and we warn all persons not to come to our peaceful firesides to slander us, and sow the seeds of discord between the master and the servant; for, as much as we deprecate the necessity to which we may be driven, we cannot be responsible for the consequences."

A committee of vigilance, consisting of thirty persons, was appointed, whose duty it was to observe and report all such persons, as should "by the expression of abolition sentiments produce a disturbance to the quiet of the citizens, or danger to their domestic relations; and all such persons, so offending shall be notified, and made to leave the territory." This committee found abundant employment, and was exceedingly active in issuing orders to all free-state men, who should dare to express a sentiment adverse to the institution of slavery, to quit the territory at a certain specified time, or suffer the penalty of death. Under its edicts many good men were driven from their homes, and their wives and children compelled to flee to distant parts for safety and protection.

Among those ordered to leave was Mr. William Phillips, a lawyer of Leavenworth, who had signed a protest against the election in that city. Upon his refusal to go, he was, on the 17th of May, seized by a band of men chiefly from Missouri, who carried him eight miles up the river to Weston, where they shaved one half of his head, tarred and feathered him, rode him on a rail, and sold him at a mock auction by a negro, all of which he bore with manly fortitude and bravery, and then returned to Leavenworth and persisted in remaining, notwithstanding his life was constantly threatened and in danger. He was subsequently murdered in his own house, by a company of "law and order" men, or "territorial militia," under command of Captain Frederick S. Emory, simply for refusing to leave the town.

On the 25th of May, just eight days after the perpetration of the outrage above narrated, another meeting was held at Leavenworth, over which R. R. Rees, a member elect of the Council presided. "This meeting," the papers say, was also "eloquently addressed by Judge Lecompte," after which the following resolutions offered by Judge Payne, a member elect of the House of Representatives, were unanimously adopted:

"*Resolved*, That we heartily endorse the action of the committee of citizens that shaved, tarred and feathered, rode on a rail, and had sold by a negro, William Phillips, the moral perjurer.

"*Resolved*, That we return our thanks to the committee for faithfully performing the trust enjoined upon them by the pro-slavery party.

"*Resolved*, That the committee be now discharged.

"*Resolved*, That we severely condemn those pro-slavery men who, from mercenary motives, are calling upon the pro-slavery party to submit without further action.

"*Resolved*, That, in order to secure peace and harmony to the community, we now solemnly declare that the pro-slavery party will stand firmly by and carry out the resolutions reported by the committee appointed for that purpose on the memorable 30th."

Meetings were also held in numerous towns in Missouri, to approve the proceedings of the invaders at the March election, at which violent addresses were made and denunciatory resolutions were passed. The following, adopted at a meeting held in Clay county, will give an idea of their general tenor:—

"Those who, in our state, would give aid to the abolitionists by inducing or assisting them to settle in Kansas, or would throw obstacles in the way of our friends, by *false* and *slanderous* misrepresentations of the acts of those who took part in and contributed to the glorious result of the late election in that territory, should be driven from amongst us as traitors to their country.

"That we regard the efforts of the northern division of the Methodist Episcopal Church to establish itself in our state as a violation of her *plighted faith*, and, pledged as its ministers must be to the anti-slavery principles of that church, we are forced to regard them as enemies to our institutions. We therefore fully concur with our friends in Platte county in resolving to permit no person belonging to the Northern Methodist Church to preach in our county.

"That all persons who are subscribers to papers in the least tinctured with free-soilism or abolitionism, are requested to discontinue them immediately."

The Missouri press was extremely vituperative against all who dared to condemn the course pursued in regard to the Kansas election. The *Brunswicker* found fault with a contemporary in the following choice terms:

"The last Jefferson *Inquirer* is down on the citizens of Missouri who took steps to secure the election of pro-slavery men to the Territorial Legislature of Kansas. This is in keeping with the *Inquirer's* past conduct. If the editor of that paper had been in Kansas on the day of election, he would have voted with the abolitionists. That he is a negro-stealer *at heart* we have no doubt."

The Platte County *Luminary*, was printed at Parkeville, Mo., and was owned by Mr. Parke, one of the oldest residents, after whom the town was named. After the March election this paper ventured to condemn, though in gentle terms, the Missouri invasion; upon which, a few days afterwards, April 14th, a company was formed at Platte City, and arming themselves for the occasion, marched to Parkeville, broke to pieces the press of the *Luminary*, and threw it, with all the material belonging to the office, into the Missouri River. They also seized Mr. Patterson, the editor, Mr. Parke being absent, and would have killed him, but for the interference of his wife, a young and beautiful woman, who threw herself about his neck, to which she clung so firmly that it was difficult to separate them. They finally relinquished their intention, released their prisoner, and permitted him to leave the place, under the penalty of losing his life should he refuse to go or dare to return.

CHAPTER VI.

Census returns, February, 1855.—The election of March 30th.—The Legislative Assembly.

GOVERNOR REEDER having ordered a census to be taken, the returns, on the 28th of February, 1855, exhibited a population, exclusive of Indians, of 8,501 souls. There were 5,128 males, 3,373 females, and 3,469 minors. 7,161 were citizens of the United States; 409 of foreign birth; 242 were slaves, and 151 free negroes. There were, at this time, but 2,905 voters, which number was somewhat increased by immigration, before the election for a Legislative Assembly, which took place on the 30th of March.

This election was controlled almost entirely by citizens of Missouri, who came into the territory in large parties, took possession of the polls, drove off the regularly appointed judges and chose others to answer their own objects, elected persons who were not and never had been citizens of Kansas; and committed other atrocities, the details of which are absolutely too disgusting to relate. It is estimated that about five thousand Missourians, led on by men claiming respectability, and certainly occupying prominent positions, visited the territory to take part in this nefarious transaction. The following extract is from the report of the Congressional Committee:

"By an organized movement, which extended from Andrews county in the north, to Jasper county in the south, and as far eastward as Boone and Cole counties, companies of men were arranged in regular parties, and sent *into every council district in the territory and into every representative district* but one. The numbers were so distributed as to control the election in each district. They went to vote, and with the avowed intention to make Kansas a slave state. They were generally armed and equipped, carried with them their own provision and tents, and so marched into the territory."

Another paragraph in the same report, which gives a detailed statement of the outrages committed at this election, carefully gathered from the examination of witnesses under oath, asserts:

"The Missourians began to leave on the afternoon of the day of election, though some did not go home until the next morning.

"In many cases, when a wagon-load had voted, they immediately started for home. On their way home they said if Governor Reeder did not sanction the election they would hang him.

"This unlawful interference has been continued in every important event in the history of the territory. *Every election* has been controlled, not by the actual settlers, but by citizens of Missouri; and, as a consequence, every officer in the territory, from constables to legislators, except those appointed by the President, owe their positions to non-resident voters."

Instead of making any attempt to conceal or deny the frauds committed at this election, the pro-slavery people of Missouri boasted of the fact, and maintained they had as much right to vote in Kansas according to the terms of the Organic Act, having been there but five minutes, as though they had been residents for as many years. The press of Missouri urged the people to go to Kansas to vote. The Liberty, Clay county, paper, contained the following:

"The election in Kansas Territory is close at hand, and we embrace this, the last opportunity we will have before the attempt, of admonishing Missouri and southerners that it is the part of wisdom as well as prudence to employ every means of preparation necessary to a successful combat for the issue which is suspended upon it."

The Weston *Reporter* of March 29th (1855), says:—

"Our minds are already made up as to the result of the election in Kansas to-morrow. The pro-slavery party will be triumphant, *we presume*, in nearly every precinct. Should the pro-slavery party fail in this contest, it will not be because Missouri has failed to do her duty to assist friends. It is a safe calculation that two thousand squatters have passed over into the promised land from this part of the state within four days."

After the election, the Missouri papers were filled with jubilant expressions of victory. The Platte *Argus* says: "It is to be admitted that they—the Missourians—have conquered Kansas. Our advice is, let them hold it or die in the attempt."

Protests from several of the election districts, numerously signed, having been forwarded to the governor, he refused issuing certificates to the members whose seats were thus contested, whereupon an open war was declared upon him by the pro-slavery party. A meeting was held at the seat of government at which the right of the governor to call a new election was denied, and a resolution passed saying that "in the event a new election shall be ordered by the governor in any district, we recommend to every law-abiding and order-loving citizen of Kanzas Territory not to attend said election, but rely on the returns already made to sustain the claims of those returned heretofore to their seats in each house."

The governor, notwithstanding, did order a new election in six of the contested districts, which called forth the fury of the Missouri papers. Of the articles published, the following from the *Brunswicker* is a choice specimen:

> "We learn, just as we go to press, that Reeder has refused to give certificates to four of the Councilmen and thirteen members of the House. He has ordered an election to fill their places on the 22d of May. This infernal scoundrel will have to be hemped yet."

The pro-slavery party took no interest in the May election, having determined not to recognize it, except in the Leavenworth district, where they re-elected their candidates by Missouri votes. In all the other districts free-state men were elected. But upon the assembling of the Legislature their seats were refused them, and given to those elected on the 30th of March. There was but one free-state member whose seat could not be deprived him upon any pretence whatever, and this he voluntarily resigned, leaving the entire assembly of the same political complexion.

The Kansas Legislative Assembly, elected by Missouri votes, convened, agreeably to the order of Governor Reeder, at Pawnee City, near Fort Riley, in the interior of the territory, on the 2d of July, 1855. On the 4th, an act was passed to remove the seat of government to Shawnee Mission, near the Missouri border. This bill was vetoed by Governor Reeder, but was subsequently adopted by a two-third majority, and became a law.

This body was in session less than fifty working days; but in looking over the published records of the amount of labor it performed, it might be regarded as the most industrious legislative assembly that ever had an existence. Besides its journals, embracing two good sized duodecimo volumes of several hundred pages, it discussed and adopted laws filling more than a thousand octavo pages. How this was accomplished would be a mystery to the uninitiated; for it would have required all the time occupied by the meetings to read, at a rapid rate, even a part of the enactments; but the mystery is revealed when it is understood that the Missouri code was adopted without the laborious formality of reading, with the simple instructions to the clerks to substitute the name of "Kansas Territory" wherever the "State of Missouri" occurred. There were, however, some additions made that never could have received the sanction of a Missouri Legislature. These were test and election laws, so odious that even the Kansas officials, corrupt as they were, did not attempt their enforcement, and hence remained dead letters upon the statute book. The person claiming to be the author of these laws says he wrote them when under the evil influence of bad whiskey, and that they passed the Houses when the other members were in about the same condition as he was when they were written and presented. This was as rational an explanation as could have been given for their conception and adoption.

The Legislature adjourned on the 30th of August, having fixed the permanent seat of government at Lecompton. This was about as inaccessible and inconvenient a place as could have been chosen in the territory; but, as it is maliciously affirmed, that the members received from the town company liberal grants of town lots as the price of their votes, they could afford to travel somewhat out of the ordinary way, and suffer a few trifling discomforts, especially as the public welfare was thus to be promoted.

CHAPTER VII.

Removal of Governor Reeder.—Secretary Woodson.—Assumption of power by the Legislature.—Office-holders all pro-slavery men.—Free-state mass meetings and conventions.—Elections for delegate to Congress.—Free-state Constitution adopted.—Dr. Charles Robinson elected governor.—Meetings of the State Legislature.—Arrest of Robinson and others for high treason.—The Topeka Legislature dispersed by Col. Sumner.

GOVERNOR REEDER made a visit to Washington in the spring of 1855, leaving Kansas on the 19th of April, to consult with the administration on the affairs of the territory. When about to take his departure for the west, on the 11th of June following, he received a letter from Secretary Marcy, charging him with irregular proceedings, in the purchase of Indian lands. The governor replied to this letter, after he had again reached Kansas, explaining the circumstances in question, and showing that the charge had no foundation other than in the fact that he was one of a company who had proposed to purchase a portion of the Kaw lands, provided the sanction of the government could be obtained, otherwise the purchase was of no avail. Although this pretended speculation was the ostensible ground for his removal, of which he received official information on the 31st of July, it was evident that other reasons, not made public, had influenced the action of the administration. He did not please the southern wing of the Democratic party, and the leading pro-slavery men clamored for his dismissal. From these he had suffered every possible annoyance, even to having been assaulted and beaten in his own office by Gen. B. F. Stringfellow, for having, as was alleged, spoken unfavorably, when in the east, of border ruffianism. The Legislative Assembly also sent a memorial to Washington, preferring charges against him, which were not received until after his removal. The speculation in the half-breed lands, therefore, while it furnished a pretext, was not the real cause for the removal of Reeder.

The secretary of the territory, Daniel Woodson, was, agreeably to a provision in the organic law, acting governor, from the 31st of July, until Wilson Shannon, the successor to Reeder, arrived in the territory on the 1st of September. Woodson was all that the pro-slavery party desired. There was nothing in which he was not willing and ready to do their bidding. He was emphatically a man after their own heart. And so well pleased were they with his soundness and pliancy, that petitions were forwarded to Washington, to obtain for him the appointment of governor. There was no possible reason to fear that he would be guilty of the commission of any act that would favor the free-state people, or that would not have for its chief object the advancement of the pro-slavery cause.

Previous to the removal of Reeder, the Legislative Assembly had passed enactments stripping the governor of almost every vestige of power, attempting even to deprive him of the privileges granted by the organic act. They arrogated to themselves the appointment of all the territorial officers, and selected none but persons of their own class, and those who were known to be of the most ultra character. In this they had strictly followed the policy of the administration, all whose appointments were of the same description; so that, after the removal of Reeder, there was but one man, and he the postmaster at Lawrence, who held an office, either under the federal government, or by appointment of the legislature, or through their agents, who was not in favor of introducing slavery into the territory, and through any means by which it could be effected.

The free-state settlers, believing themselves the subjects of a cruel persecution; feeling they could not obtain any sympathy from the general government; and knowing they might look in vain for justice at the hands of the territorial officers, held mass meetings and conventions, to discuss with each other the subject of their grievances. At one of these meetings, a resolution was passed, requesting "all *bona fide* citizens of Kansas Territory, of whatever political views or predilections, to consult together, in their respective election districts," and elect "delegates to assemble in convention, at the town of Topeka, on the 19th day of September, 1855, then and there to consider and determine upon all subjects of public interest, and particularly upon that having reference to the speedy formation of a state constitution, with an intention of immediate application to be admitted as a state into the Union of the United States of America."

A convention, numerously attended, was held at Big Springs, on the 5th of September, at which it was resolved, that the Legislative Assembly had been fraudulently elected; "that its laws had no validity or binding force; and that every freeman was at liberty, consistently with his obligations as a citizen and a man, to defy and resist them." A resolution was also passed denunciatory of the judiciary, for entering "into a partisan contest, and, by extra-judicial decision, giving opinions in violation of all propriety." It was further resolved to endure and submit to the laws of the spurious legislature "no longer than the best interests of the territory require, as the least of two evils;" and to "resist them to a bloody issue as soon as it could be ascertained that peaceable remedies should fail, and forcible resistance furnish any reasonable prospect of success;" and, in the mean time, the resolution read, "we recommend to our friends throughout the territory, the organization and discipline of volunteer companies, and the procurement and preparation of arms." They especially repudiated the election law, determined not to meet on the day appointed for election, but resolved themselves to "fix upon a day for the purpose of electing a delegate to Congress."

Agreeably to this last resolve, the 9th day of October was set apart for the election of a delegate to Congress, at which election Governor Reeder received two thousand eight hundred and sixteen free-state votes, the pro-slavery party taking no part in the election. This party had already held an election on the first of the month, when Whitfield received over three thousand votes, more than eight hundred of them, as before, polled by invaders from the neighboring state. The free-state people kept away from the polls on that occasion.

Both Whitfield and Reeder presented themselves in Washington, and claimed their seats as delegates. After a careful investigation of the circumstances, both were rejected, though each received his mileage.

At the same time the free-state election for delegate to Congress was held, delegates to form a constitutional convention were also elected. This convention assembled at Topeka, on the 23d of October, 1855, at which a state constitution was adopted, the important feature of which is, that "slavery shall not exist in the state."

This Constitution was submitted to the people for ratification, on the 15th December, 1855, when it received a respectable popular vote. At some of the election districts, disturbances were created, and at Leavenworth, the poll-books were seized and destroyed. But as a general thing, the election was permitted to go off even more quietly than could, under the agitated condition of the territory, have been reasonably expected.

Just one week after this December election, a caucus meeting was held in Lawrence to nominate a free-state ticket for state officers under the Topeka Constitution. At this meeting, Dr. Charles Robinson, received the nomination for governor, who with the other candidates then nominated, was subsequently elected.

The newly elected State Legislature, assembled at Topeka on the 1st of March, 1856, and proceeded to organize a state government. Dr. Robinson took the oath of office and delivered his inaugural address. A committee was appointed to frame a code of laws for the future state, during the adjournment of the Legislature. Andrew H. Reeder and James H. Lane were elected United States Senators, to take their seats when the new state should be admitted into the Union. After the transaction of this, and other important business, the Legislature adjourned until the following 4th of July.

Sheriff Samuel J. Jones, whose name must necessarily figure somewhat in these pages, as a prominent agitator in all the Missouri-Kansas troubles, was present at the above meeting, busily employed in taking notes, and especially registering the names of the most prominent participants. Through his instrumentality, Robinson and others who were active in the movement, were subsequently arrested and held in confinement a period of four months, on the charge of high-treason. These men frequently demanded a trial; but the government was never ready. At length, Judge Lecompte, hearing that James H. Lane was marching with a large army to set them at liberty, consented to discharge them upon bail. This will be the end of the matter, as it was never any part of the programme to give them a trial. Since the above was written, and after the prisoners had been held in bail a period of full eight months, the district attorney, as was predicted, entered *nolle prosequies* in their cases, and they were discharged.

Previous to the 4th of July, threats were freely uttered by the pro-slavery party, that the free-state legislature should not assemble, at that time, according to its adjournment. Their first intention was to disperse the members by an armed force of their own people; but they afterwards determined upon a wiser and safer course of action. In consequence of these threats, the free-state men began to assemble at Topeka in considerable numbers as early as the 2d of July. Some of the most prominent of the party being still in prison, and others having been driven from the territory, they were undecided in regard to the policy best to be pursued. Both branches of the State Legislature consequently met in convention on the evening of July 3d, and resolved to assemble in regular session, agreeably to adjournment, at noon on the following day.

In the mean time, a large United States force, under command of Col. E. V. Sumner, consisting of seven companies of dragoons from Fort Leavenworth, and four companies from Fort Riley, had encamped close to Topeka, both to the north and the south of the town. Secretary Woodson, who in the absence of Shannon, was again acting-governor, accompanied the troops, as did also the United States Marshal, Israel B. Donalson.

On the evening of the 2d, a committee of free-state men had been appointed to correspond with Col. Sumner, and ascertain, if possible, the object of this extraordinary warlike demonstration on the part of the United States. On the 3d, the committee received from Col. Sumner the following letter:

"Head Quarters, First Cavalry,
"Camp at Topeka, K. T., July 3, 1856.

"Gentlemen: In relation to the assembling of the Topeka Legislature (the subject of our conversation last night), the more I reflect on it the more I am convinced that the peace of the country will be greatly endangered by your persistence in this measure. Under these circumstances I would ask you and your friends to take the matter into grave consideration. It will certainly be much better that you should act voluntarily in this matter, from a sense of prudence and patriotism, at this moment of high excitement throughout the country, than that the authority of the general government should be compelled to use coercive measures to prevent the assemblage of that Legislature.

"I am, gentlemen, very respectfully, your obedient servant,
"E. V. Sumner,
"Col. First Cavalry Commanding."

Early on the morning of the 4th the convention again assembled in one of the rooms appropriated to the Legislature, when they were visited by Marshal Donalson, accompanied by ex-judge Elmore, who by request of the marshal, explained the object of their errand. He read, among other things, a proclamation of President Pierce, issued on the preceding February, in which he declared that the laws of the Legislative Assembly as adopted at the Shawnee Mission, should be sustained and enforced by the entire force of the government, and concluded by delivering a proclamation to the same effect from the secretary of the territory, the acting-governor.

This ceremony concluded, the marshal and judge took their departure. The excitement in the town was intense, and the entire population, embracing two volunteer companies, who were out on parade, were assembled in and about the legislative hall. A short time before the hour appointed for the meeting, Colonel Sumner, at the head of about two hundred dragoons, was seen approaching at a rapid rate. Having posted two field pieces so as to command the principal avenues, he drew his forces up in front of the hall and entered the building; and addressing the people who were there assembled, he informed them that under the proclamation of the President, he had come to disperse the Legislature, which duty, though the most painful of his life, he was compelled to perform, even if it should demand the employment of all the forces in his command. The members present readily consented to obey his orders, and no attempt was made at an organization. The colonel was heartily cheered as he left the hall; and when he was about marching off at the head of the troops, three groans for Franklin Pierce were given with such an unanimity and hearty good will by the assembled multitude, as fairly to shake the building, startle the horses of the soldiers, and betoken anything but a friendly feeling toward the existing administration.

CHAPTER VIII.

The Kansas Legion.—Patrick Laughlin.—The murder of Collins.—Outrages upon J. W. B. Kelley.—Rev. Pardee Butler set adrift in the Missouri River on a raft.—Disputes about land claims.—The murder of Dow.—Portrait of Sheriff Jones.—Arrest and rescue of Jacob Branson.

It is not to be presumed that all the outrages and crimes committed in Kansas Territory were the work of the pro-slavery party. That party will have a terrible catalogue for which to account; but in the great day of retribution their political opponents will not entirely escape condemnation. The pro-slavery men were doubtless the original aggressors; but their unworthy example was too eagerly followed by many claiming to be the advocates of freedom. The one party burned houses, and robbed and murdered unoffending people; and the other, in retaliation, committed the same atrocities. Buford collected a regiment of men in Alabama, South Carolina, and Georgia; and Jones, Whitfield and others, bands of desperadoes in Missouri, which they brought into Kansas to pillage and destroy; whilst Lane marched in his famous "Army of the North," whose path was also marked with desolation and ruin. The slavery faction established its "Blue Lodges," and their opposers organized their "Kansas Legion," both of which were secret associations, bound together by solemn oaths, and having signs and pass-words of recognition. The only difference was, that the largest and most respectable portion of the free-state party condemned the "Kansas Legion," and took no part in its operations; whilst the "Blue Lodges" originated with, and received their chief encouragement and support from the most prominent, wealthy and leading pro-slavery men, not only in the territory, but in various states of the Union.

In the summer of 1855, an Irishman, named Patrick

Laughlin, who had formerly lived in Missouri, pretended to have become a convert to the free-state principles, and was received into the fellowship of the "Kansas Legion." He became a very active member, and was deputized to open encampments in sundry free-state towns. After acquainting himself with all the mysteries and thoroughly understanding the working of the entire machinery, Patrick returned to the pro-slavery party and made an *exposé* of the whole affair, telling perhaps all the truth and adding much of his own invention. He also became an active persecutor of the free-state men, towards whom he exhibited the most violent hostility. This led to a personal altercation between Laughlin and a man named Collins, both of whom resided at Doniphan.

They met in the vicinity of Collins' saw-mill, where himself, sons and nephews were at work, Laughlin having with him several friends. All the parties were armed. After a wordy quarrel they were about separating, upon which Laughlin reiterated some offensive language, and Collins turned toward him. One of the pro-slavery men fired, hitting Collins, who returned the shot without effect, upon which Laughlin fired his pistol at Collins and killed him instantly. A general fight then ensued, in which bowie-knives and pistols were freely used. Several on both sides were wounded, and Laughlin seriously. He was carried to Atchison, and has entirely recovered. This scene occurred on the 25th of October.

The pro-slavery residents of Atchison had previously resolved to rid that place of all free-state settlers, and accordingly, on the 8th of August, they seized Mr. J. W. B. Kelley, and after having beaten and otherwise abused him, they drove him from the town.

Soon after this occurrence, Rev. Pardee Butler, a preacher from Missouri, visited Atchison, and having expressed himself rather freely in condemnation of the outrage upon Kelley, he was forthwith disposed of in a summary and somewhat novel manner. The following is the *Squatter Sovereign's* relation of this affair:—

"On Thursday last one Pardee Butler arrived in town with a view of starting for the East, probably for the purpose of getting a fresh supply of free-soilers from the penitentiaries and pest-holes of the northern states. Finding it inconvenient to depart before morning, he took lodgings at the hotel, and proceeded to visit numerous portions of our town, everywhere avowing himself a free-soiler, and preaching the foulest of abolition heresies. He declared the recent action of our citizens in regard to J. W. B. Kelley, the infamous and unlawful proceedings of a mob; at the same time stating that many persons in Atchison, who were free-soilers at heart, had been intimidated thereby, and feared to avow their true sentiments; but that he (Butler) would express his views in defiance of the whole community.

"On the ensuing morning our townsmen assembled en masse, and, deeming the presence of such persons highly detrimental to the safety of our slave property, appointed a committee of two to wait on Mr. Butler and request his signature to the resolutions passed at the late pro-slavery meeting held in Atchison. After perusing the said resolutions, Mr. B. positively declined signing them, and was instantly arrested by the committee.

"After the various plans for his disposal had been considered, it was finally decided to place him on a raft composed of two logs firmly lashed together; that his baggage and a loaf of bread be given him; and having attached a flag to his primitive bark, emblazoned with mottoes indicative of our contempt for such characters, Mr. Butler was set adrift in the great Missouri, with the letter R legibly painted on his forehead.

"He was escorted some distance down the river by several of our citizens, who, seeing him pass several rock-heaps in quite a skilful manner, bade him adieu, and returned to Atchison.

"Such treatment may be expected by all scoundrels visiting our town for the purpose of interfering with our time-honored institutions, and the same punishment we will be happy to award all free-soilers, abolitionists, and their emissaries."

Butler states that Robert S. Kelley, the junior editor of the *Squatter Sovereign* was one of the most active members of the mob that committed this disgraceful act, and that he assisted to tow the raft out into the stream, where he was set adrift, with flags bearing the following strange inscriptions: "Eastern Emigrant Aid Express. The Rev. Mr. Butler for the Underground Railroad." "The way they are served in Kansas." "For Boston." "Cargo insured—unavoidable danger of the Missourians and the Missouri River excepted." "Let future emissaries from the north beware. Our hemp crop is sufficient to reward all such scoundrels."

Many of the personal rencontres in Kansas, grew out of

the unsettled condition of affairs in regard to the possession of lands. Most of the "claims" had been staked out by persons living in Missouri, who, paying no proper regard to the requirements of the pre-emption laws, had no possible right to the property they assumed to own. These claims were, beyond all question, legally open for the actual settler. Such was the condition of a large tract of valuable woodland, at Hickory Point, bordering on the Wakarusa, on the Santa Fe road. A free-state man, named Jacob Branson, occupied a claim in this vicinity, upon which he was living, was improving, and his right to which was not disputed. The adjoining claim was vacant, and Branson invited a young man from Ohio, named Dow, to take it up, which he did, and commenced making improvements.

The pro-slavery squatters in the neighborhood determined to drive off these free-state settlers, and sent an anonymous letter to Branson, filled with threats of violence, and ordering him to leave; whilst they maintained that Dow's claim belonged to a William White, of Westport, and persisted in cutting timber from it and otherwise annoying Dow, with the obvious and avowed purpose of creating a difficulty. Dow at length gave them notice that he would not longer submit to these abuses, but would adopt measures to defend his rights.

The principal aggressors in this matter were three pro-slavery men, named Franklin M. Coleman, Josiah Hargis, and Harrison W. Buckley. On the 21st of November, Dow had an errand to a blacksmith shop in the vicinity, to which place he was followed by these three men, who there provoked a quarrel with him about the claim, in the course of which Buckley cocked his gun and presented it at Dow, who entreated him not to shoot. He then left the shop and proceeded along the Santa Fe road toward the house of Branson, at which he boarded. Coleman followed, and soon overtook him, the other two keeping a short distance behind. Upon reaching Coleman's house they separated, Dow walking slowly on. As soon as he reached his house, Coleman raised his gun, and aiming at Dow's back, pulled the trigger. The noise of the exploding cap, the gun not discharging, startled Dow, who suddenly turned towards Coleman, and threw up his arms imploring him not to fire; when Coleman deliberately put on a new cap, raised his gun and discharged a heavy load of buckshot and slugs, which entered the breast and heart of Dow, killing him instantly. The other two parties to this atrocious murder, soon joined Coleman, and the three appeared to rejoice over the fiendish deed. The body of Dow lay in the road, where it fell, during the whole afternoon, when Branson, hearing of the affair, had it removed to his own dwelling. This occurrence was witnessed by a man named Moody and a wagoner.

The authorities took no action in the matter, and on the 26th of the month, a meeting of settlers was held at Hickory Point to take it into consideration. This meeting was conducted with the utmost propriety, simply passing resolutions condemning the murder, and appointing a committee to take the necessary steps to bring the criminals to punishment. A proposition was made to burn their houses, but this act was almost universally condemned and deprecated by a resolution.

Meanwhile, Coleman had fled towards Westport, and thrown himself upon the protection of the renowned Sheriff Jones, whom he met near Shawnee Mission, and who it is time should be properly introduced to the reader.

Samuel J. Jones is, perhaps, over thirty years of age, and about six feet in height, though not stoutly built. His hair is light, his complexion cadaverous, and his features irregular and unprepossessing. His eye is small, and when in repose, dull and unmeaning. He seldom looks those with whom he is conversing full in the face, though his eye constantly wanders about as if he was apprehensive of some unknown danger. His conversation is in short and broken sentences, always well interspersed with oaths, and generally relates to his own exploits against the free-state people, of whom he has been one of the most relentless persecutors. He delights in conveying the impression that he bears a "charmed life," and in proof of his many "hair-breadth 'scapes," will occasionally exhibit a broken watch chain or a hole in his garment, effected by a ball aimed at him by some unseen enemy. He is now suffering from a pistol ball, lodged somewhere about the spinal column, which he received at night while in a tent at Lawrence. Every attempt, in which the free-state men were most active, to discover the perpetrator of this outrage, proved futile, and even the most rabid friends of Jones failed to make any great capital out of the affair. He seems to have pretty well understood the case, for he has since asserted that he believes the shot was fired by a man with whose wife he had been fooling.

Sheriff Jones is one of the most zealous of the pro-slavery men, and has done as much to create and perpetuate the difficulties that have disgraced Kansas, as any other individual. He has led in bands of invaders to prevent the citizens from giving a fair expression of their opinions at the ballot-box; interfered with the elections on every possible occasion; assisted in the destruction of property; and done everything in his power to harass and distress free-state people, by whom he is generally held in detestation. In none of the outrages in which he has taken an active part, however, has he exhibited evidences of that bravery his friends attribute to him; for in no instance has he ever interfered with, or shown fight to his political opposers, excepting when the odds were decidedly in his favor, as respected arms and physical and numerical strength. Jones is held in the highest estimation by his party, and is always consulted when there is any mischief in contemplation. He owns some real estate, all of which is encumbered to nearly if not its full value, and his name stands upon the bail-bonds of some of the worst men that have yet been indicted for crime by the grand juries.

When Coleman told his story to Jones, the sheriff accompanied him to Shawnee Mission, where by advice, he surrendered himself to Governor Shannon, and then accompanied Jones towards Lecompton, to be examined. Upon reaching Franklin, this party were joined by Hargis and Buckley, when a most interesting scheme was concocted. Buckley was induced to swear that his life was in danger from threats made by old Jacob Branson, the friend of young Dow, and to effect the arrest of Branson, Jones induced a justice of the peace, named Hugh Cameron, to issue a peace-warrant for Branson's arrest, which was given to the sheriff for execution. A party of fifteen was then obtained as a *posse*, including Jones and the two accessories to the murder of Dow, who reached Branson's house toward midnight of the 26th, the same day upon which the meeting at Hickory Point was held. The door was burst open, and Branson arrested while in bed.

In the meantime, the free-state settlers in the neighborhood, ascertained what was going on, and hastily forming a company, posted themselves at Blanton's Bridge, where they knew Jones must pass with his prisoner. Here the parties met about two hours after midnight, and the free-state men demanded the surrender of Branson. Jones first swore terrifically, and then coaxed the rescuers to allow him to proceed, as he was the sheriff of Douglas county, and in discharge of his official duty. The opposite party were inexorable and demanded that Jacob Branson should be delivered into their hands. The sheriff then declared he would fire into them if they persisted, to which he received the reply that he might fire and be d—d; that at that game both parties might take a hand. Branson then left the sheriff's party, and, without any attempt at violent detention, joined his friends, who, leaving Jones mad with anger, and loudly vaporing in the road, marched triumphantly toward Lawrence, which town they entered before the sun had risen.

A number of affidavits were made in regard to the arrest and rescue of Branson, by Hargis, Buckley, and Jones, of the pro-slavery, and sundry individuals of the free-state party, all of which substantiate the above relation, the principal difference being in the unimportant fact, that the rescuing company, agreeably to the account of the sheriff and his friends, were exaggerated to the number of thirty or forty, while themselves claim, which seems to be the true state of the case, only fourteen men.

Coleman was taken to Lecompton, where he was discharged from custody upon entering bail in the sum of five hundred dollars. Just before the murder of Dow he had been commissioned as a justice of the peace by Governor Shannon.

CHAPTER IX.

Governor Wilson Shannon.—Consequences of the arrest and rescue of Branson.—Meeting at Lawrence.—Military organization for defence.—Sheriff Jones requires three thousand men.—The governor orders out the militia.—A general call to arms.—The governor issues a proclamation.—War excitement in Missouri.—The invading army.—Governor Shannon's excuse.

WILSON SHANNON, at the time of the occurrences narrated in the last part of the preceding chapter, was Governor of Kansas, having arrived in the territory and assumed the executive functions on the 1st of September, 1855. The objects of his appointment at that peculiar period, to such an important trust, though inexplicable to all who knew his qualifications, was doubtless well understood by the administration. He had previously held several responsible public positions, in neither of which he did any great credit to himself or to the appointing power. He was decidedly a pro-slavery man, though hailing from a free state, and in a speech he made at Westport, before entering the territory, proclaimed his determination to exert to the utmost of his abilities, in his official capacity, all his influence and power to promote the interests of the pro-slavery cause. But he lacked the moral courage to accomplish the work he had promised and was expected to perform. The leaders of the free-state party soon understood the weak points of his character, and by appealing successfully to his grosser passions, caused him so to vacillate as to render him a subject of their own ridicule and the contempt of those whom he desired to serve. He soon lost the confidence of all classes. The free-state people were content to have him retained in office, as they considered him less dangerous to their interests than one entertaining the same sentiments but greater force of character; but those of the opposite side required a man who would stand firmly by them in every critical emergency. Hence they not only sought his removal, and left no means untried to annoy and embarrass him, but actually at last, succeeded in terrifying him to such an extent, that he fled alone from the territory with the apprehension that his life was really in danger from their hands.

The arrest and rescue of Branson led to many serious difficulties. It was, in fact, the beginning of the war which was subsequently waged with such frightful consequences. Soon after he reached Lawrence, a meeting of the citizens was held, at which S. N. Wood, the leader of the rescuing party presided, and at which, because of the fierce threats of Sheriff Jones, it was resolved to form a military organization, and to prepare to defend the town against an expected assault. Dr. Charles Robinson was chosen commander-in-chief of the volunteer forces, and Col. James H. Lane to be the second in command. A large fortification was thrown up on Mount Oread, a prominence commanding the main entrances to the city, in various parts of which earthen breastworks, or redoubts, were constructed.

Sheriff Jones hastened from the scene of his discomfiture to the town of Franklin, where he raved like one bereft of his reason, and swore terrifically that he would have revenge before he returned to Missouri. He forthwith sent a messenger to Col. A. G. Boone, of Westport, and another to Governor Shannon, with the following dispatch:—

"Douglas County, K. T., Nov. 27, 1855.

"SIR: Last night I, with a *posse* of ten men, arrested one Jacob Branson, by virtue of a peace-warrant regularly issued, who, on our return, was rescued by a party of forty armed men, who rushed upon us suddenly from behind a house upon the road-side, all armed to the teeth with Sharpe's rifles.

"You may consider an open rebellion as having already commenced, and I call upon you for *three thousand men* to carry out the laws. Mr. Hargis (the bearer of the letter) will give you more particularly the circumstances.

"Most respectfully, SAMUEL J. JONES,
"Sheriff of Douglas Co.

"To his Excellency, WILSON SHANNON,
"Governor of Kansas Territory."

This requisition for three thousand men might excite ridicule were it not known that Jones had already laid his plans to obtain them from Missouri; and of such a class as he knew would be willing to do his bidding. At this time the governor had no Kansas militia to furnish the sheriff, no organization having ever been effected, and the entire territorial military force consisted of a few generals and other commissioned officers. The governor, however, desirous of gratifying the sheriff to the full extent of his means, issued the following dispatch to William P. Richardson, a citizen of Missouri, but a member of the Kansas Council and major general of the territorial militia. The governor dates, in true military style, from *Head Quarters*:—

"Head Quarters, Shawnee Mission, K. T.,
"Nov. 27, 1855.

"MAJOR-GENERAL WILLIAM P. RICHARDSON,

"Sir: Reliable information has reached me that an armed military force is now in Lawrence, or in that vicinity, in open rebellion against the laws of this territory; and that they have determined that no process in the hands of the sheriff of that county shall be executed. I have received a letter from S. J. Jones, the sheriff of Douglas county, informing me that he had arrested a man under a warrant placed in his hands; and while conveying him to Lecompton, he was met by an armed force of some forty men, who rescued the prisoner from his custody, and bid open defiance to the law. I am also duly informed that a band of armed men have burned a number of houses, destroyed personal property, and turned whole families out of doors. This has occurred in Douglas county; warrants will be issued against these men and placed in the hands of Mr. Jones, the sheriff of that county, for execution; who has written to me, demanding three thousand men to aid him in preserving the peace and carrying out the process of the law.

"You are hereby ordered to collect together as large a force as you can in your division, and repair without delay to Lecompton, and report yourself to S. J. Jones, sheriff of Douglas county. You will inform him of the number of men under your control, and render him all the assistance in your power, should he require your aid in the execution of any legal process in his hands.

"The forces under your command are to be used for the sole purpose of aiding the sheriff in executing the law, and for none other.

"I have the honor to be your obt. servt.,

"WILSON SHANNON."

A similar order was addressed on the same day to Adjutant General Hiram J. Strickler. The brigadier general of the second division, residing at Leavenworth City, also a member of the Council and editor of the *Leavenworth Herald*, had received a dispatch by a special messenger, from Head Quarters, and on the 28th issued the following order:—

"Head Quarters of Second Brigade of Northern Division of Kansas Militia, Leavenworth City, Nov. 28, 1855.

"*To the Militia of the Second Brigade:*

"Information has been received by me that a state of open rebellion is now in existence in Douglas county, Kansas Territory. This is, therefore, to command the militia of my brigade of the Northern Division to meet at Leavenworth City, on Saturday, 1st day of December, 1855, at 11 o'clock, A. M., armed and equipped according to law, and to hold themselves in readiness, subject to the order of Major-General W. P. Richardson.

"Bring your arms and ammunition along.

"LUCIAN J. EASTIN,

"Brig. Gen. of 2d Brigade, Northern Division Kansas Militia."

The following hand-bill was posted in various prominent places:—

"TO ARMS! TO ARMS!

"It is expected that every lover of law and order will rally at Leavenworth on Saturday, December 1st, 1855, prepared to march at once to the scene of rebellion, to put down the outlaws of Douglas county, who are committing depredations upon persons and property, burning down houses, and declaring open hostility and resistance to the laws, and have forcibly rescued a prisoner from the sheriff. Come one, come all! The laws must be executed. The outlaws, it is said, are armed to the teeth, and number one thousand men. Every man should bring his rifle, ammunition, and it would be well to bring two or three days' provisions. Let the call be promptly obeyed. Every man to his post, and to his duty.

"MANY CITIZENS."

A proclamation was issued by the governor on the 29th, setting forth that the sheriff had been molested in the discharge of his official duties, a prisoner rescued from his hands, and his life endangered, and calling upon all good citizens to come forward to assist in reclaiming the said prisoner, and to disperse a "numerous association of lawless men, armed with deadly weapons, and supplied with all the implements of war, combined and confederated together for the avowed purpose of opposing, by force and violence, the execution of the laws of this territory."

Col. Boone, having received the dispatch of Sheriff Jones, immediately called upon sundry prominent men of Independence, Mo., for help, and upon receiving a letter asking further information, replied as follows:—

"Shawnee Mission, Nov. 30, 5 A. M.

"To Dr. McMurry and Col. Sam'l Woodson:

"Your favor was received. I thought I was too well known in the community to be thought capable of practising a hoax. The marshal has a requisition from the governor to arrest forty-two men in Lawrence, and they refuse to give them up, and he calls for volunteers, and if the citizens refuse to aid him, I cannot help it. They also say publicly that they will take Coleman and Jones, and hang them both.

"They are drilling in the open prairie every day, and have five fine pieces of artillery, and openly bid defiance to the laws.

"A large number of them were seen crossing from Delaware and Leavenworth yesterday, going to Lawrence.

"A member of the Legislature was from there yesterday morning for guns. We can only send twenty. Jones also sends for a wagon-load of ammunition and cannon.

"Now act, or not, as you please. If you will send the cannon here, I will take it there myself. In haste.

"A. G. Boone."

Upon the receipt of this, the following circular was published and widely circulated.—

"Independence, Mo., Dec. 2.

"An express, in at ten o'clock last night, says all the volunteers, ammunition, &c., that can be raised will be needed. The express was forwarded by Gov. Shannon to Col. Woodson, and by Woodson to this place, to be transmitted to various parts of the county. Call a meeting, and do everything you can.

"Drs. McMurry and Henry."

The Col. Woodson here named, is a member of Congress from Missouri, but has on several occasions taken an active part among the Missouri invaders of Kansas. On the next day, another circular, still more inflammatory, and numerously signed by *respectable* citizens, was published at Independence, of which the following is a copy:—

"Independence, Dec. 3, 8 P. M.

"Jones will not make a move until there is sufficient force in the field to ensure success. We have not more than three hundred men in the territory. You will, therefore, urge all who are interested in the matter to start immediately for the seat of war. *There is no doubt in regard to having a fight, and we all know that a great many have complained because they were disappointed heretofore in regard to a fight. Say to them, now is the time to show game, and, if we are defeated this time, the territory is lost to the South.*"

From Kansas City, the following dispatch was sent to Platte county, to encourage the people of that neighborhood, and it was there circulated, accompanied with appeals for men, arms, money and provisions:—

"Kansas City, Mo., Dec. 3, 8 P. M.

"Mr. Payne, the mayor of this city, went to Liberty to-day, and succeeded in raising two hundred men and one thousand dollars for the assistance of Jones."

Many documents of this description were widely spread all along the western border of Missouri. The result was that about fifteen hundred men were gathered in that state, who entered Kansas, and encamped on the Wakarusa, a few miles from the town of Lawrence. Concerning this invading army, Gov. Shannon uses the following apologetic language, which more than his acts, exhibits his weakness and incompetency to govern under the trying circumstances in which he suffered himself to become involved, by heeding the counsels and yielding to the mandates of a rash, passionate, and arbitrary subordinate.

"These men," he says, "came to the Wakarusa camp to fight; they did not ask peace; it was war—*war to the knife.* They *would* come; it was impossible to prevent them. What, then, was my policy? Certainly this; to mitigate an evil, which it was impossible to suppress, by bringing under military control these irregular and excited forces. This was only to be accomplished by permitting the continuance of the course which *had already been adopted,* without my knowledge, by Generals Richardson and Strickler; that is, to have the volunteers incorporated, as they came in, into the already organized command. A portion of these men, who were mostly from Jackson county, Mo., reported themselves to Sheriff Jones, by giving in a list of their names, as willing to serve in his *posse;* and he, after taking legal advice upon the question, determined to receive them. They were accordingly enrolled."

CHAPTER X.

The governor calls upon Colonel Sumner for United States troops.—Proposition for the Lawrence people to surrender their arms.—The governor makes a treaty with the free-state generals.—Dispersion of the militia.

GOVERNOR SHANNON discovered that it was easier to raise than allay a storm among the excitable people with whom he had to deal, and was alarmed at the probable consequences of his own hasty action. He was sensible of the difficulty he would have to control the lawless invaders whom he had caused to be enrolled as Kansas militia. Some of the more judicious of the pro-slavery leaders saw the subject in its true and frightful aspects, and began to suggest measures to end the troubles without the threatened loss of life and property. Hence General Eastin dispatched the following advice to Governor Shannon:—

"Leavenworth, K. T., Nov. 30, 1855.

"GOVERNOR SHANNON:

"Information has been received here direct from Lawrence, which I consider reliable, that the outlaws of Douglas county are well fortified at Lawrence with cannon and Sharpe's rifles, and number *at least* one thousand men. It will, therefore, be difficult to dispossess them.

"The militia in this portion of the state are entirely unorganized, and mostly without arms.

"I suggest the propriety of calling upon the military at Fort Leavenworth. If you have the power to call out the government troops, I think it would be best to do so at once. It might overawe these outlaws and prevent bloodshed.

"L. J. EASTIN,
"Brig. General, Northern Brigade, K. M."

The governor adopted this suggestion as the easiest means of freeing himself from his unfortunate dilemma, and immediately forwarded several dispatches to Colonel Sumner, commanding at Fort Leavenworth, asking him to interpose the United States troops between the opposing parties, and thus prevent a collision. To all of which the colonel replied that he did not feel justified to act "in this matter until orders were received from the government." Some of the leaders of the Wakarusa army had attempted to intercept Shannon's dispatches to Colonel Sumner, in order to prevent the interference of the United States forces, until they could destroy the town of Lawrence. The following letter from Colonel Joseph C. Anderson, of Lexington, Missouri, indicates the feelings of the invading army:—

"MAJOR-GENERAL WILLIAM P. RICHARDSON:

"Sir: I have reason to believe from rumors in camp that before to-morrow morning the *black flag* will be hoisted, when nine out of ten will rally round it, and march without orders upon Lawrence. The forces at the Lecompton camp fully understand the plot, and will fight under the same banner.

"If Governor Shannon will pledge himself not to allow any United States officer to interfere with the arms belonging to the United States now in their possession, and, in case there is no battle, order the United States forces off at once, and retain the militia, provided any force is retained—all will be well, and all will obey to the end, and commit no depredation upon private property in Lawrence.

"I fear a collision between the United States soldiers, and the volunteers, which would be dreadful.

"Speedy measures should be taken. Let the men *know at once—to-night*—and I fear that it will even then be *too late to stay the rashness of our people.*

"Respectfully, your obedient servant,

"J. C. ANDERSON."

General Richardson was beginning to open his eyes, and to see that an attack upon Lawrence might not, after all, be an entirely one-sided battle. It had been ascertained, in the Wakarusa camp, that Robinson and Lane had not been wholly idle, but had collected a force of over one thousand men, many of them armed with Sharpe's rifles, and having in possession several cannon, and that they seemed as anxious for an opportunity to resist as were their enemies to attack. Hence the general proposed to the governor, that, instead of assaulting Lawrence, it would be better, in order to prevent the effusion of blood, simply to demand of the citizens to surrender their arms.

But the governor could not clearly perceive how the course suggested by his friend, would tend to "prevent the effusion of blood and preserve the peace of the territory." He knew the people of Lawrence too well to suppose they would peaceably surrender their arms, and thus expose themselves, in a defenceless condition, to the tender mercies of the fierce men who were thirsting for their blood; and he felt quite well assured that an attempt to deprive them of those arms by force, might lead to anything but the most desirable results. He, therefore, preferred to follow the more sensible advice of Colonel Sumner, who said: "I would respectfully suggest that you make your application to the government extensively known, at once; and I would countermand any orders that may have been given for the movement of the militia, until you receive the answer."

Accordingly, his excellency addressed communications to General Richardson and Sheriff Jones, ordering them to proceed no further until he should receive instructions from Washington, in reference to the employment of the United States troops. Richardson readily acquiesced; but Jones, whose voice was "still for war," addressed the following rather indignant reply to the governor:—

"Camp, at Wakarusa, Dec. 4, 1855.

"HIS EXCELLENCY, GOVERNOR WILSON SHANNON:

"Sir: In reply to your communication of yesterday I have to inform you that the volunteer forces, now at this place and at Lecompton, are getting weary of inaction. They will not, I presume, remain but a very short time longer, unless a demand for the prisoner is made. I think I shall have a sufficient force to protect me by to-morrow morning. The force at Lawrence is not half so strong as reported; I have this from a reliable source. If I am to wait for the government troops, more than two-thirds of the men now here will go away, very much dissatisfied. They are leaving hourly as it is. I do not, by any means, wish to violate your orders, but I really believe that if I have a sufficient force, it would be better to make the demand.

"It is reported that the people of Lawrence have run off those offenders from that town, and, indeed, it is said that they are now all out of the way. I have writs for sixteen persons, who were with the party that rescued my prisoner. S. N. Wood, P. R. Brooks, and Saml. Tappan are of Lawrence, the balance from the country round. Warrants will be placed in my hands to-day for the arrest of G. W. Brown, and probably others in Lawrence. They say that they are willing to obey the laws, but no confidence can be placed in any statements they may make.

"No evidence sufficient to cause a warrant to issue has as yet been brought against those lawless men who fired the houses.

"I would give you the names of the defendants, but the writs are in my office at Lecompton.

"Most respectfully yours,

"SAMUEL J. JONES,

"Sheriff of Douglas county."

Affairs remained unchanged until the 6th of the month, when the governor called a convention of officers, to consult with them in regard to his desires and purposes. They convened at his quarters, when, after defining his position, he "soon discovered," as he says, "but one person present who fully approved of the course which he desired to pursue. The

6

others wished to go further. Some would hear of nothing less than the destruction of Lawrence and its fortifications, the demolition of its printing presses, and the unconditional surrender of the arms of its citizens. Others, more moderate, expressed a willingness to be satisfied, if the free-state party would give up their Sharpe's rifles and revolvers. Under these unfavorable circumstances, the conference broke up at midnight, having accomplished nothing beyond the interchange of opinions on either side."

On the morning of the 7th, the governor visited Lawrence, and, in a lengthy interview with Robinson and Lane, suggested, as a means of safety to the citizens and of peace to the territory, that they should surrender their arms to General Richardson, which proposition was positively declined.

On the following day, prominent men of the pro-slavery party informed the governor that if the citizens of Lawrence did not give up their arms, the place would be attacked, and that he had better consult his own safety and keep out of danger.

His excellency, therefore, again hastened to Lawrence, where he found that the people had held a meeting, on the previous evening, and submitted to writing the terms on which they proposed to treat. These, with few alterations, were agreed to, and received the signatures of the contracting parties, as follows:—

"*Whereas*, there is a misunderstanding between the people of Kansas, or a portion of them, and the governor thereof, arising out of the rescue at Hickory Point of a citizen under arrest, and other matters: *And whereas*, a strong apprehension exists that said misunderstanding may lead to civil strife and bloodshed: *And, whereas*, as it is desired by both Governor Shannon and the citizens of Lawrence and its vicinity, to avoid a calamity so disastrous to the interests of the territory and the Union; and to place all parties in a correct position before the world: Now, therefore it is agreed by the said Governor Shannon and the undersigned citizens of the said territory, in Lawrence now assembled, that the matter is settled as follows, to wit:

"We, the said citizens of said territory, protest that the said rescue was made without our knowledge or consent, but that if any of our citizens in said territory were engaged in said rescue, we pledge ourselves to aid in the execution of any *legal* process against them; *that we have no knowledge of the previous, present, or prospective existence of any organization in the said territory, for the resistance of the laws;* and we have not designed and do not design to resist the execution of any legal service of any criminal process therein, but pledge ourselves to aid in the execution of the laws, when called upon by *the proper authority*, in the town and vicinity of Lawrence, and that we will use our influence in preserving order therein, and declare that we are now, as we have ever been, ready to aid the governor in securing a *posse* for the execution of such process; *provided*, that any person thus arrested in Lawrence or its vicinity, while a foreign foe shall remain in the territory, shall be only examined before a United States District Judge of said territory, in said town, and admitted to bail; *and provided further*, that all citizens arrested without legal process, shall be set at liberty; *and provided further*, that Governor Shannon agrees to use his influence to secure to the citizens of Kansas Territory remuneration for any damage suffered in any unlawful depredations, if any such have been committed by the sheriff's *posse* in Douglas county. And further, Governor Shannon states, that he has not called upon persons, residents of any other states to aid in the execution of the laws; that such as are here are here of their own choice, and that he does not consider that he has any authority to do so, and that he will not call upon any citizens of any other state who may be here.

"We wish it understood, that we do not herein express any opinion as to the validity of the enactments of the Territorial Legislature.

"WILSON SHANNON,
"CHARLES ROBINSON,
"J. H. LANE.

"Done in Lawrence, K. T., Dec. 8, 1855."

The next day, December 9th, his excellency issued orders to Generals Richardson and Strickler and to Sheriff Jones, to disband their forces. His order to Sheriff Jones was in the words following:—

"Having made satisfactory arrangements by which all legal process in your hands, either now or hereafter, may be served without the aid of your present *posse*, you are hereby required to disband the same."

The most singular part of this whole history is, that, while on a visit to Lawrence, and when stipulating a treaty with the free-state commanders, Governor Shannon furnished them with the following document:—

"TO C. ROBINSON AND J. H. LANE, COMMANDERS OF THE ENROLLED CITIZENS OF LAWRENCE:

"You are hereby authorized and directed to take such measures and use the enrolled forces under your command in such manner, for the preservation of the peace and the protection of the persons and property of the people in Lawrence and its vicinity, as in your judgment shall best secure that end.

"WILSON SHANNON.

"Lawrence, Dec. 9, 1855."

Governor Shannon had proclaimed the people of Lawrence

to be an "association of lawless men," in open rebellion against the laws, and armed with the accustomed implements of war, to resist the officers of the territory in the prosecution of their duty. He had caused their city to be besieged by a large army of infuriated men from a neighboring state, whom he had enrolled as his own militia, to subdue and disarm the rebels. But after continuing the siege nine or ten days, he visits these "lawless men," who invite him to a "convivial party," in the midst of which, when the enraged army outside was for the time being forgotten, and all was hilarity and joy, the good-natured governor signs a paper authorizing the commanders of the rebels to "use the enrolled forces under their command" in such manner as their own judgment should dictate, to *resist his own forces* should they attempt to prosecute the object for which they were called into the field. Generals Robinson and Lane were skilful tacticians, and Shannon a most accommodating governor. No wonder that Sheriff Jones should feel aggrieved and angry at being thus despoiled of his contemplated revenge.

But it is due to the governor that he should be allowed to give his own explanation of this strange precedure. He says:

"In the evening I was invited to attend *a social gathering of ladies and gentlemen of the town of Lawrence*, at the Emigrant Aid Society Hotel, which I accepted. There were but two rooms finished in the hotel; they were small, and in the third story, and were, therefore, very much crowded by the company assembled. The time was spent in the *most friendly and social manner*, and it seemed to be a matter of congratulation on every side that the difficulties so lately threatening had at length been brought to a happy termination. In the midst of *this convivial party*, and about ten o'clock at night, Dr. C. Robinson came to me, in a state of apparent excitement, and declared that their picket guard had just come in and reported that there was a large irregular force near the town of Lawrence, who were threatening an attack; adding that the citizens of Lawrence claimed the protection of the executive, and to this end desired me to give himself and Gen. Lane written permission to repel the threatened assault. I replied to Dr. Robinson that they did not require any authority from me, as they would be entirely justified in repelling by force any attack upon their town; that the law of self-preservation was sufficient, and that any authority which I might give would add nothing to its strength. The doctor replied that they had been represented as having arrayed themselves against the laws and public officers of the territory, and that he therefore wished me to give him written authority to repel the threatened assault, so that it might appear hereafter, if a renconter did take place, that they were not acting *against*, but *with*, the approbation of the territorial executive.

With this view, *amid an excited throng, in a small and crowded apartment, and without any critical examination of the paper* which Dr. Robinson had just written, I signed it; but it was distinctly understood that it had no application to anything but the threatened attack on Lawrence that night.

"It did not for a moment occur to me that this pretended attack upon the town was but a device to obtain from me a paper which might be used to my prejudice. I supposed at the time that I was surrounded by gentlemen and by grateful hearts, and not by tricksters, who, with fraudulent representations, were seeking to obtain an advantage over me. I was the last man on the globe who deserved such treatment from the citizens of Lawrence. For four days and nights, and at the cost of many valuable friends, whose good will I have forfeited by favoring too pacific a course, I had labored most incessantly to save their town from destruction and their citizens from a bloody fight."

The sheriff's army disbanded agreeably to orders, the greater portion of it returning disgusted and enraged to Missouri, while the people of Lawrence, in anticipation of another visit at no distant day, went quietly though busily to work at increasing and strengthening their fortifications.

CHAPTER XI.

THE MURDER OF THOMAS W. BARBER.

THUS ended the Wakarusa war, but not till a most fearful tragedy had been enacted. About one o'clock on the afternoon of December 6th, three men, named Thomas W. Barber, Robert F. Barber and Thomas M. Pierson, left Lawrence to proceed to their houses, about seven miles distant. They had progressed nearly four miles, when they saw a party of from twelve to fifteen horsemen, travelling the road leading from Lecompton to the Wakarusa camp. These were subsequently ascertained to be pro-slavery men, and among them were Gen. Richardson, commander of the Kansas militia; Judge S. G. Cato, of the Supreme Court of the territory; Jno. P. Wood, probate judge and police magistrate of Douglas county; Col. J. N. Burns, a lawyer of Weston, Mo., and Major George W. Clarke, U. S. Agent for the Potawattomie Indians.

The Barbers, who were brothers, and Pierson, their brother-in-law, had just left the main road and taken a nearer path to the left. Upon perceiving this movement, Clarke and Burns put spurs to their horses, and dashed across the prairie, with the obvious intention to intercept them. The Barbers, therefore, slackened their pace, when Clarke, getting within speaking distance, ordered them to halt, a summons which they immediately obeyed. Richardson, Cato, and the remainder of Clarke's party, continued in full sight and at but a short distance. Clarke, who is a thick set man, about five feet three inches in height, exceedingly loquacious, and consequential in his manners, and notorious for his violent opposition to free-state people, commenced interrogating the Barbers, demanding to know who they were, where they were from, and where they were going; to all of which questions Thomas W. Barber made mild and truthful replies. Clarke then ordered them to turn their horses heads and go with him and Burns, to which demand Barber answered, "We wont," when Clarke drew his pistol, and taking deliberate aim, fired at Thomas W. Barber. Burns discharged his pistol almost at the same instant. Robert F. Barber then returned the shots, firing three times in rapid succession without effect. Pierson had with him a small revolver, but could not get it out. Thomas W. Barber was without arms of any description. The parties then separated, taking opposite directions and galloping their horses. They had proceeded but a short distance, when Thomas W. Barber remarked to his brother, with a smile, "That fellow shot me," and placed his hand against his side. Robert, perceiving that he had dropped the reins and was riding unsteadily, hastened to his assistance and attempted to support him; but in a little while he slipped from his saddle and fell to the ground. His brother and Pierson immediately dismounted; but Thomas was dead. They were about to place the body upon a horse and convey it home, when looking around they saw the other party again in pursuit, and to save their lives, they left it where it lay, hastily mounted and fled. They had not gone far when the horse of Robert gave out, and upon an examination he was found to have been shot, doubtless by Burns, just behind the fore-shoulder on the right side. He died during the night. The body of Barber was afterwards carried to Lawrence, where it was buried. A fouler murder than this, or one for which there was so little excuse, has not been committed during all the Kansas excitement.

The pro-slavery men's account of this transaction is as follows. They state that they were on their way from Lecompton to Franklin, and seeing Barber's party turn aside from the road, "Colonel Burns and Major Clarke were detailed and rode to overtake the free-state men. This they did; and, after halting them, a conversation ensued, in which the free-state men not only declared that there was no law nor order in the territory, but declined to surrender themselves in compliance with the demands of Clarke and his companions. Upon this both parties commenced drawing their arms, with the exception of one of the free-state men (who was most probably the man killed); this person sat on his horse a little apart from his companions. He had a switch in his hand, but drew no arms, nor did he appear to have any. Both parties 'squared to each other' and fired pistols, being the only weapons used. On the part of the pro-slavery men, Clarke was armed with a small five-inch Colt's revolver, while Colonel Burns had a navy revolver, which is heavier, and carries a much larger ball. After exchanging shots, the free-state men galloped off. Burns proposed to send a long shot after them with his rifle; but Clarke objected, saying, 'Let them go.' Burns is said to have admitted that he thought he hit the man he fired at, as he saw him press his hand to his side, or, as others state it, 'saw the fur fly from his old coat.'"

It is of little consequence which of the two men fired the fatal shot. Both were alike guilty, and both fired with the intention to kill. The testimony of Pierson and Robert F. Barber seems to fix the crime directly upon Clarke, who, it is said, and none who know the man will discredit the story, boastingly declared, when he entered the Wakarusa camp, "I have sent another d—d abolitionist to h–ll!"

A writer, who is decidedly pro-slavery in his tendencies, gives the following account of a visit, a short time afterwards, to the widow of the murdered man. After describing the dreary house, into which he entered, he says:—

"Between a heavy pine table, on which a flaring tallow candle stood flickering and sweltering in its socket, and the half-curtained window, against which the sleet and biting winter wind beat drearily, sat a woman of some forty years of age, plainly clad in a dress of coarse dark stuff. She was leaning forward when we entered, and seemed unmindful of all about her. It needed no introduction to tell us that this was the widow of Thomas W. Barber. No, the thin hand which supported the aching head and half shielded the tear-dimmed eyes, as well as the silent drops that came trickling down those wasted cheeks, had already told the story. What could *we* say in the way of consolation? What was the cause of Kansas and liberty to *her?* Could the success of a party or the advancement of a principle dry those burning tears? Could *they* soothe the sorrows of what she herself has called a poor heart-broken creature? Oh, ye demagogues! ye peace-breakers! ye incendiary orators of both north and south, whose aim is to urge on a strife, that you yourselves are not slow to avoid! could you but have stood beside us, in her once happy home, and have listened to the broken sentences, uttered with all that unstudied pathos which an agonized and grief-torn spirit alone can give, we hope, for the sake of our common humanity, that the lesson would have sunk deep into your hearts. Hear what she says:

"'*They* have left me a poor forsaken creature, to mourn all my days. Oh, my husband! They have taken from me all that I held dear—one that I loved better than I loved my own life.' These are her very words. We have added nothing to them, nor have we taken aught from them.

"There are circumstances connected with the life and character of the man Barber, which make his death more particularly to be deplored. He adds another to the long list of victims who have been sacrificed to the demon of political excitement. Barber is spoken of as a quiet, inoffensive, and amiable man; domestic and unexceptionable in his habits, and deeply attached to his wife to whom he had been married between nine and ten years. He was, moreover, the leading man among the agriculturists in his neighborhood; a lover of fine stock; and a careful pains-taking farmer. Such at least is the reputation he bore in Ohio, the state from whence he emigrated. He was unarmed when he received his death wound, and on his way to his home. His wife, to whom he had written to inform her of his coming, was expecting him. She is said to have loved her husband with more than ordinary devotion. Her sister-in-law tells us that they used to rally her, upon her almost girlish affection and solicitude for Thomas. It was her habit, when she saw him coming back from his work, to leave the house, and go forth to meet him on his way. If he failed to return at the time indicated, she grew anxious; and if his stay was prolonged, oftentimes passed the night in tears; when ill—the same informant tells us—she would hang over his bed, with all the anxiety of a mother for her child. She would seem, too, to have had a presentiment of some impending evil, for after exhausting every argument to prevent her husband from going to join the free-state forces in Lawrence, she said, 'Oh, Thomas, if you should be shot, I should be all alone indeed; remember I have no child—nothing in the wide world to fill your place.' And this was their last parting. The intelligence of his death was kept from her—in mercy—through the kindness of her friends, but only to be announced, without the slightest preparation, by a young man, who had been sent out from Lawrence, with a carriage, to bring her in to the Free-State Hotel, where her husband's body had been laid. Upon arriving at the house where Mrs. Barber was, he rode up, most unthinkingly, and shouted, 'Thomas Barber is killed.' His widow heard the dreadful tidings, rushed to the door, cried, 'Oh, God! what do I hear?' and then filled the room with her shrieks. We have heard, too, a description of the heart-rending scene, which took place when they brought her into the apartment where her husband's body lay; of her throwing herself upon his corpse, and kissing the dead man's face; of the fearful imprecations, which, in her madness, she called down upon the heads of those who had separated her from all that she held dear; and these things were related to us by men, who turned shudderingly away from the exhibition of a sorrow which no earthly power could assuage. It is, moreover, stated that her companions were obliged to hold her forcibly down in the carriage, from whence her frantic exclamations rang out along the prairie, as they conveyed her from her home to the chamber of the dead."

And what became of him who thus wantonly destroyed the life of an innocent and inoffensive man, and made such sad havoc of that poor woman's peace? As the pretended conservator of "law and order," he might subsequently have been seen at the head of bands of kindred spirits, traversing the country, venting, as once did Saul of Tarsus, threats of slaughter and destruction; robbing stores and burning dwellings; in the camps of infuriated armies bent upon ruin and desolation; in the legislative halls, the most active of those assembled, helping to enact laws for the oppression of free men; writing inflammatory articles for incendiary newspapers; and finally, at the seat of the general government, in daily intercourse with the president and his cabinet, the new governor and secretary of Kansas, consulting and advising as to the policy to be pursued for the government of that abused territory.

This man boasts of his willingness and anxiety to be tried for the terrible crime of which he stands accused. And this he may do with perfect safety. Such a trial before a judge who was a witness, if not a party to his guilt, would be but mockery and a farce. But he must yet appear before that Supreme Judge, at whose dread tribunal no false witness will be heard and no quibbles of law can screen the guilty soul. There the blood of the murdered man, and the tears and sighs, shrieks, groans and terrible agonies of that distracted widow, will appeal and not in vain, for retributive justice upon the destroyer's head. "Vengeance is mine!—I will repay, saith the Lord!"

CHAPTER XII.

Pro-slavery mob at Leavenworth.—Ballot-box stolen and clerk beaten.—The jail and printing office destroyed.—The election and fight near Easton.—Murder of Capt. E. P. Brown.—Shannon receives authority to employ the troops.—Congressional Committee.—Arrival of Buford and his southern regiment.—Sheriff Jones shot at Lawrence.—Rev. Pardee Butler tarred and feathered.

It would be impossible, in the limits allotted to this work, and to carry out its intentions, to give more than a mere passing notice of the most important events that occurred prior to Governor Geary's arrival in the territory. Party spirit increased daily in violence, new accessions were constantly being made to each of the contending factions, and hordes of desperadoes rushed into the country to take advantage of its disturbed condition, simply to plunder and destroy, regardless of the consequences, or of who might be the sufferers. Brutal and shocking crimes were of daily occurrence, and a state of affairs existed too disgusting and deplorable for language properly to describe.

The Topeka Constitution being submitted to the people, an election was held in regard thereto on the 15th of December. This went off quietly, excepting at Leavenworth City. Here a drunken mob from Platte county, Missouri, with horrid yells, curses and threats, attacked the house in which the votes were being polled, and beating one of the clerks almost to death, seized and carried off the ballot-box. Three days afterward they assailed the Leavenworth jail, and after releasing one of their companions who was held a prisoner, burned it to the ground; and on the 20th of the month a similar mob, infuriated by evil passions and bad whiskey, destroyed the printing office of the *Territorial Register*, the free-state newspaper at that place.

An election for officers under the Topeka Constitution was ordered for the 15th of January, 1856. The Mayor of Leavenworth, a pro-slavery man, elected by force and fraud, forbid such election being held in that city. It was therefore adjourned for that district to the 17th, at a house near Easton, twelve miles from Leavenworth. At that time armed parties of pro-slavery men stationed themselves at various places on the road, and intercepted the passage of the free-state people, whom they disarmed and drove back from the place of voting. Threats being made to take and destroy the ballot-box, and a dispatch having been sent to Kickapoo for a company of the "Rangers" to assist in that work, a party of twenty free-state men remained, after the polls were closed in the evening, to protect the box. Late at night three of these, Mr. Stephen Sparks, his son, and nephew, supposing the danger over, started for their homes. When close to Easton, through which they had to pass, they were assailed by a party of a dozen armed men, who rushed upon them from a grocery where they were drinking and carousing. Mr. Sparks and his son retreated into a fence corner, where they drew their revolvers and kept their enemies at bay. The nephew made his escape, and spread the alarm among the free-state people, and Captain E. P. Brown, with fifteen mounted men, speedily came to the rescue of their friends. As they approached, the pro-slavery party retreated. At that moment a large body of the Kickapoo Rangers rushed upon the scene, and commanded Brown and his party to surrender. This being refused, the Rangers commenced firing, which was promptly returned by Brown's men, and a general fight ensued, in the course of which both parties retreated to some empty houses, from which they continued their fire upon each other. This fight lasted over two hours, during which a pro-slavery man named Cook was killed, and several on each side were wounded.

A short time after this rencontre, Brown, with seven others, left for their homes near Leavenworth, in a buggy and a one horse wagon. They had not proceeded far when a wagon filled with armed men passed them in the road, without anything being said on either side. Scarcely had they passed, when, at a bend in the road, two other wagons appeared, and also a party of mounted men. These were the Kickapoo Rangers, who had thus fairly entrapped Brown and his party. Escape was impossible, and as resistance would have been certain destruction, Brown yielded to the wishes of his friends, and surrendered. Then commenced a series of cruelties never exceeded by the wildest savages. Capt. Martin, of the Rangers, being unable to restrain his men, after numerous efforts, turned away in disgust from their wanton atrocities. While, however, the most of them were engaged in tormenting Captain Brown, Martin succeeded in aiding the other prisoners, who, in the meantime, had been confined in the store of a man named Dawson, to make their escape. The ruffians assaulted their unarmed prisoner with kicks and blows, and finally, after amusing themselves for some time in this way, literally hacked him to pieces with their hatchets, which, in imitation of the less savage Indians, they always carried. The fatal blow was given by a man named Gibson, who buried his hatchet in the side of Brown's skull, sinking it deep into the brain. Before life was extinct, his murderers carried him to his own house, when meeting his wife on the threshold, he exclaimed, "I have been murdered by a gang of cowards in cold blood," and instantly fell dead in her arms. Can Heaven look upon such deeds and bless the cause in which they were committed?

February 16*th*, 1856.—Governor Shannon, in reply to his dispatches to Washington, received authority from the Federal Government to employ the United States troops to enforce the laws of the Shawnee Legislature. The President, in the meantime, had issued a proclamation denouncing the acts of the Topeka Assembly, and endorsing those of the pro-slavery party. The Secretary of War had also forwarded orders to the commander of the military department of the west to support Shannon in his efforts to enforce the enactments of the Shawnee Assembly, and to disperse the Topeka Legislature.

March 19.—The House of Representatives appointed an Investigating Committee to inquire into the validity of the Shawnee Legislature, and of the election as a delegate of Gen. Whitfield. This committee arrived in Lawrence on the 17th of April. During its sittings numerous attempts were made by pro-slavery men to interfere with the investigations, and threats were freely uttered against the personal safety of free-state men who should furnish them with evidence. A Mr Mace, having been before the commission, was on the same night shot at and wounded in his own house. Whilst Governor Reeder was before the committee as a witness at Tecumseh, a subpœna was served upon him by Deputy Marshal Fain, who demanded his immediate presence at Lecompton, to appear before the grand jury. Reeder, knowing that the sole object was to embarrass the investigation, refused to obey this summons. Mr. Howard, the chairman of the commission, could scarcely imagine it possible that these apparent attempts were actually intentions to interfere with their proceedings, but declared that if they were thus to be molested, he would call to their aid a sufficient force to arrest and send the offending parties as prisoners to Washington. After a lengthy and thorough examination, this commission published a voluminous report, clearly setting forth the facts of the election outrages which have been briefly narrated in this book, and showing conclusively that General Whitfield and the Kansas Legislature were alike elected by violence and fraud.

Early in the month of April, Colonel Buford arrived in Kansas, with a regiment of men from Alabama, Georgia, and South Carolina. The most inflammatory appeals had been made to the patriotism of these people, and flattering promises of reward given to induce them to enlist in this service, the avowed objects of which were to drive the abolitionists out of the territory and make Kansas a slave state. Some of these proved to be worthy men, and afterwards became good citizens. But the vast majority were "lewd fellows of the baser sort," who were qualified and prepared for the practice of any villany, however enormous. They disgraced themselves by their violence and depredations before they reached the territory, and, passing through Missouri, were a terror to some of its inhabitants. After their arrival in Kansas, Marshal Donalson took them into pay as his *posse*, and Shannon armed them with United States muskets, furnished for the use of the militia of the territory. Many of these men subsequently traversed the country as bands of highwaymen and robbers.

After Governor Shannon had received authority from Washington to employ the United States troops to enforce the enactments of the Legislative Assembly, Sheriff Jones was in his glory. Writs were obtained for the arrest of numerous free-state men, who were charged with sundry trivial offences, and the sheriff trooped about the country executing these writs, with companies of dragoons following at his heels. He several times visited Lawrence, where, although his very presence was considered an insult and an outrage, he succeeded in making arrests without resistance. The people, though not acknowledging his authority, bowed in submission to the government forces.

On the 23d of April, the sheriff entered Lawrence, with a large force of United States dragoons, and arrested a number of persons, who were held as prisoners in the tents of the soldiers. At night, Jones was in his own tent, which was lighted, and, when stooping down, some person from the outside fired at him, and the ball took effect in his back. The wound, though severe, did not prove mortal.

This affair created a lively sensation in Lawrence. Much as the citizens despised Jones, they were averse to any outrage being committed upon him in that place, as they well knew nothing would have proved more gratifying to their enemies. They consequently held a public meeting, at which the attempt upon the life of Jones was censured in the severest terms, and a reward of five hundred dollars offered for the detection of the intended assassin.

Jones and his party determined to make capital out of this affair. Although he does not seem to have been seriously injured, dispatches were forwarded to Washington on the subject, and even the president considered it of sufficient importance to elicit his official action. Communications, at the same time, were circulated through Missouri, and the pro-slavery papers teemed with inflammatory articles. Of these, the following is but a fair and even moderate specimen:—

"Kansas is once more in commotion. The traitors of Lawrence have again set the laws of the territory at defiance, and this time have added murder to their crime. Sheriff Jones, of Douglas county, than whom a braver man never lived, has been murdered while in the performance of his official duties—shot down by the thieving paupers of the north, who are shipped to Kansas to infringe upon the rights of southern settlers, murder them when opportunity offers, steal their property, and if possible, to raise a storm that will cease only with the Union itself.

"The excitement in this city, during the past week, has been very great. Rumors of various kinds have reached us, and although we believed a difficulty had occurred, we were not prepared to hear of such lamentable news,—the death of the patriot Jones. His death must be avenged, his murder shall be avenged, if at the sacrifice of every abolitionist in the territory. If the pro-slavery party will quietly sit still and see our friends, one by one, murdered by these assassins, without raising their arms to protect them, we much mistake their character. Will they again allow a northern governor to cheat them out of their just revenge? We answer emphatically, no! If the governor of this territory and the administration at Washington any longer attempt to force us to assume the position of outlaws before we can have justice done us, the sooner such a contingency arises the better. We are now in favor of levelling Lawrence, and chastising the traitors there congregated, should it result in the total destruction of the Union. If we are to have war, let it come now! While the memory of our murdered friends, Clarke and Jones, is fresh in our memories, we can coolly and determinedly enter into the contest, let it result as it may. We do not approve of the course of the governor, in calling out the United States troops to enforce the laws of the territory. It looks to us as a virtual admission that the law and order party of Kansas are not strong enough within themselves to enforce the law."

The sacking of free-state towns—the burning of free-state houses—the ravishing and branding of free-state women, and turning them and their helpless children naked upon the prairies—the murders of free-state men and shocking mutilations of their dead bodies,—were all nothing, and less than nothing, when weighed in the balance against this villanous attempt to take the life of Sheriff Jones. That gentleman, however, was less violent than his friends and associates, in regard to this transaction; and he was far less anxious than they, for secret reasons of his own, to discover and arrest his assailant.

On the 30th of April, the Rev. Pardee Butler, having terminated safely his voyage on the raft, again ventured to cross the Missouri River, and make his appearance in the pro-slavery town of Atchison, when, as he says, "I spoke to no one in town save two merchants of the place, with whom I had business transactions since my first arrival in the territory. Having remained only a few minutes, I went to my buggy to resume my journey, when I was assaulted by Robert S. Kelly, junior editor of the *Squatter Sovereign*, and others; was dragged into a grocery, and there surrounded by a company of South Carolinians, who are reported to have been sent out by a Southern Emigrant Aid Society."

Here they exposed him to every sort of indignity, calling him a d—d abolitionist, and many of them insisting upon his being instantly shot or hung. There were present those, however, who protested strongly against the outrage, when Kelly, who was the prime mover in the business, fearing the consequences of murdering his victim, said he "did not take Butler to be hanged, only tarred and feathered." To this some demurred, calling it a "milk-and-water-style" of doing things. Eventually they concluded upon their arrangements, and, as Mr. Butler himself says:—

"They stripped me naked to the waist, covered my body with tar, and then, for the want of feathers, applied cotton-wool. Having appointed a committee of three to certainly hang me the next time I should come to Atchison, they tossed my clothes into the buggy, put me therein, accompanied me to the suburbs of the town, and sent me naked out upon the prairie.

"I adjusted my attire about me as best I could, and hastened to rejoin my wife and two little ones, on the banks of the Stranger Creek. It was rather a sorrowful meeting after so long a parting. Still, we were very thankful that, under the blessing of a good Providence, it had fared no worse with us all.

"The first mob that sent me down the Missouri River on a raft—always excepting Robert S. Kelly—were courteous gentlemen compared with this last one. When I was towed out into the middle of the stream. I do not remember to have heard a word spoken by the men on shore. This last mob, when they left me on the border of the town, shrieked and yelled like a pack of New Zealand cannibals. The first mob did not attempt to abridge my right of speech. In reply to all the hard and bitter things they said against me they patiently heard me to the end. But these men, who have come to introduce into Kansas that order of things that now exists in South Carolina, savagely gagged me into silence by rapping my face, choking me, pulling my beard, jerking me violently to my seat, and exclaiming, 'D—n you, hold your tongue!' All this was done while my arms were pinioned behind me.

"Many will ask now, as they have asked already, what is the true and proper cause of all these troubles which I have had in Atchison. 'The head and front of my offending hath this extent, no more': I had spoken among my neighbors favorably for making Kansas a free state, and said in the office of the *Squatter Sovereign*, I am a free-soiler, and intend to vote for Kansas to be a free state. It is true that Kelly, by an after-thought, has added two new counts to his bill of indictment against me. The first is that I went to the town of Atchison last August, talking abolitionism. I have not the honor of being an abolitionist. And, second, that I spoke, somehow or other, improperly in the presence of slaves. All this is not only utterly false, but the charges are ex-post facto; for not a word was said of this the day they put me on the raft."

CHAPTER XIII.

Charge of Judge Lecompte to the Grand Jury.—Presentment.—Arrests at Lawrence.—Travellers interrupted on the highways.—The murder of Jones and Stewart.—The sacking of Lawrence.—Burning of the hotel and destruction of printing offices.

On the 5th of May, Judge Lecompte delivered a charge, highly partisan in its character, to the grand jury of Douglas county, of which, the following extract is in his own words:—

"This territory was organized by an act of Congress, and so far its authority is from the United States. It has a Legislature elected in pursuance of that organic act. This Legislature, being an instrument of Congress, by which it governs the territory, has passed laws; these laws, therefore, are of United States authority and making, and all that resist these laws, resist the power and authority of the United States, and are, therefore, guilty of high treason. Now, gentlemen, if you find that any persons *have* resisted these laws, then must you, under your oaths, find bills against such persons for high treason. If you find that no such resistance has been made, but that combinations have been formed for the purpose of resisting them, and individuals of influence and notoriety have been aiding and abetting in such combinations, then must you still find bills for constructive treason, as the courts have decided that to constitute treason the blow need not be struck, but only the *intention* be made evident."

The grand jury accordingly made a presentment, as follows:—

"The grand jury, sitting for the adjourned term of the First District Court in and for the county of Douglas, in the Territory of Kansas, beg leave to report to the honorable court that, from evidence laid before them, showing that the newspaper known as *The Herald of Freedom*, published at the town of Lawrence, has from time to time issued publications of the most inflammatory and seditious character, denying the legality of the *territorial authorities*, addressing and commanding forcible resistance to the same, demoralizing the popular mind, and rendering life and property unsafe, even to the extent of advising assassination as a last resort;

"Also, that the paper known as *The Kansas Free State* has been similarly engaged, and has recently reported the resolutions of a public meeting in Johnson county, in this territory, in which resistance to the *territorial laws* even unto blood has been agreed upon; and that we respectfully recommend their abatement as a nuisance. Also, that we are satisfied that the building known as the 'Free-State Hotel' in Lawrence has been constructed with the view to military occupation and defence, regularly parapeted and port-holed for the use of cannon and small arms, and could only have been designed as a stronghold of resistance to law, thereby endangering the public safety, and encouraging rebellion and sedition in this country; and respectfully recommend that steps be taken whereby this nuisance may be removed.

"OWEN C. STEWART, Foreman."

In order to accomplish the objects of this presentment, which was simply a declaration of war against Lawrence, a number of writs were made out and placed in the hands of the marshal for the arrest of prominent citizens of that place. Although it is asserted that no attempts were made to resist the marshal's deputies in serving these writs, the marshal, on the 11th of May, issued the following proclamation:—

"TO THE PEOPLE OF KANSAS TERRITORY:

"Whereas, certain judicial writs of arrest have been directed to me by the First District Court of the United States, etc., to be executed within the county of Douglas, and whereas an attempt to execute them by the United States Deputy Marshal was evidently resisted by a large number of the citizens of Lawrence, and as there is every reason to believe that any attempt to execute these writs will be resisted by a large body of armed men; now, therefore, the law-abiding citizens of the territory are commanded to be and appear at Lecompton, as soon as practicable, and in numbers sufficient for the execution of the law.

"Given under my hand, this 11th day of May, 1856.

"I. B. DONALSON,
"United States Marshal for Kansas Territory."

Previous to the publication of this proclamation, Buford's regiment, and other armed bands, had taken up positions in the vicinity of Lawrence, who were not only committing depredations upon the property of the settlers, but were intercepting, robbing, and imprisoning travellers on the public thoroughfares, and threatening to attack the town, in consequence of which a meeting was held, and a committee appointed to address Governor Shannon, stating the facts in gentle terms, and asking his protection against such bands by the United States troops at his disposal.

To this respectful application the committee received the following reply:—

"Executive Office, May 12, 1856,
"Lecompton, K. T.

"Gentlemen: Your note of the eleventh inst. is received, and, in reply, I have to state that there is no force around or approaching Lawrence, except the legally constituted posse of the United States Marshal and Sheriff of Douglas county, each of whom, I am informed, have a number of writs in their hands for execution against persons now in Lawrence. I shall in no way interfere with either of these officers in the discharge of their official duties.

"If the citizens of Lawrence submit themselves to the territorial laws, and aid and assist the marshal and sheriff in the execution of processes in their hands, as all good citizens are bound to do when called on, they, or all such will entitle themselves to the protection of the law. But so long as they keep up a military or armed organization to resist the territorial laws and the officers charged with their execution, I shall not interpose to save them from the legitimate consequences of their illegal acts.

"I have the honor to be yours, with great respect,
"Wilson Shannon.

"Messrs. C. W. Toplief, John Hutchinson, W. Y. Roberts."

Still desirous of averting the impending difficulties, the citizens of Lawrence held another meeting on the 13th, when the following preamble and resolution were adopted, copies of which were immediately forwarded to Marshal Donalson and Governor Shannon:—

"Whereas by a proclamation to the people of Kansas Territory, by I. B. Donalson, United States Marshal for said territory, issued on the 11th day of May, 1856, it is alleged that 'Certain judicial writs of arrest have been directed to him by the First District Court of the United States, etc., to be executed within the county of Douglas, and that an attempt to execute them by the United States Deputy Marshal was violently resisted by a large number of the citizens of Lawrence, and that there is every reason to believe that any attempt to execute said writs will be resisted by a large body of armed men; therefore,

"*Resolved*, By this public meeting of the citizens of Lawrence, held this thirteenth day of May, 1856, that the allegations and charges against us, contained in the aforesaid proclamation, are wholly untrue in fact, and the conclusion which is drawn from them. The aforesaid deputy marshal was resisted in no manner whatever, nor by any person whatever, in the execution of said writs, except by him whose arrest the said deputy marshal was seeking to make. And that we now, as we have done heretofore, declare our willingness and determination, without resistance, to acquiesce in the service upon us of any judicial writs against us by the United States Deputy Marshal for Kansas Territory, and will furnish him with a *posse* for that purpose, if so requested; but that we are ready to resist, if need be, unto death, the ravages and desolation of an invading mob.

"J. A. Wakefield, President."

On the 14th, still another meeting was held at Lawrence, and a letter, signed by a large and respectable committee appointed for the purpose, was sent to the marshal, in which it was affirmed "that no opposition will now, or at any future time, be offered to the execution of any legal process by yourself, or any person acting for you. We also pledge ourselves to assist you, if called upon, in the execution of any legal process.

"We declare ourselves to be order-loving and law-abiding citizens; and only await an opportunity to testify our fidelity to the laws of the country, the constitution, and the Union.

"We are informed, also, that those men collecting about Lawrence openly declare that it is their attention to destroy the town and drive off the citizens. Of course we do not believe you give any countenance to such threats; but, in view of the excited state of the public mind, we ask protection of the constituted authorities of the government, declaring ourselves in readiness to co-operate with them for the maintenance of the peace, order, and quiet, of the community in which we live."

In reply to this the marshal sends a lengthy communication, intended to be bitterly sarcastic, which he closes with these words:—

"You say you call upon the constituted authorities of the government for protection. This, indeed, sounds strange from a large body of men armed with Sharpe's rifles, and other implements of war, bound together by oaths and pledges, to resist the laws of the government they call on for protection. All persons in Kansas Territory, without regard to location, who honestly submit to the constituted authorities, will ever find me ready to aid in protecting them; and all who seek to resist the laws of the land, and turn traitors to their country, will find me aiding and enforcing the laws, if not as an officer as a citizen."

Whilst these documents were passing, the roads were blockaded by the marshal's *posse* of southern volunteers, upon which no man without a passport could safely venture. Captain Sam uel Walker, who had carried one of the above-mentioned letters to Lecompton, was fired upon on his return to Lawrence. Mr. Miller, who with two others had gone up to negotiate with the governor for an amicable adjustment of the pending troubles, was taken prisoner by a detachment of Buford's South Carolinians near Lecompton, who knowing him to have been from their own state, tried him for treason and sentenced him to be hung. He contrived, somehow, to get away with the loss of his horse and purse. Mr. Weaver, a sergeant-at-arms of the Congressional Committee, was arrested while in the discharge of his duty, and carried across the Kansas River, to the South Carolinian camp, where after a critical examination of his papers, he was discovered to be in the service of the United States, and released, the officer in command giving him a pass, and kindly advising him to answer promptly, if challenged, otherwise he might be shot. Outrages of this kind became so frequent that all travel was at last suspended.

On the 17th of May the citizens of Lawrence, through a committee, again addressed the United States Marshal, in the words of the following letter :—

"Lawrence, K. T., May 17, 1856.

"I. B. DONALSON, U. S. MARSHAL OF K. T.

"Dear Sir: We desire to call your attention, as citizens of Kansas, to the fact that a large force of armed men have collected in the vicinity of Lawrence, and are engaged in committing depredations upon our citizens; stopping wagons, arresting, threatening and robbing unoffending travellers upon the highway, breaking open boxes of merchandise, and appropriating their contents; have slaughtered cattle, and terrified many of the women and children.

"We have also learned from Governor Shannon, 'that there are no armed forces in the vicinity of this place but the regularly constituted militia of the territory—this is to ask if you recognise them as your *posse*, and feel responsible for their acts. If you do not, we hope and trust you will prevent a repetition of such acts, and give peace to the settlers.

"On behalf of the citizens,

"C. W. BABCOCK,
"LYMAN ALLEN,
"J. A. PERRY."

To this communication no reply was given. In the mean time, preparations were going forward, and vigorously prosecuted, for the sacking of Lawrence. The pro-slavery people were to "wipe out" this ill-fated town under authority of law. They had received the countenance of the president—the approbation of the chief justice—the favorable presentment of the grand jury—the concurrence of the governor—the orders of the marshal,—and were prepared to consummate their purpose with the arms of the government, in the hands of a militia force gathered from the remotest sections of the Union.

They concentrated their troops in large numbers around the doomed city, stealing, or, as they termed it, "pressing into the service," all the horses they could find belonging to free state men, whose cattle were also slaughtered, without remuneration, to feed the marshal's forces; and their stores and dwellings broken open and robbed of arms, provisions, blankets and clothing. And all this under the pretence of "law and order," and in the name and under the sanction of the government of the United States.

The marshal's army had a gallant host of commanders. There was General Atchison, with the Missouri Platte County Rifles, and two pieces of artillery; Captain Dunn, with the Kickapoo Rangers; General Stringfellow, and Colonel Abel, his law-partner, aided by Doctor John H. Stringfellow and Robert S. Kelly, editors of the *Squatter Sovereign*, with the forces from Doniphan, Atchison and Leavenworth; Colonel Boone, with sundry aids, at the head of companies from Westport, Liberty and Independence; Colonels Wilkes and Buford, with the Carolinians, Georgians and Mississippians; Colonel H. T. Titus, in command of the Douglas County Militia; and many others, too numerous to mention.

The heart of the marshal must have swelled with triumphant pride when he looked upon this *posse comitatus*, comprising in all not less than eight hundred warlike men. The governor must have reviewed them with that satisfaction which governors only can feel when about to accomplish a mighty undertaking, with the certainty of success. This patriotic host was about to engage in an enterprise that was to redound to their everlasting glory—one of the most noble actions that ever called warriors to the field of battle. But where, all this time, was Sheriff Jones, the life and spirit and power of all this chivalric host? Why had he not made his appearance, to encourage with his presence, and cheer with his voice and smiles, these patriotic forces? By some it was still supposed that he was either dead or dying of the wound in his back. Jones was still behind the scenes. The time for his appearance upon the stage had not arrived, and he patiently awaited his proper cue.

On the 19th of May, while these forces were collecting for

the destruction of Lawrence, a young man from Illinois, named Jones, had been to a store near Blanton's Bridge, to purchase flour, when he was attacked by two of the marshal's party, who were out as scouts. To escape these men, Jones dismounted and entered the store, into which they followed, and there abused him. He again mounted his horse and left for home, the others following, and swearing that the d——d abolitionist should not escape. When near the bridge, they levelled their guns (United States muskets), and fired. Jones fell mortally wounded, and soon expired.

On the following morning, the 20th, several young men, hearing of this transaction, left Lawrence to visit the scene of the tragedy. One of these was named Stewart, who had but recently arrived from the State of New York. They had gone about a mile and a half, when they met two men, armed with Sharpe's rifles. Some words passed between them, when the two strangers raised their rifles, and, taking deliberate aim at Stewart, fired. One of the balls entered his temple. The work of death was instantly accomplished, and another accusing spirit stood before the bar of God.

Soon after sunrise, on the morning of the 21st, an advanced guard of the marshal's army, consisting of about two hundred horsemen, appeared on the top of Mount Oread, on the outskirts of the town of Lawrence, where their cannon had been stationed late on the preceding night. The town was quiet, and the citizens had resolved to submit without resistance to any outrage that might be perpetrated. About seven o'clock, Doctor Robinson's house, which stood on the side of the hill, was taken possession of, and used as the headquarters of the invaders. At eight o'clock, the main body of the army posted themselves on the outer edge of the town. Deputy Marshal Fain, with ten men, entered Lawrence, and, without molestation, served the writs in his possession, and arrested Judge G. W. Smith and G. W. Deitzler. Fain and his companions dined at the free-state hotel, and afterwards returned to the army on Mount Oread. The marshal then dismissed his monster posse, telling them he had no further use for them.

It was nearly three o'clock in the afternoon, when suddenly another actor appeared upon the stage. The "dead" and "dying,"—the immortal Sheriff Jones,—rode rapidly into Lawrence, at the head of twenty-five mounted men; and as he passed along the line of the troops, he was received with deafening shouts of applause. His presence was the signal for action, and a sanction for the outrages that ensued.

Atchison then addressed his forces, in language not sufficiently well selected for ears polite, and then marched the whole column to within a short distance of the hotel, where they halted. Jones now informed Col. Eldridge, the proprietor, that the hotel must be destroyed; he was acting under orders; he had writs issued by the First District Court of the United States to destroy the Free-State Hotel, and the offices of the *Herald of Freedom* and *Free Press.* The grand jury at Lecompton had indicted them as nuisances, and the court had ordered them to be destroyed. He gave Col. Eldridge an hour and a half to remove his family and furniture, after which time the demolition commenced, and was prosecuted with an earnestness that would have done credit to a better cause.

In the mean time the newspaper offices had been assailed, the presses broken to pieces, and these, with the type and other material, thrown into the Kansas River. The following extract from the report of these transactions, given in the columns of the *Lecompton Union*, the most rabid pro-slavery paper in Kansas, the *Squatter Sovereign* excepted, is too significant not to be read with interest:—

"During this time appeals were made to Sheriff Jones to save the Aid Society's Hotel. This news reached the company's ears, and was received with one universal cry of 'No! no! Blow it up! blow it up!'

"About this time a banner was seen fluttering in the breeze over the office of *The Herald of Freedom.* Its color was a blood-red, with a lone star in the centre, and South Carolina above. This banner was placed there by the Carolinians — Messrs. Wrights and a Mr. Cross. The effect was prodigious. One tremendous and long-continued shout burst from the ranks. Thus floated in triumph the banner of South Carolina,—that single white star, so emblematic of her course in the early history of our sectional disturbances. When every southern state stood almost upon the verge of ceding their dearest rights to the north, Carolina stood boldly out, the firm and unwavering advocate of southern institutions.

"Thus floated victoriously the first banner of southern rights over the abolition town of Lawrence, unfurled by the noble sons of Carolina, and every whip of its folds seemed a death-stroke to Beecher propagandism and the fanatics of the east. O! that its red folds could have been seen by every southern eye!

"Mr. Jones listened to the many entreaties, and finally replied that it was beyond his power to do anything, and gave the occupants so long to remove all private property from it. He ordered two companies into each printing office to destroy the press. Both presses were broken up and thrown into the street, the type thrown in the river, and all the material belonging to each office destroyed. After this was accomplished, and the private property removed from the hotel by the different companies, the cannon were brought in front of the house and directed their destructive blows upon the walls. The building caught on fire, and soon its walls came with a crash to the ground. *Thus fell the abolition fortress;* and we hope this will teach the Aid Society a *good lesson for the future.*"

Whilst the work of destruction was going on at the printing-offices, the bombardment of the hotel, a strongly constructed three-story stone building, commenced. Kegs of gunpowder had been placed inside and the house fired in numerous places; and whilst the flames were doing their destructive work within, heavy cannon were battering against the walls without; and amid the crackling of the conflagration, the noise of falling walls and timbers, and the roar of the artillery, were mingled the almost frantic yells of satisfaction that constantly burst from the "law and order" lovers of Kansas Territory. Jones himself was in ecstasies. He sat upon his horse, contemplating the havoc he was making, and rubbing his hands with wild delight, exclaimed: "This is the happiest day of my life. I determined to make the fanatics bow before me in the dust, and kiss the territorial laws; and I have done it—by G—d, I have done it!"

And then followed scenes of reckless pillage and wanton destruction in all parts of that ill-fated town. Stores were broken into and plundered of their contents. Bolts and bars were no obstacles to the entrance of drunken and infuriated men into private dwellings, from which most of the inhabitants had fled in terror. From these everything of value was stolen, and much that was useless to the marauders was destroyed.

The closing act of this frightful drama was the burning of the house of Dr. Robinson on the brow of Mount Oread. This was set on fire after the sun had gone down, and the bright light which its flames shed over the country illuminated the paths of the retreating army, as they proceeded toward their homes, pillaging houses, stealing horses, and violating the persons of defenceless women. All these dreadful deeds were done by human authority. There is yet an account to render to a Higher Power!

During the perpetration of these atrocities, one of the pro-slavery intruders accidentally shot himself on Mount Oread.

another was killed by the falling of a brick from the free-state hotel, and a third had his leg crushed and broken by falling from his horse when gallopping in pursuit of an unoffending man, whom he had mistaken for Governor Reeder.

CHAPTER XIV.

Murderous assault on a pro-slavery company.—Captain John Brown.—The Potawattomie murders.—Outrages of Captain Pate at Osawattomie.—Battle of Palmyra.—Fight at Franklin.—General Whitfield's army.—Colonel Sumner disperses the contending armies.—Murder of Cantral.—Sacking of Osawattomie.—The murder of Gay, an Indian agent.—Outrages at Leavenworth and on the Missouri River.

AFTER the sacking of Lawrence, parties of free-state men were organized and armed with the determination to continue the war which had now begun in earnest. Some of these committed depredations upon their political opponents under the pretence of recovering horses and other property of which themselves and neighbors had been robbed. They attacked the pro-slavery men in the roads and at their dwellings, and committed most flagrant outrages. These organizations and their actions were condemned by the prominent and more respectable portions of the free-state party, and very few of the actual settlers of the territory had any lot or part in their proceedings. They were chiefly composed of men of desperate fortunes, who were actuated in many instances as much by a disposition to plunder as from a spirit of retaliation and revenge for insults and injuries they had received.

A detachment of one of these parties, eight in number, secreted themselves in a ravine near the Santa Fe road, where they laid in wait for a company of eighteen pro-slavery men who they had understood were coming in that direction on a marauding expedition, and as they approached, a fire was poured into them from their ambushed enemies, killing three and wounding several more. The remainder, not knowing the strength of their assailants, fled in dismay. Other instances of the kind were constantly occurring. Indeed, it seemed as though each party was determined to vie with the other in the number of outrages it could commit.

Captain John Brown, who lived near Osawattomie, was the

leader of one of these free-state guerilla bands. He was a Vermonter by birth, an old soldier, and had served through the war of 1812. He was a resolute, determined and brave old man; but fierce, passionate, revengeful and inexorable. His hatred for the border-ruffians had reached so high a degree, that he could emulate the worst of them in acts of cruelty, whilst not one among them was his equal as a tactician, or possessed as much courage and daring. Hence his name soon became a terror, and not a few unsuccessful attempts were made to effect his capture.

Old Brown, as he was familiarly called, is said to have been the leader of a band, who on the night of the 26th of May, attacked a pro-slavery settlement at Potawattomie, and cruelly murdered a Mr. Doyle and his two sons, Mr. Wilkinson and Wm. Sherman. The excuse given for this act, is, that the persons killed were there assembled to assassinate and burn the houses of certain free-state men, whom they had notified to quit the neighborhood. These five men were seized and disarmed, a sort of trial was had, and in conformity with the sentence passed, were shot in cold blood. This was doubtless an act of retaliation for the work done but a few days before at Lawrence.

Captain H. C. Pate, who was in command of a predatory band of about sixty Missourians, called "Shannon's Sharp Shooters," resolved to capture Capt. John Brown, and with this intent visited Osawattomie on the last day of May. Old Brown was absent, and Captain Pate succeeded without resistance, in taking prisoners two of his sons, whom he found engaged in their peaceful occupations. Captain Pate's men burned the store of a German named Winer, who was supposed to have been in the Potawattomie affair, and also the house of young John Brown, the captain's son. After committing these and other depredations upon the free-state settlers, the most of whose houses they entered and robbed, Pate and his company left the place, taking with them their prisoners. These they delivered to a company of United States dragoons, whom they found encamped on the Middle Ottawa Creek.

When Captain Brown learned of the visit of Pate, he gathered a company of about thirty men, and hastening in pursuit, overtook him on the 2d of June, near Palmyra, about fifteen miles from Lawrence.

Pate was encamped when Brown appeared, and having been informed of his approach, had fortified his camp by drawing together some heavy wagons. Brown soon made his arrangements, and notwithstanding the disparity of their forces, commenced the attack, when a spirited battle ensued. This lasted about three hours, when Captain Pate sent out a flag of truce, and unconditionally surrendered. Some of his men had ridden off during the fight, as was also the case with some of Brown's command. Several were severely wounded on both sides, but none were killed. Brown took thirty-one prisoners, a large number of horses, some wagons, arms, munitions, and a considerable amount of plunder that had been seized at various places by Pate's men. Soon after the surrender of Pate, Brown was reinforced by a Captain Abbott, with a company of fifty men from the Wakarusa, who had come to his assistance.

Whilst Brown was in pursuit of Captain Pate with the free-state men from Osawattomie, other parties from Lawrence and the Wakarusa were planning an attack on Franklin, where a number of the pro-slavery rangers had remained since the sacking of Lawrence. Franklin is about four miles from the latter town, near the Wakarusa, and on the road to Westport. It was a sort of Missouri head-quarters, where the forces were accustomed to assemble whenever a descent upon Lawrence was contemplated. Having settled the preliminaries to their satisfaction, a company of the attacking party entered Franklin about two o'clock on the morning of June 4th. The night was extremely dark, and everything in and about the town was wrapped in the most profound stillness. Yet the pro-slavery forces had been apprised of the intended visit, and were prepared to give the intruders a warm reception. The latter, numbering about fifteen men, proceeded directly to the guard house and demanded a surrender, which was answered by the discharge of a cannon planted in the door, that had been loaded heavily with every imaginable sort of missile that could be crammed into its muzzle. The noise of the explosion was like the loud roar of thunder in the very midst of the town. Fortunately for the assailants, the gun was not properly pointed, and its infernal contents passed harmless over their heads. Then came on the battle. A volley from the Sharpe's rifles of the free-state men was poured into the guard-room door, simultaneously with which, many shots came down from the neighboring houses. The attacking party threw themselves upon the ground, and without any regular order, kept up a random fire as rapidly as they could load their pieces, their enemies constantly returning their shots. In the meantime, reinforcements had entered the town, but in consequence of the extreme darkness and the uncertainty of the positions of the contending forces, they could take no part in the fight, not being able to distinguish their foes from their friends. They nevertheless made the best of their time, having broken into the stores and loaded their wagon, which had been brought for the purpose, with ammunition, rifles, guns, provisions and such other articles as they desired, the greater part of which were Buford's stores, previously captured from free-state people. The firing continued on both sides until nearly daylight, when the pro-slavery men retired, leaving their enemies in possession of the town. In this affair a pro-slavery man named Teschmaker was killed, and three or four wounded. One man had his ear shot off. The assailants received no injury whatever. One remarkable feature in all these Kansas battles, is, that although many persons were sometimes engaged, who fought with passions inflamed to the most violent pitch, the loss on either side was almost invariably quite insignificant. Those who suffered death were generally murdered, not in the heat of battle, but deliberately and in cold blood, when the fights were over.

General Whitfield, in the meantime, had collected a large force, chiefly from Jackson county, Mo., with which, accompanied by General Reid, and other prominent members of his party, professedly to relieve Captain Pate, and attack and capture Brown, he entered the territory and encamped near Palmyra. Whilst this army was assembling, the free-state bands were also concentrating and moving towards the same neighborhood.

These latter, says one of their own writers, "were a harum-scarum set, as brave as steel, mostly mere boys, and did not consider it a sin to 'press' a pro-slavery man's horse. At various times they have made more disturbance than all other free-state men together. They were under no particular restraint, and did not recognise any authority—military, civil, or otherwise—any further than suited their convenience. While they went around the country skirmishing, and carrying on the war against the pro-slavery men on their own hook, and in their own time and way, they were at the same time quite willing to lend a hand in more systematic and important fighting when there was an opportunity. These boys have been most bitterly maligned, and the free-state men, or conservative free-state men, were not slow to denounce them. Resolutions were passed by the sensitively moral free-state people, or the *sensitively timid*, declaring that these daring young guerillas were a nuisance, and that they, the conservative class, did not wish to be held responsible for them. To all this moralizing these young braves turned up their noses, ironically recommending all who were too cowardly to fight to 'keep right on the record.' For their own part, they regarded the war as begun, and would wage it against the pro-slavery men as the pro-slavery men waged it against their free-state friends."

This was the state of affairs near Hickory Point on the morning of the 5th of June. Whitfield was encamped behind Palmyra with near three hundred men. The free-state camps mustered, or mustering, on that day, were about two hundred strong, and two companies were marching from Topeka with fifty more, who arrived the day after.

The governor, in view of this condition of things, issued a proclamation on the 4th, "commanding all persons belonging to military companies unauthorized by law to disperse, otherwise they would be dispersed by the United States troops." Col. Sumner, at the head of a large force of dragoons, proceeded towards Hickory Point to enforce the order. He went directly to the camp of Brown, on Ottawa Creek, who consented to disband, but not until he was assured by Sumner that Whitfield's army should be dispersed. Pate and the other prisoners were then set at liberty, and their horses, arms, and other property restored. Captain Pate received a severe rebuke for invading the territory without authority, and especially for being in possession of the United States arms. Col. Sumner next visited the camp of Whitfield, who promised to return with his men to Missouri, and at once moved down the Santa Fe road, and encamped about five miles below Palmyra on the Black Jack.

Early on the following morning, June 6th, this army separated into two divisions, one half of it under General Reid, with Captain Pate, Bell, Jenigen, and other prominent leaders, moving towards Osawattomie, whilst the others, under Whitfield, started for Westport. They had, in their march on the day previous, taken several prisoners, and before they divided, held a court among themselves and tried one of these, a free-state man named Cantral, whom they sentenced to death, carried into a deep ravine near by, and shot. His body was subsequently found, with three bullet holes in the breast. The executioner in this case is said to have been a man named Forman, of Pate's company, belonging to Westport, Missouri.

On the 7th, Reid, with one hundred and seventy men, marched into Osawattomie, and without resistance, entered each house, robbing it of everything of value. There were but few men in the town, and the women and children were treated with the utmost brutality. Stores and dwellings were alike entered and pillaged. Trunks, boxes, and desks were broken open, and their contents appropriated or destroyed. Even rings were rudely pulled from the ears and fingers of the women, and some of the apparel from their persons. The liquor found was freely drunk, and served to incite the plunderers to increased violence in the prosecution of their mischievous work. Having completely stripped the town, they set fire to several houses, and then beat a rapid retreat, carrying off a number of horses, and loudly urging each other to greater haste, as "the d—d abolitionists were coming!"

There are hundreds of well authenticated accounts of the cruelties practised by this horde of ruffians, some of them too shocking and disgusting to relate, or to be accredited, if told. The tears and shrieks of terrified women, folded in their foul embrace, failed to touch a chord of mercy in their brutal hearts, and the mutilated bodies of murdered men, hanging upon the trees, or left to rot upon the prairies or in the deep ravines, or furnish food for vultures and wild beasts, told frightful stories of brutal ferocity from which the wildest savages might have shrunk with horror.

On the 21st of June, an Indian agent, named Gay, was travelling in the vicinity of Westport, and was stopped by a party of Buford's men, who asked if he was in favor of making Kansas a free-state. He promptly answered in the affirmative, and was instantly shot dead. Such was the only crime for which this soul was hurried into the eternal world.

Whilst these events were transpiring on the south side of the Kansas river, Col. Wilkes, Captain Emory, and other prominent pro-slavery men, were actively employed in persecuting the free-state citizens of Leavenworth. Notices were served on them to quit the city; some were violently seized and imprisoned, and still others carried to the levee, having been deprived of all their property and the greater part of their clothing, placed on board of steamers, and thus compelled to leave the country. At the same time the steamboats coming up the river continued to be boarded at every stopping place, the free-state passengers insulted, their trunks broken open and robbed, and their arms taken from them; after which they were put upon return boats, and forced to go back.

CHAPTER XV.

Removal of Colonel Sumner and appointment of General P. F. Smith.—Free-state refugees driven from Fort Leavenworth.—Immigration from the North.—Destruction of pro-slavery forts by free-state bands.—Murder of Major Hoyt.—Defeat of the pro-slavery forces at Franklin.—Colonel Titus captured by Captain Walker, and his house burned.—Alarm at Lecompton.—Governor Shannon makes another treaty with the Lawrence people.

COL. SUMNER, in consequence of the strict impartiality with which he discharged his duties, failed to give satisfaction to the pro-slavery party, who having all the official power in Kansas, backed up by still greater power at Washington, had no difficulty in effecting his removal from the territory. He was superseded in July, 1856, by General Persifer F. Smith, whose quarters were at Fort Leavenworth. The general was born in Pennsylvania, but has spent much of his time in Louisiana, and is decidedly a pro-slavery man in feeling and sentiment. His appointment was highly gratifying to those who had so strongly desired to get rid of Sumner. Soon after his arrival, General Smith, whose health had been failing for some time, became quite ill, and until the time that he left Kansas in February, 1857, was closely confined to his apartments, so that he was not able to take any active part in the affairs of the territory. Hence, after the removal of Shannon on the 21st of August, when Secretary Woodson became acting governor, until the arrival of Governor Geary in September, the belligerents had matters pretty much their own way, and the ruffians improved the time, under pretence of authority from Woodson, to perpetrate with impunity the most shocking barbarities. During this period Gen. Smith received much censure from the free-state people. Emory, Wilkes, Stringfellow, and others, were driving these from their homes at Leavenworth and other places, and many of them hastily fled in terror for protection within the enclosures of the fort; when the general caused hand-bills to be posted over the grounds commanding them to leave before a certain specified time, and gave orders to his subordinates to enforce this command. These unfortunate people, among whom were men of the highest respectability, and even women and children, were compelled, some of them without money or suitable clothing, to take to the prairies, exposed at every step to the danger of being murdered by scouting or marauding parties, or at the risk of their lives, effect their escape upon the downward bound boats. Some of these were shot in the attempt upon the river banks, whilst others were seized at Kansas City and other Missouri towns, brought back as prisoners, and disposed of in such a manner as will only be made known at that great day when all human mysteries will be revealed. There is many an unhappy wife and mother in the states looking anxiously, and hoping against hope, for the return of an adventurous husband or son, whose bones are bleaching upon the prairies or mouldering beneath their sod.

In August the troubles had reached their culminating point. The free-state immigrants had opened a new route into the territory through Nebraska and Iowa, and large and well-armed companies came pouring in, many of them of irreproachable character, who came to the relief of the oppressed; and others of desperate fortunes, eager to take part in the disturbances from a spirit of revenge or a love of the excitement; and still others, perhaps, for the sole purpose of plunder. These bands were generally under the direction of Lane, Redpath, Perry, and other prominent free-state leaders.

The pro-slavery marauders south of the Kansas River had established and fortified themselves at the town of Franklin; at a fort thrown up near Osawattomie; at another on Washington Creek, twelve miles from Lawrence; and at Colonel Titus's house, on the border of Lecompton. From these strongholds they would sally forth, "press" horses and cattle, intercept the mails, rob stores and dwellings, plunder travellers, burn houses, and destroy crops.

The fort near Osawattomie, in consequence of outrages committed in the neighborhood, and at the solicitation of the settlers, was attacked by a company of free-state men from Lawrence, on the 5th of August. A party of Georgians who held this position, upon the approach of the enemy, fled without firing a gun, leaving behind a large quantity of plunder. The fort was then taken and demolished.

The defeated party retreated to the fort at Washington Creek, and thence continued their depredations upon the neighboring inhabitants. On the 11th the people of Lawrence sent Major D. S. Hoyt, a peaceable man, who was greatly respected, to this camp to endeavor to make some sort of armicable arrangement with Colonel Treadwell, the commander. On his way home he was waylaid and shot, his body being fairly riddled with bullet holes.

This news so enraged the people of Lawrence, that on the 12th they attacked the pro-slavery post at Franklin. The enemy was strongly fortified in a block-house, and had one brass six-pounder. This battle lasted three hours, and was conducted with great spirit on both sides. The free-state men, at length, drew a wagon load of hay against the house, and were about to set it on fire when the inmates cried for quarter. They then threw down their arms and fled. In this engagement the free-state men had one killed and six wounded. The other side had four severely wounded, one of them mortally. The cannon taken was one that had been used to batter down the walls of the Lawrence hotel.

A general panic seized the Missouri and other southern intruders on learning these repeated free-state successes. On the 15th the Georgian camp at Washington Creek broke up in great confusion, its occupants flying in hot haste as the Lawrence forces approached. This fort was entered without resistance; large quantities of provisions and goods taken at Lawrence were recovered; the building was set on fire and entirely consumed.

The next blow was struck at Colonel Titus's fortified house, near Lecompton. This was one of the boldest strokes of the Kansas war. Lecompton was the stronghold of the pro-slavery party. It was the capital of the territory, the headquarters of Governor Shannon, and within two miles of the house of Titus a large force of United States dragoons was encamped. Captain Samuel Walker, a Pennsylvanian, and as brave a man as ever lived, commanded the attacking army. With about four hundred men and one brass six-pounder, he took up a position upon an elevated piece of ground near the house soon after sunrise on the morning of the 16th of August. The fight, which was a spirited one, immediately commenced, and resulted in the capture of Titus, Captain William Donaldson, (who also had rendered himself notorious at the sacking of Lawrence and elsewhere), and of eighteen others. Five prisoners, previously taken by Titus's party, were released, one of whom had been sentenced to be shot that very day. One of his men was killed in this engagement and several others wounded. Titus was shot in the shoulder and hand. Walker's cannon was loaded with slugs and balls cast from the type of the

Herald of Freedom, fished out of the Kansas River, where it had been thrown on the day that Lawrence was sacked. Walker set fire to the house of Titus, which was completely destroyed, and carried his prisoners to Lawrence.

The time occupied by this battle was greatly magnified by Titus in his account of the affair, as he maintains that he held out for six hours, and did not surrender until a wagon load of hay was brought up to burn the building. He says that he came out to capitulate with Walker when he received his wounds. On the other hand, Walker thinks the action lasted short of half an hour, which was also the opinion of Woodson, whose house was but half a mile distant, and of Major Sedgwick, of the United States dragoons, who hastened to the rescue as soon as he heard the firing, but did not reach the scene of action until the assailants had retired. Walker also states that Titus was found hid under the floor when his party surrendered.

Nothing could exceed the consternation that prevailed in Lecompton during this engagement. A universal stampede succeeded the firing of the first gun. The stoutest and most noisy boasters of the town rushed to the river, some on foot and others on horseback, and in their fright and hurry jumped into the water to swim across. Governor Shannon, when Major Sedgwick arrived, was sought for, and after considerable difficulty was found concealed in the bushes on the river bank. He was prevailed upon to accompany the dragoons in pursuit of Walker, and after proceeding a few miles, he saw him and his army leisurely crossing the prairies. Major Sedgwick asked for orders to make an attack and rescue the prisoners. But the governor, looking at the formidable force before him, thought it better not to venture an engagement, and gave orders for an immediate return to Lecompton.

He thence proceeded to the house of General George W. Clarke, a short distance from the capital, to ascertain whether that had also suffered damage. He found that the general had rapidly fled with his family, not taking time to remove an article or even to fasten or close his doors. Ever since the murder of Barber, Clarke has evinced an almost painful nervousness. He is exceedingly restless, and terribly alarmed at the slightest appearance of danger. Is it the ghost of the murdered man haunting the guilty soul? His house was fortified, a large number of arms collected there, and guards stationed during the nights. He was in everlasting fear of an attack from some unknown source. On one occasion, his wife had sent for a party of neighbors to protect them from some imaginary danger. It was dark when they arrived. Clarke hearing them coming, rushed out of the back door with a loaded gun, fired it at the party, and lodged its contents in the leg of one of his own friends. This is his statement of the affair. Others assert that he accidentally wounded his friend in an attempt to shoot a free-state man.

Titus had been one of the most active of the assailants in the sacking of Lawrence. On that occasion he rode through the town, giving his orders in a loud voice, and urging on his men to the work of destruction. When Walker brought him into that town, a wounded prisoner, he compelled Titus to sit up in the wagon and look around him, and as he carried him past the ruined buildings, would stop and ask him to contemplate his work. At length, when they reached the spot where the hotel had stood, Titus was informed that they intended to put him to death, when no man ever supplicated more pitifully to be spared. After being sufficiently tormented, he was conveyed to a place of confinement and attention given to his wounds. Captain Shombre, of the free-state party, was wounded in the attack upon Titus, and died on the evening of the 17th of August.

On that day, it being Sunday, Governor Shannon, Dr. Rodrique and Major Sedgwick, visited Lawrence, as a committee from Lecompton, to make a treaty; when the terms submitted to must have been most humiliating to his excellency. It was agreed that no more arrests should be made of free-state people under the territorial laws; that five free-state men arrested after the attack on Franklin should be set at liberty; and that the howitzer taken by Jones from Lawrence, should be restored; upon which degrading conditions, Titus and his band were released, and permitted to return to Lecompton.

CHAPTER XVI.

Atchison and Stringfellow call on Missourians for assistance.—Mr. Hoppe and a teamster scalped.—A German murdered at Leavenworth.—Outrages upon a young female.—Shannon removed, and Woodson acting-governor.—Atchison concentrates an army at Little Santa Fe.—General L. A. Maclean his commissary.—He robs the settlers and the United States mails.—Reid attacks Brown at Osawattomie, who retreats and the town is sacked and destroyed.—Murder of Frederick Brown and insanity of his brother John.—Lane drives Atchison into Missouri.—Outrages at the Quaker Mission.—Burning of free-state houses.—Lane threatens Lecompton.—Dead bodies found and buried.—Captain Emory murders Philips, and drives free-state residents from Leavenworth.

INFORMATION of the occurrences related in the foregoing chapter, soon reached the prominent leaders of the slavery faction, who lost no time in spreading them out before the people of Missouri, with any amount of exaggeration. On the 16th of August, Atchison and Stringfellow issued a circular at Westport, stating that Lane had entered Kansas at the head of a large army, had taken Lecompton, conquered the dragoons, liberated the treason prisoners, and committed other great and daring deeds; and concluding by calling upon the border ruffians for men and arms to drive the invaders from the territory.

On the 17th, a shocking affair occurred in the neighborhood of Leavenworth. Two ruffians sat at a table in a low groggery, imbibing potations of bad whiskey. One of them, named Fugert, belonging to Atchison's band, bet his companion six dollars against a pair of boots, that he would go out, and in less than two hours bring in the scalp of an abolitionist. He went into the road, and meeting a Mr. Hoppe, who was in his carriage just returning to Leavenworth from a visit to Lawrence, where he had conveyed his wife, Fugert deliberately shot him; then taking out his bowie-knife whilst his victim was still alive, he cut and tore off the scalp from his quivering head. Leaving the body of Hoppe lying in the road, he elevated his bloody trophy upon a pole, and paraded it through the streets of Leavenworth, amid the shouts of the "law and order" militia, and the plaudits of some who are denominated the noblest specimens of "southern chivalry," and regarded as men of respectability. On the same day, a teamster, who was approaching Leavenworth, was murdered and scalped by another human monster.

A poor German, when the scalp of Hoppe was brought into Leavenworth, was imprudent enough to express his horror of the shocking deed, when he was ordered to run for his life, in attempting which a number of bullets sped after him, and he fell dead in the street. The pro-slavery men aided Fugert to escape from the territory by sending him down the river, and furnishing him with money. He wore, upon his departure, the boots he so nobly won.

On the following day, a young lady of Bloomington was dragged from her home by a party of merciless wretches, and carried a mile or more into the country, when her tongue was pulled as far as possible from her mouth and tied with a cord. Her arms were then securely pinioned, and, despite her violent and convulsive struggles——but let the reader imagine, if possible, the savage brutality that followed. She had been guilty of the terrible offence of speaking adversely of the institution of slavery.

August 21st.—Governor Shannon receiving official notice of his removal, Secretary Woodson took charge of the government. This was a signal for great rejoicing among the pro-slavery people. Woodson was a creature of their own, and they felt assured that they would now be endowed with legal authority to continue the acts of rapine that had previously been committed without the shadow of law. The acting governor came up to all their expectations. He forthwith issued a proclamation, declaring the territory in a state of rebellion and insurrection, and called for help from Missouri, to drive out and exterminate the destroyers of the public peace. Atchison and Stringfellow soon responded to this call, and concentrated an army of eleven hundred men at Little Santa Fe, on the Missouri border.

General L. A. Maclean, chief clerk of Surveyor-General Calhoun, who subsequently served as adjutant-general under Brigadier-General Heiskell in the contemplated attack upon Lawrence, of September 1856, was the commissary of this invading army. He delights to boast of the skilful manner in which he performed his duties.

In the office of Governor Geary, on the morning of February 24th, 1857, Maclean, who was disposed at certain times to be loquacious, was in one of his vaporing moods, and the governor's private secretary, who appeared to be pursuing his usual avocation, took notes of a conversation, of which the following is a part:—

MACLEAN.—I was lying in my tent, one night, on the broad of my back, smoking my pipe, and enjoying myself over a bottle of good whiskey, when Generals Reid and Strickler, and several other officers, entered, apparently in great distress. They said they had over a thousand men to feed, and not a d——d ounce of rations for the next day. After much talk, I consented to act as commissary. They wanted me to get up and go to work, but I kept my place, as though utterly unconcerned, and continued to whiff away at my pipe; telling them that the rations would all be ready at an appointed hour in the morning. They didn't know what to make of my coolness—thought I was either drunk or crazy, and went off somewhat disappointed and evidently vexed.

GOV. GEARY.—Well, were the rations ready?

MACLEAN.—Yes, by G–d! Ready that morning, and every other, so long as we were in camp, about two weeks.

GOVERNOR.—But how did you manage it?

MACLEAN.—That was d——d easy. I was up before daylight; got out a number of wagons, and started parties in every direction, with orders to go to the stores and dwellings, get all the provisions they could find, and drive in all the cattle; and they returned with a pretty generous supply.

GOVERNOR.—How did you raise the funds to pay for all this?

MACLEAN.—Funds! by G–d, we didn't pay a d——d cent! We "pressed" it all! In these expeditions, which were continued every day, we got some useful information, too. We seized the mails going to and from Osawattomie, and more than a half bushel of letters fell into my hands, in examining which, I found many of them directed to, and others written by, some of the most wealthy and influential citizens of Boston and other parts of the northern and eastern states.

Maclean is a Scotchman, and has been but a short time in America. He is over six feet high, and proportionably stout; is the constant companion of Sheriff Jones, General Clarke, and others of that class, and is among the most prominent of the Kansas mischief-makers. He may always be found in the Lecompton post-office, at the opening and closing of the mails, and generally manages to acquaint himself with their contents, for the benefit of his party. He makes inflammatory speeches at pro-slavery meetings; is extremely violent in denunciations

of free-state men; always urging others to unlawful and atrocious acts; but never venturing to place his own person in the place of danger.

A detachment of Atchison's army, under General Reid, numbering about three hundred men, with one piece of artillery, attacked Osawattomie on the 30th of August. Brown was in command at the time, and, having only between thirty and forty men, he retreated to the timber on the river or creek known as the Marais Des Cygnes. The battle which ensued lasted about three hours, Brown having a decided advantage. He was overpowered, however, by superior numbers and driven to the river, in crossing which he suffered some loss from the enemy. Two free-state men were killed in this fight; but the loss of the other party was much greater, though its precise amount has never been ascertained. It has been stated that more than thirty men were killed and as many wounded, but this is probably an exaggeration. It was the most disastrous battle during the Kansas war.

After the retreat of Brown, Reid's forces burned some twenty or thirty houses, robbed the post-office and stores, took possession of all the horses, cattle and wagons in the town, and committed many other depredations. They found a man named Garrison concealed in the woods, whom they killed, and wounded another by the name of Cutter, whom they supposed to be dead, but who has since recovered. A Mr. Williams, a pro-slavery man, was murdered by them in mistake.

Early in the morning, about 6 o'clock, of the same day, Frederick Brown, a half-witted young man, and son of old Captain Brown, was killed in the road near his father's house, by Martin White, a member from Lykens county of the Kansas Legislature, and formerly a clergyman. White's own account of this transaction, is, that sometime previous, Captain Brown had stolen some of his horses, and on the morning of his death, Frederick was seen by him, riding one of these stolen horses and leading another; that he ordered young Brown not to approach or he would shoot him. This warning was unheeded, but Brown came on, apparently feeling in his breast for a weapon, when he, White, raised his gun, fired, and shot him.

Captain John Brown, Jr., is a maniac in consequence of the cruel treatment he received while a prisoner of Pate. His arms were so firmly bound with cords as to cut into the flesh, in which condition he was compelled to travel in front of the horses for a number of miles under a burning sun, and often forced to run to keep from under the horses' feet. He was also kept without food and water. During these sufferings and privations, his reason forsook him and has never been restored.

On the same day of the battle at Osawattomie, Lane, with about three hundred men, marched in pursuit of Atchison, who was encamped with the main body of his army on Bull Creek. Atchison would not stop to fight, but retreated into Missouri, and Lane on the following day returned to Lawrence.

Whilst these things were occurring, a party of pro-slavery men entered the Quaker Mission, on the Lawrence road, near Westport, plundered it of everything worth carrying away, and brutally treated the occupants. At the same time, Woodson's "territorial militia" were amusing themselves by burning the houses of the free-state settlers between Lecompton and Lawrence. Seven buildings were destroyed, among which were the dwellings of Captain Walker and Judge Wakefield The deputy marshal, Cramer, whose features are almost as hard as his heart, was one of the most active of these incendiaries.

Because of these outrages, and the seizure of some free-state prisoners, Lane, with a large force, proceeded to Lecompton, on September 4th, and before any intimation was received by the citizens, his cannon were frowning upon their houses from the summit of Court House Hill. General Richardson, who was in command of the pro-slavery forces, refused to defend the town, having no confidence in the courage of the inhabitants, who were flying in all directions, in confusion and alarm, and he therefore resigned his commission. General Marshall being next in command, held a parley with Lane, who demanded the liberation of the free-state prisoners. This was agreed to. Lane returned to Lawrence, and the next day, the prisoners came down with an escort of United States dragoons.

At Leavenworth and vicinity, outrages had been renewed, and were being committed, if possible, with increased ferocity. As Governor Shannon afterward remarked, "the roads were literally strewn with dead bodies." A United States officer discovered a number of slaughtered men, thirteen, it is stated, lying unburied, who had been seized and brained, some of them being shot in the forehead, and others down through the top of the skull, whilst some were cut with hatchets and their bodies shockingly and disgustingly mutilated.

On the first of September, Captain Frederick Emory, a United States Mail Contractor, rendered himself conspicuous in Leavenworth, at the head of a band of ruffians, mostly from western Missouri. They entered houses, stores, and dwellings of free-state people, and, in the name of "law and order," abused and robbed the occupants, and drove them out into the roads, irrespective of age, sex or condition. Under pretence of searching for arms, they approached the house of William Phillips, the lawyer who had previously been tarred and feathered and carried to Missouri. Phillips, supposing he was to be subjected to a similar outrage, and resolved not to submit to the indignity, stood upon his defence. In repelling the assaults of the mob, he killed two of them, when the others burst into the house, and poured a volley of balls into his body, killing him instantly in the presence of his wife and another lady. His brother, who was also present, had an arm badly broken with bullets, and was compelled to submit to an amputation. Fifty of the free-state prisoners were then driven on board the Polar Star, bound for St. Louis. On the next day a hundred more were embarked by Emory and his men, on the steamboat Emma. During these proceedings, an election was held for Mayor, and William E. Murphy, since appointed Indian agent by the President, was elected "without opposition."

At this time civil war raged in all the populous districts. Women and children had fled from the territory. The roads were impassable. No man's life was safe, and every person, when he lay down to rest at night, bolted and barred his doors, and fell asleep grasping firmly his pistol, gun or knife.

CHAPTER XVII.

Appointment of Governor Geary.—His departure for Kansas.—Arrival at Jefferson City.—Interviews with Governor Price.—Removal of obstructions on the Missouri River.—Departure on steamboat Keystone.—Scenes at Glasgow.—Captain Jackson's Missouri volunteers.—What Reeder did.—Arrival at Kansas City.—Description of Border Ruffians.—Who comprise the Abolitionists.—Appearance and condition of Leavenworth City.

COL. JOHN W. GEARY, of Westmoreland county, Pennsylvania, received information of his appointment as Governor of Kansas in the latter part of July, 1856, and in a few days after, was confirmed, without the usual reference to a committee, by a unanimous vote of the Senate. He immediately hastened to Washington City, to receive instructions and make the necessary arrangements, and early in September proceeded to take charge of the office to which he had been chosen. He reached Jefferson City, Mo., on the 5th of that month, and passed the greater portion of the 6th, in consultation with Governor Sterling Price, in relation to the policy he was about to adopt and the means he purposed to employ to restore tranquillity and peace to the territory. Gov. Price coincided in his opinions, heartily approved the indicated course, and promised such assistance as might be desired and he had the power to render. From these considerations and mutual understandings, measures were adopted, and successfully carried out, to remove the obstructions, that until this time existed, against the free-state emigrants passing up the Missouri River on their way to Kansas. In no instance were the emigrants subsequently interfered with upon the steamboats on the river.

On the night of Sept. 6th, accompanied by his private secretary, and several friends, Governor Geary took passage on the steam packet Keystone, for Fort Leavenworth, and about noon of the 7th, it being Sunday, arrived at Glasgow in Missouri. On approaching this town, a most stirring scene was presented. The entire population of the city and surrounding neighborhood was assembled upon the high bank overlooking the river, and all appeared to be laboring under a state of extraordinary excitement. Whites and blacks,—men, women, and children, of all ages, were crowded together in one confused mass, or hurrying hither and yon, as though some terrible event was about to transpire. A large brass field-piece was mounted in a prominent position, and ever and anon belched forth a fiery flame and deafened the ear with its thundering warlike sounds. When the Keystone touched the landing a party of about sixty, comprising Captain Jackson's company of Missouri volunteers for the Kansas militia, descended the hill, dragging their cannon with them, and ranged themselves along the shore; the captain, after numerous attempts, failing to get them into what might properly be termed a line. He got them into as good a military position as possible, by backing them up against the foot of the hill. They were as raw and undisciplined a set of recruits as ever shouldered arms. Their ages varied, through every gradation, from the smooth-faced half-grown boy to the grey-bearded old man; whilst their dresses, which differed as much as their ages, gave unmistakable evidences, that they belonged to any class of society, excepting that usually termed respectable. Each one carried some description of fire-arm, not two of which were alike. There were muskets, carbines, rifles, shot-guns, and pistols of every size, quality, shape and style. Some of them were in good condition, but others were never intended for use, and still others unfit to shoot robins or tomtits. It would have been an afflictive sight to witness the numerous friends of this patriotic band, shaking them affectionately by the hand and pronouncing their blessings and benedictions, had they been enlisted in their country's cause, to repel invasion, or battle with a foreign foe; but knowing the character of their enterprise, the feeling inspired was anything but one of admiration or even sympathy.

While these parting ceremonies were being performed, a steamboat, bound down the river, and directly from Kansas, came alongside the Keystone. Ex-governor Shannon was a passenger, who, upon learning the close proximity of Governor Geary, sought an immediate interview with him. The ex-governor was greatly agitated. He had fled in haste and terror from the territory, and seemed still to be laboring under an apprehension for his personal safety. His description of Kansas was suggestive of everything that is frightful and horrible. Its condition was deplorable in the extreme. The whole territory was in a state of insurrection, and a destructive civil war was devastating the country. Murder ran rampant, and the roads were everywhere strewn with the bodies of slaughtered men. No language can exaggerate the awful picture that was drawn; and a man of less nerve than Governor Geary, believing it not too highly colored, would instantly have taken the backward track, rather than rush upon the dangers so eloquently and fearfully portrayed.

During this interview, Captain Jackson embarked his company, cannon, wagons, arms and ammunition on board the Keystone, and soon after, she was again on her way. Opportunities now occurred for conversation with the volunteers. Very few of them had any definite idea of the nature of the enterprise in which they had embarked. The most they seemed to understand about the matter, was, that they were to receive so much per diem for going to Kansas to hunt and kill abolitionists. What this latter word meant they could not clearly define. They had been informed that abolitionists were enemies to Missourians, some of whom had been killed, and they were hired to revenge their deaths. More than this they neither knew nor cared to know. A vague notion prevailed among them, that whatever an abolitionist was, it was a virtue to kill him and take possession of his property. They seemed to apprehend no danger to themselves, as they had been told the abolitionists would not fight; but being overawed by the numbers and warlike appearance of their adversaries, would escape as rapidly as possible out of the territory, leaving behind them any quantity of land, horses, clothing, arms, goods and chattels, all of which was to be divided among the victors. They crowded around Governor Geary, wherever he might chance to be, eager to ask questions, volunteer advice, and ascertain satisfactorily, whether, in their own chaste phrase, he was "sound on the goose." One, more importunate than the rest, and who was a sort of spokesman for his companions, having made sundry efforts to receive convincing proofs of the latter named fact, very knowingly remarked, after putting an unusually large plug of tobacco into his mouth, and winking to those around him, as though he would say, "I'll catch him now; just listen!"—

"Wall, govner, as yer gwoin to Kanzies to be govner, I hope ye'll not do what Reeder done."

The governor very quietly asked, "What was it that Reeder did?"

This was a poser.

"Whoy," said the inquisitor, breathing less freely, and shifting the plug of tobacco to the opposite side of his huge jaws, as if to awaken a new thought,—"whoy, Reeder, you see—Reeder, he—wall, Reeder, then Reeder, he didn't do nothin!"

"In that case," answered the governor, "I'll endeavor not to do as Reeder did!"

This answer was perfectly clear and satisfactory. The governor was "sound," and the inquisitorial party adjourned to the bar to drink the health of the new governor, who was all right, as he didn't intend to do as Reeder had done.

Active preparations for war were discernible at all the river towns. At Lexington, a large crowd was assembled on the levee, many of the persons composing it loaded with arms. But at Kansas City, the warlike demonstrations were still greater. This town is on the southern side of the mouth of the Kansas River, which, at this point, separates Missouri from the territory of Kansas. It is situated about five miles from Westport, near the eastern boundary of Kansas, where the Missouri army was concentrating, preparatory to an invasion of the territory. Both of these towns have become notorious as places of refuge for the most desperate characters, whose almost nameless crimes have blackened the annals of Kansas, and as being the resorts of numerous combinations which have been congregated to plot against its peace. In a word, they are the strongholds of the worst of the "Border Ruffians."

Let it not be understood that this latter term is considered by those to whom it is applied as one of reproach. On the contrary, they boast of it, are proud of it, glory in it, and do all in their power to merit it; and very many of them have been eminently successful. In their manner, they assume the character of the ruffian; in their dress, they exhibit the appearance of the ruffian; and in their conversation they labor to convey the impression that they are ruffians indeed. They imitate and resemble the guerillas, ladrones or greasers of Mexico; the brigands of Spain or Italy; or the pirates, robbers and murderers of the theatre.

On the levee at Kansas City stood a sort of omnibus or wagon, used to convey passengers to and from Westport, upon either side of which was painted in flaming capitals the words "BORDER RUFFIAN." Standing about in groups, or running in every direction, were numbers of the men who claim for themselves that gentle appellation. A description of one of these will give the reader some idea of their general characteristics. Imagine a man standing in a pair of long boots, covered with dust and mud and drawn over his trousers, the latter made of coarse, fancy-colored cloth, well soiled; the handle of a large bowie-knife projecting from one or both boot-tops; a leathern belt buckled around his waist, on each side of which is fastened a large revolver; a red or blue shirt, with a heart, anchor, eagle or some other favorite device braided on the breast and back, over which is swung a rifle or carbine; a sword dangling by his side; an old slouched hat, with a cockade or brass star on the front or side, and a chicken, goose or turkey feather sticking in the top; hair uncut and uncombed, covering his neck and shoulders; an unshaved face and unwashed hands. Imagine such a picture of humanity, who can swear any given number of oaths in any specified time, drink any quantity of bad whiskey without getting drunk, and boast of having stolen a half dozen horses and killed one or more abolitionists, and you will have a pretty fair conception of a border ruffian, as he appears in Missouri and in Kansas. He has, however, the happy faculty of assuming a very different aspect. Like other animals, he can shed his coat and change his colors. In the city of Washington, he is quite another person. You will see him in the corridors of the first-class hotels—upon Pennsylvania avenue—in the rotunda of the capitol, or the spacious halls of the White House, dressed in the finest broad cloths and in the extreme of fashion; his hair trimmed, his face smoothed and his hands cleansed; his manner gentle, kind and courteous; his whole deportment that of innocence, and his speech so smooth, studied and oily as to convince even the sagacious President himself that he is a veritable and a polished gentleman, and obtain from the wise heads that form the cabinet the most important posts of trust, honor and emolument in the gift of the nation.

The Keystone no sooner touched the shore at Kansas City, than she was boarded by a half dozen or more of the leading ruffians, who dashed through the cabins and over the decks, inspecting the passengers and the state-rooms to satisfy themselves that no abolitionists were on board. And here let it be distinctly observed that an abolitionist, in border-ruffian parlance, is not simply a man opposed to the extension of slavery, or who favors its abolishment from the states; but every person born in a free state, who is unwilling to give indubitable evidences that he will do all in his power to assist in making Kansas a slave state, by means either fair or foul, at any sacrifice and at every hazard. It is of little consequence what have been and still are his political predilections on every great national question. He must know but one issue—that issue, slavery—or be branded, in the language of a resolution unanimously passed by the Legislative Assembly, as an "ally of abolitionism." It will not do to assume a neutral ground; it is not sufficient to asseverate that you will give your influence to the cause of slavery. All this may be done, and you will be regarded with suspicion and treated as an enemy. More substantial proof of being "sound on the goose" is demanded. You must join the "Blue Lodges"—take their solemn oaths—bind yourself to murder any man who is opposed to making Kansas a slave state, and invoke upon yourself their horrible penalties in case of failure. You must steep your hands in crime deeper than the most rabid of the fire-eaters of the south. You must place yourself utterly in their power, so that you dare not quail, or hesitate, or fail to do their bidding. You must become yourself a slave, bound by stronger bonds than any that holds in servitude the veriest negro wretch—else you are *an abolitionist.* And there are men in Kansas, who, though born in free states, are sold, body and soul, to the slave interest; men who have taken the oaths of the Blue Lodges—who boast, to prove themselves "sound," of the number of crimes they have committed; the horses they have stolen; the women they have outraged; the houses they have robbed; the murders they have done:—men, in fact, who have become so deeply steeped in infamy that they dare not now stop, even should they never so much desire; but who find themselves precisely in the condition of Macbeth, when he exclaimed

> "I am in blood,
> Stept in so far, that, should I wade no more,
> Returning were as tedious as go o'er."

The abolitionists of Kansas are all northern-born men, who will not thus prostitute, degrade and destroy themselves in support of the slave power; but who have the honesty and independence to be free, and to maintain their freedom.

The Keystone remained at Kansas City only long enough for Captain Jackson to land his company with its paraphernalia of war, and to undergo a thorough inspection of the border ruffian inquisitors, when she proceeded up the river for Fort Leavenworth. She left Kansas City late on the evening of the 8th, and soon after day-break of the 9th, reached the landing at Leavenworth City, three miles below the fort. Here was given another exhibition of the wretched condition of the country and deplorable spirit of the times. In front of the grog-shops, and these comprised nearly every house on the river front; on piles of wood, lumber and stone; upon the heads of whiskey barrels; at the corners of the streets; and upon the river bank,—lounged, strolled, and idled, singly or in squads, men and boys clad in the ruffian attire, giving sure indication that no useful occupation was being pursued, and that vice, confusion and anarchy, had undivided and undisputed possession of the town. Armed horsemen were dashing about in every direction, the horses' feet striking fire from the stones beneath, and the sabres of the riders rattling by their sides. The drum and fife disturbed the stillness of the morning, and volunteer companies were on parade and drill, with all the habiliments and panoply of war. The town was evidently under a complete military rule, and on every side were visible indications of a destructive civil strife. The whole scene was calculated to excite feelings of commiseration, if not disgust for the parties, who, actuated by pride, avarice, or other even worse passions, should suffer themselves to sink so low in the scale of humanity, as to become entirely unmindful of all that elevates and dignifies the character of man.

CHAPTER XVIII

Arrival at Fort Leavenworth.—General P. F. Smith.—Free-state men driven from Leavenworth City.—Pressed horses.—John D. Henderson.—Violation of United States safeguard.—Arrest of Captain Emory.—Character of his company.—Governor Geary's letter to Col. Clarkson.—Rev. Mr. Nute.—District Attorney Isacks.

THE governor and his party landed at 8 o'clock on the morning of September 9th at Fort Leavenworth, where they were cordially received and hospitably entertained by Gen. Smith. The general was very feeble in health, and confined to his quarters. Many free-state people, who had been threatened with personal violence and driven from their homes in Leavenworth City, had taken refuge within the enclosures of the fort, and were seated on the grass plots or strolling about the grounds. A handbill was posted in sundry places ordering them to leave the premises on the following day.

Several of these persons directed the writer's attention to four horsemen who were passing in front of the general's quarters, and asserted that the horses were their own property and stolen by the riders. The leader of the mounted party was John D. Henderson, editor and proprietor of the *Leavenworth Journal*, and a rabid pro-slavery man.

"Captain," said a gentleman who had heard the story of the refugees, and addressing Henderson, "that is a fine horse you are riding."

"Yes," was the reply. "He is a splendid animal. He is a *pressed* horse. All these horses are pressed."

"Pressed! What does that mean?"

"Oh, pressed into the service."

"In other words, I suppose you mean the horses are stolen. Who are the owners?"

"Why, those d——d abolitionists over there. We don't call it stealing to take possession of their property."

This man Henderson is by birth a Pennsylvanian; but having affiliated with the Kansas pro-slavery party, and connected himself with the Blue Lodges, was among those northern born men who were compelled to do extraordinary things, and even boast of those still more remarkable which they had not courage to perform, in order to give satisfactory assurance of their entire soundness on the "goose." Hence "Jack," as his associates call him, delights to tell of his valiant deeds in pressing horses, burning houses, and killing abolitionists; and his course has been so thoroughly approved that he has been elevated to the dignified position of chairman of the central committee of the pro-slavery, misnamed the "National Democratic Party of Kansas."

A few hours after the arrival of Governor Geary at Fort Leavenworth, a sergeant belonging to the United States troops entered the general's quarters with a serious complaint against certain of the men who claimed to be the militia, or "law and order" party of the territory. He had been appointed a *safeguard* to escort Samuel Sutherland, E. B. Whitman, and Abraham Wilder along the public highway to Fort Leavenworth, and when within a few miles of that place a party of armed men belonging to Captain Frederick Emory's company stopped him on the road, and violated the safeguard, by forcibly taking from him the three men named, whom they carried as prisoners, with their horses, wagons, and other property, into Leavenworth City.

General Smith expressed himself with considerable warmth against this outrage, appeared anxious to bring the offenders to punishment, and readily granted a requisition from Governor Geary for a detachment of United States troops to proceed at once to Leavenworth City and arrest Emory and his company, and rescue the three men they had imprisoned.

This detachment was forthwith dispatched, and in a few hours returned to the fort with the free-state prisoners and Emory and his company, numbering twenty men. Upon appearing before General Smith, Emory produced James Withrow, George H. Perrin, L. S. Boling, T. J. Clyde, D. Scott Boyle, John J. Benz, and J. M. Branaman, as the persons who had commited the alleged outrage. He spoke in rather insolent terms; said he was not present himself, but that he approved the act and held himself responsible. The general very mildly reprimanded him, informed him that he was under arrest; then dismissed him and suffered him to return to Leavenworth City, to laugh over the silly farce in which he had been compelled to be an actor.

Emory's company were all mounted upon "pressed" horses, the owners of some of which were present to point out and claim them; but as there existed no courts or judges from whom the necessary legal process could be obtained, and as Gen. Smith would not listen to their complaints, they had no means by which to recover their property. Most of them preferred to submit quietly to the loss of their horses, rather than risk their lives by making any effort for their recovery.

Emory and his company held their headquarters at Leavenworth City, whence they sallied into the surrounding country to "press," not steal the horses, cattle, wagons, and other property of free-state men, to whom they had become a terror. It was during these excursions that Major Sackett, of the United States army, found in the road near Leavenworth City a number of bodies of men who had been seized, robbed, murdered, mutilated, and left unburied by the wayside. It was this same Emory and company that made the attack on Phillips's house, when Phillips was killed and his brother severely wounded. They were also present when the assassin of Hoppe brought in his reeking scalp, elevated upon a pole, and applauded the savage deed. They were exceedingly active in warning free-state men to leave the city, on pain of death, and in placing them upon steamboats without money or proper clothing, after breaking into their stores and houses and seizing on their effects, not even sparing the wearing apparel of women and children. Emory was a contractor for carrying the mails, and the fidelity with which he discharged this trust is evinced in the fact that on more than one occasion the mails submitted to his charge were broken open and robbed. All these things, however, seem to have met the approbation of the judicial and other constituted authorities, and for his extraordinary and valuable services Captain Emory has been appointed by President Buchanan as Register of the Land Office of the Western Land District of Kansas.

The next day after the events above narrated the governor addressed the following letter to Colonel Clarkson, who had command of the territorial militia stationed at Leavenworth City:—

"Fort Leavenworth, K. T., Sept. 10, 1857.

"Col. Clarkson:

"Dear Sir:—It seems necessary that I should address you, relative to an unpleasant occurrence that took place yesterday. Not doubting that you are actuated by a desire to maintain the public peace and promote the prosperity of this territory, I am sure you will at once perceive and properly appreciate the motives which prompt me to call your attention to the fact above hinted at, and the suggestions I am about to offer.

"Three men, having a passport from General Marshall, and under the *safeguard* of a sergeant of the United States army, were yesterday seized by a troop of your men, and carried as prisoners into Leavenworth City. The only excuse that can be offered for an outrage of this character, is the plea of ignorance as to the position of the party to whom reference is made. The men in your militia may not have been satisfied that the person from whom they took their prisoners, was, in truth, a United States sergeant. But in that case, their plain duty would have been to accompany him to the fort to ascertain that fact.

"You will please guard against errors of this description as far as possible in future. I also request that you will at once take the necessary measures to have returned to the three persons who were seized by Captain Emory's men, their horses, wagons, and other property, precisely in the condition in which they were found. You will send these effects to General Smith, who will see them duly restored to their proper owners.

"Trusting that hereafter the safeguard of the United States army, and everything else in which the honor of the nation is concerned, will be held by you sacred and inviolable,

"I am, truly yours,

"John W. Geary,

"Governor of Kansas Territory."

Soon after the troops left the fort to arrest Emory, a scene occurred there strongly illustrative of the times. Rev. E. Nute, a Unitarian clergyman, had several times been arrested and imprisoned on the grave charge of being an abolitionist. He had also been robbed, almost starved, and otherwise cruelly abused, and had just made his escape from his persecutors and fled for safety to the fort. Whilst relating his adventures to an admiring company of his associates and friends, who like himself were refugees from oppression, he espied a wagon passing along the road towards Leavenworth, drawn by two horses, and containing beside the driver, two women and a goodly supply of household furniture and other movables. The reverend gentleman immediately recognised the horses as a favorite pair that had been pressed from him when last taken prisoner. Without waiting for a legal process, he summoned to his assistance a half-dozen friends, and demanded the driver of the wagon to halt. He then deliberately unhitched the horses and drove them away in triumph, amid the congratulations and shouts of the bystanders, leaving the driver and his female companions in their wagon in the middle of the road in a mute state of consternation. Chief Justice Lecompte and associate justice Cato, would have pronounced this act unlawful and unwarrantable, and all the judges and lawyers in the land would have agreed in the decision. Mr. Nute should have appealed to a court, or some judicial functionary—made affidavit in regard to his stolen horses—obtained a warrant for the arrest of the thief and the restoration of his property—placed this in the hands of the marshal or sheriff, and waited patiently for its execution. Such would have been the process in ordinary communities, where the laws are made for the protection of the people—where courts are occasionally held—where judges deal out even-handed justice—and where officers of the law can be induced to execute writs against culprits of their own political faith. But such was not the condition of things in Kansas. There the balance of legal justice had but one scale, and Mr. Nute occupied the opposite side of the beam. Had he asked the courts or the judges, the marshals or the sheriffs, for the restoration of his horses, he might have been regarded as a madman, or at least been ridiculed for his presumption. And had he waited until they reached Leavenworth City to recover them, he could only have made the attempt at the hazard if not the sacrifice of his life.

At Fort Leavenworth, the governor endeavored to impress

the United States District Attorney, A. J. Isacks, with the importance of resurrecting the courts, holding more frequent terms, and arresting, bringing to trial, and legally punishing the numerous criminals that were committing with impunity atrocious outrages and disturbing the peace of the country. Mr. Isacks could not agree with the governor in regard to the course of policy he advised. He was for war—war to the knife—war to the death. There was no law that could absolutely rid the country of abolitionists. They must be killed or driven out by force. Like other prominent pro-slavery men, he was fully imbued with the idea that no person had a right in Kansas who was not favorable to making it a slave state; and he is said to have been one of the leaders of the secret band of "Regulators," whose business was to call in disguise at the houses of free-state men and order them to quit the territory, and threaten them with assassination in case of their refusal. Although he received the pay of the government to prosecute offences against the laws of the territory, he seldom, if ever, was present to perform that duty on the few occasions that it suited the convenience of the supreme judges to hold, for a few days, a district court.

CHAPTER XIX.

Fort Leavenworth.—Departure for Lecompton.—Barricade at Leavenworth City.—Excuse for Border Ruffian outrages.—Terror of James H. Lane.—Hair breadth escapes.—Anecdotes of the times.—Robbery at Alexandria.—A chase and race.—The robbers overtaken.—Arrival at Lecompton.—Letter to the Secretary of State.—Two men shot at Lecompton.

Fort Leavenworth is situated on an elevated piece of land on the west side of the Missouri River, three hundred and ninety-eight miles above its mouth, and thirty-one miles from the mouth of the Kansas. It is just four miles below the town of Weston, Missouri, in lat. 39° 21′ 14″ N. and long. 94° 44′ W. It was established in 1827. The enclosed grounds are spacious and beautiful, and command a delightful view of the surrounding country, of many miles in extent. The buildings, all of which are constructed of brick and stone, are substantial and well arranged, and present quite an imposing appearance. The quarters for the officers and men, are commodious and comfortable. There is a spacious hospital, constructed at a cost of $15,000. The grounds adjacent belong to the government, and comprise a farm, nine square miles in extent, of rich, well improved and highly cultivated lands.

The governor left the fort at about 10 o'clock on the morning of September 10th, for Lecompton, the capital of the territory. He was accompanied by the writer, three friends, and Lieutenant Drum of the army, all of whom occupied an ambulance, drawn by four horses. The lieutenant was in command of an escort, consisting of a mounted sergeant of dragoons, and six infantry soldiers, who rode in a covered army wagon.

The road passes a short distance westward of Leavenworth City, which was barricaded by a line of heavy transportation wagons, drawn close together, and extending along the whole western border of the town. These were intended as a protection against an expected assault from Lane; but to a military eye, it was evident that a barricade of pipe-stems would have answered a far more useful purpose. The wagons would have proved more serviceable to the attacking than to the repelling forces.

It is due to the pro-slavery party of Leavenworth to give the reasons they assigned for their atrocities against the free-state people. The former were laboring under a serious apprehension that Lane was about to attack them with a large army, and their fears caused them to regard all free-state men as spies or allies of Lane; hence the determination to drive them from the city, or assassinate them in case of their refusal to depart. The very name of Lane was a terror, and it was only necessary to get up a rumor that he was within a hundred miles, to produce a universal consternation. And when it was reported that he was actually approaching a pro-slavery town, a general panic and stampede was the result. Vaporing generals, colonels, captains and privates, suddenly stopped in the midst of their stories of valiant deeds, and remembering that they had forgotten their needed arms or ammunition, or that the women and children must be carried to a place of safety, off they ran for shelter in the woods or elsewhere, creeks and rivers furnishing no obstacles to their flight. When the dreaded danger was over, or they had discovered the alarm to be unfounded, they would re-assemble, each ready to boast over his bad whiskey, what terrible deeds he would have accomplished, had the cowardly abolitionist dared to make his appearance. It was amusing to hear the many stories of hair-breadth 'scapes these men had made. There was scarcely one among them who did not seem to carry a charmed life; for, almost every day they had been shot at, the balls whizzing past their heads or through their clothing. According to their accounts, their adversaries must have been the worst shots that ever handled fire-arms. The deputy marshals and sheriffs exibited bullet-holes in their clothing, or through their hats, as evidences of the terrible risks they had run, in the discharge of their hazardous duties. Should one of them, at any time, hear the discharge of a gun within a mile of him, his vivid fancy readily imagined that he could distinctly see the ball strike somewhere near his person. On one occasion, one of these officials was relating a wonderful escape he had just effected. A man, he said, had fired at him in the road several successive shots, and as evidence of the narrowness of his escape, he presented his hat, showing two holes in it, one in front and the other in the back.

"Why," said a listener, "it is strange that the ball should have gone through your hat so low down, without also passing through your head!"

"Oh," replied he, nothing disconcerted, "I held my hat in my hand when he fired. But I fixed him. I returned the shot, and I saw him stagger into the bushes and fall."

The body, it is scarcely necessary to add, was never found, nor could any traces of blood be discovered.

Many anecdotes were constantly occurring, which, had they been collected, would have made an interesting volume. It was customary for the "Regulators," and others of the slavery party, to go through the streets of Leavenworth, blowing a horn, and ordering free-state men to leave in the next steamer. At one time, two Jews were attracted to the door of their house by this strange proceeding:

"What dosh all dat meansh, Hans?" asked one.

"It meansh dat all who doshent like schlavery mush go down de rivers, and all who dosh like schlavery may staysh."

"Well, Hans, den I tinks schlavery is de besht, so we will staysh."

He was like many others, who adopted the slavery side of the question, as a matter of policy, to escape persecution and subserve personal interests.

A Pennsylvanian who had done good service in the Mexican war, and whose testimony can be relied upon, related the following:

"Upon arriving in the territory, I established my residence in Leavenworth City, where I was solicited to take command of a company of the territorial militia, or "law and order" party. The company consisted of twenty mounted border ruffians. One night it became my duty to guard the main entrance to the city, and I took up my position in a prominent place on the road, at about one mile distant. It was a very dark night, and it was difficult to discern objects even close at hand; my men amused each other and myself, relating the daring deeds they had accomplished, and telling what great things they would do, in case of an assault. About midnight, we heard the distant sounds of horses' feet approaching at a rapid rate. A perfect stillness took possession of my men. Not a word was uttered. Nearer and nearer, came on the advancing party. At length, one of my men exclaimed, 'Lane is coming, by G–d!' and instantly, the whole company broke and ran for the town. In vain I ordered a halt. As well might I have attempted to turn back the current of the river, as to arrest their flight. I stood alone to await the approach of the enemy, whom I found to be four scouts of our own party, returning to the city. I immediately resigned my office, feeling assured that no dependence could be placed in the courage of the men I had been chosen to command. They are great braggarts, but they will not fight. They make good assassins, but bad soldiers."

The governor and party crossed the Stranger River, about noon, thirteen miles from Leavenworth, at a place called Alexandria. The town consists of two houses, used as a post-office and stores. These had been robbed about an hour before our arrival. Several whiskey barrels, with their heads broken in, lay in the road. A young man in attendance, gave a deplorable account of the robbery. He said the attack was made by about one hundred and fifty of Lane's men, all mounted, who came with two wagons, which they filled with goods, broke open the post-office box and robbed it of letters and postage stamps, and destroyed such articles as they could not carry away. The proprietor, to save his life, had fled to the hills and hid himself in the bushes, and he was threatened with death if he should give information concerning the robbery. The governor, who had been accustomed to examine "moccasin tracks," made a careful investigation of the premises, and at once assured Lieutenant Drum that the statements of his informant were false. He pointed out distinctly the fact that the traces upon the ground indicated the late presence of certainly not over a dozen horsemen. He then ordered the young man to take a seat in the ambulance, to point out the direction taken by the robbers, and hastened in pursuit of them. Along the road were exhibited fearful evidences of ruffian violence. Almost every house had been destroyed, and the sites they had occupied were marked only by solitary chimneys standing in the midst of heaps of ashes. The first dwelling approached was about three miles from Alexandria, where the governor halted and inquired of the settler if he had seen a large body of men pass during the morning. He was promptly answered that only six horsemen had passed that way, about half an hour previous. The governor then asked the man in company why he had attempted to mislead him with a lying statement. The fellow had nothing to reply, and, after a severe rebuke, was permitted to return to Alexandria. As a reward for having told the truth, the settler's house was attacked a day or two after, and burned to the ground; his wife and half dozen children being turned out upon the open prairie, and his crop of corn destroyed.

The governor increased his speed, and having travelled two miles further, upon reaching an elevated piece of ground, saw six horsemen crossing the prairie at the distance of about half a mile. Upon observing the carriage, they turned toward it, putting their horses to a gallop, with the evident intention to attack and rob it. As they came within a few hundred yards, and preparations were being made to give them a warm reception, the covered wagon ascended the hill, thus exhibiting the character and strength of the governor's party, when the intended assailants instantly turned and fled in the opposite direction. They were pursued by the sergeant, the only mounted man in the company, and a more interesting chase was never witnessed. The horses were put to their utmost speed, their tails standing straight out, and making time rarely equalled on a race-course. Four of them succeeded in reaching a wooded ravine, but the other two, whose horses were not equal to that rode by the sergeant, were overtaken and commanded to halt. Upon being questioned, they represented themselves as free-state men who had been driven from their homes by a party of border ruffians. The sergeant, however, recognised them as two of a party of six men whom he had that morning seen leave Leavenworth City. It was subsequently ascertained that the leader of the party was a citizen of Missouri; a prominent member of the Legislative Assembly of Kansas, and the alleged author of most of the odious election and test laws passed by that body during its session of 1855. This person has boasted that he "pressed" from free-state men several valuable horses, which he had carried for safe keeping into Lexington, Missouri.

Upon reaching the Kansas River, ferriage was difficult, in consequence of the low stage of the water, and it was some hours before the governor reached the opposite shore. An armed and mounted sentinel guarded the Lecompton landing, and demanded to know who the new-comers were. The only hotel in the place was reached at about eleven o'clock, where the governor was introduced to Secretary Woodson, Ex-Judge Elmore and other prominent citizens. The town was in a great state of excitement, produced by a recent visit of Lane, at the head of five hundred men, who had come to demand the release of the free-state prisoners, but who had already been discharged, by Judge Lecompte, on bail, after hearing of Lane's approach.

Previous to his departure from Fort Leavenworth, the governor addressed the following communication to Secretary Marcy, in which he clearly expresses his opinions concerning the condition of the territory at that time:—

"Fort Leavenworth, Kansas Territory,
"Sept. 9, 1856.

"Hon. Wm. L. Marcy,

"Dear Sir: I arrived here this morning, and have passed the day mostly in consultation with Gen. P. F. Smith, in relation to the affairs of the territory, which, as I am now on the spot, I begin more clearly to understand. It is no exaggeration to say that the existing difficulties are of a far more complicated character than I had anticipated.

"I find that I have not simply to contend against bands of armed ruffians and brigands, whose sole aim and end is assassination and robbery—infatuated adherents and advocates of conflicting political sentiments and local institutions—and evil-disposed persons, actuated by a desire to obtain elevated positions; but worst of all, against the influence of men who have been placed in authority, and have employed all the destructive agents around them to promote their own personal interests, at the sacrifice of every just, honorable and lawful consideration.

"I have barely time to give you a brief statement of facts as I find them. The town of Leavenworth is now in the hands of armed bodies of men, who, having been enrolled as militia, perpetrate outrages of the most atrocious character under shadow of authority from the territorial government. Within a few days these men have robbed and driven from their homes unoffending citizens; have fired upon and killed others in their own dwellings; and stolen horses and property under the pretence of employing them in the public service. They have seized persons who had committed no offence; and after stripping them of all their valuables, placed them on steamers, and sent them out of the territory. Some of these bands, who have thus violated their rights and privileges, and shamefully and shockingly misused and abused the oldest inhabitants of the territory, who had settled here with their wives and children, are strangers from distant states, who have no interest in, nor care for the welfare of Kansas, and contemplate remaining here only so long as opportunities for mischief and plunder exist.

"The actual pro-slavery settlers of the territory are generally as well-disposed persons as are to be found in most communities. But there are among them a few troublesome agitators, chiefly from distant districts, who labor assiduously to keep alive the prevailing sentiment.

"It is also true that among the free-soil residents are many peaceable and useful citizens; and if uninfluenced by aspiring demagogues, would commit no unlawful act. But many of these, too, have been rendered turbulent by officious meddlers from abroad. The chief of these is Lane, now encamped and fortified at Lawrence, with a force, it is said, of fifteen hundred men. They are suffering for provisions, to cut off the supplies of which, the opposing faction is extremely watchful and active.

"In isolated or country places, no man's life is safe. The roads are filled with armed robbers, and murders for mere plunder are of daily occurrence. Almost every farm-house is deserted, and no traveller has the temerity to venture upon the highway without an escort.

"Such is the condition of Kansas, faintly pictured. It can be no worse. Yet I feel assured that I shall be able ere long to restore it to peace and quiet. To accomplish this, I should have more aid from the general government. The number of United States troops here is too limited to render the needed services. Immediate reinforcements are essentially necessary; as the excitement is so intense, and citizens generally are so much influenced by their political prejudices, that members of the two great factions cannot be induced to act in unison, and therefore cannot be relied upon. As soon, however, as I can succeed in disbanding a portion of those now in service, I will from time to time cause to be enrolled as many of the *bona fide* inhabitants as exigencies may seem to require. In the meantime, the presence of additional government troops will exert a moral influence that cannot be obtained by any militia that can here be called in requisition.

"In making the foregoing statements, I have endeavored to give the truth, and nothing but the truth. I deem it important that you should be apprised of the actual state of the case; and whatever may be the effect of such relations, they will be given, from time to time, without extenuation.

"I shall proceed early in the morning to Lecompton, under an escort furnished by Gen. Smith, where I will take charge of the government, and whence I shall again address you at an early moment.

"Very respectfully, your obedt. servt.,

"Jno. W. Geary,

"Governor of Kansas."

On the 10th of September, an altercation took place at Lecompton between two South Carolinians. They were personal friends, but had been drinking too freely. One of them, incensed at some remark of the other, drew his pistol and fired, and was about to repeat the shot, when his companion, after warning him, discharged into his body the contents of a gun loaded with buckshot. The wounded man lingered three or four days, in great agony, the other watching and waiting upon him during his sufferings. He was never tried for the murder, but set at liberty at an examination before one of the justices.

Two or three days later, another serious shooting affair occurred in the same town. A free-state man living in the vicinity, brought in a load of beef for sale. He proceeded to one of the stores, where, meeting a number of the citizens, he got into conversation, during which he denounced the institution of slavery, an offence unpardonable in Lecompton. A quarrel and fight ensued, when the free-state man ran for his life. He was pursued to a cluster of woods on the edge of the town, his pursuers firing at him a number of times, he turning to fire back. He at length dodged behind a tree, whence he fired a few more shots. Some of his assailants had run for guns, and succeeded in shooting him three times, as he attempted to make his escape, the balls having entered his back, abdomen, and side. He was laid, dangerously, though not mortally wounded, upon the beef on his wagon, and brought into town with his ox-team. Here his wounds were dressed. These occurrences had become so common that they attracted but little attention. Whilst this man was writhing apparently in the agonies of death on one side of the street, the groggeries opposite were filled with loungers too unconcerned to take any special notice of the circumstance.

CHAPTER XX.

The town of Lecompton.—Its location and moral character.—The accounts of their grievances by the pro-slavery party.—Policy indicated by that party for Governor Geary.—The Inaugural address.—Proclamations ordering the dispersion of armed bodies, aud for organizing the militia of the territory.

LECOMPTON is situated on the south side of the Kansas River, about fifty miles from its junction with the Missouri, and forty miles in a south-westerly direction from Leavenworth City, upon as inconvenient and inappropriate a site for a town as any in the territory; it being on a bend of the river, difficult of access, and several miles beyond any of the principal thoroughfares. It was chosen simply for speculative purposes. An Indian 'floating claim' of a section of land was purchased by a company of prominent pro-slavery men, who found it easy to induce the legislative assembly to adopt it for the location of the capitol, by distributing among the members, supreme judges, the governor, secretary of the territory, and others in authority, a goodly number of town lots, upon the rapid sale of which each expected to realize a handsome income. It contained, at the time of Governor Geary's arrival, some twenty or more houses, the majority of which were employed as groggeries of the lowest description. In fact, its general moral condition was debased to a lamentable degree. It was the residence of the celebrated Sheriff Jones (who is one of the leading members of the town association), and the resort of horse-thieves and ruffians of the most desperate character. Its drinking saloons were infested by these characters, where drunkenness, gambling, fighting, and all sorts of crimes were indulged in with entire impunity. It was and is emphatically a border ruffian town, in which no man could utter opinions adverse to negro slavery without placing his life in jeopardy. The corporators, who are the contractors, have expended the $50,000 appropriated by Congress for the erection of the capitol building, for which sum they can now exhibit the foundations for a house, some iron castings and tin cornices.

Upon the governor's arrival he was surrounded by the leading men of the place, who kindly volunteered their friendly advice and instructions in regard to the policy to be pursued.

To insure his own comfort and safety, and accomplish any good whatever in the territory, he was given to understand that it was absolutely necessary to identify himself with the pro-slavery party, and aid it with his influence and power to "wipe out the d—d abolitionists." These were represented as the most wicked wretches that ever disgraced the earth. Upon their shoulders were heaped all imaginable offences. There was no crime of which they had not been guilty. Every enormity committed in Kansas was charged to their account; whilst their accusers were and had ever been peace-loving and law and order citizens, who with Christian forbearance and Job-like patience had meekly submitted to outrages that no pencil could portray nor language properly depict. It was really painful to hear their plausible stories of the sufferings they had quietly and patiently endured at the hands of their northern oppressors and fiendish persecutors.

The governor was too perverse and obstinate to believe that the wrong was altogether on one side, or that the cause of humanity or the welfare of the country was to be promoted by the course of policy he was so eloquently and earnestly solicited to adopt and pursue. Hence he issued the following address, in which he expressed a determination to know no party, and to recognise no sectional prejudices, but in the exercise of his official functions to do equal and exact justice to all classes of the community—a resolution to which he rigidly adhered during his entire administration:—

"FELLOW CITIZENS:

"I appear among you a stranger to most of you, and for the first time have the honor to address you, as Governor of the Territory of Kansas. The position was not sought by me; but was voluntarily tendered by the present chief magistrate of the nation. As an American citizen, deeply conscious of the blessings which ever flow from our beloved Union, I did not consider myself at liberty to shrink from any duties, however delicate and onerous, required of me by my country.

"With a full knowledge of all the circumstances surrounding the executive office, I have deliberately accepted it, and as God may give me strength and ability, I will endeavor faithfully to discharge its varied requirements. When I received my commission I was solemnly sworn to support the Constitution of the United States, and to discharge my duties as Governor of Kansas with fidelity. By reference to the act for the organization of this territory, passed by Congress on the 30th day of March, 1854, I find my duties more particularly defined. Among other things, I am 'to take care that the laws be faithfully executed.'

"The Constitution of the United States and the organic law of the territory, will be the lights by which I will be guided in my executive career.

"A careful and dispassionate examination of our organic act will satisfy any reasonable person that its provisions are eminently just and beneficial. If this act has been distorted to unworthy purposes, it is not the fault of its provisions. The great leading feature of that act is the right therein conferred upon the actual and *bona fide* inhabitants of this territory 'in the exercise of self-government, to determine for themselves what shall be their own domestic institutions, subject only to the constitution and the laws duly enacted by Congress under it.' The people, accustomed to self-government in the states from whence they came, and having removed to this territory with the *bona fide* intention of making it their future residence, were supposed to be capable of creating their own municipal government, and to be the best judges of their own local necessities and institutions. This is what is termed '*popular sovereignty.*' By this phrase we simply mean the right of the majority of the people of the several states and territories, being qualified electors, to regulate their own domestic concerns, and to make their own municipal laws. Thus understood, this doctrine underlies the whole system of republican government. It is the great right of self-government, for the establishment of which our ancestors, in the stormy days of the revolution, pledged 'their lives, their fortunes, and their sacred honor.'

"A doctrine so eminently just should receive the willing homage of every American citizen. When legitimately expressed, and duly ascertained, the will of the majority must be the imperative rule of civil action for every law-abiding citizen. This simple, just rule of action has brought order out of chaos, and by a progress unparalleled in the history of the world, has made a few feeble, infant colonies, a giant confederated republic.

"No man, conversant with the state of affairs, now in Kansas, can close his eyes to the fact that much civil disturbance has for a long time past existed in this territory. Various reasons have been assigned for this unfortunate condition of affairs, and numerous remedies have been proposed.

"The House of Representatives of the United States have ignored the claims of both gentlemen claiming the legal right to represent the people of this territory in that body. The Topeka Constitution, recognised by the House, has been repudiated by the Senate. Various measures, each in the opinion of its respective advocates, suggestive of peace to Kansas, have been alternately proposed and rejected. Men, *outside of the territory*, in various sections of the Union, influenced by reasons best known to themselves, have endeavored to stir up internal strife, and to array brother against brother.

"In this conflict of opinion, and for the promotion of the most unworthy purposes, Kansas is left to suffer, her people to mourn, and her prosperity is endangered.

"Is there no remedy for these evils? Cannot the wounds of Kansas be healed, and peace be restored to all her borders?

"Men of the north—men of the south—of the east, and of the west.

in Kansas, you, and you alone, have the remedy in your own hands. Will you not suspend fratricidal strife? Will you not cease to regard each other as enemies, and look upon one another as the children of a common mother, and come and reason together?

"Let us banish all *outside influences* from our deliberations, and assemble around our council board with the constitution of our country and the organic law of this territory, as the great charts for our guidance and direction. The *bona fide* inhabitants of the territory *alone* are charged with the solemn duty of enacting her laws, upholding her government, maintaining peace, and laying the foundation for a future commonwealth.

"On this point let there be a perfect unity of sentiment. It is the first great step towards the attainment of peace. It will inspire confidence amongst ourselves and insure the respect of the whole country. Let us show ourselves worthy and capable of self-government.

"Do not the inhabitants of this territory better understand what domestic institutions are suited to their condition—what laws will be most conducive to their prosperity and happiness, than the citizens of distant, or even neighboring states? This great right of regulating our own affairs and attending to our own business, without any interference from others, has been guaranteed to us by the law which Congress has made for the organization of this territory. This right of self-government—this privilege guaranteed to us by the organic law of our territory, I will uphold with all my might, and with the entire power committed to me.

"In relation to any changes of the laws of the territory which I may deem desirable, I have no occasion now to speak; but these are subjects to which I shall direct public attention at the proper time.

"The territory of the United States is the *common property* of the several states, or of the people thereof. This being so, no obstacle should be interposed to the free settlement of this common property, while in a territorial condition.

"I cheerfully admit that the people of this territory, under the organic act, have the absolute right of making their own municipal laws. And from citizens who deem themselves aggrieved by recent legislation, I would invoke the utmost forbearance, and point out to them a sure and peaceable remedy. You have the right to ask the next legislature to revise any and all laws; and in the meantime, as you value the peace of the territory and the maintenance of future laws, I would earnestly ask you to refrain from all violations of the present statutes.

"I am sure that there is patriotism sufficient in the people of Kansas to induce them to lend a willing obedience to law. All the provisions of the Constitution of the United States must be sacredly observed—all the acts of Congress, having reference to this territory, must be unhesitatingly obeyed, and the decisions of our courts respected. It will be my *imperative* duty to see that these suggestions are carried into effect. In my official action here, I will do justice at all hazards. Influenced by no other considerations than the welfare of the whole people of this territory, I desire to know no party, no section, no north, no south, no east, no west—nothing but Kansas and my country.

"Fully conscious of my great responsibilities in the present condition of Kansas, I must invoke your aid, and solicit your generous forbearance. Your executive officer can do little without the aid of the people. With a firm reliance upon Divine Providence, to the best of my ability, I shall promote the interests of the citizens of this territory, not merely collectively, but individually, and I shall expect from them, in return, that cordial aid and support, without which the government of no state or territory can be administered with beneficent effect.

"Let us all begin anew. Let the past be buried in oblivion. Let all strife and bitterness cease. Let us all honestly devote ourselves to the true interests of Kansas; develope her rich agricultural and mineral resources; build up manufacturing enterprises; make public roads and highways; prepare amply for the education of our children; devote ourselves to all the arts of peace; and make our territory the sanctuary of those cherished principles which protect the inalienable rights of the individual, and elevate states in their sovereign capacities.

"Then shall peaceful industry soon be restored; population and wealth will flow upon us; 'the desert will blossom as the rose;' and the State of Kansas will soon be admitted into the Union, the peer and pride of her elder sisters.

"JNO. W. GEARY."

Simultaneously with this address, clearly developing the policy by which his official action was to be guided and controlled, the governor published the following proclamations:—

"PROCLAMATION.

"WHEREAS, A large number of volunteer militia have been called into the service of the Territory of Kansas, by authority of the late acting governor, for the maintenance of order, many of whom have been taken from occupations or business, and deprived of their ordinary means of support and of their domestic enjoyments; and

"WHEREAS, The employment of militia is not authorized by my instructions from the general government, except upon requisition of the commander of the military department in which Kansas is embraced; and

"WHEREAS, An authorized regular force has been placed at my disposal, sufficient to insure the execution of the laws that may be obstructed by combinations too powerful to be suppressed by the ordinary course of judicial proceedings; now

"*Therefore*, I, JOHN W. GEARY, Governor of the Territory of Kansas, do issue this, my proclamation, declaring that the services of such volunteer militia are no longer required; and hereby order that they be immediately discharged. The secretary and the adjutant-general of the territory will muster out of service each command at its place of rendezvous.

"And I command all bodies of men, combined, armed and equipped with munitions of war, without authority of the government, instantly to disband or quit the territory, as they will answer the contrary at their peril.

"In testimony whereof, I have hereunto set my hand, and affixed the seal of the Territory of Kansas.

"Done at Lecompton, this eleventh day of September, in the year of our Lord one thousand eight hundred and fifty-six.

"JNO. W. GEARY,
"Governor of Kansas Territory."

"PROCLAMATION.

"WHEREAS, It is the true policy of every state or territory to be prepared for any emergency that may arise from internal dissension or foreign invasion;

"*Therefore*, I, John W. Geary, Governor of the Territory of Kansas, do issue this, my proclamation, ordering all free male citizens, qualified to bear arms, between the ages eighteen and forty-five years, to enrol themselves, in accordance with the act to organize the militia of the territory, that they may be completely organized by companies, regiments, brigades, or divisions, and hold themselves in readiness, to be mustered, by my order, into the service of the United States, upon requisition of the commander of the military department in which Kansas is embraced, for the suppression of all combinations to resist the laws, and for the maintenance of public order and civil government.

"In testimony whereof, I have hereunto set my hand and the seal of the Territory of Kansas.

"Done at Lecompton, this eleventh day of September, in the year of our Lord one thousand eight hundred and fifty-six.

"JNO. W. GEARY,
"Governor of Kansas Territory."

CHAPTER XXI.

Gloomy prospect for Governor Geary's administration.—Determination to make Kansas a slave state.—Opposition to the new governor.—Address to the people of the slave states.—Secretary Woodson's proclamation.

No man ever commenced the discharge of official duties under such discouraging auspices, or in the face of so many embarrassments, difficulties, and dangers, as did Governor Geary. The bitterness of party spirit had reached its acme.

Every class of the community either was or pretended to be suffering grievances that cried aloud for vengeance. All means at pacification were regarded as fruitless. and the leaders of the conflicting parties neither saw nor recognised any hope of redress or peace except in the extermination of the other. The free-state people had no reason to expect even a show of justice from the administration at Washington. Every federal officer in the territory and every territorial officer, whether appointed or elected, from the supreme judges and secretary to the deputy marshals, sheriffs and clerks, were wedded to the slave power, and pledged at all hazards to its extension. And the free-state party, judging from the uniform policy of the general government, very naturally supposed that the new governor was but another instrument chosen for their oppression and persecution. It was by no means remarkable, therefore, that they should not only withhold from him everything like a cordial welcome, but regard him with distrust and suspicion, and determine to throw every possible obstacle in the way of his administration. Even President Pierce and his cabinet appear to have made a mistake in the appointment of Governor Geary; for subsequent events prove, that although he succeeded in restoring peace to the territory, he failed to accomplish the object of their desires; and when they discovered his unwavering determination to do equal justice to all the citizens, they withdrew from him, at the time it was most needed, their protecting care.

The pro-slavery party, on the other hand, had selected a governor for themselves, and were resolved not to receive with favor any other than the man they had chosen. This was John Calhoun, the surveyor-general of Kansas and Nebraska. He had been well tried, and found to be entirely "sound on the goose." Of his attachment to their interests there was no room to doubt. Like all others of their party born in free states, he was willing and ready to commit excesses at which even the most rabid of themselves would hesitate. He considered it no crime to murder northern men, and declared that he would kill an abolitionist with less compunction than he would a rat. He had the bestowment of an immense patronage, which he took great care to render subservient to the interests of his party. His clerks and other attachés, paid by the government to survey the lands, were enlisted in the Missouri army of invasion, and the horses and wagons belonging to his department were employed to transport provisions and ammunition for its use. He would have made just such a governor as his party needed, and great dissatisfaction was the result of his failure to receive the appointment.

The broad ground assumed by the rabid leaders of the pro-slavery party in Kansas was that an equilibrium of the slave power must be maintained at any sacrifice in the American Union, and this could only be effected by increasing the slave states in proportion with the free. As Nebraska will unquestionably enter the Union a free State, Kansas must be admitted with a constitution authorizing slavery. Whilst, therefore, the south was willing to give Nebraska to the north, they asked and demanded that Kansas should be ceded to the south. It was of little consequence what number of northern men located themselves in Kansas. It was assumed that they had no right to come there, unless with the intention of assisting to make it a slave state. If they would not pledge themselves to that object they were abolitionists, allies of disunionism, and deserving of death; and so far from being a crime, it was a virtue to kill them. This was the doctrine, openly and boldly advocated, that led to the commission of the most horrid atrocities that blackened the annals of the territory.

Hence, when Governor Geary's appointment was announced, and it was understood that he was determined not to affiliate with either of the opposing factions, but purposed to hold the scales of justice with an even hand, and to support and carry out the doctrine of popular sovereignty in the territory, not only much dissatisfaction but considerable consternation was the result. It was feared that every darling scheme and infamous attempt to force the institution of slavery into Kansas would be frustrated by his acknowledged integrity and well-known sagacity, industry and energy. Measures were immediately adopted to circumvent his plans, in anticipation of his coming. Active preparations were commenced, and carried forward with surprising energy, to gather an army in Missouri and other slave states with which to overrun the territory and drive out or annihilate all the free-state people, before the new governor could be on hand to intervene his authority and prevent the execution of so diabolical a purpose. An inflammatory address was prepared and published, signed by Atchison, Stringfellow, Tebbs, Anderson, Reid, Doniphan, and a host of kindred spirits, most of them Missourians, accusing the free-state people of the very outrages which themselves were daily committing, and calling for assistance to punish the traitors, assassins, and robbers who had invaded the territory from the north. This address was exceedingly plausible, and deceived many an honest man into the espousal of a cause which he subsequently abandoned in horror and disgust. The following extracts will give a proper idea of the general tenor of this document:—

"We have asked the appointment of a successor, who was acquainted with our condition; who, a citizen of the territory, identified with its interests, familiar with its history, would not be prejudiced or misled by the falsehoods which have been so systematically fabricated against us—one who, heretofore a resident as he is a native of a non-slaveholding state, is yet not a slaveholder, but has the capacity to appreciate, and the boldness and integrity requisite faithfully to discharge his duty, regardless of the possible effect it might have upon the election of some petty politician in a distant state.

"In his stead we have one appointed who is ignorant of our condition, a stranger to our people; who we have too much cause to fear will, if no worse, prove no more efficient to protect us than his predecessors.

"With, then, a government which has proved imbecile—has failed to enforce the laws for our protection—with an army of lawless banditti overrunning our country—what shall we do?

"Though we have full confidence in the integrity and fidelity of Mr. Woodson, now acting as governor, we know not at what moment his authority will be superseded. We cannot await the convenience in coming of our newly appointed governor. We cannot hazard a second edition of imbecility or corruption.

"We must act at once and effectively. These traitors, assassins, and robbers must be punished; must now be taught a lesson they will remember.

"We wage no war upon men for their opinions; have never attempted to exclude any from settling among us; we have demanded only that all should *alike* submit to the law. To all such we will afford protection, whatever be their political opinions. But Lane's army and its allies must be expelled from the territory. Thus alone can we make safe our persons and property—thus alone can we bring peace to our territory.

"To do this we will need assistance. Our citizens unorganized, many of them unarmed, for they came not as soldiers—though able heretofore to assemble a force sufficient to compel the obedience of the rebels, now that they have been strengthened by this invading army, thoroughly drilled, perfectly equipped, mounted, and ready to march at a moment's notice to attack our defenceless settlements—may be overpowered. Should we be able even to vanquish this additional force, we are threatened with a further invasion of like character through Iowa and Nebraska.

"This is no mere local quarrel; no mere riot; but it is a war! a war waged by an army! a war professedly for our extermination. It is no mere resistance to the laws; no simple rebellion of our citizens, but a war of invasion—the army a foreign army—properly named the 'army of the north.'

"It is then not only the right but the duty of all good citizens of Missouri and every other state to come to our assistance, and enable us to expel these invaders.

"Mr. Woodson, since the resignation of Governor Shannon, in the absence of Governor Geary, has fearlessly met the responsibilities of the trust forced upon him, has proclaimed the existence of the rebellion, and called on the militia of the territory to assemble for its suppression.

"We call on you to come! to furnish us assistance in men, provisions, and munitions, that we may drive out the 'army of the north,' who would subvert our government and expel us from our homes.

"Our people though poor, many of them stripped of their all, others harassed by these fiends so that they have been unable to provide for their families, are yet true men; will stand with you shoulder to shoulder in defence of rights, of principles in which you have a common if not deeper interest than they.

"By the issue of this struggle is to be decided whether law or lawlessness shall reign in our country. If we are vanquished you too will be victims. Let not our appeal be in vain!"

The *Squatter Sovereign*, an incendiary newspaper, published and edited by Messrs. Stringfellow and Kelly, at Atchison, in Doniphan county, also lent its aid to increase the excitement and embarrass the action of the governor, whose arrival was daily expected. Its articles were highly inflammatory, calling loudly for war and the extermination of the free-state people. Its complaints against the administration for the appointment of Geary, were uttered in no stinted terms. "No northern man," it alleged, "was fit to govern Kansas." John H. Stringfellow, one of the editors, is notorious for his violence. He has been arrested and indicted on sundry charges of horse-stealing and other crimes; whilst Robert S. Kelly, his associate, who was so conspicuous in the outrages upon Rev Pardee Butler, declared that he could never die happy until he had killed an abolitionist. "If," said he, "I can't kill a man, I'll kill a woman; and if I can't kill a woman, I'll kill a child!" That such men should do all in their power to embarrass an impartial executive and prevent the restoration of peace, is no subject for astonishment.

But the most reprehensible character in the drama being enacted, all things considered, was the secretary of the territory, then acting-governor. Without a will of his own, he became the subtle tool of the designing men with whom he was surrounded, and was inveigled into the commission of an act which words can scarcely condemn with sufficient severity. More than three weeks after Governor Geary had received his commission, and Secretary Woodson had every reason to believe that he was on his way to the territory, that weak-minded, if not criminally defective officer, issued the following:—

"PROCLAMATION.

"*By the acting governor of the Territory of Kansas.*

"WHEREAS, satisfactory evidence exists that the territory of Kansas is infested with large bodies of armed men, many of whom have just arrived from the states, combined and confederated together, and amply supplied with all the munitions of war, under the direction of a common head, with a thorough military organization, who have been and are still engaged in murdering law-abiding citizens of the territory, driving others from their homes, and compelling them to flee to the states for protection, capturing and holding others as prisoners of war, plundering them of their property, and in some instances burning down their houses and robbing United States post offices, and the local militia of the arms furnished them by the government, in open defiance and contempt of the laws of the territory, and of the constitution and laws of the United States, and of civil and military authority thereof—all for the purpose of subverting by force and violence, the government established by law of Congress in this territory.

"Now, therefore, I, Daniel Woodson, acting governor of the territory of Kansas, do hereby issue my proclamation declaring the said territory to be in a state of open insurrection and rebellion; and I do hereby call upon all law-abiding citizens of the territory to rally to the support of their country and its laws, and require and command all officers, civil and military, and all other citizens of the territory to aid and assist by all means in their power, in putting down the insurrectionists, and bringing to condign punishment all persons engaged with them, to the end of assuring immunity from violence, and full protection to the persons, property, and civil rights to all peaceable and law-abiding inhabitants of the territory.

"In testimony whereof, I have hereunto set my hand and caused to be attached the seal of the territory of Kansas.

{SEAL.} "Done at the city of Lecompton, this 25th day of August, in the year of our Lord, eighteen hundred and fifty-six, and of the independence of the United States the eightieth.

"DANIEL WOODSON,
"Acting Governor, K. T."

This proclamation, calling for volunteer militia from Missouri and elsewhere out of the territory, exhibits an utter lack of sound judgment, and came nigh proving more disastrous to the country than all the events combined that have yet transpired. Not satisfied, however, with the proclamation, which, of itself, was sufficiently mischievous, he wrote private letters to parties in Missouri, calling for men, money and munitions of war, to carry out his partisan purposes. This proclamation and these letters called together thousands of men, mostly from Missouri, with passions inflamed to the highest degree, and whose only thought and full determination, was wholesale slaughter and destruction. From the hour they entered the territory until they again passed its borders, their path was marked with bloodshed and ruin. There was scarcely a crime in the vast category of crimes that they did not commit with a brutality scarcely conceivable in beings bearing the human form. It would be disgusting and sickening to recapitulate the wanton atrocities, the hellish cruelties, perpetrated by these bands of volunteer militia. When Governor Geary appeared among them at their camp at Franklin, as will hereafter be related, and made known his purpose to disband them, it was with difficulty that their leaders could restrain their fiendish appetites and prevent the consummation of their shocking designs. The presence of the governor there was most opportune. An hour or two later, the town of Lawrence would have been in ashes; every man, woman and child in it, would have been ruthlessly slaughtered; and several thousands of human bloodhounds thirsting for vengeance, would have been let loose upon the territory with uncontrollable fury, to lay waste and desolate whatever came in their way. It is impossible to imagine the extent of the calamities and horrors that would have ensued. The alarm would have spread beyond the boundaries of Kansas to every state and territory of the Republic; the tocsin of war would have sounded from one extremity of the Union to the other; and as bloody a civil strife as the world has ever known must have been the result. For this act of the secretary, which, but for the timely interference of Governor Geary, would have been productive of unspeakable evils, President Buchanan, with characteristic generosity, has rewarded Mr. Woodson with the office of receiver for the Delaware Land District.

CHAPTER XXII.

The Missouri army.—Orders to the adjutant and inspector-generals of the territory.—Dispatch to Secretary Marcy.—Dispatches from General Heiskell.—Message from the governor's special agent.—Requisition for troops.—Visit of the governor to Lawrence, and return to Lecompton.

It was the fixed purpose of Secretary Woodson to keep Governor Geary in ignorance of the extensive preparations that were being made to attack and destroy the free-state settlements. As yet, the governor had not seen Woodson's proclamation, and he regarded the demonstrations on the Missouri River more in the light of a farce than a dangerous reality. When, upon entering the steamer, at Jefferson City, he was accosted by an armed ruffian, who assured him that if, upon his arrival in Kansas, he attempted to interfere with the arrangements of the pro-slavery party, he would be assassinated, he treated the warning with contempt, as he did others of a similar character, made at different stages of his journey. But at Lecompton everything assumed so quiet an aspect, and the secretary appeared so composed and placid, that the governor had no reason to suspect that a conspiracy was then being consummated on a grand and terrible scale, to thwart the objects of his mission and deluge the country in blood.

Without, therefore, perceiving the heavy cloud that was rapidly increasing in magnitude and darkness, and about to break with frightful fury over the territory, the governor was proceeding deliberately to institute the policy made known in his inaugural address, and to disband the militia of the territory, in common with other armed bodies, in accordance with his proclamation. To this end he verbally instructed Secretary Woodson, and issued the following orders to the proper military officers:—

"Executive Department,
"Lecompton, K. T., Sept. 12, 1856.

"Adjt.-Gen. H. J. Strickler:

"Dear Sir:—You will proceed without a moment's delay to disarm and disband the present organized militia of the territory, in accordance with the instructions of the President, and the proclamations which I have issued, copies of which you will find enclosed. You will also take care to have the arms belonging to the territory deposited in a place of safety and under proper accountability.

"Yours, &c.,
"Jno. W. Geary,
"Governor of Kansas Territory."

"Executive Dapartment,
"Lecompton, K. T., Sept. 12, 1856.

"Inspector-Gen. Thos. J. B. Cramer:

"Sir:—You will take charge of the arms of the Territory of Kansas, now in the hands of the militia about to be disbanded and mustered out of the service by the adjutant-general. You will also carefully preserve the same agreeably to the 15th section of the act of assembly, to organize, discipline, and govern the militia of the territory.

"Yours, &c.,
"Jno. W. Geary,
"Governor of Kansas Territory."

Notwithstanding the positive character of these orders, they were utterly disregarded by the parties to whom they were addressed, who lingered about Lecompton with an air of self-satisfaction which could only be regarded as disrespectful and insulting to the governor, who not only administered to them a severe rebuke, but, suspecting that treachery was somewhere at work, he forthwith dispatched confidential messengers on the road toward Westport, to ascertain, if possible, what operations were going forward in that vicinity.

He likewise, on the same day, forwarded the following letter to the secretary of state:—

"Executive Office,
Lecompton, K. T., Sept. 12, 1856.

"Hon. Wm. L. Marcy,
"Secretary of State, Washington, D. C.

"My dear Sir:—I arrived here late on the night of the 10th inst., having crossed from Fort Leavenworth with an escort furnished me by General Smith. On the road, I witnessed numerous evidences of the atrocities that are being committed by the bands of marauders that infest the country. In this place everything is quiet; which is attributable to the presence of a large force of United States troops. The trial of the United States prisoners was to have taken place on the day of my arrival; but in consequence of the absence of the district-attorney, and the non-appearance of witnesses, it was deferred until the next regular term of the court, Judge Lecompte admitting the prisoners to bail in the sum of five thousand dollars each. They departed on the same day for Lawrence, where Lane still continues in force.

"Accompanying this you will find printed copies of my inaugural address and my first proclamations, which will exhibit the policy I have thus far thought proper to pursue.

"I have determined to dismiss the present organized militia, after consultation with and by the advice of General Smith; and for the reasons that they were not enrolled in accordance with the laws; that many of them are not citizens of the territory; that some of them were committing outrages under the pretence of serving the public; and that they were unquestionably perpetuating, rather than diminishing, the troubles with which the territory is agitated.

"I have also, as you will see, taken the proper steps to enroll the militia of the territory, agreeably to the act of assembly, and to your instructions of September 2d. I trust that the militia, thus organized, may be rendered serviceable to the government. It is probable also that these proclamations may have the tendency to disband the free-state organizations at Lawrence.

"Nothing of material importance has occurred, or come under my notice, since I last addressed you. I shall continue to keep you apprised of all matters that I may deem of sufficient interest to communicate.

"As there is no telegraphic communication nearer than Boonville, I am compelled to trust my dispatches to the mails, which are now in this region somewhat uncertain.

"Most truly and respectfully, your obedient servant,

"Jno. W. Geary."

At the time of writing the above, the strength, movements and designs of the Missouri army were unknown to Governor Geary; but soon afterwards their plans and operations began to be developed. Shortly after midnight, on the morning of September 13th, the governor received a messenger bearing the following remarkable dispatch :—

"Head Quarters, Mission Creek, K. T.,
"11th September, 1856.

"To His Excellency, J. W. Geary,
"Governor of Kansas Territory.

"Sir: In obedience to the call of Acting-Governor Woodson, I have organized a militia force of about eight hundred men, who are now in the field, ready for duty, and impatient to act. Hearing of your arrival, I beg leave to report them to you for orders. Any communication forwarded to us, will find us encamped at or near this point.

"I have the honor to be, respectfully, your obdt. servant,

"Wm. A. Heiskill,
"Brig Gen. Commanding First Brigade,
"Southern Division, Kansas Militia.

"By order,
"L. A. Maclean, Adjutant."

Not more than an hour after the receipt of the foregoing, a second messenger arrived, himself almost exhausted with a long and fast ride and his horse nearly broken down, and presented the following:—

"Head Quarters, Mission Camp,
"12th September, 1856.

"To His Excellency, J. W. Geary,
"Governor of Kansas Territory.

"Sir: Yesterday I had the honor to report to you my command of Kansas Militia, then about eight hundred strong, which was dispatched *via* Leavenworth. In case it may not have reached you, I now report one thousand men as territorial militia, called into the field by proclamation of Acting-Governor Woodson, and subject to your orders.

"I have the honor to be, respectfully, your obedt. servt.,
"Wm. A. Heiskell,
"Brig. Gen. Commanding First Brigade,
"Southern Div., Kansas Militia.

"By order,
"L. A. Maclean, Adjutant."

Without a moment's hesitation, the governor determined at once to disband these troops and send them back to their homes; and he accordingly answered the dispatches of General Heiskell, as follows:—

"Executive Office, Lecompton, K. T.,
"September 12, 1856, 1½ o'clock.

"Brig. Gen. Wm. A. Heiskell.

"Sir: Your first and second dispatches have been received. I will communicate with you through the person of either the secretary of the territory, or the adjutant-general, as soon as he can reach your camp, he starting from this place at an early hour this morning.

"Very respectfully yours,
"Jno. W. Geary,
"Governor of Kansas Territory."

Whilst the foregoing was being written, a message was received from a special agent of the governor, dated at Lawrence, in which he says:—

"I arrived here a few moments ago, and distributed the address and proclamations, and found the people prepared to repel a contemplated attack from the forces coming from Missouri. Reports are well authenticated, in the opinion of the best men here, that there are within six miles of this place a large number of men—three hundred have been seen. * * At this moment one of the scouts came in, and reports the forces marching against them at Franklin, three miles off, and all have flown to their arms to meet them."

This message was enclosed with the following dispatch, and sent immediately to Colonel Cook, commanding United States forces near Lecompton:—

"Executive Office, Lecompton, K. T.,
"Sept. 13, 1856, at 1½ o'clock, A. M.

"COL. P. ST. GEORGE COOK.

"Dear Sir: The accompanying dispatch, just received from Lawrence, gives sufficient reason to believe that trouble of a serious character is likely to take place there. Mr. Adams, the writer of the dispatch, is the special agent whom I sent down last evening to ascertain the state of affairs. I think you had better send *immediately* to Lawrence a force sufficient to prevent bloodshed, as it is my orders from the President to use every possible means to prevent collisions between belligerent troops. If desirable, I will accompany the forces myself, and should be glad to have you go along.

"Truly yours,
"JNO. W. GEARY,
"Governor of Kansas Territory."

About one hour after this dispatch was sent to the camp of Colonel Cook, say at half-past two o'clock, on the morning of September 13th, that officer, with three hundred mounted soldiers and four pieces of artillery, and accompanied by Governor Geary, left for Lawrence, which town they reached at early sunrise. Here they learned that the danger was not so imminent as had been apprehended. The city was fortified at every point, and the inhabitants generally under arms. There were not over three hundred men in the city. These were assembled together, and addressed at great length by the governor, who cautioned them against the commission of any unlawful acts, and promised them ample protection in case they should be attacked.

He was received with much cordiality, listened to with marked attention and respect, and heartily cheered at the conclusion of his speech. Finding no immediate necessity for his presence, and receiving intelligence that he was needed at Lecompton, in consequence of serious difficulties that had sprung up in that neighborhood, the governor made all proper arrangements for any emergency that might arise at Lawrence, and with Colonel Cook, and his command, returned to Lecompton in the afternoon of the same day.

CHAPTER XXIII.

Excitement at Lecompton.—Affidavit of W. F. Dyer.—Requisition for troops.—The battle at Hickory Point.—Arrest of one hundred and one free-state prisoners.—The killing of Grayson, a pro-slavery man.—Treatment of the prisoners.—Conduct of Judges Lecompte and Cato.—Trial and sentence of the prisoners, and their subsequent treatment.

UPON his return to Lecompton, the governor found his office beset with crowds of persons, all of them greatly excited, and many seriously alarmed, in consequence of a supposed intended assault by a large body of men belonging to Lane's party, on the pro-slavery settlements at Hardteville, (known as Hickory Point,) Osawkee, and the surrounding neighborhoods. It was alleged that on that day, and several days previous, stores had been broken into and robbed, horses had been stolen, cattle driven off, and other similar outrages committed; and that there was abundant reason for apprehension that additional atrocities were about to be committed. The inhabitants had hastily fled in terror from their dwellings, fearful that their lives were in danger, and numbers had made their way to Lecompton to seek protection and redress from the governor.

Among the most importunate of the complainants was Dr. William H. Tebbs, a prominent member of the pro-slavery party. He, among others, insisted upon some immediate action being taken to secure the persons complained of, and to save the property declared to be endangered. It was quite late in the evening when the governor arrived, and during the night the excitement increased, as other settlers came in, each having some tale of horror to relate. There were no courts in session—no judges or magistrates at hand to hear these complaints and issue process against the offenders, in legal form. After much difficulty, a Mr. Dyer succeeded in finding a justice of the peace, before whom he swore and subscribed to the following affidavit, which he placed in the hands of the governor on Sunday morning, September 14th:

"Territory of Kansas, Douglas County.

"Personally appeared before a justice in and for Douglas county, Kansas Territory, William F. Dyer, and being duly sworn, says, that Col. Whipple, at the head of a hundred or more men, among whom were J. Ritchie, Ephraim Bainter, J. O. B. Dunning, Captain Jamison, and others not known to him, did, on Monday, September 8, 1856, rob him of six head of mules and horses, and various articles of merchandise, amounting in value to more than a thousand dollars; and on Tuesday following, it being the 9th of September, 1856, the same men robbed him of various articles of merchandise, amounting in value to over three thousand dollars; and that this day, it being Saturday, September 13, 1856, the same men were assembled at Osawkee, about 8 o'clock, A. M., as he believed for the purpose of robbing and burning the town and country round about, and attacking the town of Hardtville this evening.

"W. F. DYER.

"Subscribed and sworn this 13th day of September, 1856, before me,
R. R. NELSON,
"Justice of the Peace."

Upon the receipt of this affidavit, the statements of which were confirmed by other reliable witnesses, a requisition was made upon Colonel Cooke, as follows:—

"Executive Department,
"Lecompton, K. T., Sept. 14, 1856.

"COL. P. ST. G. COOK:

"Dear Sir: You will perceive by the accompanying affidavit, and from verbal statements that will be made to you by Dr. Tebbs, that a desperate state of affairs is existing at Osawkee and its vicinity, which seems to require some action at our hands. I strongly recommend that you send a force, such as you can conveniently spare, to visit that neighborhood, at the earliest moment. If such a force cannot succeed in arresting the perpetrators of the outrages already committed, and of which complaint has been made in due form, it may at least tend to disperse or drive off the band or bands of marauders who are threatening the lives and property of peaceable citizens. The deputy marshal will accompany such troops as you may judge expedient to detail on this service.

"Very respectfully and truly yours,
"JNO. W. GEARY,
"Governor of Kansas Territory."

Colonel Cook immediately detailed a squadron of United States dragoons to pursue the alleged marauders, and protect the threatened neighborhood. They forded the river at Lecompton a little before sunset, and about midnight fell in with a party of men, of whom they made one hundred and one prisoners, without resistance. This party was mostly mounted, and well armed with rifles, pistols and bowie-knives, and had one brass field-piece and several wagons, all of which were captured and brought into Lecompton early on the morning of Monday, September 15th. They were said to be a detachment of Lane's forces, under command of Captain Harvey, and had come from Lawrence on Saturday the 13th, with a view to join a large body from Topeka. They had been engaged in an affray at Hickory Point, about twelve miles from Lecompton, and one mile from the place at which they were taken, on the afternoon of Sunday. The full particulars of this fight and capture of the prisoners will be found in the governor's dispatch to Secretary Marcy, of the 16th September. The prisoners at first denied having been guilty of any overt act, and claimed to have been peaceable citizens, banded together for mutual protection. But upon being taunted by some prominent pro-slavery men in regard to the dilemma in which they were placed, they acknowledged the whole story of the Hickory Point fight, and made themselves merry in describing what they pronounced the cowardice of the opposite party. They called it a 'free-fight,' in which they said all concerned were equally at fault. They seemed to apprehend no serious results from their capture; and some of them even proposed to the persons who were taking advantage of their helpless condition to insult them, that they should be allowed another opportunity to fight the matter out. "We will give you two to one in numbers," says one, "and an equality of arms, if you will only give us an open field and fair play." Being asked if they had not read the governor's proclamation, one of the leaders readily and wittily replied, "Oh, yes, and before we commenced our fire upon the border-ruffians, we read the proclamation to them, and commanded them to surrender in the name of the governor."

A man named Grayson was killed by a soldier shortly after the capture of these prisoners. He was a pro-slavery man, and had been acting as a guide to the troops. He attempted to pass the guard during the night, which was dark, when being hailed, he supposed he was accosted by an enemy, and suddenly turned and shot the sentinel in the shoulder. Another of the guard, witnessing the transaction, immediately discharged his pistol, the ball from which took effect in the breast of Grayson, killing him instantly.

The prisoners were conducted to the United States encampment on the outskirts of Lecompton, where they were detained some time without proper shelter from the weather or sufficient rations. Their preliminary examination was procrastinated to an unreasonable and almost criminal length of time by the supreme judges. A hearing was eventually given them by Judge Cato, which was somewhat partial in its character, the prosecuting attorney being the celebrated Joseph C. Anderson, of Lexington, Mo., a member of the Kansas Legislature, the author of some of its most obnoxious laws, and notorious for his complicity with many of the grossest outrages committed by the pro-slavery party. The judge, who but a short time previous had been found in the encampment of as lawless men as those under examination, committed the whole party for trial on the charge of murder in the first degree. Nothing would be heard in mitigation of their offence; nor would either Judge Cato or Judge Lecompte permit them to be discharged from custody, upon any amount or character of bail, although it was notoriously true that every pro-slavery man that had been arrested in the territory, no matter how heinous the crime or positive the proof, for which he was committed, had been set at liberty upon worthless bail, by these same officials; the murderers of Barber, of Phillips, of Buffum, and others, were all liberated upon "straw bail," and some of them are now holding offices of responsibility under the federal government.

It was quite palpable that some of these prisoners were comparatively if not entirely innocent of any crime; but this fact had no weight upon the judges. They were free-state men, and that, in their estimation, was a crime sufficient to condemn them to imprisonment and death. There were many cases of peculiar hardship, one of which may be related. A poor German, who scarcely understood the nature of the political contest that was waging in the territory, was working in his field with a wagon and two horses, when the party for Hickory Point passed his house. Some of these being on foot, jumped into his wagon, and compelled him to drive them to the scene of action. This fact was clearly established, and the wretched wife of the prisoner came on foot a distance of nearly twenty miles, bringing with her six almost naked and bare-footed children, to plead to the governor in behalf of her husband. She told the story as it really occurred; represented her husband as an industrious and peaceable man, who had taken no part in any of the disturbances; and declared that unless he was set at liberty, to procure them a livelihood, herself and children were in danger of actual starvation. Notwithstanding all this was satisfactorily established, and responsible gentlemen were willing to enter bail for the prisoner's appearance at court, the judges were inexorable, and refused, upon any terms, to discharge the unfortunate man.

Colonel Cook finding it inconvenient to keep the prisoners

at the encampment, and General Smith having issued an order for their removal, they were taken to a dilapidated house in Lecompton, and guarded by a company of militia under command of Colonel H. T. Titus. Here their condition was truly deplorable. The building was insufficient in capacity for so many men, while no adequate means were at hand to provide them with food, clothing or bedding. Hence they were nearly starved; subject to constant insults from their guards; living in actual filth; overrun with vermin; and exposed to all the changes of the weather in the most severe and inclement season of the year.

The prisoners received their trial at the October term of the first district court, when some of them were acquitted, and others convicted of various degrees of manslaughter. These were sentenced to terms of confinement varying from five to ten years, at hard labor, and to wear a ball and chain.

Sheriff Jones, who was disappointed in not being allowed by the verdict to hang these prisoners, agreeably to his expressed desire, was nervously anxious to see the ball and chain applied, and accordingly wrote to Governor Geary, then at Fort Leavenworth, as follows:—

"Lecompton, Nov. 17, 1856.

"Sir:—It is indispensably necessary that balls and chains should be furnished for the safety of the convicts under my charge, and understanding that the same can be procured by your application to General Smith, I will request that you will procure and have them sent over at the earliest day possible.

"Very respectfully, your obedt. servt.,

"SAML. J. JONES,

"Sheriff of Douglas county.

"His Excellency, Governor Geary,

"Fort Leavenworth."

To this application the governor replied, upon reaching Lecompton:

"Executive Department,

"Lecompton, K. T., Nov. 21, 1856.

"SAMUEL J. JONES, Esq.,

"Sheriff of Douglas county.

"Sir: In reply to yours of the 17th instant, received by me while at Fort Leavenworth, I have to remark that the master of convicts—a just and humane man—with the aid of such guard as he may require, will take care of the convicts, who are, or may be placed under his charge, in such manner as may be deemed most advisable for the public interests.

"General Smith has no balls and chains for the purpose indicated in your request—nor is it deemed advisable to procure any, while the trial of the remainder of the Hickory Point prisoners is unfinished.

"Very respectfully, your obedt. servt.,

JNO. W. GEARY,

"Governor of Kansas Territory."

On the next day, the governor addressed the following communication to Captain L. J. Hampton, whom, in accordance with an act of the territorial legislature, creating that office, he appointed master of convicts. The remission of the ball and chain penalty excited the unconcealed anger of Jones, Clarke and other leaders of the pro-slavery party, whose maledictions against the governor, for his clemency, were loud and unstinted. The *Lecompton Union*, over which they had control, was unsparing in its denunciations:—

"Executive Department,

"Lecompton, K. T., Nov. 22, 1856.

"L. J. HAMPTON, Esq.,

"Master of Convicts:

"Sir: I have been requested by Sheriff Jones to procure balls and chains, in accordance with 2d section, 22d ch. Kansas Statutes, for the safety of the prisoners recently convicted for manslaughter for participation in the Hickory Point fight.

"Reposing especial trust and confidence in your integrity, humanity, and discretion, I have, in pursuance of the statutes, appointed you master of convicts, and placed them under your supervision.

"By the organic act, I am authorized to grant pardons and reprieves for 'all offences against the laws of the territory;' and esteeming the punishment as described in the said section as cruel and unusual, and especially inappropriate to the prisoners alluded to, I hereby remit that portion of their sentence requiring the use of 'balls and chains,' and desire you to treat the prisoners with every humanity consistent with their safe-keeping.

"Your obedient servant,

"JNO. W. GEARY,

"Governor of Kansas Territory."

These prisoners were not all rough and desperate adventurers. Some of them were gentlemen of polished education, who had graduated in the best institutions of learning, and belonged to the most respectable families in the country. It is true, they were convicted of the commission of an unlawful act; but, in order to understand the merits of their case, it is necessary that all the circumstances connected with it should be fairly weighed and duly considered. The territory was in a state of insurrection and rebellion. The whole community was in arms. Aggressions had been committed by various parties, which had aroused on all sides a spirit of retaliation and revenge. These same prisoners had suffered many and great abuses from their pro-slavery enemies; and at the very time they attacked the settlement at Hickory Point, these latter were marching in great force to effect their utter annihilation.

Upon the disbanding of the militia in December, those of the prisoners that were left, one having died of privation and exposure, and others having made their escape despite the vigilance of their guards, were placed in charge of the master of convicts. Captain Hampton was a Kentuckian by birth, and a pro-slavery man; but possessed an honest heart and generous disposition. He treated the prisoners as though they were human beings, and with as much kindness and consideration as their relative positions would permit. He soon gained their confidence, and having no proper place for their safe confinement, and being required to keep them at work when labor could be obtained, he allowed them to go at large without a keeper, relying upon their own promise to return to his charge at any specified time.

This conduct called down upon Hampton the vengeance of leading members of his party, who denounced him fiercely for his leniency, complained of him to the governor, and loudly demanded his removal from office. The most violent of those who condemned him were Sheriff Jones, the editors of the *Lecompton Union*, and L. A. Maclean, chief clerk of Surveyor Calhoun, every one of whom was guilty of greater offences against the laws than the worst man then in charge of the master of convicts. When the pro-slavery convention, which baptized itself into the name of the "National Democracy of Kansas," met in Lecompton, in January, Captain Hampton was violently assailed by Maclean, Jones and Stringfellow, and his seat as a delegate contested, because, as it was maintained, his kind treatment of the free-state prisoners afforded ample proof that he was not and could not be a pro-slavery man. And for the same reason the Legislative Assembly refused to confirm his appointment.

A good anecdote is told by a gentleman from one of the southern states, in regard to these free-state prisoners, when under the charge of Captain Hampton. Soon after his arrival at Lecompton, he called upon the governor, and, in the course of conversation, expressed himself with considerable warmth against the prisoners who had committed such atrocious crimes as were charged against them in certain newspapers that he had read. So horrible an idea had he conceived of the character of the men in question, that he could not find terms sufficiently strong to express his execration of their deeds. He unquestionably and honestly imagined that they were moral monsters of enormous magnitude. Having expressed a desire to see these terrible robbers and murderers and assassins, as he styled them, the governor directed him to the prison, and assured him that by paying it a visit he might gratify his curiosity.

He immediately started, and after reaching the designated neighborhood, and looking in vain for anything that resembled a prison, he approached two men, who were enjoying themselves with a game of quoits.

"Can you tell me," he enquired, "where the prison is in which those great robbers and murderers are confined?"

"That's it," said one of the men, pointing to a house near at hand.

"What! that old building, falling to pieces, without either doors or windows? You don't want to tell me that they keep murderers and thieves and other criminals there?"

"That is the only prison we have here," replied the man, deliberately pitching his quoit.

"Well," says the southern gentleman, "I want to see those desperate murderers and assassins."

"I am one of them," says the quoit-player, "and that is another," pointing to his companion.

"What! you convicted felons? You the terrible murderers about whom I have heard so much?"

"Yes; we are certainly two of them. The others are gone over to the House of Representatives, to hear the members abuse the governor."

"But," says the old gentleman, "they don't allow convicted murderers to go about in this way, without a guard to watch them?"

"Oh, yes," says the man interrogated; "they used to send a guard with us, whenever we went over to the Legislative Halls, to protect us against violence from the members; but they found that too troublesome and expensive; so they gave each of us a revolver and bowie-knife, and told us we should hereafter be required to protect ourselves."

"But why don't you run away? You have every opportunity. There is nothing to prevent you."

"Why, to tell the truth, we have often been persuaded to do that; but then, you see these rascally legislators have been threatening to assassinate the governor, and we have determined to remain here to watch them, and protect him."

The old gentleman had no desire to see any more of those desperate thieves, robbers, murderers and assassins.

There were but seventeen convicts remaining in the custody of Captain Hampton on the 2d of March, at which time they were all freely pardoned by the governor, in compliance with numerous petitions, in which it was alleged that the prisoners had, previous to the difficulty for which they were arrested, uniformly "maintained good reputations; that the offence for which they were convicted, was committed in one of those political contentions, in which a great portion of the people of the territory took an active part, many of whom, though equally, if not more guilty, were still at liberty, and could never be brought to punishment; that they had already suffered an imprisonment of nearly six months; and that their continued punishment could neither subserve the ends of justice, nor the interests of the territory."

It might, with propriety, have been added, in palliation of their offence, that the most of those with whom they had the affray at Hickory Point, comprised a company of pro-slavery men, under the command of one Captain Robinson, who were then on their way to join the Missouri army, about to destroy Lawrence, and that in their march from the northern portion of the state, they had committed many and grievous depredations upon the free-state settlers, and the attack upon them was partly in retaliation for the wrongs they had inflicted.

CHAPTER XXIV.

The Missouri army of invasion.—Letter from Theodore Adams.—Governor Geary proceeds with troops to Lawrence, and protects the town.—The governor visits the camp of the Missourians, addresses the officers, and disbands the forces.

WHILST the governor was making his arrangements for quelling the disturbances at Osawkee and Hickory Point, difficulties of a more serious nature were demanding his attention in a different direction. Messengers were constantly arriving from Lawrence, bringing intelligence that a large army from Missouri was encamped on the Wakarusa River, and was hourly expected to attack the town. As these men styled themselves territorial militia, and were called into service by the late acting-governor Woodson, Governor Geary commanded that officer to take with him Adjutant-General Strickler, with an escort of United States troops, and disband, in accordance with the proclamations issued, the forces that had so unwisely been assembled. Woodson and Strickler left Lecompton in the afternoon, and reached the Missouri camp early in the evening.

Here Woodson found it impossible to accomplish the object of his mission. No attention or respect was paid to him by those having command of the forces. The army he had gathered, refused to acknowledge his authority. He had raised a storm, the elements of which he was powerless to control. Neither could the officers be assembled to receive the governor's orders from the adjutant-general. The militia had resolved not to disband; the officers refused to listen to the reading of the proclamation; they were determined upon accomplishing the bloody work they had entered the territory to perform. Nothing but the destruction of Lawrence, and the other free-state towns, the massacre of all the free-state residents, and the appropriation of their lands and other property, could satisfy them. Vengeance was theirs—they had now the power—and it should be executed. Governor Geary was denounced by such men as Clarke, Maclean, Stringfellow and Jones, and sentence of death was freely uttered against him, along the whole line of the encampment, should he dare to interfere. Nothing, now, could satisfy them but abolition blood. This they intended to wade through, and drink to satiety; nor would they stop at anything short of the utter extermination or "wiping out" of Kansas, everything bearing the vestige of free-soilism. Never was collected together such a fierce and furious band. Little did they imagine that for every abolitionist they "wiped out," a hundred others would arise to revenge his death! Little did they think that for every drop of blood they shed, rivers of their own would have been caused to flow! Had Governor Geary permitted them to execute their fiendish work, the sword of retribution would long since have fallen with dreadful power upon that murderous crew. The measure of their iniquity would have been full, and Heaven could no longer have held back the avenging arm of justice; and ere now, the slave power, which has so long been bullying the freemen of the land, would have been swept into the ocean of eternity! The delusive hope that the north will not fight, would have been dispelled; for the weight would have been felt, of thousands of more powerful and mighty arms than any that have ever laid the lash upon negroes' backs. The entire people of the south—every man, woman and child, of the slavery party—owe a debt of gratitude which never can be paid, to Governor Geary, for his timely presence and arrest of the bloody purpose of these hot-brained madmen!

Mr. Adams, who accompanied Secretary Woodson to the Missouri camp, dispatched the following:—

"Lawrence, 12 o'clock, midnight,
"September 14, 1856.

"His Excellency, Governor Geary:

"Sir: I went as directed to the camp of the militia, and found at the town of Franklin, three miles from this place, encamped three hundred men, with four pieces of artillery. One mile to the right on the Wakarusa, I found a very large encampment of three hundred tents and wagons. They claim to have two thousand five hundred men; and from the appearance of the camp I have no doubt they have that number. General Reid is in command. I saw and was introduced to General Atchison, Colonel Titus, Sheriff Jones, General Richardson, &c. The proclamations were distributed.

"Secretary Woodson and General Strickler had not, up to the time I left, delivered their orders; but were about doing so as soon as they could get the officers together.

"The outposts of both parties were fighting about an hour before sunset. One man killed of the militia, and one house burned at Franklin.

"There were but few people at Lawrence, most of them having gone to their homes after your visit here.

"I reported these facts to the officer in command here, and your prompt action has undoubtedly been the means of preventing the loss of blood and saving valuable property.

"Secretary Woodson thought you had better *come* to the camp of the militia as soon as you can. I think a prompt visit would have a good effect. I will see you as you come this way, and communicate with you more fully.

"Very respectfully, your obedt. servt.,

"THEODORE ADAMS."

Before this dispatch reached Lecompton, the governor had departed, with three hundred United States mounted troops and a battery of light artillery, and riding speedily, arrived at Lawrence early in the evening of the 14th, where he found matters precisely as described. Skilfully stationing his troops outside the town, in commanding positions, to prevent a collision between the invading forces from Missouri and the citizens, he entered Lawrence alone, and there he beheld a sight which would have aroused the manhood of the most stolid mortal, and which another writer has thus eloquently described:—

"About three hundred persons were found in arms, determined to sell their lives at the dearest price to their ruffian enemies. Among these were many women, and children of both sexes, armed with guns and otherwise accoutred for battle. They had been goaded to this by the courage of despair. Lawrence was to have been their Thermopylæ, and every other free town would have proved a Saragossa. When men determine to die for the right, a hecatomb of victims grace their immolation; but when women and children betake themselves to the battle-field, ready to fight and die with their husbands and fathers, heroism becomes the animating principle of every heart, and a giant's strength invigorates every arm. Each drop of blood lost by such warriors becomes a dragon's tooth, which will spring from the earth, in all the armor of truth and justice, to exact a fearful retribution. Had Lawrence been destroyed, and her population butchered, the red right hand of vengeance would have gleamed over the entire South, and the question of slavery have been settled by a bloody and infuriated baptism. There are such examples in history, and mankind have lost none of their impulses or human emotions.

"Gov. Geary addressed the armed citizens of Lawrence, and when he assured them of his and the law's protection, they offered to deposit their arms at his feet and return to their respective habitations. He bid them go to their homes in confidence, and to carry their arms with them, as the Constitution of the Union guaranteed that right; but to use those arms only in the last resort to protect their lives and property, and the chastity of their females. They obeyed the governor and repaired to their homes."

Early on the morning of the 15th, having left the troops to protect the town of Lawrence, the governor proceeded alone to the camp of the invading forces, then within three miles, and drawn up in line of battle. Before reaching Franklin, he met the advance guard, and upon inquiring who they were and what were their objects, received for answer, that they were the territorial militia, called into service by the governor of Kansas, and that they were marching to "wipe out Lawrence and every d—d abolitionist in the country." Geary informed them that he was now Governor of Kansas, and commander-in-chief of the territorial militia, and ordered the officer in command to countermarch his troops back to the main line, and conduct him to the centre, that being his proper position, which order, after some hesitation, was reluctantly obeyed.

The scene that was presented as the governor advanced, was one that no time nor circumstance can ever erase from his mind. The militia had taken a position upon an extensive and beautiful plain near the junction of the Wakarusa with the Kansas River. On one side towered a lofty hill, known as the Blue Mound, and on the other Mount Oread showed its fortified summit. The town of Franklin, from its elevated site, looked down upon the active scene, while beyond, in a quiet vale, the more flourishing city of Lawrence reposed as though unconscious of its threatened doom. The waters of the Kansas River might be seen gliding rapidly toward the Missouri, and the tall forest trees which line its banks, plainly indicated the course of the Wakarusa. The red face of the rising sun was just peering over the top of the Blue Mound, as the governor with his strange escort of three hundred mounted men, with red shirts and odd-shaped hats, descended upon the Wakarusa plain. There, in battle array, were ranged at least three thousand armed and desperate men. They were not dressed in the usual habiliments of soldiers; but in every imaginable costume that could be obtained in that western region. Scarcely two presented the same appearance, while all exhibited a ruffianly aspect. Most of them were mounted, and manifested an unmistakable disposition to be at their bloody work. In the background stood at least three hundred army tents and as many wagons, while here and there a cannon was planted ready to aid in the anticipated destruction. Among the banners floated black flags to indicate the design that neither age, sex, nor condition would be spared in the slaughter that was to ensue. The arms and cannon also bore the black indices of extermination.

In passing along the lines, murmurs of discontent and savage threats of assassination fell upon the governor's ears; but heedless of these, and regardless, in fact, of everything but a desire to avert the terrible calamity that was impending, he fearlessly proceeded to the quarters of their leader.

This threatening army was under the command of General John W. Reid, then and now a member of the Missouri Legislature, assisted by ex-senator Atchison, General B. F. Stringfellow, General L. A. Maclean, General J. W. Whitfield, General George W. Clarke, Generals William A. Heiskell, Wm. H. Richardson, and F. A. Marshal, Col. H. T. Titus, Captain Frederick Emory, and others of similar character. Some of these men have since been rewarded by the present administration with lucrative offices, if not for the valuable services they were about to render in this affair, at least for some others which the government has considered important.

Governor Geary at once summoned the officers together, and addressed them at length and with great feeling. He depicted in a forcible manner the improper position they occupied, and the untold horrors that would result from the consummation of their cruel designs: that if they persisted in their mad career, the entire Union would be involved in a civil war, and thousands and tens of thousands of innocent lives be sacrificed. To Atchison, he especially addressed himself, telling him that when he last saw him, he was acting as vice-president of the nation and president of the most dignified body of men in the world, the senate of the United States; but now with sorrow and pain he saw him leading on to a civil and disastrous war an army of men, with uncontrollable passions, and determined upon wholesale slaughter and destruction. He concluded his remarks by directing attention to his proclamation, and ordered the army to be disbanded and dispersed. Some of the more judicious of the officers were not only willing, but anxious to obey this order; whilst others, resolved upon mischief, yielded a very reluctant assent. General Clarke said he was for pitching into the United States troops, if necessary, rather than abandon the objects of the expedition. General Maclean didn't see any use of going back until they had whipped the d—d abolitionists. Sheriff Jones was in favor, now they had a sufficient force, of "wiping out" Lawrence and all the free-state towns. And these and others, cursed Governor Geary in not very gentle expressions, for his untimely interference with their well laid plans. They, however, obeyed the order, and retired, not as good and law-loving citizens, but as bands of plunderers and destroyers, leaving in their wake ruined fortunes, weeping eyes, and sorrowing hearts.

The question has been asked, why was this army dispersed, and permitted to depart for their homes, whilst that at Hickory Point was captured, imprisoned, tried and convicted of a criminal charge? The answer is simple. These men had been called into service by the late acting-governor, and by him given authority as the duly constituted militia of the territory. As such Governor Geary was compelled to recognise them. They had committed no overt act against the laws of which they were accused and of which he could properly take cognisance, and all that he could do was to order them to disperse. Had they refused, and still kept up their military organization, they would have been placed in quite a different position, and Governor Geary could then have arrested them as violators of the peace. But they obeyed his order and disbanded. On the other hand, the party at Hickory Point, though morally as good, if not better men, were in arms not only without the sanction, but in open violation of law. With the governor's proclamation in their hands, commanding all unauthorized armed bodies instantly to disband or quit the territory, they marched against and stormed a settlement, killing one man and wounding several others, and almost in the very commission of this unlawful and overt act, they were captured by the government troops. The whole difference, therefore, between the two parties, is, not that one was morally worse than the other, but because one was acting by and the other against legal authority.

On the 16th of September, the governor dispatched the following letter to Secretary Marcy:—

"Executive Department, Lecompton, K. T.,
"Sept. 16, 1856.

"Hon. Wm. L. Marcy, Secretary of State:

"My Dear Sir:—My last dispatch was dated the 12th instant, in which I gave you a statement of my operations to that date. Since then, I have had business of the deepest importance to occupy every moment of my attention, and to require the most constant watchfulness and untiring energy. Indeed, so absolutely occupied is all my time, that I scarcely have a minute to devote to the duty of keeping you apprised of the true condition of this territory. I have this instant returned from an expedition to Lawrence and the vicinity, and am preparing to depart almost immediately for other sections of the territory, where my presence is demanded.

"After having issued my address and proclamations in this city, copies of which have been forwarded to you, I sent them with a special messenger, to Lawrence, twelve miles to the eastward, where they were made known to the citizens on the 12th instant. The people of that place were alarmed with a report that a large body of armed men, called out under the proclamation of the late acting-governor Woodson, were threatening them with an attack, and they were making the necessary preparations for resistance. So well authenticated seemed their information, that my agent forwarded an express by a United States trooper, announcing the fact, and calling upon me to use my power to prevent the impending calamity. This express reached me at half-past one o'clock, on the morning of the 13th instant. I immediately made a requisition upon Colonel Cook, commander of the United States forces stationed at this place, for as many troops as could be made available, and in about an hour was on my way towards Lawrence, with three hundred mounted men, including a battery of light artillery. On arriving at Lawrence we found the danger had been exaggerated, and that there was no immediate necessity for the intervention of the military. The moral effect of our presence, however, was of great avail. The citizens were satisfied that the government was disposed to render them all needed protection, and I received from them the assurance that they would conduct themselves as law-abiding and peace-loving men. They voluntarily offered to lay down their arms, and enrol themselves as territorial militia, in accordance with the terms of my proclamations. I returned the same day with the troops, well satisfied with the result of my mission.

"During the evening of Saturday, the 13th, I remained at my office, which was constantly thronged with men uttering complaints concerning outrages that had been and were being committed upon their persons and property. These complaints came in from every direction, and were made by the advocates of all the conflicting political sentiments, with which the territory has been agitated; and they exhibited clearly a moral condition of affairs, too lamentable for any language adequately to describe. The whole country was evidently infested with armed bands of marauders, who set all law at defiance, and travelled from place to place, assailing villages, sacking and burning houses, destroying crops, maltreating women and children, driving off and stealing cattle and horses, and murdering harmless men in their own dwellings and on the public highways. Many of these grievances needed immediate redress; but unfortunately the law was a dead letter, no magistrate or judge being at hand to take an affidavit or issue a process, and no marshal or sheriff to be found, even had the judges been present to prepare them, to execute the same.

"The next day, Sunday, matters grew worse and worse. The most positive evidence reached me, that a large body of armed and mounted men were devastating the neighborhoods of Osawkee and Hardtville, commonly called Hickory Point. Being well convinced of this fact, I determined to act upon my own responsibility, and immediately issued an order to Colonel Cook for a detachment of his forces, to visit the scene of disturbance. In answer to this requisition, a squadron of eighty-one men were detached, consisting of companies C. and H. 1st cavalry, Captains Wood and Newby, the whole under command of Captain Wood. This detachment left the camp at two o'clock, P. M., with instructions to proceed to Osawkee and Hickory Point, the former twelve, and the latter eighteen miles to the northward of Lecompton. It was accompanied by a deputy marshal.

"In consequence of the want of proper facilities for crossing the Kansas River, it was late in the evening before the force could march. After having proceeded about six miles, intelligence was brought to Captain Wood, that a large party of men, under command of a person named Harvey, had come over from Lawrence, and made an attack upon a log house at Hickory Point, in which a number of the settlers had taken refuge. This assault commenced about eleven o'clock in the morning, and continued six hours. The attacking party had charge of a brass four-pounder, the same that was taken by Colonel Doniphan at the battle of Sacramento. This piece had been freely used in the assault; but without effecting any material damage. As far as has yet been ascertained, but one man was killed, and some half-dozen wounded.

"About eleven o'clock in the evening, Captain Wood's command met a party of twenty-five men, with three wagons, one of which contained a wounded man. These he ascertained to be a portion of Harvey's forces, who had been engaged in the assault at Hickory Point, and who were returning to Lawrence. They were immediately arrested, without resistance, disarmed and held as prisoners. Three others were soon after arrested, who also proved to be a portion of Harvey's party.

"When within about four miles of Hickory Point, Captain Wood discovered a large encampment upon the prairie, near the road leading to Lawrence. It was the main body of Harvey's men, then under command of a man named Bickerton, Harvey having left after the attack on Hickory Point. This party was surprised and captured.

"After securing the prisoners, Captain Wood returned to Lecompton, which place he reached about day-break, on Monday the 15th instant, bringing with him one hundred and one prisoners, one brass field-piece, seven wagons, thirty-eight United States muskets, forty-seven Sharp's rifles, six hunting rifles, two shot guns, twenty revolving pistols, fourteen bowie knives, four swords, and a large supply of ammunition for artillery and small arms.

"Whilst engaged in making preparations for the foregoing expedition, several messengers reached me from Lawrence, announcing that a powerful army was marching upon that place, it being the main body of the militia called into service by the proclamation of Secretary Woodson, when acting-governor.

"Satisfied that the most prompt and decisive measures were necessary to prevent the sacrifice of many lives, and the destruction of one of the finest and most prosperous towns in the territory, and avert a state of affairs, which must have inevitably involved the country in a most disastrous civil war, I dispatched the following order to Colonel Cook:—

"'Proceed at all speed with your command to Lawrence, and prevent a collision if possible, and leave a portion of your troops there for that purpose.'

"Accordingly, the entire available Uuited States force was put in motion, and reached Lawrence at an early hour in the evening. Here, the worst apprehensions of the citizens were discovered to have been well founded. Twenty-seven hundred men, under command of Generals Heiskell, Reid, Atchison, Richardson, Stringfellow, and others, were encamped on the Wakarusa, about four miles from Lawrence, eager and determined to exterminate that place and all its inhabitants. An advanced party of three hundred men had already taken possession of Franklin, one mile from the camp, and three miles from Lawrence, and skirmishing parties had begun to engage in deadly conflict.

"Fully appreciating the awful calamities that were impending, I hastened with all possible dispatch to the encampment, assembled the officers of the militia, and in the name of the President of the United States, demanded suspension of hostilities. I had sent in advance, the secretary and adjutant-general of the territory, with orders to carry out the spirit and letter of my proclamations; but up to the time of my arrival, these orders had been unheeded, and I could discover but little disposition to obey them. I addressed the officers in council at considerable length, setting forth the disastrous consequences of such a demonstration as was contemplated, and the absolute necessity of more lawful and conciliatory measures to restore peace, tranquillity, and prosperity to the country. I read my instructions from the president, and convinced them that my whole course of procedure was in accordance therewith, and called upon them to aid me in my efforts, not only to carry out those instructions, but to support and enforce the laws, and the constitution of the United States. I am happy to say, that a more ready concurrence in my views was met, than I had at first any good reason to expect. It was agreed, that the terms of my proclamations should be carried out by the disbandment of the militia; whereupon the camp was broken up, and the different commands separated, to repair to their respective homes.

"The occurrences, thus related, are already exerting a benificent influence; and although the work is not yet accomplished, I do not despair of success in my efforts to satisfy the government that I am worthy of the high trust which has been reposed in me. As soon as circumstances will permit, I shall visit, in person, every section of the territory, where I feel assured that my presence will tend to give confidence and security to the people.

"In closing, I have merely to add, that unless I am more fully sustained hereafter by the civil authorities, and serious difficulties and disturbances continue to agitate the territory, my only recourse will be to martial law, which I must needs proclaim and enforce.

Very respectfully, &c.

"JNO. W. GEARY.

Governor of Kansas Territory."

CHAPTER XXV.

Improved condition of things.—Attempt to resurrect the courts and incite the judges to the performance of their duty.—Judges Burrell, Cato and Lecompte.—The examination and trial of free-state prisoners.—Directions to Judge Cato.—Letters to the Supreme Judges.—Replies of Judges Cato and Lecompte.—Great criminals permitted to run at liberty.—Discharge of free-state men on bail.—Judge Lecompte's defence.

THE dismissal of the Missouri invaders, the arrest of Harvey's party, and the departure of Col. Lane (which took place about this time) from the territory, were followed with the most beneficial effects. The prompt, bold, rapid, and decisive movements of the governor struck the numerous predatory bands with terror, and they either dispersed, or fled the country; and a happier condition of things began to be apparent on every hand.

The next important measure for the governor, was to resurrect, if possible, the courts, and infuse new life and spirit and energy into the judiciary, who had not only been entirely neglectful of their duties, but were actually responsible for a great portion of the evils that had so long existed. The President cannot be reprehended for not appointing men of superior legal attainments, or more than ordinary talent, to these offices; for the inducements to accept them were insufficient for men of that description. Hence, he was in a measure compelled to make his selections from other material. But still he could have obtained men of mediocre ability, who possessed at least a small amount of integrity and legal knowledge, and some disposition to hold the scales of justice with an even hand. He certainly could not have chosen worse than he did for the necessities of the times and territory, had he canvassed the entire country with that sole determination.

Judge Burrell was in the territory about ten days of the two years he held his appointment, the remainder of his time being passed at his residence in Greensburg, Pa., where he recently died.

When Governor Geary visited the camp of Reid, as already related, he found his honor, Judge Cato, performing the duties of a soldier in that ruffian army, and brought him thence to Lecompton, where, a short time afterwards, being in a tent of the militia, who had got possession of the arms of the free-state prisoners, and were making selections to appropriate to their own use, the judge was shot in the ankle by the accidental discharge of a revolver in the hands of a drunken fellow, named Hull. This disabled him for a considerable length of time; but, after his recovery, he became the constant companion of the most worthless characters in Lecompton, was the daily associate of George W. Clarke and L. A. Maclean, and the room-mate, mess-mate and bed-fellow of Jones and Bennett of the *Lecompton Union*, the honor of writing and supervising the scurrilous and lying productions of which false and abusive sheet he was shrewdly, and perhaps not unjustly, accused of sharing with Surveyor Calhoun and the other worthies named. His knowledge of law was extremely meagre, and his sense of justice by no means delicate or refined.

Chief-Justice Lecompte was a third or fourth-rate lawyer, from Maryland; and though notoriously indolent and sluggish, has, during his two years' residence in Kansas, accumulated in valuable property a fortune of considerable magnitude. In most of the towns laid out by pro-slavery men he owns a goodly share of choice lots, presented to him, doubtless, more in regard to his virtues and talents, than for any favors he had bestowed, or was expected to bestow, in the discharge of his judicial functions. The judge owns a handsome place near Leavenworth City, to which he is so devotedly attached, that he finds it far more convenient to discharge prisoners on straw-bail, than travel twenty or more miles to hold courts and go through the troublesome forms of trial. He can always find time to strike a profitable bargain, make a good land speculation, or engage in any operation that will put money in his purse; but the duties of a judge are too insignificant to receive any special amount of attention; hence he troubles himself but little with the matter of holding courts. An anecdote, somewhat characteristic, is almost universally told, and very generally believed, of him in Kansas. He adjourned the spring term of his court, it is said, to plant potatoes; the summer term to hoe his potatoes; the fall term to dig his potatoes; and the winter term because he had to be at home to sell his potatoes. This, however, is probably somewhat of an exaggeration.

When the governor returned from the Missouri camp, on the 15th, bringing Judge Cato with him, he found Lecompte at the capital, in compliance with a request forwarded to him at Leavenworth to that effect. On the 16th he had an interview with these two officials, in which he endeavored to impress them with the importance to the territory and the country, of proper judicial proceedings—of opening and holding courts; not only that prisoners could be justly disposed of, but that processes could be issued and criminals arrested. This, they were assured, must be done, or military law proclaimed and adopted. They both seemingly concurred in his views, and agreed to his expressed desires.

At this time hundreds of persons were constantly pouring into the city, distracting the attention of the governor with pitiful complaints of atrocious outrages that were being committed upon their persons and property. It was the province of the judges to hear these complaints and endeavor to redress the wrongs the people were suffering, adopt and prosecute measures for the arrest and punishment of transgressors, and prevent a continuance of the crimes which were distracting the territory.

On the 17th the governor accompanied a detachment of troops to arrest a party of alleged criminals at Topeka; and upon his return, on the following day, learned, to his astonishment, that Lecompte had already left for his home in Leavenworth; and that, instead of making arrangements for the immediate examination of the great number of prisoners collected at Lecompton, he had appointed a court for that purpose, to be held three weeks subsequently, at Leavenworth City, forty miles distant, and left directions to have the prisoners conveyed there for trial. Had he adopted this procedure for the express purpose of defeating the ends of justice, and of stultifying all the exertions of the executive for the public welfare, he could not more effectually have accomplished that object. It would have been possible, though extremely difficult, and unnecessarily expensive, to carry one hundred and twenty or more prisoners, then in custody, fifty miles to accommodate Lecompte; but it would have been altogether *impossible* to give those prisoners a proper hearing and just trial at a place so far distant from where their offences were alleged to have been committed. The witnesses could not have been brought together at such a distance, in times when no unprotected traveller could pass the roads in safety, even were there in the way no other obstacles. This, Lecompte knew; and the whole arrangement afforded but another evidence, in addition to the numbers he had already given, of imbecility and worthlessness during the entire period he had been in office.

Incensed at this conduct, and determined that the prisoners should have an early hearing in Lecompton, or be set at liberty, the governor addressed the following note to associate-justice Cato:—

"Executive Department, K. T.,
"Lecompton, Sept. 20, 1856.

"JUDGE STERLING G. CATO:

"Dear Sir: You will oblige me by fixing an early day for the examination of the prisoners now held at the encampment of the United States troops in this district, and give proper and sufficient notice of the same. It is essential to the peace of the community and the due execution of the law, that this be effected at the earliest possible moment. Some of these men have already been detained as prisoners six days without even a preliminary hearing. If at the time appointed and legally notified, no prosecutor appears, the alleged criminals should be discharged and permitted to repair to their homes and lawful pursuits.

"Truly yours,
"JNO. W. GEARY,
"Governor of Kansas Territory."

In accordance with this demand, Judge Cato appointed a court and commenced an examination of the prisoners, during the prosecution of which he met with the accident mentioned, and the proceedings were postponed. The hearing and trials, however, were finally had, the result of which has been related in another place.

Resolved, if possible, to awaken the judiciary to a sense of duty and obligation, or at least to obtain from them an account of their past stewardship, the governor addressed a letter of inquiry to each of the supreme judges, of which the following is a copy:—

"Executive Department, K. T.,
"September 23, 1856.

"To the Hon. Samuel D. Lecompte,
"Chief Justice of the Supreme Court of Kansas Territory.

"Sir: Upon my arrival here I found this territory in a state of insurrection, business paralyzed, operation of the courts suspended, and the civil administration of the government inoperative and seemingly useless.

"Much complaint has been made to me against the territorial officers, for alleged neglect of duty, party bias, and criminal complicity with a state of affairs which resulted in a contempt of all authority.

"I have therefore deemed it proper to address circulars to all territorial officers, in order that, being informed of the complaints against them, they may have an opportunity to vindicate themselves through my department.

"The efficiency of the executive will be much impaired or strengthened by the manner in which his subordinates in office discharge their respective duties.

"As it is my sworn duty to see that the laws are faithfully executed, I need offer no apology for requesting categorical answers to the following interrogatories:

"1st. When did you assume the discharge of the duties of your judicial office?

"2d. What counties compose your judicial district, and how frequently have you held courts in each county or in your district?

"3d. How many bills have been presented—how many ignored in your courts—how many indictments have been tried before you, and how many convictions had, and for what offences?

"With a brief statement of other facts and circumstances, showing the manner in which you have discharged your duties, which you may be pleased to communicate.

"Very truly, your obedt. servt.,
"Jno. W. Geary,
"Governor of Kansas Territory."

Similar communications were addressed to all the territorial officers, the replies to which are not of sufficient interest to receive a place in these pages. They all amount to precisely the same thing, to wit: that not one of the officials understood his duty, or had performed it. The offices appear to have been held, not so much for any good that could be accomplished, as for their honor and emoluments.

From Judge Cato's reply, dated October 29th, it seemed that he had been in the territory about a year. He was appointed to the second judicial district, composed of eight counties. He says: "I held court in each of said counties, except Linn, last spring and summer, beginning at Franklin on the third Monday of April, and ending at Shawnee on the second Monday of June last."

The only criminal cases that he had ever tried he speaks of thus: An "adjourned term of the court for Bourbon county was held to dispose of cases on the criminal docket, and the week was occupied in the trial of one case for murder and two for assaults with intent to kill. The case for murder resulted in an acquittal; one of those for assault with intent to kill, resulted in acquittal, and the other in a mistrial. These are the only trials of criminal cases held in my district."

The answer of Chief Justice Lecompte is very wordy and lengthy, and, with accompanying documents, consisting of a defence of himself published in the newspapers, and an address to the members of the bar, would comprise a good-sized volume, all of which amounts to the simple fact, that, although he arrived in the territory in November, 1854, he had transacted no judicial business worthy of any note. He was assigned the first judicial district, comprising the counties of Doniphan, Atchison, Leavenworth, Jefferson, Calhoun and Douglas. In each of these counties one term of court, of a week's duration, was required by statute to be held during the year. "All these were holden," he says, "except that for Doniphan [in 1855], which I was not able to reach for failure of the boats;" and "except the last term for Jefferson county and for Calhoun. These I did not hold because the recent commotions had just then arisen. It was considered utterly useless to hold court at either Osawkee, the county seat of Jefferson, or Calhoun, the county seat of Calhoun, as neither juries, nor witnesses, nor suitors could be in attendance."

"In almost all the criminal cases," he says, "presented anterior to the publication of the statute, *nolle prosequies* were entered by direction of the district attorney of the United States for the territory, upon the ground taken by him, that there was no law in force in the territory to punish them. The consequence is that few trials arose. * * * The only convictions I remember are, one for horse-stealing in Doniphan, and some three or four for assuming office; one for maliciously killing a horse in Atchison county; one in Jefferson county for selling liquor to Indians; and perhaps some eight or ten in different counties, for selling liquor without license."

Thus it appears that, although crimes of the blackest dye were daily and hourly being committed, and many of the criminals were arrested and indicted, the only convictions that could be obtained by the district courts, with three supreme judges, and a United States district attorney, in the space of two years, was one for stealing and another for killing a horse; three or four for assuming office; and some eight or ten for selling liquor without license.

What became of the incendiaries, the robbers, the ravishers and assassins? These were permitted to run at large, to burn houses and crops; plunder stores and dwellings; violate and brand women; steal horses and cattle; and murder defenceless men in their own homes or on the public highways, with impunity! Or if they were arrested, they were immediately set at liberty again, upon worthless bail, by faithless judges, or discharged because of a *nolle prosequi* entered by the United States District Attorney, or acquitted by a verdict easily obtained from a packed jury of criminals like themselves. Supreme judges and district attorneys had plenty of leisure and admirable opportunities to secure comfortable building lots and eligible claims, and to grow rapidly rich upon salaries insufficient to meet their daily wants; whilst the worst felons ran at large, laughing to scorn the laws, and the holding of courts were nothing better than shameless farces, in which all interested found abundant sources of amusement.

The judge's account of the dismissal upon bail of the prisoners indicted for high treason, is sufficiently interesting to present to the reader. He says—

"It occurs to me as proper to add something in relation to the last term of court in Douglas county. This occurred soon after the late serious disturbances in the territory, the most serious part of which existed, as always, in this county. It seemed perfectly certain to me before I left home, that there was no probability of being able to dispose of any business. I deemed it my duty, nevertheless, in view of the peculiar importance of those cases pending under indictments for treason, to attend, the more particularly as the persons so indicted were held in confinement.

"As I went I met large numbers of persons coming from Lecompton towards Leavenworth, and when I reached Lecompton, I found it almost deserted. No full jury, either grand or petit, was in attendance; indeed not enough of both to constitute one. The country, it was well understood, was equally abandoned by all those law and order men from which a jury could be selected. Under these circumstances it was perfectly clear that no business could be done.

"The cases of Robinson and others, indicted for treason, were called. They tendered themselves ready for trial. The government was not ready; nor was there any officer to represent the government upon the trial. A motion was made by a gentleman deputed for that purpose, simply to continue the causes. I saw no alternative, but a trial, which, without readiness on the part of the government under the most peculiar circumstances, would have amounted to an acquittal, almost to a farce, and on the other hand, a continuance. The latter ultimatim was adopted. The question then remained, what was to be done with the prisoners? As they tendered themselves ready for trial, I believed that to continue them in confinement would be oppression. I therefore discharged them on bail."

The United States Attorney, instead of being at Lecompton to try these cases, was in the border-ruffian army, marching towards Lawrence to massacre its inhabitants; and the "*law and order*" men, who alone were fit, according to Judge Lecompte, to sit upon a jury, were flying in terror from Lecompton, because of the reported approach of Lane. And on the afternoon of the same day upon which the alleged traitors were so generously set at liberty on bail, the guns of Lane were pointing over the town, to discharge the prisoners, had they not already been dismissed, without the legal form of a bail-bond. How far this fact influenced the action of the judge, he has not thought proper to state. One thing is certain; these men had already been held in custody for months without a trial; and it is quite probable that the government would *never have been ready for trial,* if its Kansas ministers could have continued the prisoners in confinement with any degree of safety to themselves. Had the accused been pro-slavery men, there would have been no lack of *readiness* on the part of the government to try the cause, nor any difficulty on that of the court to secure an acquittal.

An extract from that portion of the letter of Chief-Justice Lecompte, in which he attempts to repel the charges of official defection, will afford the reader some amusement even should it fail to convince him of the entire purity of the judge's ermine :—

"As to the charge of 'party bias,' he says, if it means simply the fact of such bias, I regard it as ridiculous; because I suppose every man in this country, with few exceptions indeed, entitled to respect, either for his abilities, his intelligence, or his virtue, has a 'party bias.' I am proud of mine. It has from my first manhood to this day, placed me in the ranks of the democratic party. It has taught me to regard that party as the one, *par excellence*, to which the destinies of this country are particularly intrusted for preservation.

"If it be intended to reach beyond that general application, and to charge a pro-slavery bias, I am proud, too, of this. I am the steady friend of southern rights under the Constitution of the United States. I have been reared where slavery was recognised by the constitution of my state. I love the institution as entwining itself around all my early and late associations; because I have seen as much of the nobility of the human heart in the relation of master and servant, and on the part of the one as well as of the other, as I have seen elsewhere. I have with me now an old woman who left all to come with me, when it was purely at her discretion. Another who did the same have I lost and buried with care and decency, at Fort Leavenworth. An old man has lately come to me under the care of a youthful nephew, within a few days, all the way from Maryland, and passing through every intervening free state, with a perfect knowledge of the fact, and making his own way through various interferences by his own ingenuity.

"If it mean more than the fact, and to intimate that this 'party bias' has affected the integrity of my official action, in any solitary case, I have but to say that it is false—basely false.

"In relation to the other of 'criminal complicity with a state of affairs which terminated in a contempt of all authority,' I will content myself with saying that it, too, is false—basely false, if made in relation to me, and to defy the slanderer to the proof of a solitary act to justify the deepest villain in such an assertion."

Who, after that stout denial, will dare to question the integrity or *impartiality* of Chief Justice Lecompte? Who can any longer doubt that to the abolitionist he has always meted out the same mercy and justice that he has bestowed upon his opponents? Who will pretend to affirm that Hays, the murderer of Buffum, would not have been as readily discharged from custody even had he been a free-state man or an abolitionist? The judge really seems to think himself innocent of the charge of "party bias;" yet the *loved institution of slavery* is entwined around all his affections, and he could not hold his court because *"the law and order men"* from which only he could select a jury, had fled from Lecompton

---

CHAPTER XXVI.

The murder of Buffum.—Warrant for the arrest of the murderer.—Partial conduct of the marshals.—Reward offered.—Indignation of free-state citizens.—Arrest of Charles Hays.

WHEN the army from Missouri was disbanded on the morning of the 15th September, the great body of it returned at once to that state, by the Westport road, committing every atrocity in their power as they passed along. They burned the saw-mill at Franklin, stole a number of horses, and drove off all the cattle they could find.

A detachment, calling themselves the "Kickapoo Rangers," numbering about two hundred and fifty or three hundred men, under command of Col. Clarkson, took the road for Lecompton, where they forded the river early in the afternoon, on their way to the northern part of the territory. This party was mounted and well armed, and looked like as desperate a set of ruffians as ever were gathered together. They still carried the black flag, and their cannon, guns, swords and carriages were yet decorated with the black emblems of their murderous intentions.

Six men of this detachment, when within a few miles of Lecompton, halted by a field where a poor inoffensive lame man, named David C. Buffum, was at work. They entered the field, and after robbing him of his horses, one of them shot him in the abdomen, from which wound he soon after died. The murderer also carried away a poney, belonging to a young girl, the daughter of a Mr. Thom, residing in the neighborhood.

Almost immediately after the commission of this wanton crime, Governor Geary, accompanied by Judge Cato, arrived upon the spot, and found the wounded man weltering in his blood. Although suffering the most intense agony, he was sensible of his condition, and perfectly mindful of the circumstances that had transpired. Judge Cato, by direction of the governor, took an affidavit of the unfortunate man's dying declarations. Writhing in agony, the cold sweat-drops standing upon his forehead, with his expiring breath he exclaimed, "Oh, this was a most unprovoked and horrid murder! They asked me for my horses, and I plead with them not to take them. I told them that I was a cripple—a poor lame man—that I had an aged father, a deaf-and-dumb brother, and two sisters, all depending upon me for a living, and my horses were all I had with which to procure it. One of them said I was a God d—d abolitionist, and seizing me by the shoulder with one hand, he shot me with a pistol that he held in the other. I am dying; but my blood will cry to Heaven for vengeance, and this horrible deed will not go unpunished. I die a martyr to the cause of freedom, and my death will do much to aid that cause." The governor was affected to tears. He had been on many a battle-field, and been familiar with suffering and death; but, says he, "I never witnessed a scene that filled my mind with so much horror. There was a peculiar significance in the looks and words of that poor dying man that I never can forget; for they seemed to tell me that I could have no rest until I brought his murderer to justice. And I resolved that no means in my power should be spared to discover, arrest, and punish the author of that most villanous butchery."

On his arrival at Lecompton, the governor immediately had a warrant drawn and placed in the hands of the United States marshal, for the arrest of the murderer, for the execution of which warrant the whole of the United States force was at his disposal. Several days elapsed, and no return was made, nor had any disposition been discovered to effect the governor's wishes in the matter.

In the mean time the marshal and his deputies were extremely active in obtaining and executing warrants against free-state men, some of them upon the most trivial and unwarrantable charges. To accomplish this object, requisitions were daily made upon the governor for troops, until it became so annoying to himself, and evidenced so clearly a spirit of persecution on the part of the officials, that he was compelled to refuse compliance with these requisitions. Charges for offences alleged to have been committed months before, were trumped up, and the accused were hunted down, and thrust into prison, and there held until released by the intercession of the governor, or upon an examination being demanded, no accuser or witness appeared. Mr. C. W. Babcock, postmaster at Lawrence, and several other respectable gentlemen, were arrested at Topeka, and brought to Lecompton as prisoners. As their names did not appear in the warrant held by the deputy-marshal who made the arrests, inquiry was instituted in regard to his conduct, when it appeared they were seized under the general appellation of "others," the warrant demanding the arrest of certain parties named, "and others." They were free-state men, or abolitionists, and that fact was sufficient to justify the outrage.

Whilst these proceedings were being conducted with surprising and admirable industry and activity, and additions were almost every hour being made to the swelling crowd of free-state prisoners, not one arrest had yet been made of a pro-slavery man. The murderer of Barber ran at large, and was daily in conversation with the marshal, and drinking whiskey with the sheriff. Buffum's murderer, though known, was unsought. John H. Stringfellow, Ira Morris, James A. Headley, William Martin, Captain Parker, William Simmons, and many others, all pro-slavery men, and charged with serious crimes, were at liberty, though warrants against them were in the marshal's hands, and the governor had given him requisitions upon General Smith and Col. Cook for a sufficient number of troops to secure their persons.

Justly indignant at the one-sided policy that was clearly being pursued by the territorial officers, the governor addressed the following note to Marshal Donalson:—

"Executive Department, K. T.,
"Lecompton, Sept. 18, 1856.

"I. B. Donalson, Esq.,
"United States Marshal, K. T.

"Sir: A warrant was issued a day or two since for the arrest of the murderer or murderers of Mr. Buffum at or near the residence of Mr. Thom. Please report to me whether that warrant has been executed, or whether any attempt has been made to arrest the offenders in this case, and what has been the result.

"Yours, &c.,
"Jno. W. Geary,
"Governor of Kansas Territory."

The reply to this note showed that, while the deputy-marshals were extremely active in executing warrants against free-state men, some of whom had committed no offence, they had no time to devote to such scoundrels as the assassins of Buffum. The marshal says:—

"I have to report, that upon making inquiry of my deputy, Samuel Cramer, he informed me, that when the militia from the north side of the river were passing through this place on Monday last (returning to their homes), he made diligent inquiry, and used all the means in his power to ascertain who the murderer or murderers of said Buffum were, with a view to their arrest; but from the vagueness of the affidavit on which the warrant was procured, in which no names are mentioned, nor any particular description of their persons, or any other thing about them, except "six men" in the rear or behind a company, he failed to identify or arrest the murderer or murderers."

This reply fully satisfied the governor that every attempt to secure the murderer by means of the warrant issued, must prove futile. To put such a warrant in the hands of Samuel Cramer, whose prejudices against the free-state and in favor of the slavery party were unsurpassed in bitterness by those of any other man in Kansas, was equivalent to giving him an order for the criminal's escape. Hence other measures were pursued to accomplish the ends of justice. The governor employed secret agents to visit Atchison county, the residence of the Kickapoo Rangers, and by making careful and diligent inquiries, to obtain some clue to the perpetrators of the deed in question.

He also issued a proclamation, offering "a reward of five hundred dollars for the arrest and conviction of the murderer or murderers of David C. Buffum, of Douglas county, to be paid immediately upon the conviction of the author of this great outrage."

The consequence was, that the peace, which by his prompt, fearless, and energetic action, the governor had promoted, was again threatened and in danger. The free-state people were justly incensed at the wrongs they were suffering, and for which they saw no means for redress. Their relatives and friends were being torn from them, without cause, and incarcerated in a filthy prison, without proper food or clothing, or accommodations fitted for dogs, for weeks and months, without a conviction for crime, or even a trial, whilst well-known robbers and murderers of the opposite party were permitted to come to their very prison doors and insult them with oaths and jeers. Murmurs of discontent arose on every hand, and, like the distant hum of the ocean, or the far-off muttering of thunder, rolled into the executive office. Many who had placed implicit confidence in the governor, and who looked patiently to him for protection and redress, began to question his integrity and impartiality, and suspect him of having a secret complicity with the other federal and territorial officers, who, without an exception, were their enemies and persecutors. Even his expressed determination to secure the assassin of Buffum, and his proclamation to that effect, they began to regard as intended only to blind and deceive. The free-state people thought they saw no hope for themselves save in God and their own right hands, and they began to take down from their resting places, and make ready, their arms. They preferred to fall defending their lives and property with these, than suffer and die like slaves. Nor were they hasty or unreasonable. The wretched prison-house was crammed with their associates, many of them innocent of any offence save that of being opposed to slavery; whilst, if one of the ruffians was arrested by mistake or compulsion, he was instantly released by the judges upon what was known to be worthless bail.

At length, early in November, reliable information was received, that the murderer of Buffum was a man named Charles Hays, a member of the band of Kickapoo Rangers, and living in Atchison county. A new warrant was accordingly issued for his arrest, the marshal ordered to execute it without delay, and in a few days Hays was brought a prisoner to Lecompton. A grand jury, composed entirely of pro-slavery men, on hearing the positive and overwhelming testimony against him, found a true bill, and committed him for trial, on the charge of murder in the first degree. Whilst the governor was congratulating himself upon the certainty of bringing this murderer to punishment, and thus vindicating himself from the charge of complicity with the other officers in screening from justice all pro-slavery offenders, as well as restoring the failing confidence in his impartiality, there were parties busily at work to thwart him in his just determination, and embarrass still more than ever his administration.

CHAPTER XXVII.

Discharge of Hays by Judge Lecompte.—Order for his re-arrest.—Conduct of Marshal Donalson.—Col. Titus re-arrests Hays, who is again set at liberty by Lecompte on a writ of habeas corpus.—President Pierce and the United States Senate on the case of Lecompte.—Letter from Secretary Marcy asking explanations.—Governor Geary's reply.—Judge Lecompte's letter of vindication.

On the 10th of November several members of the free-state party, all gentlemen of intelligence and respectability, and citizens of the territory, called upon the governor to protest against the abuses they were suffering from the partial manner in which the government was conducted. They complained loudly and emphatically of the fact that while no efforts were made to arrest pro-slavery criminals, or that if arrested, they were immediately discharged on bail, numerous free-state men were being seized almost daily by the officers, thrust into prison, and there detained, all their importunities to give bail being repulsed by Judge Lecompte and other pro-slavery magistrates.

The governor was vindicating his own policy, and the impartial and independent course of the grand jury as evinced by their recent action at Lecompton. They had found true bills, he said, against a number of prominent pro-slavery men, among whom was Charles Hays for the murder of Buffum. The men indicted, he continued, are pro-slavery men, and have position and influence in the community; and yet their position has not been so exalted as to screen them from the searching scrutiny of an independent grand jury, though summoned under pro-slavery auspices.

The governor dwelt upon the murder of Buffum, described it as it really occurred, narrated the circumstances of his interview with the dying man, and said that he had left no means untried to secure the murderer, and that it was a cause of great gratulation to him that the grand jury had so promptly done their duty in the matter after the officers had succeeded in making the arrest. Now, concluded the governor, you perceive that a disposition does exist to do equal and exact justice, and that a determination prevails to bring criminals of all parties to punishment.

He had scarcely completed the last sentence when several persons entered, one of them remarking that Judge Lecompte had admitted Charles Hays, the murderer of Buffum, to bail, and that Sheriff Samuel J. Jones, a man notoriously not worth a dollar, was on his bail-bond.

The governor was astounded. He could scarcely accredit what he heard. All his arguments were scattered to the winds. He no longer doubted his true position. The cloud was dispersed, and he saw precisely where he stood. He was *alone* in the territory. He was not only not supported by a single officer sent there by the general government, but every one of them was exerting his influence and power to oppose his efforts to do justice to the people and secure the peace he had effected. He saw himself surrounded by a combination of official traitors, banded together to embarrass all his just operations for the public good. He had devoted much time, expended over two hundred dollars, and offered a reward of five hundred more, to secure the person of one of the foulest murderers that ever disgraced the human form. No sooner had he accomplished this object—at a time when it was of the utmost importance to allay the rising excitement of an aggrieved people, and to satisfy them of his honest intentions to do justice to all men—than the chief-justice steps forward and sets the criminal free. He saw at a glance that he must now assume weighty responsibilities, and act independently and for himself, as the government had surrounded him with men who were resolved upon frustrating the impartial policy he had come to enforce. No other course was left to keep down the smouldering volcano that was about to break forth with fearful violence, or prevent a civil war, the elements for which were gathering. He knew that he must act promptly and decisively, and in such a manner as to convince the people of the territory that he looked with detestation upon the conduct of Lecompte, and was disposed to annul his action. No other policy was left, else in another day a thousand bayonets would have glistened in the sunbeams, and a thousand strong hearts, aroused to vengeance, would have been marching toward Lecompton to set at liberty the free-state prisoners, and chastise, as they merited, those who held them in unjust confinement.

"You see how it is, governor," said the free-state men; "all our statements are confirmed. Did not Judge Lecompte refuse to entertain a motion to have evidence in the case of the free-state men charged with the Hickory Point murder, to ascertain whether the offence was bailable, as it afterwards turned out to be by the verdict of the jury only finding mau-slaughter? In these cases the motion to admit to bail was made *before bill found*, when the right was unquestionable; but in the case of Buffum, after the grand jury had maturely considered the matter, and found a *true bill* against Charles Hays for murder in the first degree, this murderer is immediately bailed, and without authority of law or precedent for so glaring an act, is set at large. The free-state men," continued they, "can no longer expect even-handed justice, and their only hope must be in physical force."

The governor replied that he was conscientious on the subject; he was instructed to preserve the peace of the territory, and to exercise his discretion as to the means to be employed; and was sworn to, and would at all hazards, discharge his duty as he understood it. He boldly pronounced the action of Chief Justice Lecompte in dismissing the murderer of Buffum, *after the grand jury had found a bill of indictment against him for murder in the first degree*, as a judicial outrage, and under the circumstances, without precedent, as highly discourteous to himself, he having been the means of arresting Hays, and should have been consulted; as *greatly calculated to endanger the public peace*, and to destroy the entire influence of the policy he was laboring day and night to inaugurate; and to bring the court and judiciary into contempt.

He declared that he would treat the decision of Judge Lecompte as a nullity, and proceed upon the indictment for murder to re-arrest Hays as though he had merely escaped, and would submit the matter to the president, feeling assured that he would permit no judicial officer to forget his duty and trifle with the peace of the territory by making decisions abhorrent to public justice, and grossly steeped in partiality. He accordingly issued the following warrant:

"Executive Department, K. T.,
"Lecompton, Nov. 10, 1856.

"I. B. DONALSON, Esq.,
"Marshal of Kansas Territory.

"Sir: An indictment for murder in the first degree having been duly found by the grand jury of the territory against Charles Hays, for the murder of a certain David C. Buffum, in the county of Douglas in this territory, and the said Charles Hays having been discharged upon bail, as I consider in violation of law, and greatly to the endangering of the peace of this territory:

"This is therefore to authorize and command you to re-arrest the said Charles Hays, if he be found within the limits of this territory, and safely to keep him until he is duly discharged by a jury of his country, according to law.

"Given under my hand and seal at the city of Lecompton, the day and year first above written.

{ SEAL. }

"Jno. W. Geary,
"Governor of Kansas Territory."

This warrant was handed to Marshal Israel B. Donalson, who was in the executive office during the foregoing occurrences. He, however, declined to execute it, saying he would take time to consider the matter, and give his answer in writing.

The marshal retired, and the governor immediately made out a duplicate warrant, and placed it in the hands of his special aid-de-camp, Col. H. T. Titus, with orders to take a file of men and execute it without delay, as, *while the marshal was considering the matter*, Hays would escape. Colonel Titus promptly obeyed the order, and departed on his mission, the result of which is given in the following report:—

"Lecompton, Nov. 12, 1856

"His Excellency, J. W. Geary,
"Governor of Kansas Territory.

"Sir: In pursuance of your warrant of 10th instant, I proceeded to the residence of Charles Hays and arrested him, brought him to this place, and now hold him subject to your further order.

"Your obedient servant,
"H. T. Titus."

In the meantime Marshal Donalson had considered the matter, and declined to execute the order for the re-arrest of Hays, concluding his answer in writing with the following paragraph;—

"Your determination, as expressed this evening, (if I refused to execute your order), to suspend me or procure my discharge by the president, induces me to say that I have some days since determined to discontinue my present official relations with this territory; and I now desire the favor of you to assure the president of my gratitude for his confidence and kindness, and ask him to relieve me from my present position as soon as may be convenient."

Hays remained in the custody of Colonel Titus until Governor Geary visited Leavenworth City, on the 17th November, to attend the public sales of the Delaware lands. During his absence Hays was again discharged by Judge Lecompte on a writ of habeas corpus, as shown in the subjoined communication from Colonel Titus:—

"Lecompton, Nov 21, 1856.

"HIS EXCELLENCY, JOHN W. GEARY,
"Governor of Kansas Territory.

"Sir: I have the honor to state that during your recent absence from this place, a writ of habeas corpus, issued by Chief Justice Lecompte, was served upon me, by which I was commanded to produce the body of Charles Hays before him, with the cause of his detainer:

"That in obedience to the writ, I caused the body of Hays to be produced before Judge Lecompte, and returned as the cause of his detention the finding by the grand jury of a true bill of indictment against him for murder in the first degree, committed upon the person of one David C. Buffum, together with your warrant, commanding the re-arrest of the said Hays and his detention until his discharge by a jury of his country according to law.

"I have further to state that Judge Lecompte discharged the said Hays from my custody notwithstanding my return, and that he is now at large. I have the honor to remain,

"Your obedient servant,
"H. T. TITUS."

The governor did not attempt to interfere with this writ of habeas corpus. His action in the case had satisfied the free-state people that he had no complicity whatever with the partial policy of the other officers, and that he would do them justice to the full extent of his power. He therefore contented himself with forwarding to the president and secretary his executive minutes, containing a history of the circumstances as above related, and showing the necessity for a less partial judiciary in order to preserve the peace of the territory, and enable him to enforce their own instructions.

President Pierce forthwith nominated Mr. C. O. Harrison, of Kentucky, to the Senate, as successor to Lecompte, without, however, issuing a writ of supersedeas, which was a sufficient reason for the Senate to withhold their confirmation of Mr. Harrison's appointment. Neither the president nor the Senate were disposed to assume a responsibility in the matter; and Judge Lecompte, not being superseded, remained in office, to the enthusiastic delight of the pro-slavery party, and to the still further annoyance of Governor Geary, and the embarrassment of his honest and judicious administration.

While the question was pending before the Senate, which was nothing more than one of those political farces so often enacted to dazzle the vision of the people, who are not permitted to look behind the scenes, Secretary Marcy forwarded the following dispatch to Governor Geary:—

"Department of State:
"Washington, 4th February, 1857.

"To JOHN W. GEARY, Esq.,
"Governor of Kansas, Lecompton.

"SIR:—The original letter of which the inclosed is a copy, was brought to the notice of the president, a few days since, by Hon. James A. Pearce, of the United States Senate. The discrepancies between the statements of this letter and those contained in your official communication of the 19th of September, last, are such, that the president directs me to inclose you the copy for explanation.

"I am, sir, respectfully, your obed't serv't.
"W. L. MARCY."

To this insulting epistle the governor immediately made the following laconic reply:—

"Executive Department, Kansas Territory,
"Lecompton, February 20th 1857.

"Hon. WM. L. MARCY,
"Secretary of State.

"SIR:—Your dispatch of 4th instant, enclosing me a copy of Judge Lecompte's letter in the Hays case, and calling my attention 'to the discrepancies between the statements of that letter, and those contained in your (my) official communication of 19th of September, last,' and requesting 'explanation,' was received by last mail.

"In reply, I have simply to state, that 'what I have written, I have written,' and I have nothing further to add, alter, or amend on this subject.

"My executive minutes, faithfully chronicling my official actions, and the policy which dictated them at the time they occurred, and my various dispatches to the government, contain but the simple truth, told without fear, favor, or affection, and I will esteem it a favor to have them all published for the inspection of the country.

"Your obed't servant,
"JNO. W. GEARY,
"Governor of Kansas Territory."

The letter of Lecompte embraced some twenty or more pages of foolscap, written in his usual wordy and indefinite style. That portion of it which relates directly to the Hays case, fully sustains all that was affirmed in the executive minutes concerning that subject.

He says: "I take pleasure in furnishing you the facts in the Hays case, which, I see by your letter, as well as by newspaper items, has obtained a notoriety vastly disproportioned to its real consequence.

"On the last day of the term of my court, held at Lecompton for the first district, application was made by the counsel for Hays for bail. Understanding that he was indicted for murder, I observed that I could not admit to bail, unless testimony was offered tending to acquit him of the charge. I was asked by his counsel whether I would hear such testimony. The term of the court being limited, and that being the last day of its session, I said I would. A witness was called, who stated that he was with the prisoner on the day named in the indictment, and that they were coming in company from Lecompton to Leavenworth.

"I inquired for and had called the witnesses on the part of the territory. They were not in attendance. The matter being submitted on the evidence, and some observations by his counsel, who claimed to have thus furnished proof of an *alibi*, I declined to admit him to bail, stating as my reason that I did not consider the day named as an averment material to be proved, and that, while the proof exonerated him from the charge on that day, it was possible, and consistent with the evidence offered, that he was guilty of the crime on another day, before or after, and committed him to the custody of the marshal.

"In the afternoon, by his counsel, he asked permission to offer other and additional testimony, to have a further bearing upon his application. This I granted. Some two or three (three, I think) other witnesses were sworn, who concurred in saying that they were with Hays in the ranks of the militia, returning from Lawrence to Lecompton, on the day of the murder, and that he was in the ranks during the day, and that they frequently saw him. I again had the witnesses for the government called. They not being forthcoming, I stated that I was not fully satisfied to bail. At this moment the district attorney, prosecuting on behalf of the government, arose and stated that he knew Hays well; that he was a neighbor of his; and that he had full confidence that Mr. Hays could give good bail, and should be forthcoming to answer the charge, if bail were allowed; and that he had no objection to his being admitted to bail.

"I immediately replied, that being the case, if he can give sufficient security in the sum of ten thousand dollars, I will take it. It was immediately given, and he was discharged.

"But for subsequent occurrences, I know not that I should have thought of the matter again from that day to this. It attracted no more of my attention than any other case upon

M

which I have acted. I never heard the matter mentioned, as I now recollect, except as I have detailed it. * * * *

"To my infinite surprise, I learned from the marshal, who, passing my house, called to see me the next Wednesday, that the governor had ordered him to re-arrest Hays, and that, upon his refusal, Colonel Titus had been ordered to re-arrest him, and had left Lecompton for that purpose.

"A day or two afterwards, application was made to me by Hays for an habeas corpus. This I issued. Being brought before me on the return day, and the matter being submitted, I discharged him."

Such is Chief-Justice Lecompte's version of the affair, given in vindication of his conduct—a version which must condemn him in the estimation of every man acquainted with the facts. The most of his statements are true—strictly true—and hence the less excuse for his conduct.

The history of the case is simply this. The "Kickapoo Rangers," of which company Hays was a member, left Lawrence early in the morning of the murder, reached Lecompton about noon, crossed the river shortly afterwards, and proceeded northward toward Atchison on the same day.

When near Lecompton, six of this company left the ranks, and one of them murdered Buffum, stole his horses and the horse of Miss Thom, and rejoinded the company; the time occupied in the murder and robbery not exceeding, perhaps, five minutes.

The testimony upon which Hays was committed, clearly and positively established that he left the ranks; that he was absent long enough to commit the crimes alleged; that he was seen to take Buffum by the shoulder with one hand, and to shoot him with the other, calling him, as the dying man testified, a d——d abolitionist; and that he was in possession of the stolen horses.

With these facts before him, and with which Judge Lecompte was perfectly familiar, application was made for the discharge of Hays on bail, and witnesses were offered by the district attorney, an associate of the criminal, to prove an *alibi*. The judge called the witnesses for the prosecution, knowing that they were more than fifty miles distant, and, of course, they *did not answer*. He then heard the evidence to prove an *alibi*. This went to show *precisely what the prosecution had proved*, that Hays was "*in the ranks of the militia, returning from Lawrence to Lecompton, on the day of the murder, and that he was in the ranks during the day, and that*" the witnesses "*frequently saw him;*" also, that on the afternoon of the same day, Hays was on the north side of the Kansas River, still in the ranks of the militia, marching from "*Lecompton to Leavenworth.*" All this was strictly true, and the witnesses for an *alibi* might also have added, that, when on the north side of the river, Hays had with him the stolen horses, one of which was subsequently returned to Miss Thom, the owner, by Colonel Clarkson, commander of the "Rangers," upon a requisition from Governor Geary.

How the chief-justice could discover any evidence in this testimony with which to prove an *alibi*, was a matter for wonder and amusement even to his friends. It was, however, quite sufficient to satisfy his judicial understanding, and he immediately said that if Hays could give "*sufficient security in the sum of ten thousand dollars, he would take it.*" Whereupon Samuel J. Jones, sheriff of Douglas county, offered himself as *sufficient* for that amount, (and he would have done the same had it been ten millions) and the chief justice was *satisfied*, and the murderer discharged.

The remainder of Judge Lecompte's lengthy letter, sent to Governor Geary for *explanation*, consists of little else than a wordy denial of the charge of having refused bail to free-state men, or been influenced in any way in the discharge of his judicial functions by party considerations; all of which he maintains with a pertinacity which might induce a reader not thoroughly acquainted with the man, and with his official history, to imagine that the judge was really laboring under the hallucination, that he always had been, was then, and was resolved ever after to be, a most righteous and impartial judge.

The facts in the case of Hays were misrepresented by the *Lecompton Union*, and Governor Geary's conduct, as were all his acts, made the subject of an abusive article. To this George W. Brown, who was one of the treason prisoners, replied as follows, in the *Herald of Freedom*, of which paper he is the editor. Some of the undeniable facts, stated in this article, utterly disprove Judge Lecompte's pretensions to impartiality in the discharge of his official duties:—

"The *Union* justifies Lecompte, because the defendant introduced *ex parte* evidence, and proved an *alibi*. The judge was offered proof, and in fact we did prove before him, that at the time *we* were charged with doing certain treasonable things in Kansas, and for more than one month previous, we had been out of the territory, and could not have been guilty of the crime with which we were charged. Moreover we offered to give bonds in the sum of $50,000 for our appearance at the next term of the court to answer the indictment; and yet the judge declared the offence not bailable. Four months after he took bail, however, in the sum of $5,000, basing his action upon the *laches* of the prosecution.

"In the indictment against the ninety-eight free-state prisoners he refused bail, as they were indicted for murder. He well knew that there was not a jury, however malevolent, which could be so packed as to bring in a verdict of murder, because of the absence of *malice prepense.* At best it could only amount to manslaughter, and yet the judge refused them bail.

"In the case of Buffum, it was a cold-blooded, deliberate murder. There were no extenuating circumstances. The wretches attempted to steal his horses; Mr. Buffum remonstrated, and was shot down like a wild beast. A packed pro-slavery grand jury indicted Hays for murder. Lecompte released him on bail.

"The governor was knowing to the murder of Buffum. He stood by his bed-side, and heard from the dying man, *in extremis*, a statement of facts; and with Judge Cato, took his affidavit in due form of law. Hays was proven before the grand jury to be the man who inflicted the mortal blow. Five hundred dollars reward had been offered by the governor for his apprehension, and he was arrested—arrested for wilful and deliberate murder; and Judge Lecompte, disregarding the feelings of an incensed public; disregarding his own duty as a United States judge, sworn to discharge the duties of his office with fidelity; disregarding the sanctity of his judicial robes; bound in honor as in law to know no party, and show no favoritism—released that man, whose hands were dripping with innocent blood, to go at large, and repeat the same foul crime.

"It was too much for our territorial executive to bear. He had seen the villany of that judge, and had passed him by. He had seen Judge Jeffreys' character re-enacted on the judicial bench in Kansas, and had winced at his numberless faults. But when such a high-handed and atrocious act as the one alluded to, came to his knowledge, it was too much for his equanimity to endure longer. Sworn to see that the laws were faithfully executed, and feeling the sacredness of his pledge to know no north, no south, no east, no west, but to discharge his duty honestly, as given in his inaugural, he resolved on discharging that duty, and ordered Hays again into custody. Donalson, who summoned a *posse* of half a thousand men to aid in arresting three individuals where no resistance was threatened, refused to obey the reasonable request of the governor. If Governor Geary possesses a particle of influence with the national administration, it is clearly his duty to see that these men are removed from office."

CHAPTER XXVIII.

The United States Marshal.—His deputies.—Requisitions for United States soldiers.—Visit of the governor to Topeka, and arrest of prisoners.—An address to the citizens of Topeka.—Report of the marshal.—Requisition declined, and an evil practice discontinued.

ISRAEL B. DONALSON, then United States Marshal of Kansas Territory, is considerably advanced in years, and although decidedly in favor of the slave party, and one of its members, was not of the rabid sort, and had quite a sufficiency of the "milk of human kindness" in his heart, to do justly if he could or dared. His surroundings, however, were every way unfavorable to a proper and just discharge of his duties. His deputies were all violent pro-slavery men, younger and more active than himself, and he became responsible for many of their illiberal acts. He being their authorized head, their persecutions of free-state people were chargeable to his account. The marshal himself seldom went on an expedition to execute a warrant, and his deputies, knowing that they had rendered themselves offensive by their abuses of their privileges and powers, feared to go beyond the shadow of Lecompton without being attended with a posse of United States troops. Hence, whenever a warrant was issued, the governor received from the marshal a requisition of which the following is a specimen:—

"Lecompton, Kansas Territory,
"September, 17th, 1856.

"To his Excellency, JOHN W. GEARY,
"Governor of Kansas Territory.

"SIR:—Finding the ordinary course of judicial proceedings, and the powers vested in me as United States Marshal of the territory, inadequate to execute a warrant placed in my hands, from the Hon.

Samuel D. Lecompte, Chief Justice Supreme Court of Kansas Territory, for the arrest of one Colonel Whipple and others, I respectfully request, that a posse of United States troops be furnished me to assist in making said arrests, and for the due execution of a number of other warrants, now in my hands.

"Very respectfully, your obed't serv't,

"I. B. DONALSON,

"U. S. Marshal, Kansas Territory."

In compliance with these requests, which were usually accompanied with a verbal statement of the number of soldiers the marshal supposed he would require for the particular occasion stated, the governor was accustomed to make requisition as follows upon the commanding officer nearest the place where the warrant was intended to be executed:—

"Executive Department, K. T.

"Lecompton, September 17th, 1856.

"To Col. PHILIP ST. GEORGE COOK,

"Commanding U. S. Dragoons, near Lecompton.

"SIR:—I have just been shown sundry warrants from the chief justice for the arrest of a number of persons charged with the commission of crimes in this territory. The marshal has also duly certified me, that the powers vested in him by the civil authority, is inadequate to enable him to execute the aforesaid warrants, and he requires the aid of the United States troops to enable him to execute the same. You will, therefore, please furnish the marshal with two hundred dragoons, that being the number desired by him. I will accompany them, on this occasion, in person.

"Your obed't serv't.

"JNO. W. GEARY,

"Governor of Kansas Territory."

Although, as will hereafter appear, General Smith subsequently refused to furnish Governor Geary at his request, with two companies of troops, to preserve the peace of the territory from a threatened disturbance at Lecompton, it is but justice to the general to record that neither himself, nor any officer under his command, ever hesitated to answer the governor's requisitions for soldiers to accompany the marshal or his deputies in pursuit of alleged horse-thieves or other criminals.

In compliance with the above cited requisition, Col. Cook furnished two hundred mounted men, with which force, the governor, accompanied by the marshal, left Lecompton, for Topeka, at 2 o'clock on the afternoon of the 17th of September. Soon after their departure a most violent storm of wind and rain arose, which continued during the entire evening, rendering travel almost impossible. With great difficulty, and after being thoroughly drenched, they reached Tecumseh, a distance of ten miles, and encamped for the night. Early on the following morning, they proceeded to Topeka, reaching that town about eight o'clock. Here the warrants were executed and twelve prisoners arrested. A large quantity of captured property, consisting of horses, buggies, wagons, &c., was identified and recovered. With this and the prisoners, the troops were dispatched for Lecompton, the governor remaining alone at Topeka.

The citizens here soon assembled together in town meeting. They were disposed to be refractory and some of them quite insolent. They were evidently under the influence of strong prejudices against the governor, and by no means disposed to favor his supposed policy or any of his movements. Some endeavored to annoy him with what they considered smart and perplexing questions; others proposed entering into a treaty, the terms of which they were to establish; whilst still others averred that they had a governor of their own choice, to whom and to whom only, they owed and would yield allegiance.

After listening patiently to all they had to say concerning their real or imagined grievances, and resolves in regard to their future conduct, the governor addressed them with great earnestness and at considerable length.

He informed them that it was no lot nor part of his errand to Kansas to make treaties with, but to govern its people. He did not come to Topeka to discuss with its citizens the question of his right to the office he occupied, but to let them understand that he and he only was the Governor of Kansas, appointed by the president and confirmed as such by the Senate of the United States, and that they must and should yield obedience to all his reasonable requirements. He came to enforce the principles of the Constitution of the United States, the organic law of the territory, and all the territorial statutes not conflicting therewith—to maintain the doctrines of popular sovereignty—and to support the whole people, whatever were their political predilections, in the maintenance of their lawful privileges and rights. He had no partialities—all the citizens had equal claims to his guardian care—and to all classes he would do equal and exact justice.

"Gentlemen," said he, in one of his addresses, "*I come not to treat with, but to govern you.* There is now in the territory no other governor than myself. I will protect the lives and property of every peace-loving and law-abiding citizen, with all the power I possess. I will punish every law-breaker, whatever may be his position or pretensions. I will not for a moment tolerate any questioning of my authority. All who are in favor of restoring peace to this distracted territory can range themselves under my banner; all others I will treat as bandits and robbers, and as such extirpate them at the point of the bayonet. Don't talk to me about slavery or freedom—free-state men or pro-slavery men—until we have restored the benign influences of peace to the country; until we have punished the murderer, and driven out the bandit and rabble, and returned the industrious citizens to their homes and claims. Do not, I pray you, attempt to embarrass me with your *political* disputations. You shall all, without distinction of party, be alike protected. This is no time to talk about party, when men, women and children are hourly being murdered at their own firesides, or whilst sleeping in their beds, or are being driven by merciless bands of marauders from their homes without money, food, or clothing. In God's name rise for a moment above party, and contemplate yourselves as men and patriots. I am your friend—your fellow-citizen—moved by no other impulse than the welfare of the inhabitants of this territory, and the protection of their honor, their lives and property. When peace is fairly restored and secured, I will see that every man of you is protected in his political rights."

He was listened to with profound attention, and most enthusiastically cheered at the close of his remarks, when resolutions were passed approving his course, and promising a hearty support to his administration. On the same day he returned to Lecompton.

So frequent became the marshal's applications for troops, and the governor never receiving any official report of the result of his requisitions, he at length addressed Mr. Donalson as follows:—

"Executive Department, K. T.,
"Lecompton, Sept. 25, 1856.

"I. B. Donalson, Esq.,
"United States Marshal, K. T.

"Sir: You have at sundry times made application to me for requisitions upon Col. Cook, for men to assist you in the execution of warrants upon persons charged with offences against the peace of this territory, viz:

"On the 17th inst., for two hundred dragoons to serve a writ upon one Col. Whipple and others;

"On the same day, for five dragoons to arrest certain parties not named in your application;

"On the 20th inst., for ten dragoons to execute a warrant upon Thomas Kemp and others;

"On the 22d, for six dragoons to aid in securing sundry persons charged upon the complaint of James B. Lofton; and

"On the 23d, for ten dragoons to arrest Col. Whipple and many others.

"As I have received no official information respecting the result of the above named requisitions, you will oblige me by reporting at once, in writing, whether they were complied with, and if so, whether the objects for which they were made have been accomplished, and all other information relative to the subject that you have the means to communicate. Yours, &c.,

"JNO. W. GEARY,
"Governor of Kansas Territory."

The marshal replied at considerable length, but as the following contains the entire substance of his communication, it is all that need be cited:—

"The objects for which the requisitions were made have been partially accomplished. On the requisition for two hundred dragoons, on the 17th instant, a large number implicated in the warrant have not yet been arrested, on account of the difficulty in finding their whereabouts. That for the five on the same day proved abortive. That of the 20th instant, for ten dragoons, was accomplished, or nearly so. That of the 22d, for six dragoons, succeeded in arresting two of the offenders, one more of whom has since been arrested, and one still cannot be found. No resistance has been made to the execution of any of these writs; nor is it probable that any will be made when the marshal is accompanied by a military posse."

The next day after writing the report from which the foregoing is extracted, the marshal asked for a posse to execute some half dozen or more warrants, to which the governor replied as follows:—

"Executive Department, K. T.,
"Lecompton, Sept. 27, 1856.

"I. B. DONALSON, ESQ.,
U. S. Marshal for the Territory of Kansas.

"Sir: I have just received your requisition for a posse of twenty U. S. dragoons, to aid you in the execution of certain warrants in the neighborhood of Tecumseh and Topeka.

"In reply, I have to say that there are now one hundred and fifty U. S. mounted troops in the vicinity referred to, and my advices are that peace and quiet reign there; and I believe you will have no difficulty in the discharge of your duty.

"I must therefore decline acceding to your request until I am clearly satisfied that you cannot execute your warrants by virtue of the civil authority already vested in you.

"I am very averse to the employment of the military to execute civil process, and will only do so in cases of imperative necessity.

"Very truly, your obed't servt.,

"JNO. W. GEARY,

"Governor of Kansas Territory."

This put an end to a practice that had become truly disgusting to all peaceful citizens. Deputy marshals who in some instances had rendered themselves obnoxious by their habits of partisan oppression, were, at the head of United States troops, constantly scouring the country, entering free-state towns, and under the shadow of authority and the cover of protection from the soldiers, committing offences against decency and the quiet of the community more reprehensible than those even alleged against the parties of whom, in many instances, they were in search; and they were becoming almost as great a terror to unoffending people as the hordes of banditti which had previously infested the highways. The refusal of the governor, therefore, to continue to furnish the means for these officials to pursue such practices was followed with the most beneficial results. The free-state people were no longer harassed with processes issued simply for their annoyance, and were enabled to pursue their lawful avocations with confidence and in peace; and the order and quiet which previous bold and decisive measures had effected were thus in a great measure preserved.

Lieutenant Lewis Merrill, who on one occasion had been detailed with a company of dragoons to accompany a deputy marshal on one of these expeditions to execute writs, in concluding a lengthy report of the service, remarks:—

"Not the slightest evidence was shown any where that there would have been any resistance to the civil officer under any circumstances; and I think that if he had been an efficient, energetic man, who had not by his former conduct made himself obnoxious to these people, the arrests would have been made of all the warrants called for, and without any show of resistance."

CHAPTER XXIX.

Arrival of free-state immigrants, and their treatment and discharge.

DURING the last week of September information was received at the executive office from various sources supposed to be reliable, that Colonel Lane, with a force of at least a thousand men, and several pieces of artillery, was about to invade the territory with hostile intentions, by way of Nebraska; and hence a detachment of United States troops, accompanied by Deputy Marshal Preston, was sent to watch and guard the northern frontier, with orders to arrest any illegally armed body that might be found within the limits of Kansas. The troops had scarcely reached their destination when Captain James Redpath entered the territory with one hundred and thirty men, who were armed, equipped, and organized, as was supposed, in violation of the governor's proclamation. They were consequently arrested and escorted to the vicinity of Lecompton, when the governor, in an interview with Redpath, being assured that the prisoners were a company of peaceable immigrants, they were at once permitted to go their way without further molestation.

Immediately after this, reports, apparently well authenticated, reached both Governor Geary and General Smith that Redpath's party was but an advance guard of the forces of Lane, who had contracted with the ferry-men at Nebraska City for the transit of about seven hundred men, all well armed, and having three pieces of cannon; and Colonels Cook and Johnson were forthwith dispatched, with three hundred dragoons, to intercept their passage through the territory.

On the 1st of October a deputation consisting of Major Morrow, Col. Winchel, Wm. Hutchinson, and Col. J. Jenkins, called upon the governor, stating that they had been sent by General Pomeroy and Colonels Eldridge and Perry, who were escorting three hundred emigrants into the territory by way of Nebraska; that they did not come for warlike purposes nor as disturbers of the public peace, but as *bona fide* settlers, with agricultural implements, and some guns to protect themselves and shoot game; but that in the present disturbed state of affairs they did not wish to enter the territory under any circumstances of suspicion without first notifying the governor.

Upon being asked if the party in question were in anywise connected with Lane's so-called "army of the north," a decided negative reply was given.

The governor then informed his visitors that he was determined that no armed bodies of men with cannon and munitions of war, and with hostile attitude, should enter the territory to the terror of peaceful citizens; that there was no further occasion for such demonstrations, and they would not be permitted. On the other hand, he added, he would welcome with his whole heart all immigrants who should come for peaceful and lawful purposes; that to all such the highways should not only be opened, but he would furnish them a safe escort and guarantee them his protection. He then gave the deputation a letter directing all military commanders to give to Colonel Eldridge's party a safe escort should they be, as represented, a party of immigrants coming into the territory to prosecute peaceful and lawful occupations.

On the 12th of the same month Deputy Marshal Preston reached Lecompton, bearing the following dispatch from Col. Cook:—

"Head Quarters, Camp near Nebraska River,
"K. T., Oct. 10, 1856.

"HIS EXCELLENCY, J. W. GEARY,
"Governor of Kansas Territory.

Sir: Col. Preston, Deputy Marshal, has arrested, with my assistance, and disarmed, a large body of *professed* immigrants, being entirely provided with arms and munitions of war; amongst which two officer's and sixty-one privates' *sabres*, and many boxes of new saddles. Agreeably to your requisition of September 26, I send an escort to conduct them, men, arms, and munitions of war, to appear before you at the capital. Col. Preston will give you the details.

I have the honor to be, with high respect, your obed't servant,
"P. ST. GEORGE COOK,
"Lieut. Col. 2d Dragoons, Comm'g in the Field."

The reports of Colonels Preston, Cooke, Major Sibley, and others, in respect to the arrest of this party, are too lengthy, and at this date, of too little importance, to copy. The substance of them, however, is given in the following extracts of a letter from Governor Geary to Secretary Marcy, under date of October 15th. He says:—

"Col. Wm. S. Preston, a Deputy U. S. Marshal, who had accompanied Col. P. St. G. Cook and his command to the northern frontier to look after a large party of professed immigrants, who were reported to be about invading the territory in that quarter in warlike array and for hostile purposes, returned to Lecompton on the 12th instant.

"He informed me that he had caused to be arrested, an organized band, consisting of about two hundred and forty persons, among whom were a very few women and children, comprising some seven families.

"This party was regularly formed in military order, and were under the command of General Pomeroy, Colonels Eldridge and Perry, and others. They had with them twenty wagons, in which was a supply of new arms, mostly muskets and sabres, and a lot of saddles, &c., sufficient to equip a battalion, consisting one-fourth of cavalry and the remainder of infantry. Besides these arms, the immigrants were provided with shot-guns, rifles, pistols, knives, &c., sufficient for the ordinary uses of persons travelling in Kansas, or any other of the western territories. From the reports of the officers, I learn they had with them neither oxen, household furniture, mechanics' tools, agricultural implements, nor any of the necessary appurtenances of peaceful settlers.

"These persons entered the territory on the morning of the 10th instant, and met Col. Cook's command a few miles south of the territorial line. Here the deputy-marshal questioned them as to their intentions, the contents of their wagons, and such other matters as he considered necessary in the exercise of his official duties. Not satisfied with their answers, and being refused the privilege of searching their effects, he felt justified in considering them a party organized and armed in opposition to my proclamation of the 11th September. After consultation with Col. Cook and other officers of the army, who agreed with him in regard to the character of the immigrants, he directed a search to be made, which resulted in the discovery of the arms already mentioned.

"An escort was offered them to Lecompton, in order that I might examine them in person, and decide as to their intentions, which they refused to accept. Their superfluous arms were then taken in charge of the troops, and the entire party put under arrest—the families, and all others, individually, being permitted to retire from the organization, if so disposed. Few availed themselves of this privilege.

"But little delay, and less annoyance, was occasioned them by these proceedings. Every thing that circumstances required or permitted was done for the comfort and convenience of the prisoners. Their journey was facilitated rather than retarded. They were accompanied by a squadron of United States dragoons, in command of Major H. H. Sibley. A day's rations were dealt out to them, and they were allowed to pursue the route themselves had chosen.

"Being apprised of the time at which they would probably arrive at Topeka, I forwarded orders for their detention on the northern side of the river, near that place, where, as I promised, I met them on the morning of the 14th inst.

"I addressed these people in their encampment, in regard to the present condition of the territory, the suspicious position they occupied, and the reprehensible attitude they had assumed. I reminded them that there was no possible necessity or excuse for the existence of large armed organizations at present in the territory. Everything was quiet and peaceful. And the very appearance of such an unauthorized and injudicious array as they presented, while it could do no good, was calculated, if not intended, to spread anew distrust and consternation through the territory, and rekindle the fires of discord and strife that had swept over the land, ravaging and desolating everything that lay in their destructive path.

"Their apology for an evident disregard of my proclamation, was, that they had made arrangements to emigrate to Kansas when the territory was not only disturbed by antagonistic political parties, armed for each other's destruction, but when numerous bands of marauders, whose business was plunder and assassination, infested all the highways, rendering travel extremely hazardous, even though every possible means for self-protection were employed.

"After showing the necessity of so doing, I insisted upon the immediate disbandment of this combination, which was agreed to with great alacrity. The majority of the men were evidently gratified to learn that they had been deceived in relation to Kansas affairs, and that peace and quiet, instead of strife and contention, were reigning here. My remarks were received with frequent demonstrations of approbation, and at their close the organization was broken up, its members dispersing in various directions. After they had been dismissed from custody, and the fact was announced to them by Major Sibley, their thankfulness for his kind treatment to them while under arrest, was acknowledged by giving him three hearty and enthusiastic cheers."

Soon after the letter, from which the foregoing is extracted, was forwarded to Washington, the following statement from the leaders of the party in question, was received by Governor Geary:—

"Topeka, Kansas Territory,
"October 14, 1856.

"HIS EXCELLENCY, JOHN W. GEARY,
"Governor of Kansas Territory.

"Dear Sir: We, the undersigned, conductors of an emigrant train, who entered the territory on the 10th instant, beg leave to make the following statement of facts, which, if required, we will attest upon our oaths.

"1st. Our party numbered from two hundred to three hundred persons, in two separate companies; the rear company, which has not yet arrived, being principally composed of families, with children, who left Mount Pleasant, Iowa, three days after this train which has arrived to-day.

"2d. We are all actual, *bona fide* settlers, intending, so far as we know, to become permanent inhabitants.

"3d. The blockading of the Missouri River to free-state emigrants, and the reports which reached us in the early part of September, to the effect that armed men were infesting and marauding the northern portions of Kansas, were the sole reasons why we came in a company and were armed.

"4th. We were stopped near the northern line of the territory by the United States troops, acting, as we understood, under the orders of one Preston, deputy United States marshal, and after stating to the officers who we were and what we had, they commenced searching our wagons (in some instances breaking open trunks, and throwing bedding and wearing apparel upon the ground in the rain), taking arms from the wagons, wresting some private arms from the hands of men, carrying away a lot of sabres belonging to a gentleman in the territory, as also one and a half kegs of powder, percussion caps, and some cartridges; in consequence of which we were detained about two-thirds of a day, taken prisoners, and are now presented to you.

"All we have to say is that our mission to this territory is entirely peaceful. We have no organization, save a police organization for our own regulation and defence on the way. And coming in that spirit to this territory, we claim the rights of American citizens to bear arms, and to be exempt from unlawful search and seizure.

"Trusting to your integrity and impartiality, we have confidence to believe that our property will be restored to us, and that all that has been wrong will be righted.

"We here subscribe ourselves, cordially and truly, your friends and fellow-citizens.

"S. W. ELDRIDGE, Conductor
"SAMUEL C. POMEROY.
"JOHN A. PERRY.
"ROBERT MORROW.
"EDWARD DANIELS.
"RICHARD RAELF."

CHAPTER XXX.

Peace and quiet prevailing.—Visit to Lawrence.—Proclamation of the Mayor of Leavenworth.—Suspension of the liquor traffic in Lecompton.—Organization of militia.—Escort for wagons furnished.—Another election.

So great was the change wrought in the affairs of the territory, that just three weeks from the day of his arrival, the governor was justified in forwarding the following dispatch to the secretary of state:—

"Executive Department, K. T.,
"Lecompton, Sept. 30, 1856.

"Hon. Wm. L. Marcy,
"Washington, D. C.,

"Peace now reigns in Kansas. Confidence is gradually being restored. Settlers are returning to their claims. Citizens are resuming their ordinary pursuits, and a general gladness pervades the community.

"When I arrived here, everything was at the lowest point of depression. Opposing parties saw no hope of peace, save in mutual extermination, and were employing effectual means to produce that terrible result.

"I will shortly issue a proclamation announcing the fact that tranquillity prevails, and inviting the return of all citizens who have been ejected from the territory either by force or fraud.

"Your obed't servt.,
"Jno. W. Geary,
"Governor of Kansas Territory."

On the morning of October 2d, the governor, accompanied by his private secretary and a single dragoon, made a visit to Lawrence on official business. The change in the aspect of the country appeared almost magical. Two weeks previous the journey could not have been safely made without a strong force of United States troops. The improvement manifest along the road was truly wonderful. No prowling bands of marauders were seen watching for prey upon the distant hills, or flying for safety into the deep ravines; nor travellers, fearing all who approached them to be enemies, dashing from the main roads over the extensive prairies. On the contrary, everything indicated peace, confidence and returning prosperity Females rode alone on horseback, from house to house, and wagons, unattended by guards, and loaded with provisions, household goods, men, women and children, traversed the roads without the slightest danger or cause for apprehension. Workingmen were employed in rebuilding their burned houses, and taking in and securing their ripened crops. Upon reaching Lawrence, the happy influence of restored peace was still more conspicuous. No guards surrounded the town, nor were there visible any mounted spies to watch its avenues of approach. Squads of idlers no longer hung about the streets. The stores were opened, and business had been actively resumed. Gloom had forsaken the countenances of the people, and cheerfulness pervaded the community. The governor was received with the utmost cordiality, and his visit, which continued during the day, was rendered especially agreeable. A company of militia, then being enrolled, was nearly full, and a general determination seemed to have been formed to cultivate a spirit of industry, peace and good order.

On his return route to Lecompton, the governor stopped at the houses of several of the settlers, and in every instance found the families entirely freed from all apprehensions of further disturbance, and in the enjoyment of the fullest contentment.

Notwithstanding the general peace, there still existed in various localities, many personal difficulties, growing out of the past disturbances. Letters from numerous citizens and deputations appointed for the purpose, poured into the executive office, complaining of real and imagined grievances, and appealing for redress. With a determination to bring about a proper system of civilized government, these complaints were referred back by the governor to the municipal authorities of the neighborhoods whence they emanated, with instructions that justice should be done, as far as possible, to all citizens wrongfully oppressed, and that the laws should be enforced; at the same time, he declined to interpose his own authority until the powers vested in the heads of the various municipalities had been employed and exhausted without the desired effect. This policy infused a new life into some of the corporations, and aroused the prostrated officials to prompt and healthy action. They were encouraged by the assurance of strong and efficient support to enforce and maintain the laws, which had been despised and trampled under foot, and a disposition was growing on every hand to uphold and execute them in all their power and majesty. This new condition of things infused a refreshing and invigorating influence through all the ramifications of society, and gave the promise of future and permanent prosperity to the territory.

The Mayor of Leavenworth City, to whom the governor had addressed a communication respecting certain evils complained of under his jurisdiction, promptly issued a proclamation, of which the following is an extract:—

"WHEREAS, It is the bounden duty of every citizen, and particularly of every executive officer, to comply strictly with the requirements of the late proclamation of Governor Geary:

"*Now, therefore*, I, William E. Murphy, mayor of the city aforesaid, by virtue of the power and authority in me vested, do make known and proclaim, that I will rigidly enforce the law against each and every violator thereof; and I hereby call upon all good and law-abiding citizens of this city, to frown down any secret conspiracy against law, and to give me, as their chief executive officer, that aid necessary to maintain the supremacy of the law."

The Mayor of Lecompton, also, having received a communication in regard to the numerous tippling houses existing in the city, setting forth the fact that the United States troops in the vicinity were almost unfitted for duty, in consequence of the facilities with which they obtained the means of intoxication, issued a proclamation, demanding, for a certain specified time, the entire suspension of the sale of intoxicating drinks. This proclamation being unheeded, and the evil, so far as the troops were concerned, becoming more serious, the governor sent a file of soldiers to close all the groggeries that were not properly licensed, and to destroy the liquor of those who persisted in selling contrary to law, and to the detriment of the public peace.

About this time numerous individuals, desiring to be prominent, addressed the governor, requesting him to allow them to organize militia or volunteer military companies, in order to protect the neighborhoods in which they resided. Knowing that the objects of these requests, were in the majority of instances to obtain legal authority to commit depredations on opposing political parties, the governor invariably refused to grant them. He organized, however, three companies of militia, whom he caused to be regularly mustered into the service of the United States. Two of these were stationed for protective purposes at Lecompton, and the other at Lawrence. They remained in the service until the month of December, when, it appearing that they were no longer needful, they were dismissed.

In order that perfect confidence might be had by store-keepers and others desirous of transporting goods and provisions into the territory, the governor made requisitions for United States troops to accompany wagons to and from Westport, Kansas City, and other towns on the Missouri River, all of which tended to increase the feeling of security that had sprung up, and to advance the welfare and prosperity of the people.

By proclamation of the governor, an election for members of the House of Representatives of the territory, and a delegate to Congress, was held on the 6th of October. The free-state people declined taking any part in the election, and in consequence but a small vote was polled. Whitfield, who was chosen delegate to Congress, came into the territory from Westport, at the head of a party of such notoriously bad repute, that he declared himself ashamed to be seen in their company. They came up to Lecompton, voted for Whitfield, and returned to Missouri.

CHAPTER XXXI.

NOTES OF A JOURNEY OF OBSERVATION.

October 17*th*.—Governor Geary left Lecompton early this morning on a tour of observation through the southern and western portions of the territory, escorted by a squadron of United States dragoons under command of Brevet-Major H. H. Sibley. After visiting a number of families on the way, and transacting considerable official business, he reached Lawrence in the afternoon, where he encamped for the night. He inspected Captain Walker's newly raised company of territorial troops, and was agreeably entertained by the citizens, who were in good spirits, and generally well contented at the better prospect that had been opened by the suppression of the late disturbances.

18*th*.—The escort proceeded through the Wakarusa Valley, to Hickory Point, via Blanton's Bridge, a place made celebrated by its fortifications and rifle-pits, constructed during the war by the free-state men. The governor, with his secretary and an orderly, went round by Franklin, where he had disbanded, but a few weeks before, the army of General Reid, and where he had been informed a bad state of feeling still existed. Here the people were assembled and addressed with happy effect by the governor, who was cheered at the close of his remarks. Some of the houses in the town were riddled with balls, especially that of the postmaster, Crane. Leaving Franklin, the governor called upon the settlers on the way, instructing and encouraging them to keep the peace; visited all the points of peculiar interest; and joined the troops at Hickory Point early in the evening. Here he encamped for the night, and was visited by a large number of intelligent and respectable citizens, who expressed themselves highly gratified with the policy he had pursued, and their determination to support and assist him in his just and impartial administration.

19*th.*—Whilst in camp at this place, information was received that recent depredations had been committed in this vicinity, and, upon complaint being duly made, the governor dispatched a deputy marshal with a posse of dragoons, who arrested the offenders and sent them as prisoners to Lecompton.

On the march towards Prairie City, where they halted for some time, the governor's horse planted his foot upon and crushed the head of a large rattlesnake that lay coiled in the road. May not this have been a happy omen? Passing Prairie City, reached the house of John J. Jones, extensively known in Kansas by the name of "Ottawa Jones." He resides on Ottawa Creek, and is a half-breed Ottawa Indian, educated and civilized, and the interpreter of his tribe. His wife is an intelligent white woman from the state of Maine, who came to the territory some years since, as a missionary, and to whom he was married in 1845. They have no children. Jones formerly kept a hotel of considerable dimensions and excellent accommodations, which was burned on the night of the 27th of August last, by a Captain Hays, with a company of about forty men, because of his alleged free-state proclivities. Jones escaped unharmed, though he was pursued and fired at a number of times by Hays' party. Six hundred dollars in cash was taken from his wife whilst making her escape. Jones estimates his loss at $10,000, but the chiefs value it at $6000. He has three hundred acres of land under good fence, raises four thousand bushels of grain a year, has one hundred head of cattle, and fourteen horses. He was educated at Hamilton College,

New York, and now preaches every Sunday, at the Baptist Mission. The farm of Jones is a part of the Ottawa reserve, which is ten by twelve miles square. The tribe consists of 325 souls. Ottawa Creek, which empties into the Osage River, runs through this reserve, in which, notwithstanding the lateness of the season, the governor and others of his party took a comfortable and refreshing bath.

Four miles from the house of Ottawa Jones, stands the Baptist Mission, consisting of a church and several small houses. The mission, in which sixty Indian children are being educated, is under the care of John Early, a full-blooded Indian, who was educated at the Methodist Mission, and talks good English.

Having passed this mission, crossed the Marais des Cygnes, sometimes called Osage River, and proceeding seven miles further, encamped in the valley of North Middle Creek.

20th.—Struck tents, and marched through a beautiful country to Osawattomie, situated about one mile above the confluence of the Marais des Cygnes and Potawattomie rivers, upon an extensive plain of unsurpassed fertility. It formerly contained about two hundred inhabitants, many of whom were driven away at the time of the difficulties described in another place. Near this town the governor found one family, consisting of a man, his wife, and five children, all sick in bed, whilst their oldest son, who was their only support, had been forced to fly from the territory in consequence of threats against his life made by certain pro-slavery agitators.

The people of Osawattomie were laboring under the apprehension of some undefined danger, and they welcomed the governor's arrival as the guarantee of security. He called the citizens together, irrespective of party; heard their individual complaints; gave them salutary advice; urged them, as far as possible, to bury the past, and cultivate kind relations for the future; to all of which they promised a cheerful compliance.

Leaving Osawattomie, crossed the Marais des Cygnes. This river empties into the Missouri about ten miles below Jefferson City, after receiving in its course the Potawattomie, Bull's Creek, Sugar Creek, and other respectable streams. After a brisk ride of about nine miles, over a rich and beautiful country, occasionally enlivened by the flight of immense numbers of prairie fowl, Bull's Creek was crossed, and an encampment formed at the town of Paoli, the government seat of Douglas County. The town consists of thirteen houses and a good hotel, recently built, and is located upon land belonging to an intelligent Indian of the Peoria tribe, named Baptiste. He resides at this place, and is interpreter for the Peorias, Kaskaskias, Peankeshaws and Weaws, recently united under treaty by name of the Weaws. These tribes number about three hundred souls, fifty of whom reside at Paoli. The land is apportioned among them by treaty, according to the number of each family, Baptiste having received two entire sections for special services. The Baptist Mission school, under the charge of Dr. Lykens, assisted by three white teachers, is about a mile and a half from Paoli. The school is for the education of Indian children, about thirty of whom are in daily attendance. General Maxwell McCaslin, formerly of Pennsylvania, is the agent for these tribes, and is very generally respected. Their lands possess great beauty, and are very fertile, and sufficiently well timbered.

Henry Sherman, or Dutch Henry, as he was called, lived in this vicinity on the Potawattomie. He was a pro-slavery man, and disposed to be quarrelsome. A short time previous to the governor's visit, Henry was staying at the house of a Mrs. Totten, with the body of his brother who had just died, when he was called upon by three men, with blackened faces, and ordered to quit the country instantly. Upon soliciting time to bury his brother, he was given until the following night. They took away his horse and ordered him not to remove any of his cattle. Henry was waylaid and killed in March, 1857, by a party of men, simply for his money, of which he had collected a considerable amount.

21*st.*—Previous to leaving Paoli, the governor delivered a speech at a public meeting, embracing a large number of citizens and neighbors, so effectually as to elicit repeated evidences of approbation, and upon concluding was greeted with enthusiastic cheers, and general and hearty pledges of co-operation and support. He then commissioned a justice of the peace and several other officers, thus affording the citizens the immediate means of settling their own disputes and difficulties.

Leaving Paoli, returned via Osawattomie, and crossing the Potawattomie, proceeded up the valley of that creek about eight miles, to the scene of many past disturbances and of the Potawattomie murders. The route along the Potawattomie was through a fertile region well timbered. The woods abounded with wild turkeys, the creek with geese and ducks, and the prairies with grouse. The scenery was remarkably beautiful and picturesque.

22d.—Travelled all day through a drenching rain. Crossed South Middle Creek, and Big Sugar Creek, and encamped at night on the south side of the last-named stream, near the house of Mr. Means.

23d.—Early this morning the neighbors having assembled, they listened with evident satisfaction to a spirited address from Governor Geary. Travelled over a delightful country, ten miles to Sugar Mound. Deputations of citizens joined the party at various points on the road, and accompanied it to the place named. Here, in anticipation of the governor's coming, a large number of persons had already assembled. After addressing these, and receiving universal assurances of their approbation and concurrence, he proceeded on his journey, and encamped late in the evening on Little Sugar Creek, three miles south of Sugar Mound. Here, as elsewhere, the whole neighborhood thronged to see, hear, and converse with the governor—to state their grievances and their wishes, and receive instruction and encouragement. These interchanges of views and feelings between the executive and the people were evidently working a most beneficial effect. The settlers seemed universally satisfied that impartial justice would be done them, so far as the governor possessed any power.

This region of country, which is pretty generally settled by free-state men, is equal in value to any in the territory. About Sugar Mound the land is high and open, and unsurpassed in regard to its fertility. Little Sugar Creek winds round the Mound in a sort of semicircle. There is an abundance of fine timber, consisting principally of oak, hickory, walnut, sugar-maple, &c., and the sides of the hills reveal large quarries of most excellent building stone. Beyond this, a rich undulating prairie stretches out as far as the eye can reach. The settlers in this section are prosperous and contented. They value their claims, (one hundred and sixty acres,) upon which the improvements are of little account, from eight to twelve hundred dollars. Maple sugar is manufactured to a considerable extent, and sells readily at twenty cents per pound. Mr. Temple Wayne, during the past year, produced six hundred pounds, which he sold at that price. The soil is capable of yielding as much and as good hemp, corn, rye, wheat, or any of the agricultural products, as any in the United States.

24th.—The tents were struck at an early hour and the

company about to move, when two messengers hastily arrived, announcing that a robbery and murder had been committed the night previous in the rear on Sugar Creek, and that the perpetrators, numbering seven or eight men, were still in the neighborhood threatening other outrages. A countermarch was instantly ordered, and at a brisk trot, the ten intervening miles were soon traversed. The scene of the outrage, which was less serious than had been represented, was the house of Judge Briscoe Davis, who was absent in Missouri. His sister, a Mrs. Cornet, and five daughters, four of them grown, were left in possession. Captain John E. Brown, Mrs. Brown, and her daughter, were on a visit to Mrs. Cornet. The robbers entered the house, and seizing Captain Brown and two of the young ladies, confined them in one room, under charge of a couple of sentinels. The remainder of the family were imprisoned together in another apartment. The house was then searched, and robbed of every article of value, consisting chiefly of one hundred and five dollars in gold, a watch jewelry, revolver, &c. In the morning, the ruffians compelled the ladies to prepare them a breakfast, and then rode away, taking with them a valuable horse. Captain Brown made his escape during the night, and was the means of conveying information to the governor, who dispatched scouts in every direction in pursuit of the robbers, issuing, at the same time, a proclamation, offering a reward of two hundred dollars for their apprehension. Several of them were subsequently captured.

Sunday, 25th.—A very rainy and disagreeable day. Proceeded up the Potawattomie valley, recrossed the Marais des Cygnes, passed the Baptist Mission, traversed the California road, and reached Eight Mile Creek at Centropolis, where finding plenty of wood and water, an encampment was made. The day was occupied by the governor in conversing at various points with the citizens. The community was quiet, no disturbance having occurred for more than four weeks.

26*th.*—Travelled rapidly twenty-seven miles over a monotonous rolling prairie, upon which there was not a tree or shrub to break the extensive prospect. The march, however, was enlightened, as on other occasions, by a spirited hunt. A prairie wolf was started up, when a cry was raised, the hounds were quickly in pursuit, and a half-dozen horsemen followed. Away they went, now in the hollow, now dashing across the hills. The wolf was a fine fellow, and made good time, but the dogs were too much for him, and soon had him down, and the horsemen were just in time to be in at the death. These wolves are very numerous in Kansas. They are not ferocious, and are never known to attack anything but the poultry. Even the sheep appear to be unmolested by them. They prowl about the houses of the settlers at night, not hesitating to come to the very doors in search of food. After sunset, their barking, which resembles that of a small dog, may constantly be heard. Reaching One Hundred and Ten, a celebrated stopping place on the California road, for emigrants to the far west, a number of citizens called upon and had a pleasant interview with the governor. Then proceeded in a northwesterly direction on the Fort Riley road, and going twelve miles further, encamped on the head waters of the Wakarusa.

27th.—Travelled briskly all day, and encamped at night on the head waters of the Neosha. The road is over an uninhabited and rather an inferior prairie country, along a divide between the Neosha and Wakarusa, the banks of both streams being skirted with good timber. Had several wolf-chases on the route. Flocks of brant were seen, and myriads of wild geese on the wing to more southern latitudes.

28th.—Proceeded briskly along the same divide, the country being barren and desolate, and covered with immense quarries of white limestone. The only settlements are a few families at the crossing of Clark's Creek. Crossed the Kansas River at Riley City to Pawnee City. This was accomplished with much difficulty and even danger in consequence of a freshet from Smoky Hill Fork. Pawnee City, which was Reeder's abortive seat of government, contains two houses, whilst Riley City can boast of eight. Upon the governor's arrival in the evening at Fort Riley, a salute of fifteen guns was fired, the band discoursed most eloquent music, and other honors of the most marked and gratifying character were rendered.

29th, 30th, 31st.—Remained at Fort Riley to recruit the horses, equip the troops, and prepare them for a winter campaign. The governor, during this time, visited all the places of interest in and about the fort, saw nearly all the families in the neighborhood, and received conclusive assurances of universal satisfaction with his administration. On the 29th, he reviewed the troops at the fort, and in the evening attended a ball, at which all the officers, their ladies, and the prominent people of the neighborhood, were present. This was a brilliant affair, and although gotten up in a region almost beyond the bounds of civilization, would have done credit, for the education, intelligence, refinement, and it may be added, delicacy and beauty of its female participants, to any community in the world. Numerous other entertainments were given, and the stay at the fort was made as comfortable and happy as could have been desired.

Fort Riley was constructed but lately, (in 1853), at an expense of over five hundred thousand dollars to the government. It is not located in so beautiful a country as Fort Leavenworth, but its buildings are even more spacious, imposing, and comfortable. It is in latitude 39° 03′ 38″ N., longitude 96° 24′ 56″ W., at an elevation of nine hundred and twenty-six feet above the Gulf of Mexico, and at the mouth of the Republican Fork on the Kansas River, one hundred and ten miles from its junction with the Missouri.

November 1st.—Left Fort Riley *en route* for Lecompton. Crossed the river with great difficulty at Pawnee, and encamped at Riley City, where the governor was visited, as usual, by numerous citizens.

Sunday, 2d.—Weather cold and rainy. Passing down the Kansas, crossed Clark's Creek, about four miles from Riley, then over some high barren hills, into a valley of surprising richness and fertility, in which there are large quantities of fine timber. This valley is admirably adapted for the construction of a railroad, as no grading would be required for many miles; while stone, as well as timber, exists in great abundance. Wild turkeys were plenty, and in consequence, perhaps, of the rain and cold, were so dull and stupid as to be shot with pistols. Encamped on the south side of the Kansas, opposite Manhattan. A congregation had assembled at that place to hear preaching by the Rev. Charles E. Blood, who learning of the approach of the governor, adjourned the meeting, and with other gentlemen, crossed the river in a small boat to invite him over to Manhattan to address the citizens in his stead. The reverend gentleman said that the obligations of religion could not be properly discharged unless peace and order were preserved, and he assured his excellency that a few words of advice and encouragement from him at that particular period would be of more service than any sermon he could utter. The governor complied with this request, and spoke for a long while to the people with much feeling and power; and the meeting, doubtless, resulted in doing great good. Manhattan is situated at the junction of the Big Blue with the Kansas river. The military road from Fort Leavenworth to Fort Riley and Laramie passes through this place. The Big Blue is a clear stream, differing in that respect very materially from the Kansas, and is one hundred and fifty yards wide and fifteen deep. Buffalo-fish and cat-fish, with other varieties, are found here. Deer, prairie-chickens, wild turkeys, &c., abound in the surrounding country. The town is located in a valley of great fertility, and contains about one hundred and fifty inhabitants, who are generally moral, intelligent, and industrious, and who took no part whatever in the recent disturbances. The town contains a steam saw and grist mill, three stores, and a hotel.

4th.—A snow storm, the first of the season, which occurred on the 3d, kept the party in camp all that day, where they were visited by many of the settlers. The weather to-day was cold and windy. Travelled down the Kansas valley, the governor visiting the citizens on the route. The people were quietly pursuing their ordinary vocations, and everything indicated peace and increasing prosperity. Encamped for the night at an old Indian camping ground on Mulberry Creek, where was an abundance of wood, water, and grass.

5th.—Entered the Potawattomie reserve, and tavelling rapidly, crossed Mill Creek, a beautiful clear stream, abounding in fish, and afterwards Mission Creek, and encamped for the night at the Baptist Mission. The Potawattomie reserve embraces a fertile district, on both sides of the Kansas River, thirty miles square. The tribe numbers about three thousand six hundred persons. They have a thriving town called Uniontown, and two missions; the St. Mary's, the Catholic, being on the north, and the Baptist on the south side of the river. This last is under the superintendence of Mr. Fox. About thirty Indian children are in daily attendance at the school, some of whom exhibit considerable aptness in learning.

6th.—The governor issued the following proclamation:—

"Having reached this point, after an extended tour of observation through this territory, and being now fully satisfied that the benign influences of peace reigns throughout all its borders, in consonance with general custom and my own feelings, I hereby specially set apart the 20th day of November, instant, to be observed by all the good citizens of the territory as a day of general thanksgiving and praise to Almighty God for the blessings vouchsafed to us as a people."

Proceeded to Topeka, where the people were quiet and the

town prospering. Eighty new buildings were being erected Business was in a healthy condition, and all the citizens were attending to their proper avocations. Passing through Tecumseh, Big Springs, Washington, and other smaller places, and calling at the encampment of United States troops stationed near that place, the governor reached his own residence at Lecompton late in the evening, having been absent just twenty days, during which time he visited hundreds of families, addressed many assemblies of citizens, conducted considerable official business, and laid the foundations of peace, contentment, good will and prosperity in the whole line of his travel. On the day after his return he addressed the following letter to the secretary of state :—

"Executive Department, K. T.,
"Lecompton, Nov. 7, 1856.

"HON. WM. L. MARCY,
"Secretary of State.

"Sir: I have just returned to this place after an extended tour of observation through a large portion of this territory.

"I left Lecompton on the 17th ult., *via* Lawrence, Franklin, Wakarusa Creek, Hickory Point, Ottawa Creek, Osawattomie, Marais des Cygnes, Bull Creek, Paoli, Potawattomie, North and South Middle Creeks, Big and Little Sugar Creeks, and Sugar Mound, passing westward along the California and Santa Fe road to Fort Riley; thence down the Kansas River *via* Pawnee, Riley City, Manhattan, Waubonsee, Baptist Mission, Topeka, Tecumseh, and other places. I also visited at their houses as many citizens as I conveniently could, and addressed various bodies of people, as I have reason to believe, with beneficial results.

"During this tour I have obtained much valuable information relative to affairs in Kansas, and made myself familiar with the wants and grievances of the people, which will enable me to make such representations to the next legislature and the government at Washington, as will be most conducive to the public interests.

"The general peace of the territory remains unimpaired; confidence is being gradually and surely restored; business is resuming its ordinary channels; citizens are preparing for winter; and there is a readiness among the good people of all parties to sustain my administration.

"Very respectfully, your obed't servt.,
"JNO. W. GEARY,
"Governor of Kansas Territory."

CHAPTER XXXII.

The capitol building.—Captain Donaldson dismisses Justice Nelson's court.—Captain Walker surrenders himself.—Dragoons required for detached service.—Bad postal arrangements.—Free-state prisoners removed to Tecumseh.—The governor at Leavenworth.—Report of a deputation sent to arrest marauders.

NOVEMBER 7TH, 1856.—A note having been received from Mr. Owen C. Stewart in regard to the capitol buildings, the governor addressed him in reply, as follows:—

"As your services as superintendent of the capitol buildings are no longer required, you are hereby notified that your appointment is revoked from this date."

Congress had appropriated fifty thousand dollars to erect suitable public buildings for the territory, and Dr. A. Rodrique, postmaster at Lecompton, was the principal contractor for their election. He was connected in the enterprise, some way or another, with Sheriff Jones, Governor Shannon, and other officials. The money appropriated would have been sufficient for the object if properly expended. As it is, the walls of the building have only advanced a few feet above the foundation, and the whole amount of the appropriation has been exhausted. Mr. Stewart was appointed by Governor Shannon superintendent, at a salary of one thousand two hundred dollars a year, which, although the work had long been suspended, was still running on. The same gentleman was a sub-contractor under Rodrique, and was therefore required to superintend his own work, which was a very convenient sort of an arrangement. William Rumbold was the architect, who had contracted to receive for his "compensation four per cent. on the cost of the building;" and of course it would not be to his interest to oppose any amount of expenditure upon its construction. If it is completed upon the same liberal scale as it has been commenced, so far as the outlay of money is concerned, it may be ready for roofing in by the use of another appropriation of two or three hundred thousand dollars.

On this day, R. R. Nelson, a justice of the peace at Lecompton, filed an affidavit with the governor, charging Captain John Donaldson, of the territorial militia, with having entered his court with six armed men, and rescued a soldier named

Fisher, belonging to his company, who was then receiving a hearing on the charge of larceny, taking the prisoner away and dismissing the court in a manner that would have done credit to Oliver Cromwell. A requisition was immediately made upon Colonel Cook to put Donaldson under arrest, which was accordingly done. Upon making suitable apologies, and thus appeasing the squire's wounded pride, the captain was, in a few days restored to liberty and his command.

Deputy Marshal Tebbs and probate judge John P. Wood called upon the governor for a requisition to serve a warrant upon Captain Samuel Walker, then commanding a company of militia at Lawrence. The governor assured them there need be no difficulty touching that matter; that he would answer for the appearance of Captain Walker upon his own summons, and simply addressed him a note requesting him to come forward manfully and meet the charges against him. Walker accordingly came to Lecompton, voluntarily surrendered himself, entered bail to appear at court, and returned to Lawrence. He was quite a lion during his stay at the capital.

8th.—Requisition was made upon Col. Cook for two companies of United States dragoons to proceed to Paoli, at the request of Mr. Maxwell McCaslin, Indian agent, to protect him while in charge of the public funds to pay off the Indians under his care, and also to scour the southeastern portion of the territory, where it was reported a band of thieves were prowling and committing depredations. With these troops a commissioner and deputy marshal were sent, with instructions and power to make arrests of suspicious persons, give them a preliminary hearing on the spot, and thus bring justice to the doors of the people.

13th.—The governor addressed a lengthy communication to the postmaster-general in regard to well-grounded complaints concerning the management of the postal affairs of the territory, in which he remarked:—"It requires eleven days for a letter to reach this place from Washington City, when a person travelling with expedition can accomplish the same distance in six days;" and then urges him to use his "best efforts to afford regular and prompt mail facilities for this growing territory."

15th.—The free-state prisoners, forty in number, were removed to Tecumseh, where more comfortable quarters had been prepared, and where they were to receive their trial; they were attended by an escort of United States troops under command of Lieut. Higgins.

A convict named Charles H. Calkins made his escape from prison. A requisition for troops was made by the master of convicts, and a reward of one hundred dollars offered by the governor for his capture, but without success.

16th. A company of mounted U. S. troops was granted to Gen. G. W. Clarke, Indian agent for the Potawattomies, to protect him in the payment of his annuities.

17th. The governor proceeded to Fort Leavenworth, via Lawrence, to attend the public sales of the Indian trust lands. These were owned by the Delawares, who number about one thousand persons. They are the richest tribe in Kansas, and perhaps the wealthiest community in the world.

18th. These land sales had attracted to Leavenworth City a large concourse of people, not only from every part of the territory, but from almost every state in the Union. An invitation being tendered to the governor, he attended a meeting at that place, where he was warmly welcomed, and where addresses on the all-important and all-absorbing subject of the sales and the general welfare of the country, were made by the governor, the mayor, and other prominent citizens.

26th. A large meeting of citizens of that town and vicinity was held at Tecumseh, to chose delegates to attend a convention "to be held at Leavenworth City, to consult upon and propose a policy upon which the citizens of Kansas, without distinction of party, might unite for the preservation of peace and a general reconciliation, based upon acquiescence in existing legislation, an impartial administration of justice, and opposition to external intervention in the affairs of the territory."

At this meeting, which was addressed by a number of gentlemen, both of the pro-slavery and free-state parties, the following resolutions were unanimously adopted:—

"*Resolved,* That we cordially approve any and all measures that may have a tendency to restore peace and harmony among the citizens of Kansas; that in view of the past and impressed with the importance of the present, we earnestly implore our fellow-citizens, without distinction of party, to aid in the preservation of peace and order by adopting a policy of conciliation.

"*Resolved,* That whatever difference of opinion may prevail touching the circumstances that resulted in the adoption of existing laws, we deem it the duty of every man to support and sustain these laws, in preference to having no laws at all, and continuing the anarchy that has too long prevailed.

"*Resolved,* That we believe the existing territorial laws contain provisions that should be repealed, and we have confidence that the legislature, at the next session, will, with a spirit of justice and moderation, correct oppressive legislation.

"*Resolved,* That we have confidence in the patriotic desire and ability of Governor Geary to faithfully administer the laws, and protect and enforce the rights of all the citizens of Kansas; and we cordially approve the policy that he has adopted, and which, thus far, has been attended with the happiest results towards the restoration of law and order, equality and justice."

The proceedings of this meeting were endorsed by the grand jury, who published, with the resolutions, the following, to which their names were affixed:—

"*Resolved,* That we, the undersigned grand jury for the second judicial district, do hereby approve the foregoing resolutions, and recommend them to the citizens of Kansas Territory."

29*th.* The deputation sent on the 8th instant, in pursuit of a band of alleged marauders, who were committing depredations in the south-eastern section of the territory, returned to Lecompton, and made a lengthy report of their proceedings. They succeeded in arresting seven notorious characters, one of whom, James Townsley, confessed to having been a member of the party that murdered Wilkinson, Sherman, and the Doyles, on the Potawattomie creek. Others were examined and committed for felony. The five prisoners committed were carried to Tecumseh, and there held in custody to await the action of the grand jury. The report of the commission says, "they had but fairly commenced the business with which they were charged, when Captain De Saussure informed them that he had been ordered into winter quarters at Fort Leavenworth, with his command, and that no further assistance could be rendered by him. Without a military escort no arrests could be made with certainty and safety, and further operations were therefore suspended."

A special messenger brought a dispatch to the governor, from U. S. Commissioner Edward Hoagland, informing him that a band of Missourians, in the disguise of United States soldiers, had forcibly driven a man named Holmes from the territory, that the peace was thereby again endangered, and offering his own, and the assistance of the marshal, to pursue the offenders; to which a lengthy reply was returned, of which the following is an extract:—

"In reply, I have to state, that the supposed soldiers *were real soldiers*, sent by me upon the due requisition of peaceable citizens of Missouri, accompanied by Deputy-Marshal Preston, to arrest certain horse thieves (Holmes among the number), who had been plundering the citizens of Missouri; that they did arrest Holmes, and afterwards permitted him to escape, very much to my regret; that thus far the efficiency of the military is unimpaired, and no further, and that the peace of the territory still remains upon a solid basis, as I have the most gratifying reports from all quarters."

CHAPTER XXXIII.

Pay of the militia.—Settlers ordered from Indian reserve.—Sales of Delaware trust lands.—No prison in Kansas.—The capital appropriation.—Governor Geary between two factions.—False reports.—Settlement of Hyattville.—Peace still prevailing.

THE important events in the history of the territory for the month of December, 1856, are all embraced in the following extracts from letters to the president and secretary of state. In a letter to Mr. Marcy, of December 8th, the governor says:—

"Since my dispatch of 22d ultimo, the United States troops have retired to winter quarters, and the territorial militia have been mustered out of service, as before indicated. To be discharged in mid-winter, without means of support, seemed so cruel and unjust, that at very considerable inconvenience to myself, I raised the money and paid off the disbanded militia. I therefore request, that an order be made by the proper department, authorizing the payment of the amount due to the *three* militia companies for two and a half months' service. This, I think, could be done from the general army appropriation, and I could be reimbursed at an early day.

"The commission, alluded to in my former dispatch, as sent to the southern portion of the territory, with a squadron of United States dragoons, have returned, having succeeded in breaking up, as far as I can learn, the only party of robbers infesting the territory, capturing several of them, and succeeding in arresting one man charged with participation in the murders committed on the Potawattomie, in May last, upon the Doyles, Wilkinson and Sherman. The result of this commission has fully equalled my anticipations. Much has been accomplished in a brief time, and the squadron accompanying it has retired to Fort Leavenworth for winter quarters.

"In the territory there are numerous Indian reserves, under the government of Indian agents, as entirely independent of the executive of the territory as one state is of another. Questions of jurisdiction, calculated to produce bad feeling, are constantly arising, and collisions between the agents and the citizens have ensued.

"On the 5th inst., a deputation, representing citizens of Wise county, residing near Council Grove, called upon me in behalf of numerous settlers in that vicinity, stating that the agent of the Kansas Indians had notified them to leave their claims within three days, at the peril of being forcibly ousted by United States soldiers. The petition states that the petitioners made settlements and valuable improvements, commencing in 1854, by virtue of a map issued under the authority of the Indian department, *excluding the land settled upon from the Kansas reserve*, with the assurance of the Indian agent himself, that the land was open for settlement, and that they have since been living there with their families. The statements of the petitioners seemed so equitable and reasonable, and the season of the year so inclement for their removal, that I advised the Indian agent to permit the settlers to remain undisturbed until I could lay the matter before the government, having satisfactory assurances from the settlers, that they would peaceably acquiesce in a decision from that quarter."

In a letter, dated Leavenworth City, December 15th, the governor writes to President Pierce, as follows:—

"In response to a letter from the mayor, and accompanying petition of leading citizens of Leavenworth City, I came here for the purpose of aiding with my counsel and presence, in averting a threatened disturbance. I find the public mind greatly excited in consequence of some recent instructions from the commissioner of Indian affairs, entirely changing the policy which has thus far governed the land sales, with the results so entirely satisfactory to all interests.

"Solicitude for the peace of the territory brought me to this city on the 17th of November, at the beginning of the sales. Many purchasers were here from every part of the country, invited by your proclamation, and great apprehension of difficulty between them and the squatters was entertained. The lands had been previously appraised at from one dollar and twenty-five cents to twelve dollars per acre. In accordance with his instructions, the commissioner announced that the actual *bona fide* settler would be permitted to take his land at its appraised value, and that only vacant quarter sections would be opened for competition. This announcement met with universal favor. The speculators themselves, the only parties really aggrieved, having come here hundreds of miles at heavy expense, on the invitation of the government, not only acquiesced in the decision, but actually lauded its justice; while the Indians, on the other hand, were satisfied with the price they were getting for lands only made valuable by the industry, skill and capital of the pioneers who had braved everything to improve them.

"Such of the speculators as desired farms, made satisfactory arrangements with the settlers; while others, on the faith of the policy established by the government, and acquiesced in by the Indian agent, made large investments in the lots of this city.

"In pursuance of the policy and understanding adopted at the opening of the sales, all the Delaware lands advertised for sale, including the environs of this city, and also South Leavenworth, with the exception of *the city itself*, have been sold. The large sum of nearly four hundred and forty thousand dollars has been realized, which, together with the proceeds of the sale of this city, will make over four hundred and fifty thousand dollars, to be distributed among about nine hundred Indians, who have yet a magnificent reserve, more than quadrupled in value by the sale and settlement of the trust lands.

"The city of Leavenworth has been appraised by lots, making it average thirty dollars per acre. The people here are desirous that it may be sold to the original town company by the lot, at the appraised value, which would be a much more stringent rule than that which has been applied to the rural claims. This city, containing a population of over two thousand, consists of three hundred and twenty acres, or two claims, which, by the original settlers, were thrown into a town company, and divided into shares.

"It seems clear to me that every principle of justice requires that the same rule should be applied to the claims upon which this city has been founded, as that which has been applied to other portions of the trust lands, with the additional reason in favor of the city, that on the faith of the policy previously announced by the government, large investments have been made here, and it would be a violation of public faith not to secure them.

"What has induced the commissioner of Indian affairs to send the new and special instructions for this city alone, I am at a loss to conceive; but I am clear on the point, that, if carried into effect, they will destroy the peace of the community, and for years impair the prosperity of this young metropolis of Kansas.

"A meeting of the gentlemen officially connected with the subject has been held. I strongly advised that this city should be sold to the town company, by lots or blocks, at their appraised value, in accordance with the rule that has governed the previous sales, thus giving entire satisfaction to the Indians, the original settlers and the recent purchasers, in order that the exciting question might at once be settled, and the minds of the people relieved from a heavy load of anxiety. But in this matter I have been overruled, and it was deemed advisable to send Mr. Commissioner Eddy and Colonel Russell to Washington, to lay the whole matter before the government, in order to procure more satisfactory instructions.

"This subject is difficult to comprehend by any person not on the spot, and not conversant with it in all its bearings. I have given much thought and examination to the question, and have come to the deliberate conclusion, that the peace of the territory (which I regard as of greater importance to the country than the entire value of the lands) cannot easily be maintained unless some policy be adopted which will be satisfactory to the people, the original settlers and the recent purchasers."

A letter to the secretary of state, under date of Lecompton, December 22d, with other useful information, contains the following facts and suggestions:—

"There is not a prison in the territory in which a prisoner can be safely secured for a single hour. Where crime has been so abundant, the necessity of a penitentiary is too evident to require elaboration from me. An appropriation for this purpose should immediately be made by Congress.

"The appropriation to build the capitol at this place has been nearly exhausted, and is entirely inadequate to complete the building upon the plan which has been adopted. The architect informs me that an additional appropriation of at least fifty thousand dollars will be required.

"In order that the government may fully understand my position here, and guard against rumors and reports studiously set in motion by certain parties whose political interests most strongly commit them against the policy which has been established here, it seems proper that I should make certain developments.

"Because I will not co-operate with certain efforts to establish a state government, and lend myself to carry out views which are outside of the constitution and the laws, I am misrepresented by a few ultra men of one party. Because I will not enter upon a crusade in support of *one idea*, and endorse a series of resolves passed on the night of the last session of the Kansas Legislature, making but a *single issue* in Kansas, to wit, the introduction of slavery; denouncing the national democratic party from which I have the honor to hold my appointment; and branding as abolitionists or disunionists all persons not agreeing with these principles,—I am equally the subject of misrepresentation by a few violent men on the other side. My uniform reply to all objectors, is, that my position shall not be prostituted to advance partisan ends, it being my simple duty to administer the government, and leave the people free to settle and regulate their own affairs.

"The territorial officers, with scarcely an exception, were warm partisans of the last named party organization; so much so as to deprive themselves of all ability to act as mediators between the contending factions.

"The development of my policy and its happy results has produced considerable agitation among some ultra men, and various rumors, as unfounded as they are desperate, have been put in circulation here, and exaggerated statements forwarded to Washington, directly calculated to disturb the peace of the territory, and studiously intended to produce that effect.

"The whipping of Mr. Tuton, and the threatening of Mr. John Spicer, have been greatly exaggerated. Mr. Tuton was whipped, for the reason, as it is alleged, that he was treacherous to his former associates; but he was not seriously injured; and proper measures have been taken to redress the outrage. In reply to my note, Mr. John Spicer informs me that he has not been threatened; that he lives in a peaceable community, and feels entirely secure.

"A party of some ninety men, mostly disbanded militia, have gone, in charge of Thaddeus Hyatt, Esq., with provisions and necessary tools, to found the town of Hyattville, on the south branch of the Potawattomie Creek, and make settlements there. These persons were out of employment, likely to become a charge on the town of Lawrence, and Mr. Hyatt projected this scheme, to furnish them with useful occupation, and prevent them from falling into habits of indolence and vice. He fully explained the matter to me previous to putting it into execution, and it met my approval."

On the 31st of December, the governor addressed Secretary Marcy, as follows:—

"In reviewing, on this, the last evening of the year, the events of the past four months, and contrasting the disturbed condition of affairs upon my advent with the present tranquil and happy state of things, which has held its sway for the last three months, I must congratulate the administration and the country, upon the auspicious result. Crime, so rife and daring, at the period of my arrival, is almost entirely banished. I can truthfully assure you, that in proportion to her population and extent, less crime is now being committed in Kansas, than in any other portion of the United States."

CHAPTER XXXIV.

The Topeka Legislature.—Arrest of its members.—Appropriation of Vermont Legislature for the suffering poor of Kansas.

January 6th, 1857.—This day having been appointed for the meeting of the Free-State Legislature, some of its members accordingly met at Topeka; but their numbers not being sufficient to form a quorum, no organization was effected. They held an informal meeting, and adopted a memorial to Congress.

Considerable apprehension had been entertained and expressed in regard to the probable results of this meeting, and hence, precautions had been quietly taken by the governor to guard against any unlawful or evil consequences. A confidential agent had been sent to give timely notice of whatever might transpire, and other arrangements were made for such action as exigencies might demand.

There were certain restless persons, however, about Lecompton, who were unwilling to trust the management of this affair to the discretion of the governor. They thought they perceived another opportunity for a disturbance, and their disposition for mischief was too strong to let this pass by unimproved. Sheriff Jones had been laying his plans, and fancied he had them so admirably arranged, that a failure to accomplish the object he desired, was impossible. These he kept carefully concealed from the governor, though he was a daily visitor at the executive office. Had not these plans been frustrated, the peaceful intentions of the executive would have been thwarted, and a renewal of a fierce civil conflict throughout the territory would have ensued. The most careful and constant watchfulness was, therefore, necessary, to guard against the secret and mischievous machinations of men who were determined that peace should not exist, except through the extirpation of their political opponents.

A writ, for the arrest of the Topeka legislators, had been quietly issued by Judge Cato, on the oath of Sheriff Jones, which was served by Deputy Marshal Pardee, (Jones being present to prevent any mistake,) on the members assembled, who yielded themselves prisoners, without resistance or hesitation.

This quiet submission to legal authority on the part of the Topeka Legislators, was the last thing the sheriff desired or expected. He had looked forward to the time of this meeting with the same anxiety and inward satisfaction as he had previously awaited the day appointed for the sacking of Lawrence. It was to be another jubilee. He was once more to play the part of a hero. His programme had been carefully prepared. The legislature was to have met—the marshal to serve his writs—the members would of course, refuse to recognise his authority—this would furnish a sufficient pretext for making forcible arrests, the attempt to do which would be resisted, and another violent outbreak and bloody strife be the result. The governor was to be soundly abused for permitting the illegal legislature to assemble—all the evil consequences were to be charged to his account—and a petition dispatched to Washington demanding his removal. The free-state party was thus to be crushed out by the sagacity and energy of the indomitable sheriff, who was to have been applauded to the skies for his unflagging patriotism. This scheme had cost Jones an immense amount of mental labor. It was the contrivance of several months' deep and anxious consideration and study. Sleeping or waking, it was doubtless uppermost in his thoughts. What, then, was his disappointment and mortification at its entire frustration. Just as he was raising the cup of triumph to his lips, it was suddenly dashed from his hand. Upon perceiving the completeness of his discomfiture, he quietly took his seat in his buggy, and sullenly drove from Topeka, doubtless muttering curses between his teeth against the legislature, the marshal, governor, and sundry other individuals who had aided in defeating the accomplishment of one of his dearest wishes. Upon reaching Lecompton, he retired immediately to his home, and was never afterward heard to refer to his futile visit to Topeka.

The prisoners were conveyed to Tecumseh, and retained until the following day, when they received a hearing before Judge Cato, who had been instrumental in the arrest, but who liberated them on bail, in their own recognisance in the sum of five hundred dollars each. They were, of course, never brought to trial, the district attorney entering *nolle prosequies* in theirs, as in the case of all other of the free-state treason prisoners. Thus ended in a farce, a performance which the principal actors had intended for a serious and fearful tragedy.

7*th.*—A letter was received by Governor Geary from his excellency, Governor Fletcher, of Vermont, giving information that the legislature of that state had appropriated the sum of twenty thousand dollars for the relief of the suffering poor of Kansas, "upon full and satisfactory proof of the necessity of their condition," and asking information in regard to the facts. In reply to which the following letter was dispatched to Gov. Fletcher:—

"Executive Department, K. T.,
"Lecompton, Jan. 7, 1857.

"HIS EXCELLENCY, GOV. FLETCHER,
"Burlington, Vermont.

"Dear Sir: Your favor of the 22d ultimo, with a copy of an act of the legislature of Vermont, entitled 'An act for the relief of the poor of Kansas,' has been received. I am happy to inform you that I am not aware of the existence of any condition of things in this territory that will render necessary the employment of the money you have so liberally placed at our disposal.

"There is doubtless some suffering within the limits of Kansas consequent upon past disturbances and the present extremely cold weather; but probably no more than exists in other territories or in either of the states of the Union.

"No man who is able and willing to work need be destitute of the means of a comfortable livelihood in Kansas. Laborers and mechanics are in demand, and cannot be obtained, at wages ranging from $1.50 to $3.00 per day. Indeed so far as my observation has extended, the deserving and industrious portions of our population are in the full enjoyment of more than ordinary contentment and prosperity.

"Should any facts hereafter come to my notice such as to require the aid you have so kindly offered, I will assuredly make the application you suggest.

"With assurances of the highest regard, I have the honor to subscribe myself,

"Your obedient servant,

"JNO. W. GEARY."

At the time these letters were passing there were, perhaps, two hundred men in the town of Lecompton, at least one-half of whom were out of employment, though they were evidently supplied with funds from some invisible source to supply their immediate wants and support them in idleness. Laboring men and mechanics were greatly needed, but the idlers could not be induced to work. It was much easier to lounge about the groggeries and denounce abolitionists, than make a livelihood by honest industry. Fire-wood brought readily from three to four dollars per cord, and the citizens found it difficult to obtain a supply, though the river was frozen over, and any quantity of good fuel lay upon the opposite shore a few hundred yards distant, that could have been brought over by hand on rude sledges, at which easy employment at least three dollars a day could have been earned; but it was quite apparent that the most of the people about Lecompton had not come there to work. It would, perhaps, have been a degradation for the most destitute of those gentlemen, who had come to the territory to advocate the cause of negro slavery, to resort themselves to manual labor. The settlers in the country, though many of them had suffered from the past disturbances, were generally comfortable. During Governor Geary's tour of observation, he travelled many miles, and visited hundreds of families; but found very few cases of absolute distress.

CHAPTER XXXV.

Meeting of the Territorial Legislative Assembly at Lecompton.

THE Legislative Assembly met at Lecompton on the 12th of January, and organized by appointing Rev. Thomas Johnson, of Shawnee Mission, president of the Council, and W. G. Matthias, of Leavenworth City, speaker of the House of Representatives. A committee was appointed to wait upon the governor and apprise him of the organization, which was done on the following morning, when his message was sent in and read before both houses. Orders were given to the proprietors of the *Lecompton Union*, who were elected printers for the territory, to print six thousand five hundred copies of this document; but as they had neither paper nor presses to supply the order, the copies were never printed. The government, however, which is sometimes exceedingly obliging, will pay the bill, notwithstanding the omission on the part of the public printers to supply the work. It was better, perhaps, that the circulation of the message should have been restricted to the narrowest possible limits. The members of the legislature, or rather the great majority of them, looked upon it as an insult and outrage upon all pro-slavery men, inasmuch as the governor had not endorsed the actions of the "territorial militia," or the "law and order" army, and denounced the free-state men who had taken up arms to protect the persons of their women, their property and themselves from the violence of a legalized horde of ruffians. The animadversions against his excellency on this score, were sufficiently eloquent and fierce to satisfy the most exacting of his opponents.

One of the first proceedings of this legislative body, was to hold a secret meeting, in which it was resolved, that should any act pass both houses by a majority of votes, and then be vetoed by the governor, there should be a mutual agreement to disregard the veto, and pass the act by a two-third vote, which was strictly adhered to in all their subsequent proceedings. At the previous session they had stripped the governor of every vestige of power or authority save that specially named in the organic act, and this act they caused to be so printed as to take from him the pardoning power. They now concluded to deprive him of the only privilege remaining, which was that of vetoing offensive, obnoxious and unjust enactments. The governor was apprised of this fact, but scarcely believing so infamous a measure possible, attempted to arrest several bills, by offering the most tangible objections, which only served to excite the merriment of members and call down upon his own head the most violent anathemas. Indeed, the greater portion of the time of the session was taken up, with long speeches denunciatory of his excellency for his supposed impartiality, or rather his unwillingness to "go in" heart and soul, with all his ability, influence and power, to advance the interests of the pro-slavery cause. So entirely were they devoted to this peculiar object, that it was a common expression among the idlers of the town, when no better employment was on hand, to say to each other, "Come, let us go over to the House to hear Jenkins," or Brown, or Anderson, or O'Driscoll, or Johnson, or some other prominent orator, "abuse the governor." For hours at the time, would admiring audiences stand listening to these gentlemen's vituperations. It is a great loss to the world that their speeches were not phonographed and preserved for future generations. Never again will a similar amount of that peculiar style of eloquence emanate from any legislative body. So determined were some of these gentlemen to denounce the governor, agreeably to outside instructions, that they entered upon the work with a most commendable spirit and energy whenever they could obtain the floor, or stand upon their feet, which was not always the case. On one occasion, Jenkins, who was the most violent of the violent, had advocated a certain measure with great vehemence, and supposing it would meet the governor's disapprobation, caused a vote to be passed, asking information of his excellency on the subject. It so happened that the governor agreed precisely with Mr. Jenkins, and sent in a brief message to that effect. Jenkins, however, despised listening to anything from the governor's pen, and therefore crammed his fingers into his ears until the message was read, when he suddenly sprang to his feet, and for the hundredth time repeated his tirades of abuse. He was proceeding in one of his most eloquent strains. He stamped violently upon the floor—struck the table with his fist, knocking over the inkstand, and pronounced his anathemas with a voice that fairly shook the roof overhead—when he was arrested by a loud and universal burst of laughter. He stopped and looked around as though enquiring the cause of such an unusual interruption, when the speaker informed him that he had mistaken the tenor of the governor's message, his excellency having agreed with his views in every particular. "Then," said the orator, striking the table another violent blow, "had I known that I would have taken the other side of the question!" Nothing could have been more amusing than to witness the efforts of some of these orators to preserve their equilibrium whilst delivering themselves of their wisdom. The desperate struggle to stand erect—the hiccups which interspersed the most eloquent sentences—the rocking to and fro, and grasping at the backs of chairs or tops of tables, and most of all, the palpable desire to appear sober, all conspired to furnish a most admirable study for a dramatic artist.

There were some good men in this assembly; but their number was so small, that their influence was of little avail, and they were always in the minority, when any measure was proposed to which they could not give their sanction. Some of these, in the early part of the session, retired to their homes in disgust at their associates, whilst others remained, hoping even against hope, that they might be enabled to circumvent some evil machination. But the majority of the members were of the most rabid of the pro-slavery fire-eaters, who had but one idea, and that the introduction of slavery as a permanent institution into Kansas. And it is quite probable, judging from their uniform behavior, they never for a moment supposed that any means to accomplish that end, however desperate or unlawful, was deserving of reprehension. They were mostly men of limited education, rude manners, violent character, intemperate habits, and desperate fortune. There were those, however, always at their elbows, guiding, directing and controlling their legislative conduct, sufficiently cunning, shrewd and intelligent to mould them to their will, and use them as tools to effect their purposes.

Lecompton was at that time, and now is, a sort of moral plague spot in Kansas, and as such is shunned by all good people coming into the territory. When it was first laid out for a town, Sheriff Jones declared that no free-state man should own property in it, and so infamous has been its character ever since, that none will purchase there who can succeed anywhere else. Hence, when the legislature met, there were no suitable accommodations for the visitors. The weather was severely cold, the thermometer being some nights thirty degrees below zero. Beds and bedding, as well as shelter, were scarce, and wholesome provisions could not be obtained in sufficient quantities to supply the demand at any price. There was consequently much suffering, and several deaths occurred from exposure.

A few of the most respectable members of the legislature obtained boarding at several private houses, some of them being compelled to sleep at night on the floors of the legislative halls. The great portion of the body boarded and lodged at what was called "Jack Thompson's Restaurant," the proprietor being himself a member of the House of Representatives. This was a one-story frame building, the ground floor, which was the only one, being divided into three rooms, in the principal of which the bar was kept, whilst in the others faro, draw-poker, and other gambling games were played every night and on every Sunday, for the entertainment, if not the profit, of the law-makers. There was an extensive cellar underneath this slight building, where the cooking and eating were done. The dining tables furnished lodging room for a number of boarders, who spread their blankets upon them when the dishes were removed. The bar-room also provided a number with lodging. This was generally crowded, and immense quantities were here drunk of a most infamous compound of vile drugs, the qualities and character of which were only known to the manufacturer, but which he could safely have warranted to destroy the constitution of the strongest man, in a very limited time, and which "Jack Thompson" and his bar-keepers sold for whiskey at a dime a glass. This stuff seemed to produce a very peculiar effect, and to its influence must be ascribed very many of the ferocious and insane deeds which have blackened the history of Kansas. Late at night this bar-room was covered with a few inches of saw-dust, upon which, as the outsiders withdrew, boarders, mostly legislators, would stretch themselves out and fall asleep. One night a stage driver happened to drink some of that whiskey, which, if it was not sure to kill, was certain to make drunk, and he rolled over on the floor among the members. In the morning, whilst engaged in shaking off the saw-dust, he was accosted by one of the thousand borers for bank charters, or railroad bills, or town company corporations, to obtain his influence to get an act through the legislature. This threw the stage-driver into a violent passion, and the borer came near getting a flogging. "It is bad enough," said the stage-driver, "to get drunk, and make a fool of myself, and get into bad company, but no man shall insult me by mistaking me for a member of the Kansas Legislature."

The principal business of the assembly, after that of abusing the governor, was to incorporate an almost endless number of roads, railroad, ferry, bridge, and town associations. The latter were so numerous as to elicit the suggestion from a wag, that it was highly important to offer a bill withholding a few acres of the land in the territory for farming purposes. In passing these acts, the legislature exhibited a forethought for themselves that would have done credit to the "unjust steward" so highly commended for his prudence in one of the gospel parables. The charters were closely examined, and wherever it seemed probable that the scheme would prove profitable to the corporators, the names of those contained in the bills, especially if suspected of free-soilism, were erased, and an equal number or more of those of the members, were substituted, in which form the bill would become a law. A gentleman from Missouri, with the strongest pro-slavery proclivities, who had business transactions with the legislature, remarked:—"This is the most corrupt body that ever assembled in the world. Had the Saviour came down from heaven and offered a bill that would have saved the country from irretrievable ruin, unless it could have been made clear that it would be conducive to their own immediate personal interests it would have been defeated; whilst on the other hand, they would, if liberally paid, push through the most obnoxious and infamous act, even were it presented by the very devil himself!"

CHAPTER XXXVI.

Act of the Legislative Assembly, to authorize courts and judges to admit to bail in all cases.—Veto message of the governor.—The bill passed.—Clarke and others bailed under the new law.

The first act of the Legislative Assembly was a direct attempt to recreate disturbances, by agitating anew the question of difficulty between Governor Geary and Judge Lecompte, growing out of the bailing by the latter, of the murderer of Buffum. This was the passage of a bill, intended as an endorsement of Lecompte's conduct, and disapproval of the governor's, and giving to any district judge authority to bail all persons charged with any and every crime, whether previously considered bailable or not. The following is a copy of this bill :—

"The District Court, or any judge thereof, in vacation, shall have power and authority to admit to bail, any prisoner on charge, or under indictment for any crime or offence, of any character whatever, whether such crime or offence shall have heretofore been bailable or not; such court or judge, on every such application for bail, exercising a sound discretion in the premises."

This bill was returned by the governor unsigned, with his objections, which are sufficiently important and interesting to be given to the reader:

" *To the Council and House of Representatives of Kansas Territory.*

"GENTLEMEN :—The Bill, 'To authorize Courts and Judges to admit to bail in certain cases,' has been carefully examined, and notwithstanding my earnest desire to agree with the legislature, I am compelled to return it without approval, for the following reasons :—

'The doctrine that the more certain the punishment of crime is made, the greater will be the restraints upon the evil passions of wicked men, has been established in all civilized communities, and approved by the wisdom and experience of every age of the world; and had we no other evidence of its truth, more than sufficient has been furnished in the disturbances and outrages which have so recently occurred in the Territory of Kansas; for no one can be insensible of the fact, that the impunity that has here been given to crime, has been the cause of many of the offences that have been committed. Had but a few of the early agitators, and defiants of law, been brought to punishment, the subsequent events which every good citizen deplores and condemns, would never have occurred.

"It is of the utmost importance to the safety of society that the laws should be rendered as stringent, and their execution as certain as possible; especially as regards the crime of wilful and deliberate murder. Such an offence should be guarded against with the utmost care. No door, whatever, should be opened for the escape of the criminal. Once in the hands of the proper authorities, he should there be secured until the ends of justice are effected. The man whose life has been forfeited to the law, will stop at no means within the range of human possibility to accomplish his escape; for 'what will a man not give in exchange for his life?'

"The act under consideration makes it comparatively easy for the most notorious criminal to escape the punishment his crimes have merited. Any judge of a district court is thereby allowed to set him at liberty on bail. The bill does not even establish the amount of bail required. This, as well as the propriety of bailing, is left to the discretion of the court or of the district judge. Were the bill passed expressly to tamper with and corrupt the judiciary, it could not have been more effectual. All human beings are fallible, and it is a sound principle to throw in their way to err, as few temptations as possible. No judge who has a proper regard for his own reputation, can desire the passage of a law which will render him liable to invidious imputations. If this bill becomes a law, appeals will be made to the district judge to bail every person charged with the crime of murder, and the strongest inducements will be offered to influence his action. Should he refuse to accede to the wishes of the individual accused, or his importunate friends, he will subject himself tc the charge of some unjust bias; while on the other hand, should he yield to such importunities he is almost certain of being charged with bribery and corruption; and violence towards himself might ensue in either case. The judge, therefore, would prefer to avoid the additional responsibility which this bill imposes.

"But apart from this, one tendency of the act is to corrupt the judiciary. It will not do to affirm that this is impossible. It has frequently been done to such an extent as to endanger the safety of communities, and even incite to anarchy, with all its fearful consequences. The intention of the laws have been so disregarded, that the people, in self-defence, have repudiated the courts, and in opposition to all legislative enactments, have taken upon themselves the administration of justice. Indeed, in every instance where 'lynch law' has been resorted to, the excuse given by the people has been founded upon the laxity of the courts, or the inefficiency or corruption of the judiciary.

"This want of confidence in the authorities regularly constituted for the execution of justice upon persons charged with heinous crimes, produced those terrible excitements in

California, consequent upon the organization of the memorable 'Vigilance Committee.'

"It is to be hoped that a similar condition of things may never transpire in Kansas, though it may well be anticipated, if murder is permitted by the courts to be perpetrated with impunity. The murmurings on this subject are even now loud and almost universal. Some of our best citizens have been stricken down by the hand of the assassin, whose blood has cried in vain upon the legal tribunals for justice. And although many have fallen victims to this atrocious crime, not one of its numerous perpetrators has yet suffered the just penalty of the law. The murderer, his hands still reeking with human gore, walks unmolested in our midst, laughing to scorn the laws which condemn him to an ignominious death.

"Let the law contemplated in this bill be adopted, and this evil, already sufficiently deplorable, will be rendered far worse. The slight restraints now held upon the vicious, will be almost entirely removed. No good citizen can venture in the streets or upon the highways, with a proper feeling of security. The personal safety of all who are well disposed, will be constantly endangered. The odious practice of bearing concealed weapons for self-defence will become general, and the most disastrous results will follow. Every man, conscious of the uncertainty of punishment by the courts, will take the law in his own hands, and the slayer of one individual will fall a victim to the retaliatory vengeance of another. Or should he be brought before a judge or court, and liberated upon bail, an offended people will arise in their majesty, and prevent his escape by the infliction of summary punishment.

"The fact that bail has been given, will have no tendency to prevent these results; for no one can have confidence in the security furnished by such bail as a deliberate murderer can obtain. The person who will step in between him and the execution of justice, must himself be destitute of those feelings and sentiments which will render him worthy the confidence of peace-loving citizens. Or even were it otherwise, and the murderer is substantially bailed by a wealthy relative or friend, the only object in the whole transaction is the criminal's escape; for any amount of property, under such circumstances, will be forfeited to preserve his life. But in the majority of cases the bail is entirely worthless, and its being admitted by a court or judge is equivalent to the murderer's discharge; for no one who is conscious of a conviction that will condemn him to death, will ever present himself for trial. If he has wealth, he can purchase sureties, and if he has not, he may obtain the aid of those who are worthless, or if possessed of the property to which they swear, may dispose of it at pleasure, and thus defraud the territory as well as justice. Bail-bonds, as now given, are of little value even in trivial cases; for when forfeited the amount is seldom collected. To make them of any avail, a lien should immediately be created on the lands of the persons acknowledging them, 'and the execution issued by virtue of a judgment thereon, may rightly command the taking and sale of the lands, of which defendant was seized at the time the recognisance was acknowledged.' Were this rule of law adopted, there would be some value in a bail-bond, and fewer persons would be found willing to execute it. But as the law now rests in this territory, a criminal may be bailed to-day upon what is apparently tangible security, and to-morrow, both himself and sureties dispose of all their property, and unmolested and quietly depart to another region, and thus the matter ends. In the majority of instances therefore, the taking of bail in criminal cases, only tends to defeat the ends of justice, and in every case of absolute premeditated murder, where the proof is clear, or sufficient to convict, is tantamount to an acquittal of the criminal.

"The fact that we have no sufficient prisons for the safe-keeping of the murderer, affords no argument for the passage of the bill. This want can soon be supplied, and it will be better far to commence that work at once, than to adopt a law which must remove the almost only restraint that now exists upon murderous inclinations and passions. There is no necessity for deliberate murderers to be set free, on bail or otherwise, for want of a prison to keep them in lengthy confinement. Frequent sessions of the courts, early trials, and speedy executions, will dispose of such cases, and give to the people confidence in the judiciary and the laws, and a sense of security of which they have so long been deprived.

"Remove or weaken any one of the safeguards we now possess against criminals and crime, and the peace we enjoy must measurably be shaken. Hence it becomes a subject of the utmost importance, not only to guard against such a result, but to adopt, if possible, laws which will strengthen the general confidence, by making the barriers to the escape of the criminal even more firm and impassable.

"Let it be established and universally known, that 'though hand join in hand, the guilty shall not go unpunished;' that the blood-stained murderer once in the power of the authorities, shall have no possibility or hope of escape; that he who wilfully and deliberately sheds the blood of his fellow-man shall surely suffer the penalty by which his life is forfeit, and our laws will be more respected; fewer crimes will be committed; and the community will repose in far greater security and peace.

"Jno. W. Geary.

"Lecompton, K. T., January 22d, 1857."

The bill, notwithstanding these substantial reasons for its rejection, was passed by an almost unanimous vote of both houses. On the following day, George W. Clarke, charged with the murder of Barber, Dr. J. H. Stringfellow, Captain William Martin, and other pro-slavery men, against whom unserved warrants had been in the hands of the marshal for several months, appeared voluntarily before Judge Cato, offered bail, and were discharged. The sureties in Clarke's case, were the ever-ready Sheriff Jones, and the probate-judge and United States Commissioner John P. Wood. This was the first action under the new bail law. Clarke, from that time, was daily within the bar of the house, instructing the members, until the adjournment, when he proceeded to Washington, and became an adviser of President Buchanan, the Cabinet and Robert J. Walker.

CHAPTER XXXVII.

Resolution of the legislature asking the governor's reasons for not commissioning Wm. T. Sherrard—Governor Geary's reply—Conduct of the legislators—Violence of Sherrard.

The next important legislative act was the adoption of a resolution, demanding of the governor his reasons for not having issued a commission to Wm. T. Sherrard, who had some time previous been appointed by the county tribunal, as sheriff of Douglas county, in place of Samuel J. Jones, who had resigned. The obvious design of this resolution was to inveigle the governor into a quarrel and embarrass him in the prosecution of his duties, and so it was avowed and generally understood.

It had so happened, that immediately after Sherrard had received his appointment, he called upon the governor, and somewhat insolently asked for his commission. The blanks being then in possession of the secretary of the territory, whose signature and seal were also necessary to complete the paper, and Mr. Woodson being absent from the city, the governor requested Sherrard to wait until his return, which would at the furthest be in two or three days. Soon after, Sherrard called again at the executive office, and on this occasion his conduct was so exceedingly offensive and insulting as to elicit from the governor the inquiry why he (Sherrard) should be so inimical to him. Such were his defiances and threats that even had the secretary been present, the commission would not then have been issued. Next Sherrard wrote and sent a note to the governor, informing him that if the commission was not received within a certain time, a mandamus would be obtained to compel him to render it.

In the meantime, the members of the county board, who had made the appointment, had severally visited the governor, requesting him to withhold the commission until they could have a regular meeting for the purpose of revoking the appointment, which had hastily been made at the instance of Sheriff Jones, and without a proper knowledge of the character of the applicant, who they were now convinced was utterly unfit for the office, in consequence of the violence of his disposition, his being almost daily engaged in street and tavern broils, and his threats to disturb the general peace as soon as the commission was obtained. Numerous petitions to the same effect were also received from respectable citizens of the county.

Whilst the subject was thus pending, Sherrard was proving his unfitness for the position he sought. by getting into serious difficulties with sundry persons. He boarded at the Virginia House, with a man named Locklane, at whom, while at the dining table, he threw a plate, and afterwards fired his pistol, the ball grazing Locklane's eyebrow, carrying a portion of it away. He then told Locklane to run, promising that he would not fire until he had gone ten paces. Not disposed to run, under such circumstances, Locklane stood still, with Sherrard's pistol pointed at him, for the space of nearly two hours, when he was relieved from his perilous situation by the interposition of other parties. Soon after Sherrard got into a fist fight with a man named Brooke, in which he was severely beaten, both his eyes having been blackened and shockingly swollen, and his face very much disfigured. In this condition he applied to each of the supreme judges for a mandamus to compel the governor to commission him as sheriff, but without success, the judges understanding the case too well to grant his wish, notwithstanding it was urged by Mr. David Johnson, of Leavenworth, a lawyer, and member of the legislature, whom Sherrard had employed in his behalf. He next sent General Maclean with a challenge to Dr. Brooke, the proprietor of the Lecompton Hotel, who, declining to meet Sherrard, the latter posted him in huge handbills as a liar, a scoundrel, and a coward.

Such was the state of affairs when the legislature met, to whom Sherrard preferred a complaint against the governor, and who passed and sent the following resolution to his excellency :—

"House of Representatives,
"January 19, 1857.

"*Resolved*, That His Excellency, the Governor of the Territory of Kansas, be respectfully requested to furnish the House with a statement of his reasons for not commissioning Wm. T. Sherrard as sheriff of Douglas county.

"R. C. Bishop,
"Chief Clerk."

Although this was a question with which the legislature clearly had no right whatever to interfere, rather than treat them with even seeming disrespect, the governor somewhat reluctantly furnished the following reply to their officious and insolent inquiry:—

"Executive Department, K. T.,
"Lecompton, Jan. 21, 1857.

"To the House of Representatives,
Kansas Territory.

Gentlemen: In reply to your resolution of the 19th inst., which was received late on the 20th, requesting me to furnish your body with a statement of my reasons for not commissioning William T. Sherrard, Esq., as Sheriff of Douglas county, I have the honor to state, that while I am disposed to accede to any reasonable request from the legislature, I regard that matter as a subject of inquiry only from the territorial courts.

"Prior to its announcement to me, the appointment of Mr. Sherrard was protested against by many good citizens of Lecompton and

Douglas county, as his habits and passions rendered him entirely unfit for the proper performance of the duties of that office.

"There was no intention, however, on my part, to withhold his commission; but in consequence of the absence of the secretary of the territory, it was delayed for several days, during which time I was informed by many respectable gentlemen, among whom were those of the county tribunal from which he received his appointment, that Mr. Sherrard had been engaged in several drunken broils, fighting and shooting at persons with pistols, and threatening others. I have since been informed that these facts are notorious to the citizens of the place, and can easily be substantiated by proof. Should the contrary be made clearly to appear, no one will rejoice more heartily than myself.

"But it is my desire to be distinctly understood that I will commission no one laboring under such charges as would impair, if not entirely destroy, his usefulness; or whose passions and habits would render him unfit for the proper discharge of his duties, or which might in any manner endanger the peace of the territory.

"I am instructed from the source whence I derive my appointment to pursue this course of policy. The true interests of the people of the territory require it, and it is sanctioned and approved by my own judgment.

"JNO. W. GEARY,
"Governor of Kansas Territory."

This communication was received in anything but a kindly spirit by the members of the House of Representatives. The very reasons assigned for not commissioning Sherrard, were to them sufficient reasons for his having been commissioned. They desired a man who could keep the community in a state of feverish excitement. Sherrard had declared that he would, in three weeks, renew the civil commotion. This was precisely what the legislature desired, and Sherrard was a man after their own heart. Hence the governor's reply to their resolution of inquiry was met with some of the most furious harangues that were ever heard. Jenkins foamed at the mouth. He was for hanging, quartering, burning, and utterly annihilating his excellency, body, soul, and all that belonged to him. Johnson spoke with difficulty. He had been enjoying himself with some friends; but still he had to say, that Sherrard was his client, and that Governor Geary was a d—d despot, assuming an arbitrary power from which the autocrat of Russia would have shrunk dismayed. Anderson thought the governor should be severely censured for sending such a discourteous message. And O. H. Brown—Brown walked up and down the floor, his hands thrust down into his breeches pocket, occasionally giving the unconscious boards a violent kick, as though they had been guilty of some grievous offence deserving chastisement, and then delivered himself of his most eloquent effort. "Governor Geary was a usurper, a monster, and a tyrant. He (Brown) had searched the records of ancient Greece and Rome. He had studied heathen mythology until it was familiar to his very finger ends. He had wondered at the atrocities of Nero and Caligula, but he had never seen nor heard nor read of anything so abominable and worthy of hearty condemnation and execration as this conduct of Governor Geary in withholding his commission for such reasons as he assigned, from Mr. Sherrard." This powerful effort of Brown was afterwards revised, corrected and improved, and published in the *Lecompton Union;* but as the proprietors found it difficulty to procure more paper than would suffice to print copies enough to supply the members of the Cabinet and other prominent pro-slavery men at Washington, and in the southern states, for whose especial instruction and edification the *Union* is published, a copy could not be obtained for transmission to these pages.

After these and other distinguished gentlemen had exhausted the English vocabulary of abusive epithets, well interlarded with Latin, French and Spanish maledictions, and sprinkled with specimens of the various Indian dialects, a resolution was almost unanimously passed appointing Sherrard to the office of sheriff of Douglas county, and, as such, legalizing all his acts, despite the petitions of citizens, the protest of the county board, or the refusal of the governor to commission. The Council failed to concur with this resolution of the House of Representatives, and it was, therefore, of no avail.

This refusal on the part of the Council excited the evil passions of Sherrard to a most terrible extent. He was like an untamed hyena, and ready to quarrel with and assail any one who in the slightest measure opposed his will. His threats against the governor were made wherever he went. Meeting Mr. John A. W. Jones, a member of the governor's household, and a remarkably peaceable man, of slight physical frame, and without arms with which to defend himself, Sherrard assailed and struck him, without the slightest shadow of provocation.

The next day, whilst sitting in one corner of a public saloon, between David Johnson, his counsellor, and Captain Martin, of the Kickapoo Rangers, both members of the Legislature, he saw the governor's private secretary on the opposite side of the room, and called him over, when he attempted to create a quarrel by attacking the official character of the governor. The secretary declined entering into the controversy, had turned and was about to leave, and notwithstanding he was unarmed and extremely feeble from a recent accident, Sherrard sprang to his feet and struck him upon the cheek, and seizing the handle of his pistol, dared him to resent the blow. This was southern chivalry—the courage of cowardice. The secretary told him that had he not known he was unarmed, the insult would not have been offered. There were a number of persons present, and Sherrard's friends, perceiving they were in the minority, forced him from the room. The news of this outrage soon spread through the town, and considerable excitement ensued. A Pennsylvanian, named McDonald, who had done good service in the Mexican war, hearing of the affair, went in search of and found Sherrard, and inquired of him what the disturbance meant. Sherrard immediately replied, somewhat boastingly, that he had struck the governor's private secretary.

"Then," said McDonald, fixing his keen eye upon him, and laying his hand upon his pistol, "you did a d——d cowardly act!"

The other quailed beneath the fiery glance, and coweringly sneaked into the door of the nearest groggery, followed to its threshold by a willing adversary who was in all respects his equal. Here he was among his associates, and was soon after heard to boast that he had struck two of the governor's household, and his next blow would be at the governor himself.

CHAPTER XXXVIII.

Sherrard's abettors—Attempt to assassinate Governor Geary—Action of the legislature—Conduct of Judge Cato—Public indignation meetings—Outrage at a Lecompton meeting, resulting in the shooting and death of Sherrard.

ALTHOUGH Sherrard possessed passions that were uncontrollable when once aroused, and was constantly committing acts of violence for which there could be no reasonable excuse, he was less reprehensible than certain prominent parties in Lecompton, who, having discovered his temper, used him simply as a cat's-paw to consummate some of their most infamous designs. Their cool and calculating brains conceived the deeds, which his irritable disposition could easily be provoked to perpetrate.

On the night of the assault upon the governor's secretary, there was a jollification in the office of the surveyor-general, and many were the surmises as to the final result of that affair. Sherrard was present, and so were Sheriff Jones, and A. W. Jones, of the *Lecompton Union*, and Surveyor Calhoun, his clerk Maclean, and Gen. Geo. W. Clarke. They had a merry time that night. The governor, they exultingly maintained, could not help but understand that these abuses of his subordinates were nothing more than intended insults to himself; and if repeated, he could not otherwise than attempt to resent them, and then his doom was sealed. So reasoned the conspirators; and as the room grew thick with clouds of smoke from the clay pipes, and the heads of the party still thicker with the frequent potations from the whiskey bottle, the unfortunate man who was to do their villanous work and become their victim was instigated to attempt the commission of a crime which, had it succeeded, would have involved the country in a bloody civil war.

On Monday morning, February 9th, accompanied by Dr. Gihon and Richard McAllister, Esq., the governor visited successively the Supreme Court, the Council, and the House of Representatives, all of which were in session. As they passed into the latter hall and took their seats within the bar among the members, Sherrard, who occupied a seat in one corner of the room, unseen by the governor, was observed to manifest a strange uneasiness of manner, and with a heavy scowl upon his countenance, and muttering some unintelligible words, he suddenly arose and quitted the apartment. The governor remained a half-hour or more, and then took his leave. As he was about to step from the main hall into the adjoining ante-room, Sherrard stood in the door, having gone off and procured an extra pistol to the one he usually wore, both of which, contrary to his custom, he had placed conveniently in a belt, buckled on the outside of all his clothing. In his breast he also carried a huge bowie-knife. Before the governor had closed the door, Sherrard accosted him with "You have treated me, sir, like a d——d scoundrel." The governor passed on without noticing the man, much less his opprobrious salutation. Mr. McAllister followed, and as they passed toward the outer door, his person interposed between that of Sherrard and the governor. Dr. Gihon was the last to leave the hall and enter the ante-room, when he saw Sherrard spitting after the governor, at the same time uttering oaths and threats of defiance, his right hand firmly grasping one of the pistols in his belt. Adjoining the ante-room was another small room, the door of which was partially opened, and there stood several ruffians who had been apprised of the intended assassination, and were ready to take their part in the bloody work. The governor and his friends were unarmed. Had he halted to speak to Sherrard, or turned upon him, or in any possible way given an excuse for the deed, he would have been shot down like a dog, and himself and companions riddled with balls; and the murderers only would have been left to tell the story and justify their infamous crime. To the presence of mind and cool courage of the governor, who was then in as great peril as he ever had been on the field of battle, does he owe his life. The ante-room is in the second story of the building, the stairs leading to the ground being on the outside, and as the governor descended, Sherrard stood upon the platform above, with pistol in hand, hesitating whether even yet to fire or not. He followed on, and did not abandon his purpose until the length of the building was traversed, when pronouncing an audible oath, he turned off and took a different direction. In a few moments after, he was closeted with his abettors and instigators in the office of the surveyor-general. It would be no difficult matter to prove that the extra pistol provided for this and a subsequent occasion was borrowed for the purpose by a prominent member of that establishment. The governor and his party proceeded directly to the executive office without naming this occurrence. Sherrard, on the other hand, stopped all he met, and boasted that he had endeavored, but without success, to provoke the governor to a quarrel, by spitting in his face.

Without any further information on the subject than was gained from Sherrard and his accomplices, the House of Representatives, upon whose floor the outrage and attempted assassination occurred, immediately took up the subject. A conservative member offered a resolution, mildly condemnatory of the conduct of the governor's assailant, in doing which he raised a most terrible storm. The resolution met with such violent opposition, and drew forth such vindictive denunciations against the governor, that the mover deemed it expedient to withdraw it. Joseph C. Anderson, a member from Missouri, maintained that the governor had no business in the halls of the legislature, and that he should confine himself to his executive office; whilst Johnson affirmed that he knew the assault was to be made, but did not think proper to interfere, as he did not consider it any of his business. The Council, however, passed a vote of censure against Sherrard. So evident was the disposition of many of the members of the lower house to encourage these scenes of outrage, that the governor's private secretary, whose business required him to visit the hall at least once every day, refused to perform that duty without being allowed to carry weapons, contrary to former instructions, and having the attendance of an armed United States soldier.

The governor summoned Judge Cato to his office to consult him in regard to Sherrard's conduct; but the judge seemed to think the matter of too little importance to receive any serious attention, as such outrages were beyond the pale of the law, there being no statute by which they could be punished. Other counsels prevailed at the time, and an affidavit was made out, setting forth the assaults made by Sherrard on several different persons, upon which a warrant was drawn for the purpose of arresting the offender and putting him under bonds to keep the peace. This warrant was unserved for two days, during which time, Sherrard, as usual, occupied an almost constant place in the House of Representatives. A messenger was at length sent to the judge, requesting him to have the warrant executed at once, who found Cato within the bar of the house, together with Sherrard and S. J. Jones, who, notwithstanding his pretended resignation, has always continued to exercise the functions of his office. Cato said the marshal was absent, and the writ could not therefore be served. This was clearly the duty of Sheriff Jones, then in the company of the accused and the judge. Discovering his entire indisposition to have any legal action in the matter, the governor obtained and destroyed the warrant, and took no further notice of the subject.

Not so the people. An intense excitement pervaded all peaceable classes. The prophecies and threats of the assassination of the governor, which had of late been freely made and treated with ridicule, had begun to assume a somewhat serious aspect. It was known on every hand that Sherrard, in this whole affair, was but the tool of others. Of this, there was no longer room for doubt. Citizens from different neighborhoods, irrespective of party, thronged the executive office to offer their services. Indignation meetings were held in various sections of the country, and resolutions condemning the recent assault were passed with great unanimity and sent to the governor. Of these the following is a specimen of many that were received:—

"In view of the late gross insult offered to the Governor of the Territory, and in view of the action taken by the House of Representatives virtually approving the deed, and in view of the general course and policy of the Legislature in opposing the measures recommended by Governor Geary:

"We, the citizens of Big Springs, in a public meeting called for the purpose, and held on the night of February 11th, do most heartily

"*Resolve:* That we regard the late insult upon the person of the governor, its endorsement by the House, and the continued indignities heaped upon him and his officials by the Legislature, as well as by certain individuals, as most gross and ruffianly, and worthy of the denunciation of every honorable and high-minded citizen in the territory. And we do further

"*Resolve,* That Governor Geary, in his general course of policy, has our hearty approval; and in carrying out the tone and spirit of his late message, he will have our earnest support and co-operation.

"*Resolved,* also, That we denounce the present Legislature as insurrectionary, and its spirit detrimental to the true interests of Kansas; not by any means overlooking some good men associated with that body, who labor hard to effect a beneficent legislation. These men have our gratitude; while we regard the majority as false to the true interests of the country, false to the Union, and false to the Governor, whom it is their duty to support and aid in the settlement of the difficulties of the territory. And

"*Resolved*, finally, That we tender to Governor Geary our sympathies as well as our support and co-operation, and pledge him, to the extent of our power, all the assistance in this emergency that he may ask of us, feeling very confident that the honest heart and powerful arm of every freeman in Kansas will be ready at once to respond most cheerfully to these our sentiments."

Indeed, so exasperated were very many well-disposed citizens, that had it not been for the opposition of the governor to their wishes and intentions, summary punishment would have been inflicted upon Sherrard, the *Lecompton Union* office would have been tumbled into the Kansas River, and the Legislative Assembly hastily expelled from the town. There were men ready and anxious to do this work; but the executive, learning their intentions, took proper measures to prevent its accomplishment.

A call was published for a meeting of the citizens of Lecompton, and vicinity, to be held on Saturday afternoon, the 14th of February, to publicly express their views regarding the recent outrage. Sherrard and his friends (the most prominent among them being Sheriff Jones, Bennett, of the *Union*, Maclean and Clarke) threatened to break this meeting up with violence, and prepared themselves accordingly. Just about the time it was assembling, it was announced that General Wm. P. Richardson, formerly commander of the militia, and a member of the Council, had died, and the meeting was consequently adjourned until the following Wednesday, the 18th, at two o'clock.

This announcement created considerable commotion, and the parties above-named declared in the streets and grog-shops, with many profane oaths that a respectable compositor would not wish to put in type, even should they be presented in this manuscript, that no such meeting should be held in Lecompton. Still the meeting was held. Before the hour specified, numbers of persons came pouring in from the surrounding country; and it was soon discovered that Brooke's Hotel, where the assembly was to have met, was too small to accommodate half the persons present, and it was therefore adjourned to Capitol Hill.

Just before the time appointed for organization arrived, those who had threatened to disperse the meeting by violence, discovered that they were so largely in the minority that the undertaking was to be attended with far more difficulty and danger than they had imagined possible. Yet, ashamed to shrink from the position they had assumed, they were somewhat at their wits' end. In their extremity, they sought Judge Cato, who, with a man named Boling, formerly a member of Captain Emory's company at Leavenworth, was deputed to call on the governor, to induce him to interpose his power to prevent the citizens from assembling.

Having listened to Judge Cato's representation that certain parties had determined to create a breach of the peace, should the meeting be held, and that bloodshed would probably be the result, the governor inquired of the judge, who were the parties that were threatening to deny the people by violence and bloodshed the right peaceably to assemble and express their opinions? "If," asked his excellency, "you know of persons thus contemplating a breach of the peace, is it not your duty to have legal process issued against them, and proper measures thus taken to prevent the consummation of their evil designs? So far as I am concerned," continued he, "I have no right whatever to step in between the people and the exercise of their constitutional privilege to meet together peacefully, to express their opinions upon what they consider subjects of public interest. I know not the objects of this meeting. The call is for citizens without distinction of party, to assemble for the purpose of giving their views concerning the recent outrage upon the governor and the conduct of his administration. It would ill become me to interfere with such a meeting. The object may be to condemn my own course of action. Shall I assume the part of a tyrant, and, in violation of my oath of office, and my sense of right and justice, say to these people, you shall not assemble for such a purpose? No, gentlemen; the act would no sooner be accomplished than *you* would be among the first to assail me for an assumption of arbitrary power, and use my unlawful procedure as a pretext to do me injury."

Cato hung his head with shame, acknowledged the truth of

the governor's positions, and took his leave, remarking, "I never before felt so much like a fool!"

The meeting assembled at two o'clock. Nearly four hundred persons were in attendance, composed of all classes of the community, and was organized by the appointment of Owen C. Steward, Mayor of Lecompton, a pro-slavery man, as chairman. A committee of five was then appointed to draft resolutions expressive of the sense of the meeting, who having retired, Captain L. J. Hampton, also pro-slavery, made a very mild and sensible address, which was received with universal approbation. Having concluded, R. P. Bennett, junior editor of the *Union*, obtained the stand. He had, in order to screw up his courage to the sticking point, poured down such liberal quantities of Thompson's vitriolic whiskey, that it required some considerable effort to keep his feet, for, in the language of the Psalmist, "he reeled to and fro, and staggered like a drunken man!" Bennett's speech was a gem. It was well known by all present that his object was to create a disturbance, and it was therefore resolved to pay no serious attention to anything he should say or do, as he was considered a mere boyish tool, and too insignificant of himself to merit especial notice. Hence he was permitted to amuse the assembly whilst waiting for the return of the committee.

"I tell you," said Bennett, "this meetin' is not a meetin' of gen'lemen—(hic). It aint the law 'd order party—(hic)—that's sure."

His tongue was as thick as his brain was addled, and his words were chopped off very often in the middle.

"I say—I tell yer—(hic)—this meetin's the rag—(hic)—the rag-tail and the bob-tail—(hic)—of the ab'lishonists—that's what I—(hic)—what I tell yer, and by G—d, I know it!"

As Bennett halted for breath, the boys cried out, "Go it, Bennett; that's the way to talk!" "You're one of the orators—you are!" "Have a little more whiskey, Bennett!" "Why don't you pitch into the governor?"

"I tell yer," continued the speaker, "Sherrard is—(hic)—so he is, by G—d, the soul of—(hic)—chiv'l'ry, and it's a pity he did'nt—(hic)—yes it is—for d—n Governor Geary—(hic)—. Them's my sentiments, and I don't kere a d—n who knows it!"

Whilst the speaker was proceeding in this strain, a majority of the committee announced that they were ready to report.

The minority had not agreed with them, because their resolutions did not directly denounce the violent conduct of Sherrard and his abettors, and they were still engaged in preparing resolutions for that purpose. The report of the majority was then read, as follows:

"BELIEVING, with the framers of the Constitution of our country, in 'the freedom of speech and the right of the people peaceably to assemble' and express their opinions upon all subjects of interest to themselves,

"We, the citizens of Lecompton and vicinity, without distinction of party, in view of the recent personal assault upon our worthy executive, for an act done in his official capacity, and fully justified by all the circumstances, and necessary to preserve the peace of the territory and the rights of the people, in public meeting assembled, do hereby

"*Resolve:* That we express our unqualified approbation of Governor Geary's official action; that to his impartial and vigorous administration we are pleased to attribute the present peace and prosperity of the territory, and that we believe he has not only saved us from unfortunate and destructive domestic feuds, but has also preserved the Union from a bloody civil war.

"*Resolved*, That we cordially adopt, and will cheerfully maintain, the sterling principles proclaimed by Governor Geary's message to the legislature, and that the following platform, extracted therefrom, is so admirably adapted to the present condition of Kansas, that we will maintain it at all hazards with our lives and property:—

"'Equal and exact justice' to all men, of whatever political or religious persuasion; peace, comity and friendship with neighboring states and territories, with a sacred regard for state rights, and reverential respect for the integrity and perpetuity of the Union; a reverence for the Federal Constitution as the concentrated wisdom of the fathers of the republic, and the very ark of our political safety; the cultivation of a pure and energetic nationality, and the development of an excellent and intensely vital patriotism; a jealous regard for the elective franchise, and the entire security and sanctity of the ballot-box; a firm determination to adhere to the doctrines of self-government and popular sovereignty as guaranteed by the Organic Law; unqualified submission to the will of the majority; the election of all officers by the people themselves; the supremacy of the civil over the military power; strict economy in the public expenditures, with a rigid accountability of all public officers; the preservation of the public faith, and a currency based upon, and equal to, gold and silver; free and safe immigration from every quarter of the country; the cultivation of a proper territorial pride, with a firm determination to submit to no invasion of our sovereignty; the fostering care of agriculture, manufactures, mechanic arts, and all works of internal improvement; the liberal and free education of all the children of the territory; entire religious freedom; a free press, free speech, and the peaceable right to assemble and discuss all questions of public interest; trial by jurors impartially selected; the sanctity of the Habeas Corpus; the repeal of all laws inconsistent with the Constitution of the United States and the Organic Act, and the steady administration of the government so as best to secure the general welfare.'

"*Resolved*, That we hereby tender Governor Geary, the people's friend, our earnest sympathy in the discharge of his responsible duties, and we pledge him the support of all the actual bona fide settlers of Kansas, without distinction of party, so long as he shall continue to administer the government upon the principles above declared.

JAS. H. LEGATE,
JAS. G. BAILEY,
W. ESLEY GARRETT."

No sooner were these resolutions read, than Sherrard sprang upon a pile of boards, and in a loud voice exclaimed:

"Any man who will dare to endorse these resolutions, is a liar, a scoundrel, and a coward!"

His manner was highly excited. He wore a large bowie-knife and two six-shooters in his belt, one of which had been borrowed by Maclean, for Sherrard's use, of an Englishman, also employed in the surveyor-general's office. A Mr. Sheppard, living near Lecompton, and who stood in the midst of the crowd, quietly remarked:

"I endorse them, and am neither a liar, a scoundrel, nor a coward!"

Whereupon Sherrard drew a revolver, and fired all the loads as rapidly as he could pull the trigger, aiming at Sheppard, though endangering the lives of others. Three balls took effect on Sheppard, and a fourth slightly wounded another person. As soon as Sherrard commenced firing, Sheppard pulled off his gloves, and attempted to return the shots; but his caps being wet, burst without discharging the loads; and seeing that Sherrard was about to draw his other pistol, he clubbed his revolver, rushed toward Sherrard and struck at him with the butt, Sherrard not having an opportunity to fire, returning his blows in a similar manner. They were separated, and Sheppard was removed, severely, and it was then supposed, mortally wounded. Whilst Sherrard was firing, some dozen or more shots were fired by other parties, none of which seem to have taken effect.

Shakspeare relieved the heaviness of his tragedies by the introduction of comic scenes; and this tragedy in real life was not without its laughable incidents. Bennett, who was one of the chief instigators of the mischief, and the loudest of all who boasted to break up the meeting, no sooner heard a pistol fired, than he was galvanized from a death of drunkenness to a life of sobriety. There are numerous instances on record where men have died of fright, but none where fear has brought the dead to life again. Bennett did not stop to see the effect of the firing; but, upon the principle of "self-preservation," he immediately took to his heels; and never did a pedestrian make better time. His speed was that of a greyhound; his coat-tail standing out behind, scarcely able to keep up with the wearer; and his path was as straight as the flight of an arrow; nor did he stop to take breath, as his workmen averred, until he had safely ensconsed himself behind an iron press, in his printing office, at the extreme end of the town. He did not make his appearance again until a few days afterwards he issued a circular for foreign use, which was so grossly false in all its statements, that its circulation was suppressed among the people who were actually cognisant of the facts. A company of Mississippians, who were quartered near by, also ran away, to procure their rifles, as they said, but very prudently neglected to return to the scene of disturbance.

Another amusing circumstance occurred during these serious disturbances. An old man, over seventy years of age, named Thomas W. Porterfield, was among the crowd. He was one of the prisoners taken at Hickory Point, but had been discharged. Seeing Sheriff Jones with a pistol in his hand, old Porterfield deliberately took off his spectacles, and pulling out his pocket handkerchief, wiped them carefully and again adjusted them. He then drew a navy revolver, and having examined the caps, placed the barrel upon his left arm, and took precise aim at Sheriff Jones, waiting for him to give the first shot. As the sheriff moved about, the old man steadily eyed him, keeping his pistol all the time properly aimed. Notwithstanding his advanced age, Porterfield is said to be a dead shot, and it is probable that Sheriff Jones was never in so great danger of being hurried into eternity as at that moment. Had he fired his pistol, a bullet from that of the old man would have sent him to his last account.

No sooner was Sheppard taken off than Sherrard seized his other pistol and advanced, with finger on the trigger, toward John A. W. Jones, the young man whom he had assaulted a few days before, when Jones, perceiving his danger, also drew. Several shots were then simultaneously fired, and Sherrard fell, mortally wounded. One ball had struck him in the forehead, penetrating the brain, and another had grazed his side. Who fired the fatal shot, it would be impossible to determine with certainty, though Jones was accused by the friends of Sherrard, and immediately secured by Sheriff Jones, who had taken an active part in the disturbance, who went there with that avowed purpose, accompanied by Sherrard, and who is alleged to have fired his pistol. A hue and cry was raised to hang young Jones; but his friends were too numerous, and an attempt to have done so would have been attended with rather serious consequences.

The fall of Sherrard put an end to the riot. The rioters had lost their leader, and there was no one left among them sufficiently bold and desperate to take his place; and to this fact may be attributed the defeat of a well-contrived scheme to again involve the entire community in a destructive strife. This matter had long been in agitation, and Sherrard was the chosen instrument to accomplish the mischievous purpose. His fall put an end to the plot, and saved many a valuable life. He died early on the following Saturday morning, and his remains were removed to Winchester, Va., the residence of his father, who is reputed a highly respectable gentleman. His son, naturally of uncontrollable temper, unfortunately fell into bad hands, and was the victim of evil advisers, who, after his death, were among the first to screen themselves from censure by accusing him of insane impetuosity.

Deputy-Marshal Samuel Cramer busied himself running among the groggeries, vaporing that he intended to shoot the young *assassin* Jones, at sight; and five hundred dollars reward was offered by other parties to any person who should kill him. But neither Cramer nor any other person in Lecompton was willing to hazard so dangerous an undertaking. Jones was truly in the hands of his enemies; but he was surrounded by friends sufficiently numerous to guard him against personal harm. He appeared before Judge Cato, for a hearing on the charge of shooting Sherrard, who pronounced a decision against him in insulting terms, before the first witness had spoken a hundred words. Jones, perceiving that justice in Lecompton was blind, and that his life there was in jeopardy, entered bail in the sum of five thousand dollars, crossed the river, procured a guide and a mule, passed up through the northern portion of the territory into Nebraska, and safely reached his home in Pennsylvania. In the mean time, a party, supposing he would take the river route, proceeded to Kansas City, to intercept, seize and massacre him; but, being foiled in not finding their intended victim, returned with no little chagrin to Lecompton.

CHAPTER XXXIX.

How the pro-slavery leaders in Lecompton held large and enthusiastic town meetings—Incendiary meeting at Lecompton—Calhoun's speech and sentiments—The Kansas laws not created to punish pro-slavery criminals.

Two or three evenings after the occurrences just related, Maclean, Bennett, and several others, met together in the house of Sheriff Jones, and concocted a series of resolutions, inflammatory in their character, and immensely laudatory of Sherrard, which were paraded before the public as having been adopted at a large and respectable meeting of the citizens of Lecompton.

A similar meeting was held at Kansas City, by Cramer, Anderson, Crowder, and two or three others, who accompanied the body of Sherrard to that place, the proceedings of which, being almost a copy of those published at Lecompton, were inserted in the Kansas City newspaper, as having taken place at a large meeting of the citizens, not over a half-dozen of whom were present, and they only from idle curiosity. These meetings, or pretended meetings, were intended to create an excitement among pro-slavery people against Governor Geary, and to induce southern men who did not understand the *modus operandi*, to furnish funds for the support of certain interested parties, whose advocacy of slavery was simply a matter of personal interest. They, however, entirely failed of the desired effect, and as soon as it was discovered that no capital could be made out of his death, Mr. Sherrard's body was conveyed to his home, and his pretended friends ascertained that he had always been exceedingly rash and imprudent.

This plan of holding meetings was a favorite manœuvre of the little clique of pro-slavery agitators at the capital. They numbered not over a dozen, in all. Whenever they had any mischievous object to accomplish, or desired to produce an impression in favor of their cause at Washington or in the south, or when they were in need of contributions of money, they would hold a meeting, generally in the office of the surveyor-general, who was the commander-in-chief of these little innocent political schemes and operations. General Clarke was always an active participant. Sheriff Jones's presence was indispensable. Judge Cato belonged to the coterie, though his name, for prudential reasons, did not often appear. Maclean furnished the liquor and tobacco, and did the small work. Bennett and Jones, of the *Union*, filled up important gaps. This brilliant party having got together, pipes and whiskey were supplied, and the affairs of the nation solemnly discussed. The "impartial policy" of Governor Geary was a general subject for denunciation. The magnificence of the slavery cause was the grand matter for consideration—the means to rid the country of the abolitionists, the principal object of the deliberations. The best method of obtaining liberal supplies from the south, was usually discussed. These meetings wound up, after the production of a grandiloquent preamble and flaming resolutions, which graced the columns of the next issue of the *Lecompton Union*, with the announcement that at a LARGE MEETING OF THE CITIZENS OF LECOMPTON AND DOUGLAS COUNTY, HELD ON SUCH AN EVENING, *the following resolutions were unanimously adopted with great enthusiasm. Gen'ls Calhoun and Clarke addressed the meeting with their usual eloquence and power*, &c., &c.; and yet, notwithstanding all this flourish of trumpets and beating of drums, the citizens of Lecompton were as innocent of the existence of any such meetings, until their proceedings were thus published, as were the inhabitants of Greenland or the south pole.

But there was one meeting held at Lecompton, of which the citizens *were* cognisant. It was called at the instance of General Calhoun, and for the express purpose of denouncing Governor Geary. The occasion was the re-arrest of the murderer Hays. The friends of the governor, though a hundred fold more numerous than the agitators, did not go to this meeting with knives, pistols and guns, to break it up. Nay, the most respectable portion of the citizens stayed away, refusing to give it the sanction of their presence. Judge Cato did not even call upon the governor with the information that an incendiary gathering was to take place, and urge the interposition of his authority to prevent it. No! this was a meeting to denounce, not approve, the policy and action of his excellency; and hence it was right, lawful, just and proper that it should be held, and he would have been a despot of the vilest sort, had he attempted in any way to interfere. Some impetuous friends of the governor, indignant at the outrages that were being committed, under the pretence of "law and order," did, it is true, call upon him and solicit permission to throw the *Lecompton Union* into the river, and drive Calhoun and his band of conspirators from the town; but they were severely rebuked, and commanded to preserve the peace.

The meeting was held at Brooke's Hotel. The fire-eaters were there in their glory. The assembly consisted of a dozen or more of these and the attachés of the surveyor-general's office. Calhoun was the spokesman of the day, and was in a happy vein. His sentiments were plainly told. There was no attempt at disguise. The "*impartial*" policy of the governor was denounced in unmeasured terms. It was never intended that free-state and pro-slavery men should be placed upon an equality in Kansas. The laws of the legislative assembly were not for the punishment of the pro-slavery party. The governor had made a mistake in supposing that there was an act upon the statute-book that made it criminal for one of that party to rob a free-state man of his horse, or shoot him down in cold blood, if he refused freely to give it up upon demand. Hays had committed no offence in killing Buffum; Lecompte was deserving of their gratitude in setting him free; and Geary of eternal condemnation in persisting in punishing him, and charging other pro-slavery men, who had simply taken the goods and lives of abolitionists, with crime. Such was the tenor of the surveyor-general's remarks; such the infamous doctrines which he boldly and unblushingly advocated.

Should any doubt the truth of this, they have only to read the following report of this very speech, published in the *Lecompton Union* of November 20, 1856. This paper is under the immediate control of Calhoun and his associates. Nothing finds a place in its columns that does not meet his sanction and approbation. Such of its articles as are not written by the chiefs of his department, receive at least their supervision. This report, therefore, if not from the pen of Calhoun himself, was from one that he every way approved. Let it be observed that in defending the outrages of the pro-slavery scoundrels, it is done on the ground that they were committed against bad men, incendiaries, and traitors; and let it also be observed, that in this category he classes *all free-state men*, even though as free from crime as the Saviour of the world. His special reasoning on that score will be understood at a glance by every intelligent reader. Observe, now, what the *Lecompton Union* says of its paragon:

"GENERAL CALHOUN.

"To the northern men who, with a devotion amounting to heroism, have bared their breasts and received the blows aimed at the freedom of the south, state equality, and consequently the perpetuity of the Union, are the people of this Union indebted more than any others. To this class belongs General John Calhoun, surveyor-general of Kansas. Born and raised in the north, *his sympathies are all with the south*, and he is to-day *stronger on the slavery question* than one-half of those born and raised in the south; and we say this, too, without doubting their devotion to the clime of their birth, or for want of confidence in their will to defend us when necessary against any enemy.

"He belongs to the Douglas school of politicians, the men upon whose shoulders the weight of the Union has fallen. Bold in thought,—untiring in action, and sound in principle, such men are governed by principle, not motive. There is an under-covering of common honesty in their composition that defies the corrupting influences of brain-sick abolitionism. Neither gold, the glittering prize that dazzles the ambitious eye, the fear of scorn and contumacy, can tempt them from the strict line of duty; but planted upon the rock of principle,

they resist the seductive influences of the one and defy the stings of the other.

"To such men, more especially, are the people of Kansas indebted for their firm and unwavering support, under circumstances of a peculiarly trying nature. These thoughts occurred to us after listening to the very excellent remarks of General Calhoun on last Saturday evening. We will give the substance of one or two points made by him on the occasion:—

"In the first place, he exposed the injustice and fallacy of the policy that is being carried out by the territorial magnates, *under the plausible pretext of doing justice to all parties*—the levelling idea that has, *since the advent of the last gubernatorial constellation*, loomed up in our political sky—recognising no difference between the good and the bad, but placing upon a common footing the sustainers of the laws and its violators.

"Under the workings of this new policy, *some of the best and most law-abiding citizens of the territory*, [viz.: Hays, the murderer of Buffum; Clarke, the assassin of Barber; Emory, who killed Phillips, and many others of that class,] *have been dragged before the inquisitorial court*—'spotted and stained' with indictments, and made to undergo all the vexations and delays of a legal investigation, to vindicate his honor. If he shoot down the incendiary when in the act of applying the torch to his house—or *if he jumps upon the back of the first horse that comes within reach*, or 'presses' him for the purpose of vindicating the laws of the country when trampled under foot, must he be placed on an equal footing with the wretch who applies the torch, and with the traitor who breaks the law, and be branded as a murderer and common horse thief?"

This language is used in defence of men who murdered others simply to rob them of their property, and even stole horses from women and children, not to pursue violators of the law, but to carry them for sale into the adjoining state. Such men, according to the logic of the speaker, were not to be placed on an equality with those whom they robbed and murdered. But the general exposes himself as he proceeds. It was the policy of his party to claim the character of *innocence*—of *justification by circumstances* of their unheard-of atrocities,—of their numerous robberies, house-burnings, and murders. This *could not be done, if legal investigations were had, and the damning facts be brought out before a court of law.* Their crimes exposed, they could not expect a continuance of the support and encouragement they were receiving from honest, though deceived persons at a distance. Hence the opposition to Governor Geary, who could not believe that a murderer was less a murderer because he claimed to belong to a certain party, or that he should be left on that account to run at large unwhipped of justice, or beyond the exercise of the law. The general continues:—

"Is it sufficient to inquire whether such and such an act was done without inquiring into the causes that led to its commission? What will be the effect of such policy upon our party here if persisted in? It will degrade us at home and disgrace us abroad, and it will force us to either one of two extremes, to abandon a country that punishes for sustaining its laws, and defending our lives and property when threatened, or we must make up our minds to submit to every humiliation and degradation that can be heaped upon us. What will our friends at Washington or the States who have fought our battles, say, when they hear of this? It will take from them the only weapon that they have used in our defence—*our innocence*—and place in the hands of our enemies a powerful lever to be used *against us—our guilt.*"

The general appears to have been nervously sensitive on this score. He seems to have been fully aware that their cause would be seriously injured, even in the south, if the truth should, by any chance, happen to get abroad through honest legal investigations. In that case their pretended *innocence* would no longer avail them. And hence, their greatest scoundrels must be screened and protected, and though their hands with blood were as red as scarlet, they must be made to appear as white as snow. If one of these wretches stole a horse, it was only from a seditious abolitionist, and to be used in the public service; if he robbed a house and then burned it to the ground, it was to drive out some rebel who had taken refuge there; and if he murdered an unarmed and defenceless man upon the highway or whilst sleeping in his bed, it was in self-defence. This ground must be assumed and maintained, else their cause must fall; and to maintain it, their worst criminals must be kept out of the courts, else destructive secrets would necessarily be revealed. Besides, the Blue Lodges required them to protect each other, and that was another weighty consideration. The general's speech grows richer as he proceeds:

"The question is, shall we sustain our friends, who, in obedience to the proclamation of Acting-Governor Woodson, took up arms in defence of the laws, against a set of 'dogs, scoundrels, and traitors,' who came into the country, not with the intention of supporting the laws, but armed and equipped for fight—traitors at heart, with the treasonable design of overthrowing the laws and trampling them under foot, or shall we surrender them to the mercy of such a miserable policy as is being carried out at present, OR SUSTAIN THEM TO THE LAST?

"Our position is, that the law and order party is in the right, or it is in the wrong—if the first, it should be sustained; if the last, condemned. We say it is the only true, upright, constitutional party in the country; there may be individual exceptions; we are not bound by their acts, nor do we approve of them.

"The idea of appeasing the insatiable gluttony of abolition rage and fanaticism by harassing and plastering with indictments the law and order men, under the pretence of 'impartial justice,' savors of lunacy. If one-half of the law and order men in the country should be swung up by the neck on to-morrow, the sacrifice would not in the least abate their hellish desire, but like the horse leech, they would cry give, until the life of every man that opposed them was offered up. They came into the country to disturb its peace, to break its laws, to kill, burn and plunder—outlaws and traitors, they deserve the traitor's fate."

This article indicates the character of the pro-slavery party of Kansas, and explains clearly some of the seeming mysteries in the history of the territory. A brutal murder had been committed. In the annals of crime, there is not one recorded of a more diabolical character. A poor cripple is killed in cold blood by a human monster, simply to steal his horses. With his hands still reeking with the blood of his inoffensive victim, the assassin also robs a young girl of her pet pony; and then, with his booty, joins his "law and order" comrades. The governor, with great difficulty and expense, causes the criminal to be arrested. A *partial* judge sets him free—and an *impartial* governor causes his re-arrest. A public meeting is called in consequence, by men holding prominent offices under the general government, to denounce the governor as a *lunatic*, for attempting to carry out the policy of "*impartial justice.*" The surveyor-general of the territory tells the people the laws were not made to condemn the "law and order" party for killing abolitionists. It was all right that hundreds of free-state men should be groaning and starving in a loathsome prison; but it was an offence to lay hands upon a "law and order" villain. This offence sealed the governor's doom. It was decreed that he should be removed. If the government could not be prevailed upon to dismiss him, and he could not be so harassed and embarrassed as to be forced to resign, then the hand of the assassin must do the work. And these advocates for murder, associates of murderers, and murderers themselves, succeeded. They did not simply denounce the "impartial policy," as they called it, of Governor Geary; but they determined that it should not prevail in Kansas. And hence Calhoun, and Clarke, and Emory, and Jack Thompson, hastened to Washington, and *were admitted to the presence of President Buchanan, and introduced to the members of the cabinet*, to all of whom they promised they would throw no obstacles in his way if a southern governor was sent to Kansas. And Mr. Buchanan was delighted with these assurances. They called on Mr. Robert J. Walker, and told him they would give him no trouble if he would be the governor. And Mr. Walker felt highly flattered. But they *had* thrown obstacles in the way of Governor Geary—they *had* given him trouble—they *had* annoyed and abused him to the full extent of their power—they had prevailed upon the authorities to remove from him all the means he had at command to preserve the peace and protect himself—and then surrounded him with bands of assassins, ready to consummate, at the first favorable opportunity, their nefarious designs. And why? Because Governor Geary had conceived the fallacy of exercising "impartial justice"—because he could not discriminate between murder committed by a man who added to the enormity of the crime the black falsehood that it was committed for the public good, and by one who made no such lying pretence—because, in a word, he was determined that the simple fact of being an advocate for slavery and assuming the name of "law and order," should not screen the guilty wretch from merited punishment. And these men, who for this reason and none other, so foully persecuted Governor Geary, have been rewarded with lucrative offices by the administration. Since the world was made, never were such responsible positions given, in any civilized nation on earth, to men so notoriously unworthy.

CHAPTER XL.

Meeting of a pro-slavery convention at Lecompton.—Discussion between Hampton and Maclean.—Sheriff Jones endorsed.—Organization of the national democratic party of Kansas.—A novel platform.—The national administration favors the pro-slavery movements in Kansas.—Analysis of the cabinet.—Governor Geary offered the United States senatorship.—Calhoun's address to the people of the United States.—Misrepresentations of its author exposed.

A CALL having apppeared in the *Squatter Sovereign* for the meeting of a convention, a body, in answer thereto, assembled at Lecompton on the same day that the Legislature was organized. The objects of the convention had been left for the imagination of the delegates, for they had never been publicly stated or defined. They were not destined, however, to remain long in ignorance on that particular point; for when two free-state delegates presented credentials, they were given clearly to understand that their presence and services were not required. The first question discussed regarded the *name* by which the convention should be called. A proposition to denominate it the "Law and Order Convention" was overruled by the opposition of Doctor Stringfellow, who pronounced the assembly a *pro-slavery convocation*, and offered a resolution, which was almost unanimously carried, denying a seat in the meetings to any man who was not absolutely known to be in favor of making Kansas a slave state.

The passage of this resolution brought Maclean to his feet, who, in a speech of some length, delivered in a most excited manner, declared that Captain L. J. Hampton, who claimed to be a delegate from Jefferson county, had no business in that convention, as his kind treatment, in the capacity of master of convicts, to the free-state prisoners, was quite sufficient proof that he was not a sound pro-slavery man.

To this Hampton replied, with much earnestness and eloquence, declaring that he was a Kentuckian, and had always maintained the local institutions of his native state, and affirming that he was decidedly in favor of slavery extension.

Maclean retorted, and was even more violent than before: "I don't care what Captain Hampton says. His conduct to the prisoners has been such as no pro-slavery man can sanction; and my friend over there, Samuel J. Jones, the sheriff of Douglas county, the master spirit of our party, who has fought, suffered and bled for our cause, who is a living monument of the nobility of the human soul, and whose word is the soul of honor, says that Captain Hampton is not sound; and shall we take Captain Hampton's word in preference to that of Sheriff Jones? Have we not tried Samuel J. Jones? And who will say that he was ever found wanting? No! it is our duty, as pro-slavery men, to believe Sheriff Jones's word in preference to Captain Hampton's oath; to do, without hesitation, all that Sheriff Jones wishes us to do, no matter what that may be; and as Sheriff Jones desires the exclusion from this convention of Captain Hampton, I hope that no member here will be so vile a traitor to our cause as to hesitate one moment to vote for his expulsion!"

During these remarks, which were constantly interrupted with enthusiastic applause, the sheriff, it being late in the evening, was in no mood for speech-making; but sat near his friend Maclean, almost unconscious of the extravagant laudations of which he was the subject, and nodding over the pipe that he held in his mouth, from which an occasional puff of smoke would ascend. Hampton's case was finally referred to a committee, who reported him "sound on the goose," and he was admitted as a member of the convention. But here another difficulty arose. A vote had hastily been passed inviting all the members of the Legislature to participate in the business of the convention, and it was discovered that two of the members were free-state men. After a spirited debate on the question of their admission, it was decided that they were not included in the general invitation. Nothing more was done the first evening than organize the body, and appoint the proper committees.

On the following day, the convention met in committee of the whole, when, to the astonishment of many of the delegates, a proposition was made by Doctor Stringfellow, who had never pretended to be a Democrat, to call themselves "*The National Democratic Party of Kansas Territory.*" There was some little squirming and twisting when this proposition was made; for it appeared that a majority of the delegates claimed to be old-line Whigs; but when the objects were explained, all scruples were removed, and the name was adopted. It was stated that Governor Geary must by some means be disposed of; his continuance in Kansas was an injury to the pro-slavery cause. An issue must be raised between hin and Lecompte; one or the other must fall; and Lecompte could not, under any circumstances, be spared. The question was under consideration at Washington. A protest against Lecompte's removal, and in favor of Geary's, must be sent to the national democratic administration; that administration could not with propriety pay much attention to anything emanating from a body contending for no other principle than the introduction of slavery into the territory; but it would be compelled to regard with favor whatever came to them from the "National Democratic Party of Kansas." Besides, it was argued that "a rose by any other name would smell as sweet," and by *calling* himself a Democrat, for the purpose of gaining an important point, no man was compelled to embrace democratic doctrines. He might still entertain whatever sentiments he thought proper. It was thought best, nevertheless, to secure the desired object, to adopt the Cincinnati platform—reserving to themselves the privilege of engrafting thereon their one idea of slavery in Kansas.

This was a strange procedure, and one which shows an utter disregard of moral principle, when it is understood that these very men, at the last session of the Legislature, as will be seen by reference to their published journal, passed the following:

"Mr. Speaker Stringfellow, Mr. Anderson in the chair, offered the following concurrent resolution:—

"WHEREAS, The signs of the times indicate that a measure is now on foot fraught with more danger to the interests of the pro-slavery party, and to the Union, than any which has yet been agitated, to wit: the proposition to organize a *national* democratic party; and

"WHEREAS, Some of our friends have already been misled by it; and

"WHEREAS, The result will be to divide pro-slavery Whigs from Democrats, thus weakening our party one-half; and

"WHEREAS, We believe that on the success of our party depends the perpetuity of the Union; Therefore,

"*Be it resolved*, By the House of Representatives, the Council concurring therein, that it is the duty of the pro-slavery party, the union-loving men of Kansas Territory, to know but one issue, SLAVERY, and that any party making or attempting to make any other, IS AND SHOULD BE HELD, AS AN ALLY OF ABOLITIONISM AND DISUNIONISM.

"Which was read a first time, and the rule suspended, and the resolution read a second time, and agreed to."

Such is the platform of the men, who at last, for sinister motives, styled themselves the "*National Democracy of Kansas.*" They were to know but *one issue*—that issue, *slavery!* or else be held as "allies of abolitionism and disunionism." In carrying out this principle, all the free-state Democrats of Kansas were excluded from membership with the "*National Democracy,*" not one of them being received into fellowship, or in any manner allowed to take part in its proceedings.

But, it may be asked, is this sort of Democracy acknowledged and endorsed by the administration at Washington? Yes! Mr. Buchanan has carried it out to the full measure of perfection. As far as he has had the power, he has ostracised all free-state Democrats, no matter how long or how faithfully they have served himself and their party. The most, if not all, of his appointments have been made with especial reference to the slavery question, and the pleasure of the southern wing of the Democracy. Without an exception, the Kansas appointments were well known pro-slavery men, and they of the fiercest character.

The same rule was rigidly observed in selecting the members of the cabinet. It would be an insult to the sagacity of the president to suppose that this was purely accidental, or that he had been blindfolded by his political advisers. The northern Democrats have been deluded with the pretence that a strict impartiality had been observed in this regard, and that an equal distribution of the cabinet offices had been made among parties favorable to northern and southern interests; than which nothing can be farther from the truth. So far as the settlement of the question of slavery in Kansas is concerned, the cabinet officers, who have any great influence in relation to it, are all on one side. True, there are three northern men in the cabinet, which, with Mr. Buchanan, comprise one-half the number. Two of these, however, are avowed pro-slavery men, and the other a large owner of property in a slave state. But even were this otherwise, neither of these gentlemen's positions give them any peculiar control over the affairs of Kansas Territory.

General Lewis Cass, of Michigan, the Secretary of State, has no appointments to make nor patronage to bestow, in the territory; and is very little else, so far as its interests are concerned than a medium of communication between the Governor of Kansas and the President of the United States. The Attorney General, Jeremiah S. Black, of Pennsylvania, simply occupies the position of legal adviser; whilst Mr. Isaac Toucey, of Connecticut, the Secretary of the Navy, has nothing whatever to do with Kansas.

How is it with the other members of Mr. Buchanan's cabinet? These are all southern men, and have the entire management of Kansas affairs.

The Postmaster General, Mr. Aaron V. Brown, of Tennessee, has the appointment of all the postmasters, mail-agents, mail-carriers, etc., and can bestow his immense patronage upon whom he pleases; and so well has he begun, that the only free-state post-master in the territory, Mr. C. W. Babcock, of Lawrence, who is a gentleman of unimpeachable integrity, and whose sound democracy has never been questioned, has been removed to make room for a member of the pro-slavery party.

Mr. Howell Cobb, of Georgia, the Secretary of the Treasury, has charge of the national purse, and can exercise considerable influence in supplying or withholding funds for territorial uses.

The Secretary of War, Mr. John B. Floyd, of Virginia, has the management of the army, and may send to Kansas officers to command the troops, of his own political complexion, and can, at his pleasure, deny or allow the governor the employment of the United States forces.

And last, though not the least, comes Mr. Jacob Thompson, of Mississippi, the Secretary of the Interior. This is the most important of all the cabinet officers, as regards the interests of Kansas Territory. He can control the appointment of numerous Indian agents, surveyors, etc., amounting to some hundreds of persons, through whom about three millions of dollars are annually disbursed. His influence, therefore, for good or evil, in Kansas, is almost unbounded. That he intends to employ it in favor of the pro-slavery party, is evidenced in the fact, that one of the first acts of the new administration was the removal, at the instance of George W. Clarke, of Col. Winston, of Virginia, who had been appointed to succeed Clarke, as agent for the Potawattomie Indians, and against whom there could be no other charge than that, for a southerner, he was too conservative in his views to be of service to the pro-slavery cause. Winston was superseded by William E. Murphy, who had distinguished himself for his opposition to the free-state men of Leavenworth City, and who, after the latter had been driven away by violence, was fraudulently elected mayor of that city.

What will northern Democrats think of this analysis? Alas! what have northern free-state Democrats to do with the present national Democracy? That Democracy is emphatically the pro-slavery party of the country! Mr. Buchanan's administration has adopted the platform of that party, which is, to know but *one issue*—and that issue, SLAVERY!

The machinery set in motion by the leading actors of the "National Democratic Party of Kansas," did not work so well as was anticipated. The people understood the trickery, and would not come into the proposed measures. Hence there was considerable discouragement, and a new course of policy was attempted. It was suggested that it would be a capital idea to induce the governor to give his sanction to the movement. Accordingly, a meeting was called to ratify the proceedings of the convention, and Governor Geary was formally visited by J. D. Henderson, chairman of the central committee, with the assurance, that if he would attend the meeting and identify himself with the party, he should be one of the two United States senators soon to be elected, as the convention, in conjunction with the legislature, had plans on foot which could not fail of success in making Kansas a slave state. The governor reminded Henderson, that a certain tempter once took his master to the "top of a high mountain, and showed him all the kingdoms of the world, saying, All these will I give unto you, if you will fall down and worship me." "Now," said his excellency, "the devil had as many kingdoms to give as you have senatorial honors to bestow, or ever will have, by honest means. I despise your promises of reward as much as I did your infamous threats of injury. If you approach me again with such vile offers of bribery, I will be tempted to toss you through the window." The ratification meeting was held; about a dozen persons were present; A. W. Jones endeavored to make a speech; and after passing a resolution endorsing the abuses of the *Union*, of which he was editor, adjourned, the whole affair proving a most ridiculous failure.

Before its final adjournment, this "*National Democratic* convention" appointed a committee to prepare an "address to the people of the United States." This committee consisted of the following named persons, of whom, with few exceptions, the democrats of the United States have no great reason to be proud:

John Calhoun, chairman; George W. Clarke, John W. Foreman, J. Kuykendall, John H. Stringfellow, A. B. Hazzard, John R. Boyd, E. Ranson, L. A. Maclean, H. B. Harris, A. Coffey, John Donaldson, B. J. Newsome, J. T. Hereford, J. C. Anderson, D. R. Atchison, Jeff. Buford, W. H. Tebbs, S. J. Jones, Hugh M. Moore, G. W. Perkins, A. J. Isacks.

These names are published more especially for future reference. The address was prepared by Surveyor Calhoun, and published in pamphlet form; and it would be a difficult matter to find any other publication, of an equal number of pages, containing as many gross misrepresentations. A single example of the author's veracity may here be given. Speaking of the contemplated attack upon Lawrence, he assumes that it was the desire of the free-state men to have the town destroyed (and of course themselves, women and children massacred), for political effect, and adds:—

"Lane, no doubt, abandoned the town for that purpose; but he did not comprehend that his opponents were incapable of attacking where there was no chance of defence."

The truth is, they were *never known to attack* where there *was* a chance for defence, or where the odds were not greatly in their favor. The address continues:—

"General Heiskell's forces had the town completely within their power for two days before they turned back; but the leaders of those forces saw the game as clearly as the Black Republicans themselves, and determined to prevent its destruction. To control the incensed mass of Heiskell's forces, who thought only of vengeance for outrages committed, the leaders sent to Lecompton for Governor Geary to come and disband their troops, so that they might be forced to return to their homes without entering Lawrence. This was done, and Lawrence saved by the sagacity of the leaders in Heiskell's camp."

There is not the slightest shadow of truth in this statement. The leaders of Heiskell's forces *never* sent to Governor Geary to come and disband their troops. On the contrary, Maclean, Heiskell's adjutant and Calhoun's chief clerk, most heartily cursed what he called the interference of Governor Geary. The governor was studiously kept in ignorance of the movement and intentions of these troops by Heiskell's leaders, and only discovered the facts through his own secret agents and the applications of the citizens of Lawrence for protection.

The official report of Adjutant-General Strickler, whom Governor Geary sent to disband Heiskell's forces, proves the falsity of General Calhoun's statement, made for the unworthy purpose of taking from Governor Geary the credit of a great and noble act. General Strickler's report to the governor is dated September 17, 1856, in which he says:—

"In reply to your note of this date, I have the honor to report, that in pursuance of your instructions, I proceeded to the camp at Franklin, commanded by Brigadier-General Heiskell, and made known to him your proclamation and orders for the disbandment of the Kansas militia, and requested him to publish such general orders as might be necessary to execute your commands.

"The excitement and confusion became so great in consequence of this intelligence that it was deemed advisable to request your presence; and I consider it fortunate for myself that you came to the camp; for you must be convinced from what you saw during your stay of the utter impossibility to execute your commands."

Thus it seems, by the official report, that instead of the leaders of Heiskell's forces sending for the governor to disband their troops, the adjutant-general of the territory was incapable of effecting that object, and found it necessary to send for the governor himself; and it is well known that his presence alone saved the town of Lawrence from the rapine and destruction that had been contemplated. No wonder that General Calhoun and his party should now be ashamed of, and endeavor to deny, their complicity with this most dastardly and disgraceful intention.

General Reid did not attempt to take from Governor Geary the credit of defeating the murderous intentions of his army—of saving Lawrence from destruction, and the country from a civil war, but frankly acknowledged the fact. Upon Reid's return to Missouri, he was severely censured for not consummating the purpose of the invasion, when he found it necessary to defend his conduct through the medium of the press. In one of his lengthy communications published in the *Occidental Messenger*, Independence, Mo., of September 20th, 1856, he says:—

"I have no regret that Governor Geary arrived when he did, and *interposed between us and our purpose*, and relieved us from the necessity of doing extrajudicially, that which can be done so much more effectually and satisfactorily in the name and by the authority of the law—redressing the wrong of our fellow-citizens and restoring them to their rights in Kansas.

"I have no doubt, with the men we had, of the result. I have no doubt we should have driven Lane and his band, and all confederate bands, from the soil of Kansas, but I am not prepared to say I would have preferred it so. I think it better for the peace of the country and for the good of all, that it should be as it is, and hence I then thought, and now think, *the arrival of the new governor most opportune for us, for Kansas, and for the whole country*, in suspending the strife which had been forced upon us, in such a manner as regarding our honor and our rights we could not decline it, and which threatened to involve the whole country in a civil and sectional war."

CHAPTER XLI.

Passage of the census bill.—Governor Geary's veto message.—The manner in which the census was taken.—Repeal of the test laws.—Adjournment of the Legislature.—Secretary Marcy and the Topeka Legislature.—Letter to the Secretary of State.—Arrest of a fugitive.—Rencontre at Topeka.—Complaint of prisoners.—Breaking up of the Kansas River.

THE crowning act of the legislature was the passage, near the close of its session, of what is called the "Census Bill." This was the most infamous scheme to rob thousands of freemen of their right of the elective franchise, that has ever been devised in this or any other country. The bill was created with much care and cunning, by certain prominent United States senators at Washington, and sent to Lecompton, with orders for its adoption without alteration or amendment.

It provides for the taking of a census, preparatory to an election to be held in June, 1857, for delegates to a convention to frame a state constitution, to be presented to the next Congress for its approval. At the election no citizen is allowed to vote, who was not in the territory on or before the 15th of March. The census takers and judges of election are the sheriffs and other officers appointed by the pro-slavery party, and bound to its interests.

Agreeably to this regulation, the hundreds of free-state men who had been forcibly driven from their claims and homes during the past year's disturbances, and who, in consequence of the difficulty of travel, could not return until after the 15th of March, were disfranchised, as were also the thousands of emigrants that were expected to arrive after that period, and prior to the day fixed for the election. Whilst on the other hand, thousands of Missourians could simply cross the border into the territory, register their names as voters, and return to their homes to await the election. But even that trouble was at length considered unnecessary, for the sheriffs and census takers found it more convenient to carry their books into Missouri and there record their names. Although this was really done, the names of many of the most prominent and oldest free-state residents of the territory were never registered. Under the regulations of this bill the free-state people wisely concluded to take no part whatever in the election; for it was a matter of certainty that there was no possibility of justice being done them, and their participation in the fraud in any way would only be to give it their sanction. Had they resolved to vote, and showed a majority of three to one, the judges would have had no difficulty in returning them in the minority. The past history of the officials was a sufficient guarantee of what might be expected from their future conduct. To pretend that such men as Sheriff Jones would do anything like justice to the free-state residents, is simply an insult to the common sense of all who understand the history of the country. But even the possibility of the free-state people coming forward to vote, was guarded against by the insertion of a clause in the bill, intended for their intimidation, that the voting should be *viva voce.* Another feature of the bill is, that although it was framed expressly to defraud the free-state citizens of their rights, it requires them to pay a tax to assist in the accomplishment of the fraud.

Upon ascertaining the nature of this act, Governor Geary, before its passage, sent for the chairmen of the committees of the two branches of the Legislature, General Coffey of the Council and Colonel Anderson of the House, and informed them that if they would consent to add a clause referring the constitution that might be formed by the convention to the citizens of the territory, for their sanction or rejection, before its being submitted to Congress, he would waive all other objections, and give it his approval. The reply was, that that suggestion had already been fully considered and discussed, and could not be adopted, *as it would defeat the only object of the act, which was to secure, beyond any possibility of failure, the territory of Kansas to the south as a slave state.* Any alteration in the bill would be fatal to their projects. Even should they allow the spring immigration to take part in the election, their plans would be frustrated. This, they said, was their last hope, and they could not let the opportunity pass unimproved. They had already, in anticipation of the passage of the bill, so apportioned the territory, and made such other preliminary arrangements, that the success of this grand project was placed beyond the reach of any contingency that might now occur.

The bill was passed by both houses and sent to the governor for his signature, who returned it with the following objections:—

"*Gentlemen of the Council of Kansas Territory:*

"After mature consideration of the bill entitled 'An Act to provide for the taking of a census, and election for delegates to convention,' I am constrained to return the same without my approval.

"Passing over other objections, I desire to call your serious attention to a material omission in the bill.

"I refer to the fact that the Legislature has failed to make any provision to submit the constitution, when framed, to the consideration of the people, for their ratification or rejection.

"The position that a convention can do no wrong, and ought to be invested with sovereign power, and that its constituents have no right to judge of its acts, is extraordinary and untenable.

"The history of state constitutions, with scarcely an exception, will exhibit a uniform and sacred adherence to the salutary rule of popular ratification.

"The practice of the federal and state governments, in the adoption of their respective constitutions, exhibiting the wisdom of the past, will furnish us with a safe and reliable rule of action.

"The federal constitution was first proposed by a convention of delegates from twelve states, assembled in Philadelphia. This constitution derived no authority from the first convention. It was submitted to the various states, fully discussed in all its features, and concurred in by the people of the states in conventions assembled; and that concurrence armed it with power and invested it with dignity. Article seventh of the constitution makes the ratification of nine states, three-fourths of the number represented in the convention, essential to its adoption.

"In the adoption, not only of the federal constitution, but of nearly all the state constitutions, the popular ratification was made essential; and all amendments to those of most of the states are required to pass two legislatures, and then be submitted to the people for their approval.

"In Kentucky, especially, all amendments to the constitution must pass two legislatures, and for two years be submitted to the vote of the people, upon the question of convention or no convention, on the specific amendments proposed.

"Treaties made by ambassadors are not binding until duly ratified by their respective governments, whose agents they are.

"Members of the legislature or of conventions are but the agents of the people, who have an inherent right to judge of the acts of their agents, and to condemn or approve them, as in their deliberate judgment they may deem proper.

"The fundamental law of a commonwealth so inseparably connected with the happiness and prosperity of the citizens, cannot be too well discussed, and cannot pass through too many ordeals of popular scrutiny.

"What delegates to conventions may do or what omit, cannot be known until they have assembled and developed their action. If the whole power be vested in them without recourse over to the people, there is no guarantee that the popular wishes will be fairly and fully expressed.

"Although the people may have voted for a convention to form a state constitution, yet they have by no just rule of construction voted away the usual and universal right of ratification.

"Special instructions, covering every point arising in the formation of a constitution, cannot be given in the elections preliminary to a convention; and it is, therefore, proper that the action of the convention, necessarily covering new ground, should be submitted to the people for their consideration.

"The practical right of the people to ordain and establish governments is found in the expressive and beautiful preamble to the federal constitution—'We the people,' &c., 'do ordain and establish this constitution.'

"Let the constitution of Kansas be ratified and established by the solemn vote of the people, surrounded by such safeguards as will insure a fair and unbiassed expression of the actual *bona fide* citizens, and it will remain inviolably fixed in the affections of the people.

"In his report upon the Toombs bill, its distinguished author thus logically enumerates the various steps in the formation of a constitution: 'the preliminary meetings; the calling of the convention; the appointment of delegates; the assembling of the convention; the formation of the constitution; *the voting on its ratification;* the election of officers under it.'

"In the same report, the author most justly remarks:— 'Whenever a constitution shall be formed in any territory, preparatory to its admission into the Union as a state, justice, the genius of our institutions, the whole theory of our republican system, imperatively demand that *the voice of the people shall be fairly expressed, and their will embodied in that fundamental law,* without fraud or violence, or intimidation, or any other improper or unlawful influence, and subject to no other restrictions than those imposed by the Constitution of the United States.'

"The voice of the people fairly expressed, and its embodiment in the fundamental law, should be the earnest desire of every citizen of a republic.

"But how can the voice of the people be fairly expressed, and their will be embodied in the organic law, unless that law, when made, be submitted to them to determine whether it is their will which the convention has proclaimed?

"The leading idea and fundamental principle of our organic act, as expressed in the law itself, was to leave the actual *bona fide* inhabitants of the territory 'perfectly free to form and regulate their domestic institutions in their own way.' The act confers almost unlimited power upon the people, and the only restriction imposed upon its exercise is the Constitution of the United States.

"The great principle, then, upon which our free institutions rest, is the unqualified and absolute sovereignty of the people; and constituting, as that principle does, the most positive and essential feature in the great charter of our liberties, so it is better calculated than any other to give elevation to our hopes and dignity to our actions. So long as the people feel that the power to alter the form or change the character of the government abides in them, so long will they be impressed with that sense of security and of dignity which must ever spring from the consciousness that they hold within their own hands a remedy for every political evil—a corrective for every governmental abuse and usurpation.

"'This principle must be upheld and maintained, at all hazards and at every sacrifice—maintained in all the power and fulness—in all the breadth and depth of its utmost capacity and signification. It is not sufficient that it be acknowledged as a mere abstraction, or theory, or doctrine; but as a practical, substantial, living reality, vital in every part.'

"The idea of surrendering the sovereignty of the territories, the common property of the people of the several states, into the hands of the few who first chanced to wander into them, is, to me, a political novelty. Is it just that the territories should exercise the rights of sovereign states until their condition and numbers become such as to entitle them to be admitted into the union on an equality with the original states?

"In speaking of the proper construction of the Organic Act, its distinguished author remarks:—'The act recognises the rights of the people thereof, while a territory, to form and regulate their own domestic institutions in their own way, subject only to the Constitution of the United States, and to be received into the union, *as soon as they should attain the requisite number of inhabitants, on an equal footing with the original states in all respects whatever.*'

"In the report before alluded to, the author says:—'The point upon which your committee have entertained the most serious and grave doubts in regard to the propriety of endorsing this proposition, relates to the fact that, in the absence of any census of the inhabitants, there is reason to apprehend that the territory does not contain sufficient population to entitle them to demand admission under the treaty with France, if we take the ratio of representation for a member of Congress as the rule.'

"In accordance with the foregoing views, I remarked in my first message to your body, that 'the durability and imperative authority of a state constitution, when the interests of the people require a state government, *and a direct popular vote is necessary to give it sanction and effect*, will be the proper occasion, once for all, to decide the grave political questions which underlie a well regulated commonwealth.' And in another portion of the same message, I said:—'Justice to the country and the dictates of sound policy, require that the legislature should confine itself to such subjects as will preserve the basis of entire equality; and *when a sufficient population is here*, and they choose to adopt a state government, that they shall be "perfectly free," without let or hindrance, to form all their domestic institutions in their own way, and to dictate that form of government, which, in their deliberate judgment, may be deemed proper.'

"The expressions, 'requisite number of inhabitants,' 'sufficient population,'—and others, of similar import, can have no other meaning than that given them by our leading statesmen, and by the common judgment of the country, to wit:—'the ratio of representation for a member of Congress.'

"The present ratio for a member of Congress, is 93,420 inhabitants. What, then, is the present population of Kansas; or what will it be on the 15th of March next? as after that time, no person arriving in the territory can vote for a member of the convention under the provisions of this bill.

"At the last October election, the whole vote polled for delegate to Congress, was four thousand two hundred and seventy-six; (4276;) while the vote in favor of a convention to frame a state constitution, was but two thousand six hundred and seventy. (2670.)

"It is a well known fact, to every person at all conversant with the circumstances attending the last election, that the question of a state government entered but little into the canvas, and the small vote polled for a convention is significantly indicative of the popular indifference on the subject.

"No one will claim that 2670 is a majority of the voters of this territory, though it is a majority of those voting, and it is conceded that those not voting are bound by the act of those who did.

"The bill under consideration seems to be drawn from the bill known as the Toombs Bill; but in several respects it differs from that bill, and in these particulars it does not furnish equal guarantees for fairness and impartiality. The former secured the appointment of five impartial commissioners to take and correct the census, to make a partial apportionment among the several counties, and generally to superintend all the preliminaries so as to secure a fair election, while by the present bill all these important duties are to be performed by probate judges and sheriffs, elected by and owing allegiance to a party. It differs in other important particulars. The bill of Mr. Toombs conferred valuable rights and privileges upon this territory, and provided means to pay the expenses of the convention; while this bill does neither.

"If we are disposed to avail ourselves of the wisdom of the past, we will pause some time before we throw off our territorial condition, under present circumstances, by the adoption of a state government.

"The state of Michigan remained a territory for five years after she had the requisite population, and so with other states; and when they were admitted, they were strong enough in all the elements of material wealth to be self-supporting. And hence they knocked at the door of the union with that manly confidence which spoke of equality and self-reliance.

"California was admitted under peculiar and extraordinary circumstances. Her rich mines of the precious metals attracted a teeming population to her shores, and her isolated position from the parent government, with her superabundant wealth, at once suggested the experiment of self-government; and at the time of her state constitution, ratified by the vote of the people, the population of California entitled her to two representatives in Congress.

"I observe by the message of the governor of Minnesota, that the population of that thriving territory exceeds 180,000. The taxable property amounts to between thirty and thirty-five millions of dollars. And in view of these facts, and of the large increase of agricultural products, cash capital, etc., the governor favors a change from a territorial to a state government. To this end he suggests that a convention be called *to form* a constitution; that an act be passed for the taking of a census in April, and for such other preliminary steps as are necessary; and that if the constitution be '*ratified by the people*' at the next October election, it shall be presented to Congress in December following.

"These facts furnish an additional argument why the constitution should be submitted to the people, as the majority, preferring a territorial government, and thinking a state government premature, may desire to avail themselves of that opportunity to vote against any state constitution whatever.

"Burthened with heavy liabilities; without titles to our lands; our public buildings unfinished; our jail and court-houses not erected; without money even to pay the expenses of a convention; and just emerging from the disastrous effects of a bitter civil feud; it seems unwise for a few thousand people, scarcely sufficient to make a good county, to discard the protecting and fostering care of a government, ready to assist us with her treasures and to protect us with her armies.

"JNO. W. GEARY,
"Governor of Kansas Territory.
"Lecompton, K. T., February 19, 1857."

Notwithstanding these objections, the bill was adopted, without discussion, by an almost unanimous vote of both branches of the Assembly. The pro-slavery party were in raptures. They did not pretend to conceal their exultation. They freely boasted that they had now the advantage of their political adversaries, and that the question of slavery in Kansas was no longer a matter of uncertainty. So positive were they that the whole affair was entirely at their own disposal, and that the territory would soon become a slave state, that they went to work to select officers for its management, ridiculing any expression of doubt in regard to their success.

The new secretary of the territory, Mr. Stanton, and also Governor Walker, have endeavored to convince the free-state people that it is the intention of the pro-slavery convention to submit the constitution they may frame, to the people of the territory for their ratification, previous to its being presented to Congress. If these gentlemen are sincere in the expression of this opinion, they have been most successfully blindfolded by the persons from whom they received their ideas of Kansas affairs before entering upon the duties of their mission. The very reverse of this was the avowed intention of the pro-slavery leaders. That the *people* should have no voice in the matter, was the object of their chief concern. Hence, none should vote save those who were registered as being in the territory prior to the 15th of March; and hence the early election in June, and the putting off the meeting of the convention until September, that no time would be allowed to pass between the termination of their labors and the organization of Congress. The principal operators in this scheme did not hesitate to aver that their only hope was in getting the constitution through Congress despite the wishes of the majority of the inhabitants, which would not be the case should it be submitted to the popular vote.

The fairness of their intentions may be learned from the manner in which the census has been taken, the apportionments made, and the character of the parties who are nominated as delegates to the convention. Such names as Henderson,. Calhoun, Boling, Jones, &c., should certainly encourage the free-state settlers to hope that justice will be done them. The taking of the census was a mere farce and a gross imposition. No returns were made of some of the largest towns in the territory, and even whole counties were neglected. To have carried out the letter of the law in this regard, would have been a useless trouble and expense, as the whole matter was settled when the law was passed. A writer, who dates from Lecompton, May 25, 1857, says:—

"A proclamation has been issued for the delegate election, by Mr. Stanton, as acting governor. An apportionment of representation has been made by him. Out of thirty-six counties, as organized by the authorities, only twenty-one have even a nominal representation. The census has only been taken in ten of these, and in only some portions of these ten. In six of these twenty-one counties thus reported, no census was taken, but a list of voters was taken from their old poll-books, this having been done after the time for taking the census had expired. The other five are counties forming parts of districts which are mentioned because they are connected with others; but in these no census was taken, and no former vote or representation on account of former vote, has been allowed. By this proclamation three-fifths of the settled counties of the territory are *allowed no representation*. In these there are at least two-fifths of the people in the whole territory, and including the emigration of this spring, one-half.

"There are *twenty counties* to the south of the Kansas river, lying in a great solid mass, and filled with free-state towns and settlements, teeming with active life and industry; in one-half of them the great majority of claims are taken, and all are about as well settled as the majority of counties in most of the western states, and *the whole of these are left without a particle of representation* by this proclamation!"

One part of the plan, as explained to Governor Geary, is to adopt a constitution in which no reference whatever shall be made to the subject of slavery; and this fact has been announced in the administration organs as an evidence of the conciliatory disposition of the pro-slavery party of Kansas. But the pretended merit of this scheme will disappear as soon as it is understood that slavery already exists in the territory, by statute; and even though no mention may be made of it in the constitution, it will still remain an established institution of the new state.

The pro-slavery papers of the country have also claimed for the late Legislative Assembly much credit for having repealed the odious and oppressive test and election laws created at the preceding session. But in this matter a reprehensible deception has been practised. In repealing certain sections of these enactments, the legislature took especial care to permit others to remain upon the statute books, which contain all their most obnoxious features; so that, in fact, no improvement has been made. These acts, which "are disgraceful to the age," are claimed, as has already been said, to be the production of a member from Missouri, who, in explanation of their existence, has since said: "Well, I wrote them one night when I was drunk, and presented them more for fun than anything else; but they were unanimously adopted, all the members being as drunk as myself; though none of us intended that they should ever be enforced." The plea of insanity, well sustained, is all-sufficient in a court of law; that of drunkenness does not excuse the conduct of an offender.

The Legislative Assembly adjourned at midnight, on the 21st of February, when the members of both houses, with all the clerks, door-keepers, and other attachés, called upon the governor, in a body, to pay their respects, previous to their departure for their several homes. This was a sort of salvo for the wholesale abuse of which he had been for six weeks the constant subject.

Jan. 23d.—A letter was received from Secretary Marcy, in which he expresses great concern about the meeting of the Topeka Legislature, already noticed. He says:—

"I learn, with regret, that a body of men calling themselves a Legislature, are about to assemble at Topeka. The President's views in relation to the origin and purpose of such an assemblage, assuming the name and function of a legislative body, are fully set forth in his message to Congress of the 24th day of January, 1856, a copy of which accompanied your instructions. The title used is, in itself, an unwarrantable assumption. There can be but one legal legislative assembly in Kansas, and that, the one organized under the law of Congress. The assembling of the body referred to under the name and in the character of a legislature, is a procedure which ought to receive no countenance, whatever may be the assurances of any individuals as to the acts which it will or will not do."

26th.—A dispatch from the governor to the Secretary of State, of this date, contains the following paragraph:—

"The peace of the country remains unimpaired, and I have daily the most gratifying evidence of the general feeling of security which pervades all classes of the community. Notwithstanding, there are some amongst us who cannot exist much longer without commotion. I am closely watching their movements, and am determined to maintain peace at every hazard."

In the same communication the necessity of additional land offices is urged, and also the disposal at an early day of the residue of the Delaware Trust Lands.

28th.—A requisition, through the hands of Charles P. Arnold, was received by Governor Geary from Governor Wise of Virginia, for the arrest of a fugitive from that state named J. L. McCubbin, charged with the larceny of nine hundred dollars. Governor Geary immediately dispatched a force of dragoons in company with Mr. Arnold and a deputy marshal, in pursuit of McCubbin, who was arrested, and sent back to Virginia.

31st.—A communication having appeared in the Topeka *Tribune*, written by its special correspondent, and reflecting somewhat severely upon Judge Elmore, the latter met Mr. Kagi, the author, in front of the Court House, in Tecumseh, and attempted to chastise him by striking him across the head with a cane. Kagi drew a pistol and inflicted a severe flesh wound in the thigh of Elmore, when the latter fired several shots at Kagi, who had started to run, one of which slightly wounded him in the side. Neither of them was seriously injured. An attempt to create an excitement on this occasion proved a failure.

March 3d.—The prisoners at Tecumseh petitioned Governor Geary to do something toward the amelioration of their condition. They represented that for four days the only article of subsistence they had was coffee. The person who had contracted to furnish provisions, had stopped the rations because of the marshal having neglected to pay his bills.

6th.—The ice in the Kansas river, which had been frozen over for a long while, broke up in consequence of a freshet produced by heavy rains which had continued several days.

All communication between the north and south sides of the river was, for the time being, consequently suspended.

CHAPTER XLII.

Governor Geary's instructions.—The United States troops.—Enrolment, mustering and discharge of the militia.—The troops withheld from the service of the governor.

SOON after his appointment, and before his departure for the west, Governor Geary received the following instructions:—

"Department of State:
"Washington, August 26, 1856.

"Sir: The present condition of the territory of Kansas renders your duties as governor highly responsible and delicate. In the instructions heretofore communicated to your predecessor, in February last; in the annual message to Congress of the 24th of the previous December; and in orders issued from the War Department (printed copies of which are herewith furnished), you will find the policy of the President fully presented. It is first, to maintain order and quiet in the territory of Kansas; and, second, if disturbances occur therein, to bring to punishment the offenders.

"Should the force which has been provided to attain these objects prove insufficient,. you will promptly make known that fact to the President, that he may take such measures in regard thereto as to him may seem to be demanded by the exigencies of the case.

"It is important that the President should be kept well informed as to the state of things in Kansas, and that the source of the information should be such as to insure its accuracy. You are therefore directed by him to communicate constantly with this department. Such facts as it is deemed important to have early known here, you will cause to be transmitted by telegraph as well as by mail.

"The President indulges a hope, that, by your energy, impartiality, and discretion, the tranquillity of the territory will be restored, and the persons and property of the citizens therein protected.

"I am, sir, &c.,

"W. L. MARCY."

"His Excellency, John W. Geary,
"Governor of Kansas Territory."

In order that the governor might have ample means to carry out these instructions, and *"to maintain order and quiet in the territory of Kansas, and if disturbances occurred therein, to bring to punishment the offenders,"* he was not only given discretionary powers as to the expenditure of money, but was directed, if he found the United States forces inadequate, not only to muster into the service the militia of the territory, but to avail himself of requisitions made upon the governors of other states. A letter received from the secretary of state was as follows:—

"Department of State:
"Washington, September 2, 1856.

"Sir: Reliable information having reached the President that armed and organized bodies of men, avowedly in rebellion against the territorial government, have concentrated in such numbers as to require additional military force for their dispersion, you will have the militia of the territory, completely enrolled and organized, to the end that they may on short notice be brought into the service of the United States. Upon requisition of the commander of the military department in which Kansas is embraced, you will furnish by companies, or regiments, or brigades, or divisions, such number and composition of troops, as, from time to time, you may find, on his report to you, to be necessary for the suppression of all combinations to resist the laws of the United States too powerful to be suppressed by the civil authority, and for the maintenance of public order and civil government in the territory.

"I am, sir, &c.,
"W. L. MARCY.

"To His Excellency, John W. Geary,
"Governor of the Territory of Kansas. Lecompton."

A dispatch was also forwarded to General Smith, by the secretary of war. From the instructions this contains, as well as from the tenor of other documents that will be found in this chapter, it is quite palpable that the administration at Washington had been utterly deceived in regard to the true condition of things in Kansas, and was laboring under the strange hallucination that all the difficulties existing there were attributable to free-state settlers and invaders. These were the only persons who were supposed to be violating "the peace and quiet" of the territory; these were the only offenders whom Governor Geary was expected to "bring to punishment;" these were the parties against whom the troops were to be employed; and hence it is not difficult to account for the fact that the countenance of the administration was withheld and the troops withdrawn from him, as soon as it was ascertained that he had so far misunderstood his instructions and the wishes of his employers, as to cause the arrest of a pro-slavery murderer. All went well so long as he continued to cram the filthy jail with free-state prisoners; but his fate was sealed when he exhibited a disposition to punish their political opposers. This was no part of the programme, and the powers at Washington were astonished that Geary did not understand, or, understanding, did not lend his aid to further their policy. The following is a copy of the dispatch from the secretary of war:—

"War Department:
"Washington, September 3, 1856.

"Sir: Your dispatch of 22d August and its enclosures sufficiently exhibit the inadequacy of the force under your command to perform the duties which have been devolved upon you in the present unhappy condition of Kansas by the orders and instructions heretofore communicated. To meet this exigency, the President has directed the governor of the territory to complete the enrolment and organization of the militia, as you will find fully set forth in the enclosed copy of a letter addressed to him by the secretary of state; and the president has directed me to say to you that you are authorized, from time to time, to make requisitions upon the governor for such militia force as you may require to enable you promptly and successfully to execute your orders and suppress insurrection against the government of the territory of Kansas, and under the circumstances heretofore set forth in your instructions, to give the requisite aid to the officers of the civil government who may be obstructed in the due execution of the law. Should you not be able to derive from the militia of Kansas the adequate force for these purposes, such additional number of militia as may be necessary will be drawn from the states of Illinois and Kentucky, as shown in the requisition, a copy of which is here enclosed.

"The views contained in your instructions to the officers commanding the troops, under date of August 19, are fully approved, and accord so entirely with the purposes of the executive as to leave but little to add in relation to the course which it is desired you should pursue. The position of the insurgents, as shown by your letter and its enclosures, is that of open rebellion against the laws and constitutional authorities, with such manifestation of a purpose to spread devastation over the land as no longer justifies further hesitation or indulgence. To you, as to every soldier whose habitual feeling is to protect the citizens of his own country, and only to use his arms against a public enemy, it cannot be otherwise than deeply painful to be brought into conflict with any portion of his fellow-countrymen; but patriotism and humanity alike require that rebellion should be promptly crushed, and the perpetration of the crimes which now disturb the peace and security of the good people of the territory of Kansas should be effectually checked. You will, therefore, energetically employ all the means within your reach to restore the supremacy of law, always endeavoring to carry out your present purpose to prevent the unnecessary effusion of blood.

"In making your requisitions for militia force, you will be governed by the existing organization of the army and the laws made and provided in such cases. When companies, regiments, brigades, or divisions are presented to be mustered into the service of the United States, you will cause them, before they are received, to be minutely inspected by an officer of your command, appointed for the purpose.

"Very respectfully, your obedient servant,

"JEFFERSON DAVIS,

"Secretary of War.

"Major-General Persifer F. Smith,

"Commanding Department of the West."

The following, sent by telegraph to the governor, establishes the fact beyond a doubt, that the government regarded *all the offences* as coming from *one party*, the free-state; because, while it points out, with exaggeration, outrages alleged to have been committed by that party, it makes no mention of, nor reference to, the still greater enormities perpetrated by the pro-slavery agitators and invaders:—

"Washington, September 9, 1856.

"To J. W. GEARY.

"I presume the orders sent by Colonel Emory on the 3d instant have already reached you. If the militia which those orders made subject to the requisition of General Smith are not sufficient for the exigency, notify me by telegraph. *The insurrectionary invasion of the territory by the way of Nebraska, and the subsequent hostile attacks on the post-office at Franklin, and on the dwellings of Titus and of Clarke, seem to have stimulated to unlawful acts of the same character on the borders of Missouri.* The President expects you to maintain the public peace, and to bring to punishment all acts of violence or disorder by whomever perpetrated and on whatever pretext. And he relies on your energy and discretion, and the approved capacity, decision, and coolness of character of General Smith, to prevent or suppress all attempts to kindle civil war in the territory of Kansas. A communication on the same subject has this day been telegraphed to General Smith, by the secretary of war, with positive directions that no parties or bodies of armed men shall be allowed to carry on military operations in the territory, save such persons as are enrolled by him into the service of the United States.

"W. L. MARCY,

"Secretary of State."

It is true that the honorable secretary of state here directs the governor to "*bring to punishment all acts of violence or disorder, by whomever perpetrated, and on whatever pretext;*" but, at the same time, while he distinctly points to every offence that could be charged against the free-state men, even to *a hostile attack upon the house of Clarke*, which house had never been molested, he seems to have been entirely oblivious of the fact that General Reid and Captain Pate and General Whitfield, at the head of armed bands of Missourians, had invaded the territory, sacked towns, robbed post-offices, burned houses, ravished and branded women, stolen horses and cattle, destroyed crops, and committed other enormities too horrible to imagine or describe. He seemed insensible of the fact, that a band of marauders, under the command of this very man Clarke, whose house is falsely alleged to have been assailed, had pillaged stores and dwellings, and after having murdered a man in the most brutal manner, buried him a few inches below the ground, leaving his hands sticking out for tomb-stones; and at the time the secretary was writing his dispatch, an immense army was congregating in Missouri, carrying black flags as the indices of their murderous intentions, for the purpose of invading Kansas, under the authority of the governor, to destroy free-state towns and massacre their inhabitants. These were not the men whom Governor Geary was expected to "bring to punishment;" for he no sooner dared to lay his hand upon the worst assassin of them all, than he was clearly given to understand that his services were no longer needed.

Immediately after the dismissal of the volunteers called into service by Secretary Woodson, as related in another chapter, Governor Geary gave the requisite instructions for the enrolment of all the actual citizens of the territory, with a view to the proper organization of the militia, to be mustered into the service of the government whenever exigencies should seem to require. It was soon apparent that several companies would be needed to assist the civil authorities to execute warrants, to guard the prisoners of the territory, and to aid in the maintenance of the peace in various localities. General Smith being made aware of this fact, he made requisition, as follows, upon the governor, for three companies, one of cavalry and two of infantry, to be mustered into the regular service of the United States:—

"Head Quarters, Department of the West,
"Fort Leavenworth, September 17, 1856.

"His Excellency, J. W. Geary,
"Governor of the Territory of Kansas.

"Sir: By virtue of the authority given me by the President of the United States, a copy of which is in your possession, I have the honor to make a requisition on you for two companies of militia, infantry, for the service of the United States.

"Each company to consist of one captain, one first-lieutenant, four sergeants, four corporals, two musicians, and seventy-four privates.

"The companies, when ready, will be mustered into the service of the United States by an officer who will be detailed for that purpose by Lieutenant-Colonel Cooke from his command.

"With the highest respect, your obedient servant,

"PERSIFER F. SMITH,

"Bt. Major-General commanding Department."

On the 28th, a similar requisition was made "for one company of cavalry, to consist of one captain, one first-lieutenant, one second-lieutenant, four sergeants, four corporals, two buglers, one farrier and blacksmith, and seventy-four privates."

These companies were forthwith organized and duly mustered into the service for the period of three months, by United States officers detailed for that purpose. One of these infantry companies was raised at Lawrence, and was composed entirely of free-state men, under the command of Captain Samuel Walker. The others were enrolled and stationed at Lecompton, and were all of the pro-slavery party, the mounted company commanded by Captain John Wallis, and the infantry by Captain John Donaldson. In all they numbered nearly two hundred and fifty men. Colonel H. T. Titus having been commissioned by the governor, as his aid-de-camp, had special direction of these troops.

Peace being thoroughly established in every part of the territory, and the militia wearying of their inactivity, became desirous of returning to the pursuits of civil life, and on the 19th of November the free-state company at Lawrence addressed a communication to the governor, signed by the captain and all his men, as follows:—

"The undersigned, members of the Kansas militia, mustered into the service of the United States, at Lawrence, K. T., in obedience to your call, would respectfully submit, that when our services were required, the territory was distracted with internal feuds and threatened with invasion by those from abroad who had no residence in the country, then, since, or prospectively.

"We were ready to give assistance in staying the hand of violence, which had laid this country waste, to some extent depopulated it, and made life insecure. We trusted you were sincere in your professions to act justly towards the settlers, and we cheerfully left our ordinary occupations to aid, so far as we could, in restoring peace and quiet to this unfortunate territory.

"We have watched your course since your arrival amongst us as our executive, with much anxiety, and although we have wished to see you do what you have not done, still we are sensible, and bear it in grateful remembrance, that, by your activity and energy, you have done much towards the restoration of that feeling of protection that all who live under organized governments have a right to expect. We thank you for it, and trust confidently that you may not forget that we are part and parcel of this great republic, although we may differ from our neighboring state on some political subjects.

"We now feel that you have the power and will to protect the citizens of the country, and that, therefore, our services are not required. If you think such is the case, we request to be permitted to return to our several occupations, with the assurance that should you require our assistance in the future, you may be sure that right and justice to all will always be the object of our best efforts, and should you call for them, they will be given to you with unreserved zeal and fidelity."

Upon the receipt of this petition, the governor addressed a letter to General Smith, informing him of the continuation of the general peace, and that the services of the militia could be dispensed with, and suggested "the propriety of mustering them out of the service, in order that they might retire to their homes, and gratify their desires in the pursuits of peace."

A few days afterwards, on the 25th, a similar request to that of Captain Walker, was received from Captain Donaldson and his company. This had seventy-eight signatures, and read as follows:—

"We, the undersigned, officers and members of Company A, 2d Regt. Inft. Kansas Militia, believing that the policy adopted by your excellency, which has been so rigidly carried out, has produced such happy results that we can no longer serve you to advantage; whilst, therefore, acknowledging our appreciation and admiration of that peace and quiet which has been restored once more by your noble efforts, we respectfully ask to be discharged honorably from the service."

On the same day, the following communication, signed by Captain Wallis and all his men, was also received:—

"The general peace pervading the territory, indicating that the object for which we were called into service has been accomplished, should it meet your approbation, we are now desirous of quitting the tented field, and returning to our homes, our families and friends, where we hope, under your effective administration, to be permitted peaceably and safely to attend our varied avocations. These hopes are inspired by what we have seen of your success in quelling the disturbances by which our territory has been so sadly distressed. Confiding in your integrity and ability, you have our most devout wishes that peace may attend your administration, and that the reward of patriotism may be yours."

These communications were respectively answered by the governor, their compliments to his integrity and efficiency acknowledged, and the means immediately adopted to comply with the request of the petitioners. A correspondence having been opened on the subject with General Smith, he appointed the 1st day of December, by especial desire of the governor, to muster the two pro-slavery companies out of service at Fort Leavenworth, and the other at Lawrence. It then appeared that the paymaster had no appropriation for the payment of these troops; hence the governor, in a letter to General Smith, says:—

"I send by Major S. Woods a warrant of my own private funds, payable to your order, for fifteen hundred dollars, to be handed over to the paymaster for the purpose of paying the privates and non-commissioned officers. * * * It appears to me that if application be made to the department, payment would be ordered to the volunteers, and I would be immediately reimbursed."

In reply to this the governor was informed by communication from head-quarters, that no instructions could be given for the payment of the militia "until an appropriation for that purpose is made by Congress," and hence it would be necessary for the governor "to make arrangements with some individual to disburse" the fifteen hundred dollars he had forwarded "to the men to be discharged." Secretary Woodson was accordingly chosen for that purpose, and the militia were dismissed from the service, having been paid with the governor's private funds, although mustered by direction of the president, and on requisition of the commander of the military department of the west.

Peace continuing to prevail, the governor had in the mean time announced the fact to General Smith, and suggested that, for the comfort of the regular troops, their services not being immediately required, they should be withdrawn to Fort Leavenworth for winter-quarters, which was accordingly done, one small company of infantry, under Captain Flint, being left to guard the prisoners at Tecumseh, and a company of twenty-three dragoons, under Captain Newby, being quartered on the Grasshopper Creek near Lecompton.

Such was the gratifying aspect of affairs through the entire fall and winter, until the peace was again threatened by the almost daily outrages of Sherrard and his friends, the predictions of the *Lecompton Union*, and at last, the personal insult offered to the governor on the 9th of February, and the open endorsement of that act by a large portion of the members of the legislature. Before this latter occurrence, a number of peaceful citizens had called upon the governor, urging the necessity for the presence at Lecompton of a small force of United States troops to protect them against the threatened disturbances. Finding, from his own experience, that this alarm was not altogether groundless, as he had before supposed, he dispatched a messenger with the following requisition to General Smith:—

"Executive Department, Kansas Territory,
"February 9, 1857.

'MAJOR-GENERAL PERSIFER F. SMITH,
"Commanding Department of the West.

"Dear Sir: There are certain persons present in Lecompton, who are determined, if within the bounds of possibility, to bring about a breach of the peace. During the last few days a number of persons have been grossly insulted; and to-day an insult has been offered to myself. A person named Sherrard, who some days ago had been appointed Sheriff of Douglas county, which appointment was strongly protested against by a respectable number of the citizens of the county, and I had deferred commissioning him. This, it appears, gave mortal offence to Sherrard, and he has made up his mind to *assassinate* me. This may lead to *trouble.* It must be prevented, and that by immediate action. I require, therefore, two additional companies of dragoons, to report to me with the least possible delay. *I think this is absolutely necessary, and I trust you will immediately comply with my request.* I write in great haste, as the messenger is about leaving.

"I wish you would keep an eye upon Leavenworth City, as I hear of troublesome indications there. I am confident that there is a conspiracy on foot to disturb the peace, and various pretexts *will be*, and have been used to accomplish this fell purpose.

"I am perfectly cool, and intend to keep so; but I am also more vigilant than ever.

"Very truly, your friend,
"JNO. W. GEARY."

It soon became known through the town that the governor had sent a messenger to Fort Leavenworth for troops, and the fact afforded ground for merriment to the crowds of ruffians who hung about the groggeries, ready to commit any atrocity by direction of certain prominent men; they having received later intelligence from the seat of government than his excellency, and been satisfactorily assured that the United States forces were no longer under his control. Information to this effect was conveyed to Governor Geary, who treated it with the scorn he supposed it merited. What, then, was his astonishment, when the messenger returned from General Smith with the following answer:—

"Head Quarters, Department of the West,
"Fort Leavenworth, Feb. 11, 1857.

"His Excellency, John W. Geary,
"Governor of Kansas Territory,
"Lecompton, K. T.

"Governor: I have the honor to acknowledge the receipt of your letter of the 9th instant, in which you 'require immediately, two additional companies of dragoons to report to you in consequence of your confidence that there is a conspiracy on foot to disturb the peace'—and also acknowledge the receipt of a previous letter requiring a battalion to be sent to you in view of the large immigration expected here in the spring.

"If you refer to the laws you will observe that the president is authorized to call the military and naval forces into action, to: 1st, repel invasion; 2d, to suppress insurrection; and 3d, to repress combinations to obstruct the execution of the laws, too strong for the civil power. Insults or probable breaches of the peace do not authorize the employment of the troops.

"Besides, all the forces here have just been designated by the secretary of war, and are under orders, for other service more distant; and even the companies near you will have to be recalled. They are sufficient to repress any breach of the peace, and I cannot move them until the weather improves.

"But even they are to be employed to aid the civil authority only in the contingencies mentioned in the laws above referred to. The garrisons to be left in the territory will be available if the president directs their employment.

"The contingency under which the troops were acting I consider to have ceased. Without the grossest imprudence on the part of the civil authorities in Leavenworth, I see not the slightest probability of any disturbance there; and on inquiry, I can hear of none from various inhabitants. With the highest respect,

"Your obedient servant,
"Persifer F. Smith,
"Brevet Major-General commanding."

This was the first official information he had received of the fact that the government, which had sent him to Kansas, to suppress insurrection, preserve the peace, and punish offenders, with the largest promises of support and assistance, had secretly taken from him even the means to protect his own life against assassins, who being apprised of the action at Washington, and encouraged by it, were plotting his destruction. When he took possession of the government of Kansas, he was to have control, not only of all the regular forces in the territory, to be used at *his discretion*, when *he* considered exigencies required their employment, but he was empowered to enrol *all the militia of the territory, and muster them into the service*, and to call upon the governors of Kentucky and Illinois for two additional regiments. *Now*, having conquered a peace by his indomitable energy, and saved the country from an impending civil war, and finding the peace again threatened and his own life in danger, in order to obey his instructions to "preserve the peace" he had established, and be governed by "*the exigencies of affairs as they should be presented to* HIM *on the spot*," he calls upon General Smith for a few soldiers, who, in reply, tells him that the troops are no longer under his control; "*the contingency under which they were acting I consider to have ceased;*" "*besides, all the forces here have just been designated by the secretary of war, and are under orders, for other service more distant, and even the companies near you will have to be recalled!*"

Never was a grosser insult ever offered to an official. And why? Governor Geary had accomplished the ostensible object of his mission to Kansas. He had put an end to a destructive civil war, and from chaos, confusion, and wretchedness, brought peace, prosperity and happiness. True; but he had done more than that. He had arrested a pro-slavery murderer, and when a partial chief justice had set him at liberty, he persisted in bringing him to justice and punishment, agreeably to the letter of his instructions. Other pro-slavery murderers, and the companions of such, made their complaints at Washington; Calhoun and Clarke declared that Geary should be removed for that act; they had sufficient influence to accomplish their threats, and succeeded to perfection.

Whilst things were in this condition, and the indignation meeting of honest citizens was about to be held at Lecompton on the 18th of February, Judge Cato, as has been related, called upon the governor, requesting him to interpose his authority to disperse the meeting. The judge knew that the governor had no authority to interpose—he knew that he had been stripped of all military power, and that to appear at the meeting in person, would simply have been to present a mark for the bullet of the assassin, which, of all things, was then the most desired. At that time Captain Newby's small company of dragoons was on the north side of the Kansas River, which was impassable, in consequence of the ice having just broken up, and might just as well, for all the use they could have rendered the governor, have been in the Fejee Islands; and Captain Flint's company of infantry were ten miles off at Tecumseh. Besides, both these companies were ordered to report themselves at Fort Leavenworth, as soon as the weather would permit them to travel, which they did, Captain Flint's company stopping at Lecompton, and taking with it the *only soldier* the governor had left to guard an iron safe containing the public documents, and moneys belonging to himself and others.

Shortly after the receipt of the foregoing letter of General Smith, the governor returned the following reply, which did not reach the general at Fort Leavenworth, he having departed for Washington:—

"Executive Department, K. T.,
"Lecompton, March 2, 1857.

"MAJOR-GENERAL P. F. SMITH,
"Commanding Department of the West.

"Dear Sir: Your letter of 11th February was duly received, and my most serious consideration has been given to its contents.

"I regret to be compelled to differ from you in the opinion that 'the contingency under which the troops were acting' has 'ceased.' It seems to me that a proper view of the existing condition of things in the territory would lead to a different conclusion.

"The peace that now prevails is not only threatened by irresponsible individuals, but its destruction is boldly proclaimed by the newspaper *organ* of a clique or faction of sufficient influence and numbers 'to obstruct the execution of the laws,' and 'too strong for the civil power.' That attempts have been made to execute these threats and verify these predictions, you have already received conclusive assurances.

"That the presence of the troops here has been needed up to the present moment, and that it has held in check those determined to create disturbances, is quite apparent; and that their removal at this time, when their presence is daily becoming more needful, will be attended with serious and perhaps calamitous results, is very probable.

"Besides, the large incoming immigration of peaceful settlers requires protection, which cannot be given by any civil posses that can be raised, in consequence of the bitter feelings existing among the advocates of conflicting political sentiments on the highly exciting question which so long kept the territory in a state of feverish agitation and even anarchy.

"Large combinations will doubtless be formed to resist attempted and even threatened violations of the law—and invasion and insurrection, with their fearful consequences, may be anticipated.

"The *presence* of the troops, even should their active service never be required, will be sufficient, perhaps, to 'repel invasion,' which there is reason to expect—'suppress insurrection,' which has been predicted by seeming authority—and 'repress combinations to obstruct the execution of the laws too strong for the civil power,' which seem to exist.

"The withdrawal of all the troops at this time would, in my opinion, be the signal for the lawless to commence difficulties, which their presence alone may entirely prevent. A little care to guard against evils which we can foresee, may prevent others of greater magnitude which are beyond our comprehension.

"In view of these facts, I must respectfully ask, that Captain Newby's company may be permitted to remain in this vicinity during the present month, or, at least, until I shall be able to communicate with and receive an answer from the authorities at Washington, upon the subject. The importance of the matter will doubtless suggest itself to your mind, and grant a ready compliance with this request.

"An immediate answer will oblige, most sincerely,

"Your friend and obedient servant,

"JNO. W. GEARY,

"Governor of Kansas Territory."

In view of the facts so clearly established by the foregoing documents—that General Smith had declined furnishing Governor Geary with troops at the time *he* supposed their services were needed; that the general declared the secretary of war had ordered all the forces to other and more distant service; and that even the few soldiers still near the governor had been ordered to report themselves at Fort Leavenworth, as soon as the weather would sufficiently moderate to enable them to travel,—it is somewhat remarkable that General Smith, after the resignation of Governor Geary, should have addressed the following communication to Secretary Davis:—

"Baltimore, March 28, 1857.

"HON. JEFFERSON DAVIS,

"Senator.

"Dear Sir: I received a letter a few minutes since from the editor of the *Evening Star*, requesting me to 'substantiate a contradiction you make to some assertion in the *Herald* of Governor Geary.' I happen to have my letter-book, and send you a copy of my letter to the governor when he 'required' a squadron of dragoons to be sent to him. He had already Captain Newby's and Captain Flint's companies of troops under his control, and he stated no case that would justify reinforcing them in the middle of the winter. I declined sending them, evidently without your interference in the matter, for you were in Washington. His letter is of the 9th February and my answer of the 11th. I exercised the discretion left me by the president, for I saw there was no need of them.

"I send the copy to you, for I do not think myself at liberty to publish part of an official correspondence without authority from higher authority.

"Moreover, I think your simple contradiction is sufficient; the affair will not offer to Governor Geary any advantage in pursuing it, unless he provokes proof of what the *Herald* says, and that is on record in the Department of the West.

"I have copies of my letters, but his are on file in the office of the Department of the West.

"I repeat, that with my knowledge of all that took place the governor will not pursue the matter.

"With sincere respect, your obedient servant,

"PERSIFER F. SMITH,

Bt. Maj.-Gen. Comm'g Dep't of the West."

In the general's letter to the governor he says: "All the forces here have just been designated *by the secretary of war*, and are under orders for other service more distant." In the letter to General Davis he says: "I declined sending them, evidently without your interference in the matter, for you were in Washington." What General Smith means by saying that the simple contradiction of Secretary Davis will be sufficient to disprove the fact that the troops had been withdrawn from Governor Geary's service, it would be extremely difficult to comprehend. It is certain that the troops *were* withdrawn, and from the following communication to the Adjutant-General of the United States, it would seem at the suggestion of General Smith himself:—

Head-Quarters, Department of the West,

"Fort Leavenworth, Saturday, Nov. 11.

"Colonel: Since my last communication nothing of importance has happened in the department. After the success of the measures taken a few weeks since to prevent the gross outrages on the law, then threatened, and to suppress the disorders then existing in the territory, order and tranquillity have gradually resumed their legitimate sway; the laws have again been put in operation, and the administration of justice revived. Deserted farms are again occupied, fences rebuilt, fields put under cultivation, and the ruins of houses, destroyed by fire, replaced by more durable habitations; the roads are covered with travellers, unarmed and secure; and the towns thronged with persons selling their produce and purchasing from the stores. All these evidences of restored order have enabled me, with the concurrence of the governor of the territory, to recall the troops from the active duty on which they have been employed, and to establish them again at their proper posts, where they are to pass the winter. As there are no secure prisons yet built for territorial authorities to use in the administration of justice, at his request there will remain at the disposition of the governor a few men to guard prisoners in the custody of the law and for other such contingencies.

"I am happy, then, to be enabled to announce to the War Department, and through it to the president, the entire success of the measures they directed to be taken for the suppression of insurrection and removal of obstructions to the regular administration of justice, and that this end has been attained without the shedding of blood or the exertion of any force beyond the ordinary arrest of persons accused of crimes.

"The winter has commenced with severity much earlier than usual, and it is now too late to send the companies of the Sixth Infantry to the posts further west—their original destination. From necessity they must be crowded into the quarters at Fort Leavenworth. The great reduction in the number of men in the First Cavalry will render this possible now, which it would not be if the latter regiment were full.

"Being no longer occupied with the affairs of the territory, which have caused so much uneasiness, undivided attention can be paid for punishing the Cheyennes Indians. In pursuing them in the spring, the great want will be forage and transportation for supplies. Pasturing animals in rapid movements is impossible; nor can horses perform a regular day's work on grass. In short, daily journeys, grass is sufficient, for there is time to pasture and very little labor to undergo. Additional appropriations will therefore be necessary to provide for the expedition, which must be chiefly of mounted men, and ought to be ready by the middle of April. The details of the force and the direction of the operations cannot now be determined; but a general appropriation of an additional sum—much less, however, than that given to the Sioux expedition—will be advisable.

"I will again report that I consider tranquillity and order entirely restored in Kansas. I foresee nothing in the shape of disorder that the ordinary means in the hands of the civil authority, directed by as able and energetic hands as those of the present governor, are not amply sufficient to control; and the whole time and efforts of the troops here can henceforward be devoted to the protection of the frontier.

"With the highest respect, your obedient servant,

"PERSIFER F. SMITH,

"Commanding Department."

"Colonel Samuel Cooper, Adjutant-General of the Army."

Now, from all this, it very clearly appears that, although the president had placed at the disposal of Governor Geary the United States forces in Kansas, to preserve the peace and bring offenders to punishment, and to be employed by him as *he* supposed existing circumstances should require, those forces, at the suggestion of General Smith (who had been confined, by indisposition, to his quarters during the entire term of Governor Geary's administration, and, therefore, had very limited opportunities for ascertaining the true condition of the territory, and the exigencies that might demand the use of troops), and without consulting Governor Geary on the subject, were taken from the support of the governor and ordered to other service, and that at a time when the peace of the territory and the life of the executive were alike threatened and in danger.

CHAPTER XLIII.

Resignation of Governor Geary.—His Farewell Address.

Governor Geary was not only deprived of the use of the sword at a time when he considered it needful to carry out his instructions, but the public purse-strings were also drawn against him. The following communication was received on the 13th of November:—

"Department of State,
"Washington, October 30th, 1856.

"John W. Geary, Esq.
"Governor of the Territory of Kansas.

"Sir:—I have received your letter of the 6th inst., in which you ask to be furnished with a draft for two thousand dollars for meeting the contingent expenses of the government of Kansas.

The president does not doubt the necessity that you should be put in possession of the means you have asked for, and he has gone into a careful examination of the authority he has under the laws, to comply with your request. He regrets to be obliged to state that this examination has resulted in a conviction on his part, that he has no authority to advance for the contingent expenses of the government of Kansas territory, any amount whatever, beyond the sum appropriated by Congress for that purpose. The appropriation, which was an inconsiderable sum, has been exhausted, and there is no power in the executive government of the United States to furnish you with any more. This state of things is most seriously regretted; for, situated as you are, the sum provided by Congress for the contingent expenses of the territory must fall far short of that required for the public service. The subject, will, of course, occupy the attention of

Congress at the approaching session; but what will be its decision on it cannot be foretold. I should think there could be no doubt, that the next Congress will provide the means for paying all the expenses which may be or have been properly incurred in administering the affairs of the territorial government.

"I am, sir, very respectfully, your obedient servant,

"W. L. MARCY."

Such was the encouragement received by Governor Geary from the government at Washington. It could have been nothing less than an enlarged patriotism that caused him to retain so long the most thankless and unprofitable office in the nation. For months he had labored for the public good with untiring energy, not even taking time for needed rest and sleep; deprived of all the usual comforts of life; occupying a log house, and very often unable to obtain wholesome food; vexed and harassed hourly with the complaints of an abused people; constant drafts being made by persons whom he was compelled to employ, upon his pecuniary resources; required to pay the militia called into the service by the president himself, from his own private funds; every federal officer in the territory conspiring to embarrass his administration; his mails overhauled and their contents examined by government officials; surrounded with organized bands of assassins; and without a word of comfort or a particle of aid from the general government, he still continued, with fidelity, zeal and unflagging energy, to discharge the arduous duties of his station.

Under these discouraging circumstances, he addressed a lengthy letter to Secretary Marcy, on the 22d of November, from which the following is extracted:—

"I herewith transmit you by the hands of Brevet Major H. H. Sibley, a copy of my executive minutes from the 17th day of October to the 21st day of November, inclusive. These minutes will furnish you a truthful history of Kansas affairs. They embrace a daily record of all my official transactions, and a full statement of any matters requiring explanation.

"Fully appreciating the delicate and responsible mission confided to me by the generous partiality of the president, and knowing how liable, amid the strife and prejudice which seemed to hold undisturbed sway here, a person with the most patriotic intentions might be to misrepresentation and abuse, I adopted the custom of keeping an hourly record of all events, in any manner connected with my official action, which, from time to time, I might send to you, as my best vindication to the administration and the country.

"Properly to keep my executive minutes—to answer the heavy correspondence with this department—to prepare official dispatches—to execute missions requiring secrecy and intelligence—and perform the multifarious duties devolving upon me, owing to the anomalous condition of affairs, has occupied my whole time, assisted by industrious and intelligent secretaries, whom the public exigencies required me to employ.

"As occasions arose, I did not pause to enter into any refined analysis of the nature and extent of my authority, nor to inquire where the money would come from to reimburse necessary and imperative expenditures; but at once adopted the means best calculated to secure the desired end, and paid all expenses out of my own private resources, confiding in the justice of the administration and Congress for a reimbursement and support.

"Your general instructions have been the lights by which my official action has been governed, and where the letter of instruction did not meet the crisis, I have based my action on that portion of your comprehensive dispatch of the 23d of September, in which you say:—

"'Your prompt and vigorous attention will be directed towards those who *meditate* further mischief and are *disposed to obstruct* your efforts to restore the supremacy of the civil authority! The president *relies upon your energy and discretion* to overcome the difficulties which surround you, and to restore tranquillity to Kansas. *The exigencies of affairs, as they shall be presented to you on the spot*, will indicate the course of proceeding in particular cases, calculated to such results, better than any definite instructions emanating from this department.'

"At so great a distance from the general government, and so inaccessible to speedy communications from Washington, it is absolutely indispensable for the preservation of order and the protection of life, liberty and property, that the governor of this territory should be clothed with large discretionary powers.

"When I arrived here the entire territory was declared, by the acting-governor, to be in a state of insurrection; the civil authority was powerless, and so complicated by partisan affiliations as to be without capacity to vindicate the majesty of the law and restore the broken peace.

"In this state of affairs the most vigorous and determined action on my part seemed the only remedy for the growing evils. Impartial justice will ever commend itself to every American citizen worthy to bear the name. To disband armed bodies of men assembled under color of law, and disperse others brought into antagonistic existence without authority; both inflamed by the most exciting of questions, and both committing outrages which all good men must deplore, required neither hesitation nor fear.

"I am most happy to inform you that in order to calm these disturbing elements, and bring the people back to sober reason, I have not been obliged to resort to any measures unknown to the law, and not covered by the spirit and letter of my instructions. It is also a matter of special gratification to be able to say, that since my arrival here, peace has been restored and the fierce passions of men soothed, without the shedding of *one drop* of fratricidal blood.

"The peace of the territory is now placed upon a permanent basis, all parties having at length relinquished the idea of a resort to arms, and agreeing to refer the adjustment of all political disputes to the ballot box or other lawful expedients."

Such was the condition of things until the Sherrard disturbances, which were confined to the town of Lecompton. About the time of their occurrence, Calhoun, Clarke, Emory, and others went to Washington, with the avowed purpose of so prejudicing the government against Governor Geary, as to make certain his removal, and soon after, reports were returned from them to the effect that they had been entirely successful. These were circulated through all the public places, and were boldly published in the *Lecompton Union*, and very generally believed. Several persons had been named as the probable successor. During all this the governor's dispatches and letters to the outgoing and incoming administrations, defining the true condition of affairs, and asking for information and instruction, were unanswered and apparently unnoticed.

A proper sense of honor could, therefore, dictate but one course, and that was to relinquish the difficult and thankless position which he had thus far filled with such signal success —with such immense benefit to the country and credit to himself. He, therefore, on the day of the inauguration of the new President, dispatched the following letter of resignation to Washington:—

"Executive Department, K. T.,
"Lecompton, March 4, 1857.

"HIS EXCELLENCY, JAMES BUCHANAN,
"President of the United States.

"Dear Sir:—Please accept my resignation as Governor of Kansas territory, to take effect on the 20th of the present month, by which time you will be enabled to select and appoint a proper successor.

"With high respect, your friend and obedient servant,
"JNO. W. GEARY."

For prudential reasons the governor intended to keep the fact of his resignation a secret from the people of Kansas for some days, and hence made it known only to his private secretary, who deposited the letter in the post-office, late at night, and a few moments before the mail closed. The postmaster's son, and L. A. Maclean, the latter being always in the office at the opening and closing of the mails, were the only persons then present. Yet in the morning, before he had arisen from bed, the subject of the governor's letter to Washington was the theme of universal conversation through the town. It was freely discussed upon the streets and in all the grog-shops, and was a matter of no little interest and excitement. This fact furnished another conclusive proof, in addition to many that had been constantly occurring, of the propriety of a representation of the governor, contained in an official dispatch to Secretary Marcy, as far back as the 22d of September, but which, with many similar evils of which information had been given, remained unheeded. In the dispatch referred to, Governor Geary remarked:—

"There is still another subject to which it is proper that I should call your attention. The postal arrangements of the territory are lamentably inefficient. Complaints on this subject are loud and universal, and my own experience has convinced me that these are not without sufficient cause. Every package addressed to me through the mail is broken and inspected before it reaches my hands. It is entirely unsafe to send information through the post-office, and more especially to use that medium to forward anything of pecuniary value. Postmasters are either ignorant of their duty and obligations, or being acquainted with them, act in violation of both. Indeed, I have been credibly informed that in some places, persons not connected with the offices, are permitted to enter and overhaul the mails previous to their distribution. This is a serious evil, upon which some prompt action is needed."

Governor Geary left Lecompton on the 10th of March, and reached Washington City on the 21st. Here he had interviews with the president and members of the cabinet, to whom he personally communicated his views concerning the territory He found Emory, Clarke, Calhoun, and others of his worst enemies, who had been instrumental in doing most of the mischief that had disturbed the territory, so deeply ingratiated into the confidence and good opinion of these gentlemen, that there was no room to doubt their having good authority for the information they were daily furnishing their friends and associates in Kansas, and that he had not resigned his office an hour too soon. Had any doubt remained of this fact, and of the policy intended to be pursued by the new administration, it would have been removed, by the appointments that were immediately made for the most important and lucrative offices in the territory. The only free-state democrat holding office was removed, though a man of unquestionable integrity—an Indian agent, though a Virginian, was suspected or accused of free-state proclivities, and shared the same fate—all the most objectionable of the incumbents were retained—and others even still more objectionable appointed,—men, in fact, who had *no other recommendation than their complicity with the worst outrages that had disgraced the country!*

Governor Geary found Kansas involved in insurrection and civil war—he left it in the enjoyment of uninterrupted contentment, prosperity and peace. He asked to be reimbursed a portion of the money he had expended in the good work he had performed, and to be provided with a few soldiers to preserve the better state of affairs he had effected; both of which were refused. Not a man was allowed to remain to protect even himself and household against the robber and assassin.

Upon taking leave of the territory, Governor Geary issued the following:

"FAREWELL ADDRESS.

"*To the People of Kansas Territory:*

"Having determined to resign the executive office, and retire again to the quiet scenes of private life and the enjoyment of those domestic comforts of which I have so long been deprived, I deem it proper to address you on the occasion of my departure.

"The office from which I now voluntarily withdraw, was unsought by me, and at the time of its acceptance, was by no means desirable. This was quite evident, from the deplorable moral, civil and political condition of the territory — the discord, contention and deadly strife, which then and there prevailed—and the painful anxiety with which it was regarded by patriotic citizens in every portion of the American Union. To attempt to govern Kansas at such a period and under such circumstances, was to assume no ordinary responsibilities. Few men could have desired to undertake the task, and none would have been so presumptuous, without serious forebodings as to the result. That I should have hesitated, is no matter of astonishment to those acquainted with the facts; but that I accepted the appointment, was a well-grounded source of regret to many of my well-tried friends, who looked upon the enterprise as one that could terminate in nothing but disaster to myself. It was not supposed possible that order could be brought, in any reasonable space of time, and with the means at my command, from the then existing chaos.

"Without descanting upon the feelings, principles and motives which prompted me, suffice it to say, that I accepted the president's tender of the office of governor. In doing so, I sacrificed the comforts of a home, endeared by the strongest earthly ties and most sacred associations, to embark in an undertaking which presented at the best but a dark and unsatisfactory prospect. I reached Kansas and entered upon the discharge of my official duties in the most gloomy hour of her history. Desolation and ruin reigned on every hand. Homes and firesides were deserted. The smoke of burning dwellings darkened the atmosphere. Women and children, driven from their habitations, wandered over the prairies and through the woodlands, or sought refuge and protection even among the Indian tribes. The highways were infested with numerous predatory bands, and the towns were fortified and garrisoned by armies of conflicting partisans, each excited almost to frenzy, and determined upon mutual extermination. Such was, without exaggeration, the condition of the territory, at the period of my arrival. Her treasury was bankrupt. There were no pecuniary resources within herself to meet the exigencies of the time. The congressional appropriations, intended to defray the expenses of a year, were insufficient to meet the demands of a fortnight. The laws were null, the courts virtually suspended, and the civil arm of the government almost entirely powerless. Action—prompt, decisive, energetic action—was necessary. I at once saw what was needed, and without hesitation gave myself to the work. For six months I have labored with unceasing industry. The accustomed and needed hours for sleep have been employed in the public service. Night and day have official duties demanded unremitting attention. I have had no proper leisure moments for rest or recreation. My health has failed under the pressure. Nor is this all; to my own private purse, without assurance of reimbursement, have I resorted in every emergency, for the required funds. Whether these arduous services and willing sacrifices have been beneficial to Kansas and my country, you are abundantly qualified to determine.

"That I have met with opposition, and even bitter vituperation and vindictive malice, is no matter for astonishment. No man has ever yet held an important or responsible post in our own or any other country and escaped censure. I should have been weak and foolish indeed, had I expected to pass through the fiery ordeal entirely unscathed, especially as I was required, if not to come in conflict with, at least to thwart evil machinations, and hold in restraint wicked passions, or rid the territory of many lawless, reckless and desperate men. Beside, it were impossible to come in contact with the conflicting interests which governed the conduct of many well-disposed persons, without becoming an object of mistrust and abuse. While from others, whose sole object was notoriously personal advancement at any sacrifice of the general good and at every hazard, it would have been ridiculous to anticipate the meed of praise for disinterested action; and hence, however palpable might have been my patriotism, however just my official conduct, or however beneficial its results, I do not marvel that my motives have been impugned and my integrity maligned. It is, however, so well known, that I need scarcely record the fact, that those who have attributed my labors to a desire for gubernatorial or senatorial honors, were and are themselves the aspirants for those high trusts and powers, and foolishly imagined that I stood between them and the consummation of their ambitious designs and high-towering hopes.

"But whatever may be thought or said of my motives or desires, I have the proud consciousness of leaving this scene of my severe and anxious toil with clean hands, and the satisfactory conviction that He who can penetrate the inmost recesses of the heart, and read its secret thoughts, will approve my purposes and acts. In the discharge of my executive functions, I have invariably sought to do equal and exact justice to all men, however humble or exalted. I have eschewed all sectional disputations, kept aloof from all party affiliations, and have alike scorned numerous threats of personal injury and violence, and the most flattering promises of advancement and reward. And I ask and claim nothing more for the part I have acted than the simple merit of having endeavored to perform my duty. This I have done, at all times, and upon every occasion, regardless of the opinions of men, and utterly fearless of consequences. Occasionally I have been forced to assume great responsibilities, and depend solely upon my own resources to accomplish important ends; but in all such instances, I have carefully examined surrounding circumstances, weighed well the probable results, and acted upon my own deliberate judgment; and in now reviewing them, I am so well satisfied with the policy uniformly pursued, that were it to be done over again, it should not be changed in the slightest particular.

"In parting with you, I can do no less than give you a few words of kindly advice, and even of friendly warning. You are well aware that most of the troubles which lately agitated the territory, were occasioned by men who had no especial interest in its welfare. Many of them were not even residents; whilst it is quite evident that others were influenced altogether in the part they took in the disturbances by mercenary or other personal considerations. The great body of the actual citizens are conservative, law-abiding and peace-loving men, disposed rather to make sacrifices for conciliation and consequent peace, than to insist for their entire rights should the general good thereby be caused to suffer. Some of them, under the influence of the prevailing excitement and misguided opinions, were led to the commission of grievous mistakes, but not with the deliberate intention of doing wrong.

"A very few men, resolved upon mischief, may keep in a state of unhealthy excitement and involve in fearful strife an entire community. This was demonstrated during the civil commotions with which the territory was convulsed. While the people generally were anxious to pursue their peaceful callings, small combinations of crafty, scheming and designing men succeeded, from purely selfish motives, in bringing upon them a series of most lamentable and destructive difficulties. Nor are they satisfied with the mischief already done. They never desired that the present peace should be effected; nor do they intend that it shall continue if they have the power to prevent it. In the constant croakings of disaffected individuals in various sections, you hear only the expressions of evil desires and intentions. Watch, then, with a special, jealous and suspicious eye those who are continually indulging surmises of renewed hostilities. They are not the friends of Kansas, and there is reason to fear that some of them are not only the enemies of this territory, but of the Union itself. Its dissolution is their ardent wish, and Kansas has been selected as a fit place to commence the accomplishment of a most nefarious design. The scheme has thus far been frustrated; but it has not been abandoned. You are intrusted, not only with the guardianship of this territory, but the peace of the Union, which depends upon you in a greater degree than you may at present suppose.

"You should, therefore, frown down every effort to foment discord, and especially to array settlers from different sections of the Union in hostility against each other. All true patriots, whether from the north or south, the east or west, should unite together for that which is and must be regarded as a common cause, the preservation of the Union; and he who shall whisper a desire for its dissolution, no matter what may be his pretensions, or to what faction or party he claims to belong, is unworthy of your confidence, deserves your strongest reprobation, and should be branded as a traitor to his country. There is a voice crying from the grave of one whose memory is dearly cherished in every patriotic heart, and let it not cry in vain. It tells you that this attempt at dissolution is no new thing; but that, even as early as the days of our first president, it was agitated by ambitious aspirants for place and power. And if the appeal of a still more recent hero and patriot was needed in his time, how much more applicable is it now, and in this territory!

"'The possible dissolution of the Union,' he says, 'has at length become an ordinary and familiar subject of discussion. Has the warning voice of Washington been forgotten? or have designs already been formed to sever the Union? Let it not be supposed that I impute to all of those who have taken an active part in these unwise and unprofitable discussions, a want of patriotism or of public virtue. The honorable feelings of state pride and local attachments find a place in the bosoms of the most enlightened and pure. But while such men are conscious of their own integrity and honesty of purpose, they ought never to forget that the citizens of other states are their political brethren; and that, however mistaken they may be in their views, the great body of them are equally honest and upright with themselves. Mutual suspicions and reproaches may, in time, create mutual hostility, and artful and designing men will always be found who are ready to foment these fatal divisions, and to inflame the natural jealousies of different sections of the country. The history of the world is full of such examples, and especially the history of republics.'

"When I look upon the present condition of the territory, and contrast it with what it was when I first entered it, I feel satisfied that my administration has not been prejudicial to its interests. On every hand, I now perceive unmistakable indications of welfare and prosperity. The honest settler occupies his quiet dwelling, with his wife and children clustering around him, unmolested, and fearless of danger. The solitary traveller pursues his way unharmed over every public thoroughfare. The torch of the incendiary has been extinguished, and the cabins which were destroyed, have been replaced by more substantial buildings. Hordes of banditti no longer lie in wait in every ravine for plunder and assassination. Invasions of hostile armies have ceased, and infuriated partisans, living in our midst, have emphatically turned their swords into ploughshares, and their spears into pruning-hooks. Laborers are everywhere at work—farms are undergoing rapid improvements—merchants are driving a thriving trade, and mechanics pursuing with profit their various occupations. Real estate, in town and country, has increased in value almost without precedent, until in some places it is commanding prices that never could have been anticipated. Whether this healthy and happy change is the result solely of my executive labors, or not, it certainly has occurred during my administration. Upon yourselves must mainly depend the preservation and perpetuity of the present prosperous condition of affairs. Guard it with unceasing vigilance, and protect it as you would your lives. Keep down that party spirit, which, if permitted to obtain the mastery, must lead to desolation. Watch closely, and condemn in its infancy, every insidious movement that can possibly tend to discord and disunion. Suffer no local prejudices to disturb the prevailing harmony. To every appeal to these, turn a deaf ear, as did the Saviour of men to the promptings of the deceiver. Act as a united band of brothers, bound together by one common tie. Your interests are the same, and by this course alone can they be maintained. Follow this, and your hearts and homes will be made light and happy by the richest blessings of a kind and munificent Providence.

"To you, the peaceable citizens of Kansas, I owe my grateful acknowledgments for the aid and comfort your kind assurances and hearty co-operation have afforded in many dark and trying hours. You have my sincerest thanks, and my earnest prayers that you may be abundantly rewarded of Heaven.

"To the ladies of the territory—the wives, mothers, sisters and daughters of the honest settlers—I am also under a weight of obligation. Their pious prayers have not been raised in vain, nor their numerous assurances of confidence in the policy of my administration failed to exert a salutary influence.

"And last, though not the least, I must not be unmindful of the noble men who form the military department of the west. To General Persifer F. Smith and the officers acting under his command, I return my thanks for many valuable services. Although from different parts of the Union, and naturally imbued with sectional prejudices, I know of no instance in which such prejudices have been permitted to stand in the way of a faithful, ready, cheerful and energetic discharge of duty. Their conduct in this respect is worthy of universal commendation, and presents a bright example for those executing the civil power. The good behavior of all the soldiers who were called upon to assist me, is, in fact, deserving of especial notice. Many of these troops, officers and men, had served with me on the fields of Mexico against a foreign foe, and it is a source of no little satisfaction to know that the laurels there won have been further adorned by the praiseworthy alacrity with which they aided to allay a destructive fratricidal strife at home.

"With a firm reliance in the protecting care and overruling providence of that Great Being who holds in his hand the destinies alike of men and of nations, I bid farewell to Kansas and her people, trusting that whatever events may hereafter befall them, they will, in the exercise of His wisdom, goodness and power, be so directed as to promote their own best interest and that of the beloved country of which they are destined to form a most important part.

"JNO. W. GEARY.

"Lecompton, March 10, 1857."

CHAPTER XLIV.

Election of a free-state mayor at Leavenworth.—Arrest of the murderer of Hoppe.—Resignation of Judge Cunningham.—Appointment of Judge Williams.—Removal of Judge Lecompte.—Taking of the census.—Hon. Robert J. Walker.

WM. E. MURPHY, mayor of Leavenworth, having been appointed agent for the Potawattomie Indians, an election was held in that city, and H. J. Adams, a free-state candidate, was elected by a large majority of the inhabitants. This was about the first election held in that place upon which no unfair influences were brought to bear, and with which invaders from the opposite side of the river did not attempt to interfere. Mr. Adams entered upon the duties of his office with considerable energy, and by his prompt, decisive, and just action, soon gained the confidence and respect of all classes of the peaceably disposed citizens. One of his first important acts was the arrest of the murderer of Mr. Hoppe, the following account of which was furnished by a resident of Leavenworth City to the *Missouri Democrat*, under date of 27th of May:—

"Early yesterday morning, the mayor of this city received information that Fugitt was on board of a steamer lying at the levee. An officer was called, a writ placed in his hands, and with a posse he went to the steamer and found Fugitt locked in his state-room. The door was forced open, and Fugitt was asked his name. He replied that it was 'Jones.' He tried to make his escape, but was not successful. The officer arrested him, and the prisoner was conveyed to the court-room, where an effort was made to have him released on bail, by his counsel; but Judge Lecompte refused, and gave the marshal orders to ascertain whether he could place him in confinement at the fort; if not, to put him in chains and imprison him in the town jail, to which he was conveyed, and a guard placed over him, a large chain fastened to his feet, and to a ring in the floor of his cell the wretched man was fastened.

"This Fugitt is a young man, about twenty-five years of age, well dressed, a bad look about his face. I have just returned from a visit to the cell where he is confined. The iron door and grating was swung back by the keeper, and in company with a member of the press, I entered a damp, dark room, with a few small holes in each side to admit the air and light. The inmate was upon the bed; he arose as we entered, and commenced smoking. Yesterday he was very talkative with those who called upon him; this morning he would say but little. He protests that he is innocent of the crime alleged against him in the indictment. He is confined in the same room in which the Rev. E. Nute, of Lawrence, was imprisoned by Emery's gang, last summer, during the difficulties, and which he has so accurately described in several of the eastern journals.

"Fugitt is the same person who made a bet in this city last August, that before night he would have a Yankee scalp. He got a horse and rode out into the country a few miles, and met a German, a brother-in-law of the Rev. E. Nute, named Hoppe. He asked if he was from Lawrence. Hoppe replied that he was. Fugitt immediately levelled his revolver and fired, the shot taking effect in the temples, and Hoppe fell a corpse. The assassin dismounted from his horse, cut the scalp from the back of his head, tied it to the end of a pole, and returned to town, exhibiting it to the people, and boasting of his exploit. The body of the victim was found shortly after, and buried on 'Pilot Knob,' about two miles distant from this city. This same Fugitt was one of the party who, when the widow came from Lawrence to look for her husband's corpse, forced her on board of a steamer, and sent her down the river. Now, the assassin is in safe keeping, there is hope of justice being meted out to him, and that he will soon suffer for his crime on the gallows. He is to be arraigned for trial before Judge Lecompte, on Monday next. A packed jury may bring in a verdict of not guilty; but even then he is in danger of punishment. His murderous deeds were too public, and there are too many who saw him at the time and heard his boasting, to have him escape for the want of evidence. A gentleman now living in this city saw him exhibiting four scalps at one time, during the troubles of last summer. His trial will be watched with a great deal of interest by the people.

"The city marshal last night arrested, and locked up in jail, Deputy-Sheriff David Brown, of this county, for drunkenness. Leavenworth is fast becoming an orderly and well-governed city."

As Fugitt has no personal friends of influence in the territory; as the evidences of his guilt are clear and positive; and as it can no longer be a matter of policy for his former associates to screen or protect him, his conviction and punishment are considered as certain. If this be so, he will be the first of the hundreds of murderers who will suffer the just penalty of the violated law.

Thomas Cunningham, Esq., who had been appointed to fill the vacancy occasioned by the death of the associate justice of the territory, reached Kansas in January, and remained there during the session of the Legislative Assembly, acquainting himself thoroughly with the true condition of the country and of his prospects for usefulness in that field of judicial labor. Judge Cunningham was from Beaver county, Pennsylvania; has been during his whole life an active member of the democratic party, and was one of the electors for Mr. Buchanan, in the late presidential canvass. He is a gentleman of superior legal attainments and unquestioned integrity; frank and fearless in the expression of his opinions, and manly and courteous in his whole deportment. He was not slow to discover the cause of the past and existing difficulties, and the course of conduct that exigencies demanded him to pursue. The inefficiency of his associates was apparent, as well from their want of proper legal knowledge as their partisan affiliations and complication with the disturbances that had distracted the territory. Determined to avoid the rock upon which they had split, he marked out for himself a just and honorable line of conduct, and, in the prosecution of his duties, resolved to recognise no local party, but to hold the scales of justice with an even hand; in conforming to which resolution, he refused to identify himself with the pro-slavery faction that assumed the name of the "National Democracy," or be present at any of its meetings. He, therefore, failed to meet the approbation of the Legislature, who, in apportioning him a district, took care to assign him a position which they felt assured he would not accept, as he could not occupy it with satisfaction to himself or benefit to the people. After duly considering all the circumstances connected with his situation, Judge Cunningham tendered his resignation to President Buchanan, and returned, doubtless somewhat disgusted with what he had learned, to his former home. Judge Joseph Williams, formerly of Pennsylvania, but more recently of Iowa, has been appointed his successor. This gentleman also sustains an honorable reputation, and the people of Kansas may reasonably expect from him, in his official capacity, the exercise of even-handed justice.

The removal of Chief Justice Lecompte has at length been determined upon by the president. This fact will give satisfaction to the citizens of all parties who sincerely desire the continued peace and prosperity of the territory.

A writer for the *Missouri Democrat*, under date of Leavenworth, May 28th, gives the following description of the manner in which the census has been taken, and the names of the delegates chosen from the Leavenworth district for the constitutional convention:—

"The 'National Democrats,' so called, i. e. rabid pro-slavery faction of this district, have met in convention, and made a selection of the following persons to be their nominees for delegates to the constitutional convention which is to meet at Lecompton in September next:

"John D. Henderson, editor of *The Journal;* Gen. Eastin, editor of *The Herald;* Hugh M. Moore, Jared Todd, Capt. Bill Martin, Gov. Robinson's jailor last May in this city; Joseph Hall, county commissioner; James Doniphan of Leavenworth; Gov. Wm. Walker, Wyandott; S. J. Cookagey, Easton; William Christianson, Delaware City; G. B. Redman, Delaware City, and one vacancy. The census-taker returned the names of 1837 as qualified voters in Leavenworth county, and upon those returns the governor made his apportionment, giving them twelve or one-fifth the members of the convention. About one delegate to a hundred and fifty voters. The officials at Lecompton are free to acknowledge that several of the counties remain to be taken, as no returns have been received from them. But upon the returns already made to the governor, he makes the apportionment, and those districts where the census has not been taken, can have no representation in said convention, even if desired. These districts which have been overlooked by the bogus officials are free-state. Can there be a clearer evidence of fraud than this? Lawrence is supposed to be considerable of a town, and that it contains a goodly number of inhabitants. But the census-taker could only find about a dozen names in that city to put upon his list There is a firm in that city, two brothers; they are always attending to their business, and together. One of them is a free-state man, while the other voted for Whitfield last fall, and he has his name upon the census lists, while the other has not; then the lists were not posted in accordance with the provisions of their own laws made for that purpose, and the people could not know whether their names were down or not."

Hon. Robert J. Walker, whose name is familiar to all American citizens, was appointed by the president as successor to Governor Geary. The Washington correspondent of the *New York Daily Times*, speaks of this eminent statesman in the following highly commendatory manner.:—

"It seems to be the common supposition that Mr. Walker is entirely identified with the extreme southern interest, and that his sympathies are with the school of Davis, Toombs and others of the secessionist stripe. *This is not the case*, and scarcely ought to be charged against the man who was chosen to the United States Senate, from Mississippi, as the opponent of Mr. Poindexter, in the very campaign in which the latter gentleman stumped the state under the palmetto flag, as the advocate of South Carolina nullification! Mr. Walker's course, at that time, met with the approbation of every Union man throughout the land. His standard was the flag of the Union, which he wore around his waist, in which costume he denounced disunion as treason, in every principal town and village of his adopted southern state.

"Robert J. Walker, the son of Judge Walker—one of the judges of the Supreme Court of the United States—was born in Pennsylvania, and, I believe, not far from the home of Mr. Buchanan. He studied law under his own father, and practised his profession at Pittsburgh, where he married a daughter of

Franklin Bache, of Philadelphia, and a grand-daughter of Benjamin Franklin. The first nomination of Andrew Jackson for the presidency, was made by young Walker, shortly after he was admitted to the bar, at a convention of the Pennsylvania democracy. After his emigration to Mississippi, he became identified with Texan independence, but took no leading part in national matters until the declaration of South Carolina in favor of nullification had excited his zeal in behalf of the Union. Then succeeded the famous struggle between himself and Poindexter—the latter the right hand of Calhoun in Mississippi, through whom he hoped to gain over that state to the cause of secession, or an unconstitutional states rights extreme. No Mississippian will ever forget that famous canvass, nor ought it to go out of the memory of patriots in the north. Whatever may have been the real causes of complaint against Mr. Walker since, he did his duty then manfully, triumphantly, and in a way which caused him to take his seat as an equal among the giants who composed the senatorial body of that period.

"Walker, in the Senate, soon became a confidential friend of Jackson, and took a leading part in the annexation of Texas; but be it remembered by those who distrust him on account of his supposed pro-slavery proclivities, that *he strenuously opposed Mr. Calhoun's project of making all of Texas slave territory, and was the main instrument of making the freedom of the soil of the northern portion of our newly acquired possessions a condition of annexation.*

"Walker was first requested by Mr. Polk to enter his Cabinet as Attorney-General, that post being deemed most in accordance with his tastes; but subsequent events transferred him to the Treasury Department. He then inaugurated the "Revenue," as distinguished from the "Protection" tariff system, and drew up and reported the tariff of 1846. It was a bold measure, reducing duties more than one-half, on an average, and that at a time when the country was involved in a war, and in opposition to the views of the commercial, moneyed and manufacturing classes. On the passage of the bill, Mr. Evans, Senator from Maine, and considered the financial leader of the Whigs, declared, in his place, that the revenue of the next year would not be $12,000,000. Daniel Webster left a memorandum with the clerk of the Senate, that it would not produce $14,000,000. Abbott Lawrence, and the banking interests of this city and New-England, considered the policy as destructive. Walker's recorded estimate was that it would give, in the first year, $30,000,000. It gave $29,000,000 and some hundreds of thousands, and has gone on increasing until it has reached its present prodigious amount.

"Walker is the only cabinet officer who has had his reports reprinted abroad. Sir Robert Peel had them printed for the benefit of the House of Commons, and his is the honor of being the only financial minister *whom the world has produced*, who has advanced government stocks, and maintained them above par, during a foreign war, and while it was borrowing money daily.

"If this sketch sounds like a panegyric, it is because I have cared to present only one side, and a true one, of the character of a very remarkable man, who is about to be intrusted with the practical care of settling the most important question which has agitated the country for many years, and who, it is believed *here*, will do it in the interest of the Union, in accordance with the principles of the Kansas-Nebraska law, and if the majority (as is doubtless the case) of the people of Kansas are free-state men, in a way to secure the triumph of freedom over slavery."

CHAPTER XLV.

Arrival in Kansas of Secretary Stanton and Governor Walker.—The policy of the new administration.—Disapprobation of the pro-slavery party.

Frederick P. Stanton, having been appointed secretary of Kansas, to fill the vacancy occasioned by the elevation of Mr. Woodson to the office of receiver of the Delaware land district, proceeded in advance of Governor Walker to the territory, and arrived at Lecompton on the 15th of April, where he took charge of the executive office as acting-governor.

He commenced at once to inaugurate the policy of the newly appointed governor, agreeably to his instructions previous to his departure from Washington. Mr. Stanton issued an address defining that policy, all the features of which will be found in the Inaugural of Governor Walker, which, notwithstanding its great length, is considered of sufficient importance to receive a place in the appendix to this work. The first important official act of the secretary, was to make an apportionment of delegates to the convention to frame a state constitution agreeably to the bill adopted by the late Legislative Assembly. This was done from the notoriously unfair and partial returns of the census takers. These returns might, with propriety, have been repudiated by the acting-governor, as the provisions of the census law had not been observed. This fact is sufficient to condemn the constitution that may be framed by the convention to be elected from the census returns and the apportionment of delegates made by Mr. Stanton.

Governor Walker reached Leavenworth City on the 25th of May, and was received by a large concourse of citizens. A few days afterwards, having visited Lawrence, he issued his Inaugural Address at Lecompton. This document was intended to conciliate both the prominent political parties, but it has failed to give satisfaction to either, and the Kansas difficulties are as far as ever from being amicably adjusted. The free-state people have no confidence in the assurance that the pro-slavery party will permit them to give, through the ballot-box, a fair expression of their wishes, or that the constitution to be framed by the convention to be chosen in June, will be submitted to the citizens of the territory for their ratification or rejection. This proposition had been made by Governor Geary to the legislature which passed the census act, and was indignantly rejected. Nor is the pro-slavery party willing to abandon the idea of forcing slavery upon Kansas, simply because the suggestion has been made that at some future day the institution may be established in the Indian Territory, and an equilibrium of the slave power, thus maintained. The scheme to make Kansas a slave state is too precious to be relinquished as easily as Governor Walker appears to have imagined. Hence his suggestion to refer the constitution to be formed back to the people, meets with the most decided condemnation. The Kansas pro-slavery leaders, who promised the governor that they would throw no obstacles in the way of his peaceful administration, have lost much of their enthusiastic admiration of his excellency, whilst the southern press have commenced to denounce his policy in terms that cannot be misunderstood. The Charleston *Mercury* concludes a lengthy article with the following significant paragraph :—

"Now we hold that the submitting of the constitution soon to be framed by the people of Kansas in convention assembled, back again to the people individually, for ratification, is a work of supererogation—a matter to be done or not, entirely to the discretion of the convention, as a thing of contingent expediency only, and not by any means a thing of necessity. And we cannot but look upon this suggestion of Mr. Stanton, however coupled with declarations of southern feeling, and the determination expressed by Governor Walker, as partaking of the nature of official dictation, and being in fact, a violation of the promised neutrality—an insidious and high-minded breach of faith towards the south and southern men in Kansas. We, therefore, desire in the outset to stamp this game as it deserves, and to protest against all attempts to influence the action of the convention from without, whether coming from the territorial officers appointed by the president, or the free-soil schemers of New York and Boston. The real object and end is under the guise of fair words to the south to make a free state of Kansas."

The *South*, published at Richmond, Va., is no less severe in its expressions of disapprobation, as may be seen from the following article:—

"Upon the new plan, which Governor Walker promulgates for the settlement of the Kansas difficulty, we cannot venture an opinion before we scrutinize it in detail. There is one point, however, upon which we can give an instant and emphatic judgment; and that is, the proposition to submit the constitution of Kansas to a popular vote. In respect of general policy, such a step would inevitably involve very disastrous consequences. In the first place, it would inflame and prolong the controversy, and would ultimately throw Kansas into the arms of the abolitionists. But any discussion of the measure in regard of expediency is unnecessary and irrelevant, since the convention which is to frame a state constitution for Kansas is endowed with no authority to submit their work to the popular vote. The act by which the convention is assembled ascertains and limits its powers, and in that act there is not one word about submitting the constitution to the people. The convention can do nothing for which there is not an express authority in the law; and as there is neither an express nor implied authority in the law to submit the constitution of Kansas to the vote of the inhabitants of the territory, the step would be an illegal and invalid usurpation of power. The proposition is too plain to allow of controversy. Submit it to any lawyer in the land, from Chief Justice Taney or Reverdy Johnson to the poorest pettifogger in the most obscure country village, and the instant answer will be that the convention in Kansas has no right to submit the constitution to a popular vote. The journals of the north concede the point, and declaim against the law calling the convention on the ground that it makes no provision for a popular vote on the constitution. Why then does Governor Walker raise the question? It is especially surprising that he should assume an undeniably untenable position."

There is no probability of a renewal of the civil war that disgraced the territory previous to the arrival there of Governor Geary. The recent immigration of free-state settlers has so swelled their numbers, that no attempt will again be made to drive them from the territory, coerce them into any unjust position, or in any way disturb them by armed forces from Missouri or elsewhere. It is well understood that an undertaking of this kind would inevitably result in a certain and calamitous defeat. The only ground for hope now left to the pro-slavery party, is in the action of the convention to meet in September next. Should the constitution framed by that body be rejected by Congress, as justice demands, in consequence of the illegality of the convention itself, or from any other cause, the Kansas difficulties will soon be settled, by the admission of that beautiful territory as a free state into the Union.

Note.—The report that Judge Lecompte had been removed, appears to have been without foundation. He still occupies the position of Chief Justice of Kansas. Fugitt or Fugert, charged with the murder and scalping of Koppe, was recently tried and acquitted at a court over which Lecompte presided. It is certain that no pro-slavery offender can be convicted in Kansas under existing circumstances, however heinous his crime or positive the proof of his guilt.

APPENDIX.

MESSAGE OF GOV. GEARY TO THE LEGISLATIVE ASSEMBLY.

Gentlemen of the Council and of the House of Representatives:

The All-Wise and beneficent Being, who controls alike the destinies of individuals and of nations, has permitted you to convene, this day, charged with grave responsibilities.

The eyes, not only of the people of Kansas, but of the entire Union, are upon you, watching with anxiety the result of your deliberations, and of our joint action in the execution of the delicate and important duties devolving upon us.

Selected at a critical period in the history of the country, to discharge the executive functions of this territory, the obligations I was required to assume were of the most weighty importance. And when I came seriously to contemplate their magnitude, I would have shrunk from the responsibility, were it not for an implicit reliance upon Divine aid, and a full confidence in the virtue, zeal and patriotism of the citizens, without which the wisest executive suggestions must be futile and inoperative.

To you, legislators, invested with sovereign authority, I look for that hearty co-operation which will enable us successfully to guide the ship of state through the troubled waters, into the haven of safety.

It is with feelings of profound gratitude to Almighty God, the bounteous Giver of all good, I have the pleasure of announcing, that after the bitter contest of opinion through which we have recently passed, and which has unfortunately led to fratricidal strife, that peace, which I have every reason to believe to be permanent, now reigns throughout the territory, and gladdens, with its genial influences, homes and hearts which but lately were sad and desolate; that the robber and the murderer have been driven from our soil; that burned cabins have been replaced by substantial dwellings; that a feeling of confidence and kindness has taken the place of distrust and hate; that all good citizens are disposed to deplore the errors and excesses of the past, and unite with fraternal zeal in repairing its injuries; and that this territory, unsurpassed by any portion of the continent for the salubrity of its climate and the fertility of its soil; its mineral and agricultural wealth; its timber-fringed streams and fine quarries of building stone; has entered upon a career of unparalleled prosperity.

To maintain the advance we have made, and realize the bright anticipations of the future; to build up a model commonwealth, enriched with all the treasures of learning, of virtue and religion, and make it a choice heritage for our children and generations yet unborn, let me, not only as your executive, but as a Kansan, devoted to the interests of Kansas, and animated solely by patriotic purposes, with all earnestness invoke you, with one heart and soul, to pursue so high and lofty a course in your deliberations, as, by its moderation and justice, will commend itself to the approbation of the country, and command the respect of the people.

This being the first occasion offered me to speak to the Legislative Assembly, it is but proper, and in accordance with general usage, that I should declare the principles which shall give shape and tone to my administration. These principles, without elaboration, I will condense into the narrowest compass.

"Equal and exact justice" to all men, of whatever political or religious persuasion; peace, comity and friendship with neighboring states and territories, with a sacred regard for state rights, and reverential respect for the integrity and perpetuity of the Union; a reverence for the federal constitution as the concentrated wisdom of the fathers of the republic, and the very ark of our political safety; the cultivation of a pure and energetic nationality, and the development of an excellent and intensely vital patriotism; a jealous regard for the elective franchise, and the entire security and sanctity of the ballot-

non; a firm determination to adhere to the doctrines of self-government and popular sovereignty as guaranteed by the Organic Law; unqualified submission to the will of the majority; the election of all officers by the people themselves; the supremacy of the civil over the military power; strict economy in public expenditures, with a rigid accountability of all public officers; the preservation of the public faith, and a currency based upon, and equal to, gold and silver; free and safe immigration from every quarter of the country; the cultivation of the proper territorial pride, with a firm determination to submit to no invasion of our sovereignty; the fostering care of agriculture, manufactures, mechanic arts, and all works of internal improvement; the liberal and free education of all the children of the territory; entire religious freedom; a free press, free speech, and the peaceable right to assemble and discuss all questions of public interest; trial by jurors impartially selected; the sanctity of the habeas corpus; the repeal of all laws inconsistent with the Constitution of the United States and the Organic Act, and the steady administration of the government so as best to secure the general welfare.

These sterling maxims, sanctioned by the wisdom and experience of the past, and the observance of which has brought our country to so exalted a position among the nations of the earth, will be steady lights by which my administration shall be guided.

A summary view of the state of the territory upon my advent, with an allusion to some of my official acts, may not be inappropriate to this occasion, and may serve to inspire your counsels with that wisdom and prudence, by a contemplation of the frightful excesses of the past, so essential to the adoption of measures to prevent their recurrence, and enable you to lay the broad and solid foundations of a future commonwealth which may give protection and happiness to millions of freemen.

It accords not with my policy or intentions to do the least injustice to any citizen or party of men in this territory or elsewhere. Pledged to do "equal and exact justice" in my executive capacity, I am inclined to throw the veil of oblivion over the errors and outrages of the period antecedent to my arrival, except so far as reference to them may be necessary for substantial justice, and to explain and develope the policy which has shed the benign influences of peace upon Kansas, and which, if responded to by the legislature in a spirit of kindness and conciliation, will contribute much to soothe those feelings of bitterness and contention, which in the past brought upon us such untold evils.

I arrived at Fort Leavenworth on the ninth day of September last; and immediately assumed the executive functions. On the eleventh I issued my inaugural address, declaring the general principles upon which I intended to administer the government. In this address I solemnly pledged myself to support the Constitution of the United States, and to discharge my duties as Governor of Kansas with fidelity; to sustain all the provisions of the Organic Act, which I pronounced to be "eminently just and beneficial;" to stand by the doctrine of popular sovereignty, or the will of the majority of the actual *bona fide* inhabitants, when legitimately expressed, which I characterized "the imperative rule of civil action for every law-abiding citizen." The gigantic evils under which this territory was groaning were attributed to outside influences, and the people of Kansas were earnestly invoked to suspend unnatural strife; to banish all extraneous and improper influences from their deliberations; and in the spirit of reason and mutual conciliation to adjust their own differences. Such suggestions in relation to modifications of the present statutes as I deemed for the public interests were promised at the proper time. It was declared that this territory was the common property of the people of the several states, and that no obstacle should be interposed to its free settlement, while in a territorial condition, by the citizens of every state of the Union. A just territorial pride was sought to be infused; a pledge was solemnly given to know no party, no section, nothing but Kansas and the Union; and the people were earnestly invoked to bury the past in oblivion, to suspend hostilities and refrain from the indulgence of bitter feeling; to begin anew; to devote themselves to the true and substantial interests of Kansas; develope her rich agricultural resources; build up manufactures; make public roads and other works of internal improvement; prepare amply for the education of their children; devote themselves to all the arts of peace, and make this territory the sanctuary of those cherished principles which protect the inalienable rights of the individual, and elevate states in their sovereign capacities.

The foregoing is a brief summary of the principles upon which my administration was commenced. I have steadily adhered to them, and time and trial have but served to strengthen my convictions of their justice.

Coincident with my inaugural were issued two proclamations, the one, disbanding the territorial militia, composed of a mixed force of citizens and others, and commanding "all bodies of men, combined, armed and equipped with munitions of war, without authority of the government, instantly to disband or quit the territory, as they would answer the contrary at their peril." The other, ordering "all free male citizens qualified to bear arms, between the ages of eighteen and forty-five years, to enrol themselves, that they might be completely organized by companies, regiments, brigades and divisions, and hold themselves in readiness to be mustered, by my order, into the service of the United States, upon a requisition of the commander of the military department in which Kansas is embraced, for the suppression of all unlawful combinations, and for the maintenance of public order and civil government."

The policy of these proclamations is so evident, and their beneficial effects have been so apparent, as to require no vindication.

The territory was declared by the acting-governor to be in a state of insurrection; the civil authority was powerless,—entirely without capacity to vindicate the majesty of the law and restore the broken peace; the existing difficulties were of a far more complicated character than I had anticipated; predatory bands, whose sole aim, unrelieved by the mitigation of political causes, was assassination, arson, plunder and rapine, had undisturbed possession of some portions of the territory, while every part of it was kept in constant alarm and terror by the advocates of political sentiments, uniting according to their respective sympathies, in formidable bodies of armed men, completely equipped with munitions of war, and resolved upon mutual extermination as the only hope of peace; unoffending and peaceable citizens were driven from their homes; others murdered in their own dwellings, which were given to the flames; that sacred respect for woman, which has characterized all civilized nations, seemed in the hour of mad excitement to be forgotten; partisan feeling, on all sides, intensely excited by a question which inflamed the entire nation, almost closed the minds of the people against me; idle and mendacious rumors, well calculated to produce exasperation and destroy confidence, were everywhere rife; the most unfortunate suspicions prevailed; in isolated country places no man's life was safe; robberies and murders were of daily occurrence; nearly every farm-house was deserted; and no traveller could safely venture on the highway without an escort. This state of affairs was greatly aggravated by the interference of prominent politicians outside of the territory.

The foregoing is but a faint outline of the fearful condition of things which ruled Kansas and convulsed the nation. The full picture will be drawn by the iron pen of impartial history, and the actors in the various scenes will be assigned their true positions.

I came here a stranger to your difficulties, without prejudice, with a solemn sense of my official obligations, and with a lofty resolution to put a speedy termination to events so fraught with evil, and which, if unchecked, would have floated the country into the most bloody civil war.

Hesitation, or partisan affiliations, would have resulted in certain failure, and only served further to complicate affairs. To restore peace and order, and relieve the people from the evils under which they were laboring, it was necessary that an impartial, independent and just policy should be adopted, which would embrace in its protection all good citizens, without distinction of party, and sternly punish all bad men who continued to disturb the public tranquillity. Accordingly my inaugural address and proclamations were immediately circulated among the people, in order that they might have early notice of my intentions.

On the fourteenth day of September, reliable information was received that a large body of armed men were marching to attack Hickory Point, on the north side of the Kansas River. I immediately dispatched a squadron of United States dragoons, with instruction to capture and bring to this place any persons whom they might find acting in violation of my proclamation. In pursuance of these instructions one hundred and one prisoners were taken, brought here, and committed for trial.

While a portion of the army was performing this duty, I was advised that a large body of men was approaching the town of Lawrence, determined upon its destruction. I at once ordered three hundred United States troops to that place, and repaired there in person. Within four miles of Lawrence, I found a force of twenty-seven hundred men, consisting of citizens of this territory and other places, organized as territorial militia, under a proclamation of the late acting governor. I disbanded this force, ordering the various companies composing it, to repair to their respective places of rendezvous, there to be mustered out of service. My orders were obeyed; the militia retired to their homes; the effusion of blood was prevented; the preservation of Lawrence effected; and a great step made towards the restoration of peace and confidence.

To recount my various official acts, following each other in quick succession under your immediate observation, would be a work of supererogation, and would occupy more space than the limits of an executive message would justify. My executive minutes, containing a truthful history of my official transactions, with the policy which dictated them, have been forwarded to the general government, and are open to the inspection of the country.

In relation to any alterations or modifications of the territorial statutes which I might deem advisable, I promised in my inaugural address to direct public attention at the proper time. In the progress of events, that time has arrived, and you are the tribunal to which my suggestions must be submitted. On this subject I bespeak your candid attention, as it has an inseparable connection with the prosperity and happiness of the people.

It has already been remarked that the territories of the United States are the common property of the citizens of the several states. It may be likened to a joint ownership in an estate, and no condition should be imposed or restrictions placed upon the equal enjoyment of the benefits arising therefrom, which will do the least injustice to any of the owners, or which is not contemplated in the tenure by which it is held, which is no less than the Constitution of the United States, the sole bond of the American Union. This being the true position, no obstacle should be interposed to the free, speedy and general settlement of this territory.

The durability and imperative authority of a state constitution, when the interests of the people require a state government, and a direct popular vote is necessary to give it sanction and effect, will be the proper occasion once for all, to decide the grave political questions which underlie a well regulated commonwealth.

Let this, then, be the touch-stone of your deliberations. Enact no law which will not clearly bear the constitutional test; and if any laws have been passed which do not come up to this standard, it is your solemn duty to sweep them from the statute-book.

The territorial government should abstain from the exercise of authority not clearly delegated to it, and should permit all doubtful questions to remain in abeyance until the formation of a state constitution.

On the delicate and exciting question of slavery, a subject which so peculiarly engaged the attention of Congress at the passage of our Organic Act, I cannot too earnestly invoke you to permit it to remain where the Constitution of the United States and that act place it, subject to the decision of the courts upon all points arising during our present infant condition.

The repeal of the Missouri line, which was a restriction on popular sovereignty, anew consecrated the great doctrine of self-government, and restored to the people their full control over every question of interest to themselves, both north and south of that line.

Justice to the country and the dictates of sound policy require that the legislature should confine itself to such subjects as will preserve the basis of entire equality; and when a sufficient population is here, and they choose to adopt a state government, that they shall be "perfectly free," without let or hindrance, to form all their domestic institutions "in their own way," and to dictate that form of government which in their deliberate judgment may be deemed proper.

Any attempt to incite servile insurrection and to interfere with the domestic institutions of sovereign states, is extremely reprehensible, and shall receive no countenance from me. Such intervention can result in no good, but is pregnant with untold disasters. Murder, arson, rapine and death follow in its wake, while not one link in the fetters of the slave is weakened or broken, or any amelioration in his condition secured. Such interference is a direct invasion of state rights, only calculated to produce irritation and estrangement.

Every dictate of self-respect—every consideration of state equality—the glories of the past and the hopes of the future—all, with soul-stirring eloquence, constrain us to cultivate a reverential awe for the constitution as the sheet-anchor of our safety, and bid us, in good faith, to carry out all its provisions.

Many of the statutes are excellent, and suited to our wants and condition, but in order that they may receive that respect and sanction which is the vital principle of all law, let such be abolished as are not eminently just and will not receive the fullest approbation of the people. I trust you will test them all by the light of the general and fundamental principles of our government, and that all that will not bear this ordeal, be revised, amended or repealed. To some of them which strike my mind as objectionable, your candid and special attention is respectfully invited.

By carefully comparing the Organic Act, as printed in the statutes, with a certified copy of the same from the department of state, important discrepancies, omissions and additions will be discovered. I therefore, recommend the appointment of a committee, to compare the printed statutes with the original rolls, on file in the secretary's office, to ascertain whether the same liberty has been taken with the act under which they were made.

Of the numerous errors discovered by me in the copy of the Organic Act as printed in the statutes, I will refer to one in illustration of my meaning. In the 29th section, defining the executive authority, will be found the following striking omission—"against the laws of said territory, and reprieves for offences." This omission impairs the executive authority, and deprives the governor of the pardoning power for offences committed "against the laws of the territory," which Congress, for the wisest and most humane reasons, has conferred upon him.

The Organic Act requires every bill to be presented to the governor, and demands his signature, as the evidence of his approval, before it can become a law. The statutes are defective in this respect, as they do not contain the date of approval, nor the proper evidence of that fact, by having the governor's signature.

Your attention is invited to chapter 30, in relation to county boundaries. The boundary of Douglas county is imperfect, and in connection with Shawnee county, is an absurdity for both counties. The boundary lines of all the counties should be absolutely established.

Chapter 44, establishing the probate court, also requires attention. The act is good generally, so far as it relates to the organization and duties of the court. But all provisions in this and other acts vesting the appointment of probate judges, county commissioners, and other public officers, in the Legislative Assembly, should at once be repealed, and the un qualified right of election conferred upon the people, whose interests are immediately affected by the acts of those officials. The free and unrestricted right of the people to select all their own agents, is a maxim so well settled in political ethics, and springs so legitimately from the doctrines of self-government, that I need only allude to the question to satisfy every one of its justice. The "people must be perfectly free" to regulate their own business in their own way; and when the voice of the majority is fairly expressed, all will bow to it as the voice of God. Let the people, then, rule in everything. I have every confidence in the virtue, intelligence, and "sober thought" of the toiling millions. The deliberate popular judgment is never wrong. When, in times of excitement, the popular mind may be temporarily obscured from the dearth of correct information or the mists of passion, the day of retribution and justice speedily follows, and a summary reversal is the certain result. Just and patriotic sentiment is a sure reliance for every honest public servant. The sovereignty of the people must be maintained.

Section 15th of this act allows writs of habeas corpus to be issued by the probate judge, but leaves him no authority to hear the case and grant justice; but refers the matter to the "next term of the district court." The several terms of the district court are at stated periods, and the provision alluded to amounts to a denial of justice and a virtual suspension of "the great writ of liberty," contrary to the letter and spirit of the Constitution of the United States.

Many provisions of chapter 66, entitled "elections," are objectionable. Section 11th, requiring certain "test oaths" as pre-requisites to the right of suffrage, is wrong, unfair, and unequal upon citizens of different sections of the Union. It is exceedingly invidious to require obedience to any special enactment. The peculiar features of these test oaths should be abolished, and all citizens presumed to be law-abiding and patriotic until the contrary clearly appears. Sworn obedience to particular statutes has seldom secured that object. Justice will ever commend itself to the support of all honest men, and the surest means of insuring the ready execution of law, is to make it so pre-eminently just, equal and impartial as to command the respect of those whom it is intended to affect.

Section 36th deprives electors of the great safeguard of the purity and independence of the elective franchise: I mean the right to vote by ballot; and after the first day of November, 1856, requires all voting to be *viva voce*. This provision taken in connection with section 9th, which provides that " if all the votes offered cannot be taken before the hour appointed for closing the polls, the judges shall, by public proclamation, adjourn such election until the following day, when the polls shall again be opened, and the election continued as before," &c., offers great room for fraud and corruption. Voting *viva voce*, the condition of the poll can be ascertained at any moment. If the parties having the election officers are likely to be defeated, they have the option of adjourning for the purpose of drumming up votes; or in the insane desire for victory, may be tempted to resort to other means even more reprehensible. The right of voting by ballot is now incorporated into the constitutions of nearly all the states, and is classed with the privileges deemed sacred. The arguments in its favor are so numerous and overwhelming that I have no hesitation in recommending its adoption. The election law should be carefully examined, and such guards thrown around it as will most effectually secure the sanctity of the ballot-box and preserve it from the taint of a single illegal vote. The man who will deliberately tamper with the elective franchise and dare to offer an illegal vote, strikes at the foundation of justice, undermines the pillars of society, applies the torch to the temple of our liberties, and should receive severe punishment. As a qualification for voting, a definite period of actual inhabitancy in the territory, to the exclusion of a home elsewhere, should be rigidly prescribed. No man should be permitted to vote upon a floating residence. He should have resided within the territory for a period of not less than ninety days, and in the district where he offers to vote, at least ten days immediately preceding such election. All the voters should be registered and published for a certain time previous to the election. False voting should be severely punished, and false swearing to receive a vote visited with the pains and penalties of perjury.

In this connection your attention is also invited to chapter 92, entitled "jurors." This chapter leaves the selection of jurors to the absolute discretion of the marshal, sheriff, or constable, as the case may be, and affords great room for partiality and corruption. The names of all properly qualified citizens, without party distinction, should be thrown into a wheel or box, and at stated periods, under the order of the courts, jurors should be publicly drawn by responsible persons.

Too many safeguards cannot be thrown around the right of trial by jury, in order that it may still continue to occupy that cherished place in the affections of the people so essential to its preservation and sanctity.

Some portions of chapter 110, "militia," infringes the executive prerogative, impairs the governor's usefulness, and clearly conflicts with the organic act. This act requires the executive to reside in the territory, and makes him "commander-in-chief of the militia." This power must be vested some place, and is always conferred upon the chief magistrate. Section 26 virtually confers this almost sovereign prerogative "upon any commissioned officer," and permits him, "whenever and as often as any invasion or danger may come to his knowledge, to order out the militia or volunteer corps, or any part thereof, under his command, for the defence of the territory," &c.; thus almost giving "any commissioned officer" whatever, at his option, the power to involve the territory in war.

Section 12th provides for a general militia training on the first Monday of October, the day fixed for the general election. This is wrong, and is well calculated to incite to terrorism. The silent ballots of the people, unawed by military display, should quietly and definitely determine all questions of public interest.

The other sections of the law, requiring the appointment of field and commissioned officers, should be repealed. All officers should derive their authority directly from their respective commands, by election. To make the military system complete and effective, there must be entire subordination and unity running from the commander-in-chief to the humblest soldier, and one spirit must animate the entire system.

The 122d chapter, in relation to "patrols," is unnecessary. It renders all other property liable to heavy taxation for the protection of slave property; thus operating unequally upon citizens, and is liable to the odious charge of being a system of espionage, as it authorizes the patrols, an indefinite number of whom may be appointed, to visit not only negro quarters, but "any other places" suspected of unlawful assemblages of slaves.

Chapter 131, "pre-emption," squanders the school fund, by appropriating the school sections contrary to the organic act, which provides "that sections numbered sixteen and thirty-six, in each township in Kansas Territory, shall be, and the same are hereby reserved for the purpose of being applied to schools in said territory, and in the states and territories to be erected out of the same;" contravenes the United States pre-emption laws, which forbid trafficking in claims, and holding more than one claim; and directs the governor to grant patents for lands belonging to the United States, and only conditionally granted to the territory. This act is directly calculated to destroy the effect of a munificent grant of land by Congress for educational purposes. The territory is the trustee of this valuable gift, and posterity has a right to demand of us that this sacred trust shall remain unimpaired, in order that the blessings of free education may be shed upon our children.

Every state should have the best educational system which an intelligent government can provide. The physical, moral and mental faculties should be cultivated in harmonious unison, and that system of education is the best which will effect these objects. Congress has already provided for the support of common schools. In addition to this, I would recommend the Legislature to ask Congress to donate land lying in this territory for the establishment of a university, embracing a normal, agricultural and mechanical school. A university, thus endowed, would be a blessing to our people; disseminate useful and scientific intelligence; provide competent teachers for our primary schools; and furnish a complete system of education adequate to our wants in all the departments of life.

The subject of roads, bridges and highways, merits your especial attention. Nothing adds more to comfort, convenience, prosperity and happiness, and more greatly promotes social intercourse and kind feeling, than easy and convenient inter-communication. Roads should be wide and straight, and the various rivers and ravines substantially bridged.

Railroads should be encouraged; and in granting charters, the Legislature should have in view the interests of the whole people.—The prosperity of the territory is intimately connected with the early and general construction of the rapid and satisfactory means of transit.

While on the subject of internal improvement, I would call to your notice and solicit for it your serious consideration, the opening, at the earliest period, of a more easy means of communication with the sea-board than any we at present enjoy. One great obstacle to our prosperity is the immense distance we occupy from all the great maritime depots of the country by any of the routes now travelled. This can be removed by the construction of a railway, commencing at an appropriate place in this territory, and running southwardly through the Indian Territory and Texas, to the most eligible point on the Gulf of Mexico. The entire length of such a road would not exceed six hundred miles, much less than half the distance to the Atlantic, and at an ordinary speed of railroad travel could be traversed in less than twenty-four hours. It would pass through a country remarkable for beauty of scenery, fertility of soil, and salubrity of climate, and which has properly been styled "the Eden of the world;" and would open up new sources of wealth superior to any that have yet been discovered on the eastern division of the continent. It would place Kansas, isolated as she now is, in as favorable a position for commercial enterprises as very many of the most populous states in the Union, and furnish her a sure, easy, and profitable market for her products, as well as a safe, expeditious and economical means of obtaining all her needed supplies at every season of the year. You will not fail at once to perceive the importance of this suggestion. Not only Kansas and Nebraska, but the entire country west of the Mississippi, will be vastly benefited by its adoption. The advantages to Texas would be incalculable. And should you be favorably impressed with the feasibility of the plan, I would advise that you communicate, in your legislative capacity, with the legislature of that state, and that also of the territory of Nebraska, in regard to the most effectual measures for its speedy accomplishment.

Chapter 149, permitting settlers to hold three hundred and twenty acres of land, is in violation of the pre-emption laws, and leads to contention and litigation.

Chapter 151, relating to "slaves," attacks the equality which underlies the theory of our territorial government; and destroys the freedom of speech, and the privileges of public discussion, so essential to uncloak error, and enable the people properly to mould their institutions in their own way. The freedom of speech and the press, and the right of public discussion upon all matters affecting the interests of the people, are the great constitutional safeguards of popular rights, liberty and happiness.

The act in relation to a territorial library, makes the auditor ex-officio librarian, and gives him authority to audit his own accounts. These offices should be distinct, as their duties conflict.

The congressional appropriation for a territorial library has been expended in the purchase of a very valuable collection of books.

Time and space will not permit me to point out all the inconsistencies and incongruities found in the Kansas statutes. Passed, as they were, under the influence of excitement, and in too brief a period to secure mature deliberation, many of them are open to criticism and censure, and should pass under your careful revision, with a view to modification or repeal. Some which have been most loudly complained of have never been enforced. It is a bad principle to suffer dead-letter laws to deface the statute-book. It impairs salutary reverence for law, and excites in the popular mind a questioning of all law, which leads to anarchy and confusion. The best way is to leave no law on the statute-book which is not uniformly and promptly to be administered with the authority and power of the government.

In travelling through the territory, I have discovered great anxiety in relation to the damages sustained during the past civil disturbances, and everywhere the question has been asked as to whom they should look for indemnity. These injuries, —burning houses, plundering fields, and stealing horses and other property, have been a fruitful source of irritation and trouble, and have impoverished many good citizens. They cannot be considered as springing from purely local causes, and as such, the subjects of territorial redress. Their exciting cause has been outside of this territory, and the agents in their perpetration have been the citizens of nearly every state in the Union. It has been a species of national warfare waged upon the soil of Kansas: and it should not be forgotten that both parties were composed of men rushing here from various sections of the Union; that both committed acts which no law can justify; and the peaceable citizens of Kansas have been the victims. In adjusting the question of damages, it appears proper that a broad and comprehensive view of the subject should be taken; and I have accordingly suggested to the general government the propriety of recommending to Congress the passage of an act providing for the appointment of a commissioner, to take testimony and report to Congress for final action, at as early a day as possible.

There is not a single officer in the territory amenable to the people or to the governor; all having been appointed by the Legislature, and holding their offices until 1857. This system of depriving the people of the just exercise of their rights, cannot be too strongly condemned.

A faithful performance of duty should be exacted from all public officers.

As the executive, I desire that the most cordial relations may exist between myself and all other departments of the government.

Homesteads should be held sacred. Nothing so much strengthens a government as giving its citizens a solid stake in the country. I am in favor of assuring to every industrious citizen one hundred and sixty acres of land.

The money appropriated by Congress for the erection of our capitol has been nearly expended. I have asked for an additional appropriation of fifty thousand dollars, which will scarcely be sufficient to complete the building upon the plan adopted by the architect.

Where crime has been so abundant, the necessity for a territorial penitentiary is too evident to require elaboration, and I have therefore suggested a congressional appropriation for this purpose.

The Kansas River, the natural channel to the west; which runs through a valley of unparalleled fertility, can be made navigable as far as Fort Riley, a distance of over one hundred miles, and Congress should be petitioned for aid to accomplish this laudable purpose. Fort Riley has been built, at an expense exceeding five hundred thousand dollars, with the expectation that the river was navigable to that place, and doubtless the general government will readily unite with this territory to secure this object.

A geological survey, developing the great mineral resources of this territory, is so necessary as merely to require notice. Provision for this useful work should immediately be made.

The early disposal of the public lands and their settlement, will materially advance our substantial prosperity. Great anxiety prevails among the settlers to secure titles to their lands. The facilities for this purpose, by but one land-office in the territory, are inadequate to the public wants, and I have consequently recommended the establishment of two or more additional land-offices, in such positions as will best accommodate the people.

After mature consideration, and from a thorough conviction of its propriety, I have suggested large congressional appropriations. The coming immigration, attracted by our unrivalled soil and climate, will speedily furnish the requisite population to make a sovereign state. Other territories have been for years the recipients of congressional bounty, and a similar amount of money and land bestowed upon them during a long period, should at once be given to Kansas, as, like the Eureka state, she will spring into full life, and the prosperity of the territory, and the welfare and protection of the people coming here from every state of the Union, to test anew the experiment of republican government, require ample and munificent appropriations.

As citizens of a territory, we are peculiarly and immediately under the protecting influence of the Union, and, like the inhabitants of the states comprising it, feel a lively interest in all that concerns its welfare and prosperity. Within the last few years sundry conflicting questions have been agitated throughout the country, and discussed in a spirit calculated to impair confidence in its strength and perpetuity, and furnish abundant cause for apprehension and alarm. These questions have mostly been of a local or sectional character, and as such should never have acquired general significance or importance. All American citizens should divest themselves of selfish considerations in relation to public affairs, and in the spirit of patriotism make dispassionate inquisition into the causes which have produced much alienation and bitterness among men whom the highest considerations require should be united in the bonds of fraternal fellowship. All Union-loving men should unite upon a platform of reason, equality and patriotism. All sectionalism should be annihilated. All sections of the Union should be harmonized under a national, conservative government, as during the early days of the republic. The value of the Union is beyond computation, and no respect is due to those who will even dare to calculate its value. One of our ablest statesmen has wisely and eloquently said, "Who shall assign limits to the achievements of free minds and free hands under the protection of this glorious Union? No treason to mankind since the organization of society would be equal in atrocity to that of him who would lift his hand to destroy it. He would overthrow the noblest structure of human wisdom, which protects himself and his fellow man. He would stop the progress of free government, and involve his country either in anarchy or despotism. He would extinguish the fire of liberty which warms and animates the hearts of happy millions, and invites all the nations of the earth to imitate our example."

That soldier-president, whose exploits in the field were only equalled by his wisdom in the cabinet, with that singular sagacity which has stamped with the seal of prophecy all his foreshadowings, has repudiated, as morbid and unwise, that philanthropy which looks to the amalgamation of the American with any inferior race. The white man, with his intellectual energy, far-reaching science, and indomitable perseverance, is the pecular object of my sympathy, and should receive the especial protection and support of government. In this territory there are numerous "Indian reserves," of magnificent extent and choice fertility, capable of sustaining a dense civilized population, now held unimproved by numerous Indian tribes. These tribes are governed by Indian agents, entirely independent of the executive of this territory, and are, indeed, governments within a government. Frequent aggression upon these reserves are occurring, which have produced collisions between the Indian agents and the settlers, who appeal to me for protection. Seeing so much land unoccupied and unimproved, these enterprising pioneers naturally question the policy which excludes them from soil devoted to no useful or legitimate purpose. Impressed with the conviction that the large Indian reserves, if permitted to remain in their present condition, cannot fail to exercise a blighting influence on the prosperity of Kansas, and result in great injury to the Indians themselves, I shall be pleased to unite with the legislature in any measures deemed advisable, looking to the speedy extinguishment of the Indian title to all surplus land lying in this territory, so as to throw it open for settlement and improvement.

For official action, I know no better rule than a conscientious conviction of duty—none more variable than the vain attempt to conciliate temporary prejudice. Principles and justice are eternal, and if tampered with, sooner or later the sure and indignant verdict of popular condemnation against those who are untrue to their leadings, will be rendered. Let us not be false to our country, our duty, and our constituents. The triumph of truth and principle, not of partisan and selfish objects, should be our steady purpose—the general welfare, and not the interests of the few, our sole aim. Let the past, which few men can review with satisfaction, be forgotten. Let us not deal in criminations and recriminations; but, as far as possible, let us make restitution and offer regrets for past excesses. The dead, whom the madness of partisan fury has consigned to premature graves, cannot be recalled to life; the insults, the outrages, the robberies and murders, "enough to stir a fever in the blood of age," in this world of imperfection and guilt, can never be fully atoned for or justly punished. The innocent blood, however, shall not cry in vain for redress, as we are promised by the great Executive of the Universe, whose power is almighty and whose knowledge is perfect, that he "will repay."

"To fight in a just cause and for our country's glory, is the best office of the best of men." Let "justice be the laurel" which crowns your deliberations; let your aims be purely patriotic, and your sole purpose the general welfare and the substantial interests of the whole people. If we fix our steady gaze upon the Constitution and the Organic Act as "the cloud by day and the pillar of fire by night," our footsteps will never wander into any unknown or forbidden paths. Then will this Legislative Assembly be as a beacon light, placed high in the pages of our history, shedding its luminous and benign influence to the most remote generations; its members will be remembered with veneration and respect as among the early fathers of the magnificent commonwealth, which, in the not distant future, will overshadow with its protection, a population of freemen unsurpassed by any state in this beloved Union for intelligence, wealth, religion, and all the elements which make and insure the true greatness of a nation; the present citizens of Kansas will rejoice in the benefits conferred; the mourning and gloom, which too long, like a pall, have covered the people, will be dispersed by the sunshine of joy with which they will hail the advent of peace founded upon justice; we will enter upon a career of unprecedented prosperity; good feeling and confidence will prevail; the just rule of action which you are about to establish, will be recognised; the entire country, now watching your deliberations with momentous interest, will award you their enthusiastic applause; and above and over all, you will have the sanction of your own consciences, enjoy self-respect, and meet with divine approbation, without which all human praise is worthless and unavailing.

JNO. W. GEARY.

Lecompton, K. T., Jan. 12, 1857.

INAUGURAL ADDRESS OF ROBERT J. WALKER, GOVERNOR OF KANSAS TERRITORY.

Delivered in Lecompton, Kansas Territory, May 27, 1857.

Fellow-citizens of Kansas:—At the earnest request of the President of the United States, I have accepted the position of governor of the territory of Kansas. The president, with the cordial concurrence of all his cabinet, expressed to me the conviction that the condition of Kansas was fraught with imminent peril to the Union, and asked me to undertake the settlement of that momentous question, which has introduced discord and civil war throughout your borders, and threatens to involve you and our country in the same common ruin. This was a duty thus presented, the performance of which I could not decline consistently with my view of the sacred obligation which every citizen owes to his country.

The mode of adjustment is provided in the act organizing your territory—namely, by the people of Kansas, who, by a majority of their own votes, must decide this question for themselves in forming their state constitution.

Under our practice the preliminary act of framing a state constitution is uniformly performed through the instrumentality of a convention of delegates chosen by the people themselves. That convention is now about to be elected by you under the call of the territorial legislature, created and still recognised by the authority of Congress, and clothed by it, in the comprehensive language of the Organic Law, with full power to make such an enactment. The territorial legislature, then, in assembling this convention, were fully sustained by the act of Congress, and the authority of the convention is distinctly recognised in my instructions from the President of the United States. Those who oppose this course cannot aver the alleged irregularity of the territorial legislature, whose laws in town and city elections, in corporate franchises, and on all other subjects but slavery, they acknowledge by their votes and acquiescence. If that legislature was invalid, then are we without law or order in Kansas, without town, city, or county organization; all legal and judicial transactions are void, all titles null, and anarchy reigns throughout our borders

It is my duty, in seeing that all constitutional laws are fairly executed, to take care, as far as practicable, that this election of delegates to the convention shall be free from fraud or violence, and that they shall be protected in their deliberations.

The people of Kansas, then, are invited by the highest authority known to the constitution to participate freely and fairly in the election of delegates to frame a constitution and state government. The law has performed its entire appropriate function when it extends to the people the right of suffrage, but it cannot compel the performance of that duty. Throughout our whole union, however, and wherever free government prevails, those who abstain from the exercise of the right of suffrage authorize those who do vote to act for them in that contingency, and the absentees are as much bound under the law and constitution, where there is no fraud or violence, by the act of the majority of those who do vote, as although all had participated in the election. Otherwise, as voting must be voluntary, self-government would be impracticable, and monarchy or despotism would remain as the only alternative.

You should not console yourselves, my fellow-citizens, with the reflection that you may, by a subsequent vote, defeat the ratification of the constitution. Although most anxious to secure to you the exercise of that great constitutional right, and believing that the convention is the servant, and not the master of the people, yet I have no power to dictate the proceedings of that body. I cannot doubt, however, the course they will adopt on this subject. But why incur the hazard of the preliminary formation of a constitution by a minority, as alleged by you, when a majority, by their own votes, could control the forming of that instrument?

But it is said that the convention is not legally called, and that the election will not be freely and fairly conducted. The territorial legislature is the power ordained for this purpose by the Congress of the United States; and in opposing it you resist the authority of the federal government. That legislature was called into being by the Congress of 1854, and is recognised in the very latest congressional legislation. It is recognised by the present Chief Magistrate of the Union, just chosen by the American people, and many of its acts are now in operation here by universal assent. As the governor of the territory of Kansas, I must support the laws and the constitution; and I have no other alternative under my oath but to see that all constitutional laws are fully and fairly executed.

I see in this act, calling the convention, no improper or unconstitutional restrictions upon the right of suffrage. I see in it no test-oath or other similar provisions objected to in relation to previous laws, but clearly repealed as repugnant to the provisions of this act, so far as regards the election of delegates to this convention. It is said that a fair and full vote will not be taken. Who can safely predict such a result? Nor is it just for a majority, as they allege, to throw the power into the hands of a minority, from a mere apprehension—I trust entirely unfounded—that they will not be permitted to exercise the right of suffrage. If, by fraud or violence, a majority should not be permitted to vote, there is a remedy, it is hoped, in the wisdom and justice of the convention itself, acting under the obligations of an oath, and a proper responsibility to the tribunal of public opinion. There is a remedy, also, if such facts can be demonstrated, in the refusal of Congress to admit a state into the Union under a constitution imposed by a minority upon a majority by fraud or violence. Indeed, I cannot doubt that the convention, after having framed a state constitution, will submit it for ratification or rejection, by a majority of the then actual *bona fide* resident settlers of Kansas.

With these views, well known to the president and cabinet, and approved by them, I accepted the appointment of governor of Kansas. My instructions from the president, through the secretary of state, under date of the 30th of March last, sustain "*the regular legislature of the territory*" in "*assembling a convention to form a constitution;*" and they express the opinion of the president that "*when such a constitution shall be submitted to the people of the territory, they must be protected in the exercise of their right of voting for or against that instrument; and the fair expression of the popular will must not be interrupted by fraud or violence.*"

I repeat, then, as my clear conviction, that unless the convention submit the constitution to the vote of all the actual resident settlers of Kansas, and the election be fairly and justly conducted, the constitution will be, and ought to be, rejected by Congress.

There are other important reasons why you should particip— in the election of delegates to this convention. Kansas is to become a new state, created out of the public domain, and will designate her boundaries in the fundamental law. To most of the land within her limits the Indian title, unfortunately, is not yet extinguished, and this land is exempt from settlement, to the grievous injury of the people of the state. Having passed many years of my life in a new state, and represented it for a long period in the Senate of the United States, I know the serious encumbrance arising from large bodies of lands within a state to which the Indian title is not extinguished. Upon this subject the convention may act by such just and constitutional provisions as will accelerate the extinguishment of Indian title.

There is, furthermore, the question of railroad grants made by Congress to all the new states but one (where the routes could not be agreed upon), and, within a few months past, to the flourishing territory of Minnesota. This munificent grant of four millions and a half of acres was made to Minnesota, even in advance of her becoming a state, under the auspices of her present distinguished executive, and will enable our sister state of the northwest speedily to unite her railroad system with ours.

Kansas is undoubtedly entitled to grants similar to those just made to Minnesota, and upon this question the convention may take important action.

These, recollect, are grants by Congress, not to companies, but to states. Now, if Kansas, like the state of Illinois, in granting hereafter these lands to companies to build these roads, should reserve, at least, the seven per cent. of their gross annual receipts, it is quite certain that so soon as these roads are constructed, such will be the large payments into the treasury of our state that there will be no necessity to impose in Kansas any state tax whatever, especially if the constitution should contain wise provisions against the creation of state debts.

The grant to the state of Illinois for the Illinois Central Railroad, passed under the wise and patriotic auspices of her distinguished senator, was made before the pernicious system lately exposed in Washington had invaded the halls of Congress; and, therefore, that state, unlike most others which obtained recent grants, was enabled to make this great reservation for the benefit of the state. This constitutes of itself a conclusive reason why these railroad grants should be re served in the ordinance accompanying our state constitution, so that our state might have the whole benefit of the grant, instead of large portions being given to agents appointed to obtain these grants by companies substantially in many cases for their own benefit, although in the name of the state.

There is another reason why these railroad grants should thus be reserved in our ordinance.

It is to secure these lands to the state before large bodies of them are engrossed by speculators, especially along the contemplated lines of railroads. In no case should these reservations interfere with the pre-emption rights reserved to settlers, or with school-sections.

These grants to states, as is proved by the official documents, have greatly augmented the proceeds of the sales of the public lands, increasing their value, accelerating their sale and settlement, and bringing enhanced prices to the government, whilst greatly benefiting the lands of the settler by furnishing him new markets and diminished cost of transportation. On this subject, Mr. Buchanan, always the friend of the new states, in his recent inaugural, uses the following language:—

"No nation in the tide of time has ever been blessed with so rich and noble an inheritance as we enjoy in the public lands. In administering this important trust, whilst it may be wise to grant portions of them for the improvement of the remainder, yet we should never forget that it is our cardinal policy to reserve the lands as much as may be for actual settlers; and this at moderate prices. We shall thus not only best promote the prosperity of the new states, by furnishing them a hardy and independent race of honest and industrious citizens, but shall secure homes for our children and our children's children, as well as those exiled from foreign shores, who may seek in this country to improve their condition and enjoy the blessings of civil and religious liberty."

Our American railroads, now exceeding twenty-four thousand miles completed, have greatly advanced the power, prosperity, and progress of the country, whilst linking it together in bonds of ever-increasing commerce and intercourse, and tending, by these results, to soften or extinguish sectional passions and prejudice, and thus perpetuate the union of the states. This system it is clearly the interest of the whole country shall progress until the states west of the Mississippi shall be intersected, like those east of that river, by a network of railroads, until the whole, at various points, shall reach the shores of the Pacific. The policy of such grants by Congress is now clearly established; and whatever doubts may have prevailed in the minds of a few persons as to the constitutionality of such grants, when based only upon the transfer of a portion of the public domain, in the language of the inaugural of the president, "*for the improvement of the remainder,*" yet when they are made, as now proposed in the ordinance accompanying our constitution, in consideration of our relinquishing the right to tax the public lands, such grants become, in fact, sales for ample equivalents, and their constitutionality is placed beyond all doubt or controversy. For this reason, also, and in order that these grants may be made for ample equivalents, and upon grounds of clear, constitutional authority, it is most wise that they should be included in our ordinance, and take effect by compact when the state is admitted into the Union. If my will could have prevailed as regards the public lands, as indicated in my public career, and especially in the bill presented by me, as chairman of the committee on public lands, to the Senate of the United States, which passed that body, but failed in the House, I would authorize no sales of these lands except for settlement and cultivation, reserving not merely a pre-emption, but a homestead of a quarter-section of land in favor of every actual settler, whether coming from other states or emigrating from Europe. Great and populous states would thus rapidly be added to the confederacy, until we should soon have one unbroken line of states from the Atlantic to the Pacific, giving immense additional power and security to the Union, and facilitating intercourse between all its parts. This would be alike beneficial to the old and to the new states. To the working men of the old states, as well as of the new, it would be of incalculable advantage, not merely by affording them a home in the west, but by maintaining the wages of labor, by enabling the working classes to emigrate and become cultivators of the soil, when the rewards of daily toil should sink below a fair remuneration. Every new state, besides, adds to the customers of the old states, consuming their manufactures, employing their merchants, giving business to their vessels and canals, their railroads and cities, and a powerful impulse to their industry and prosperity. Indeed, it is the growth of the mighty west which has added, more than all other causes combined, to the power and prosperity of the whole country, whilst at the same time, through the channels of business and commerce, it has been building up immense cities in the eastern, Atlantic, and middle states, and replenishing the federal treasury with large payments from the settlers upon the public lands, rendered of real value only by their labor; and thus, from increased exports, bringing back augmented imports, and soon largely increasing the revenue of the government from that source also.

Without asking anything new from Congress, if Kansas can receive, on coming into the Union, all the usual grants, and use them judiciously, she can not only speedily cover herself with a network of railroads, but, by devoting all the rest to purposes of education, she would soon have a complete system of common schools, with normal schools, free academies, and a great university, in all of which tuition should be free to all our people. In that university the mechanic arts, with model workshops, and all the sciences should be taught, and especially agriculture in connexion with a model farm.

Although you ask nothing more in your ordinance than has been already granted to the other new states, yet in view of the sacrifice of life and property incurred by the people of Kansas, in establishing here the great principles of state and popular sovereignty, and thus perpetuating the Union, Congress, doubtless, will regard with indulgent favor the new state of Kansas, and will welcome her into the Union with joyful congratulations and a most liberal policy as to the public domain.

The full benefit of that great measure, the graduation and reduction of the price of the public lands in favor only of settlers and cultivators, so often urged by me in the Senate and in the Treasury Department, and finally adopted by Congress, should also be secured in our ordinance. Having witnessed in new states the deep injury inflicted upon them by large bodies of their most fertile land being monopolized by speculators, I suggest, in accordance with the public policy ever advocated by me, that our entire land tax, under the constitution, for the next twenty years should be confined exclusively to unoccupied land—whether owned by residents or non-residents—as one of the best means of guarding against a monopoly of our choice lands by speculators. I desire, in fact, to see our convention exercise the whole constitutional power of a state, to guard our rights and interests, and especially to protect the settlers and cultivators against the monopoly of our public domain by speculators.

As regards the school lands of the new states, the following views will be found in my reports of the 8th of December, 1847, and 9th of December, 1848, as Secretary of the Treasury of the United States:

"The recommendation contained in my last report for the establishment of ports of entry in Oregon, and the extension there of our revenue laws, is again respectfully presented to the consideration of Congress, together with donations of farms to settlers and emigrants, and the grant of a school section in the centre of every quarter of a township, which would bring the school-house within a point not exceeding a mile and a half in distance from the most remote inhabitants of such quarter township."

And again:

"My last report recommended the grant of one section of land for schools in every quarter township in Oregon. * * * * * * Congress, to some extent, adopted this recommendation by granting two school sections in each township, instead of one, for education in Oregon; but it is respectfully suggested that even thus extended the grant is still inadequate in amount, whilst the location is inconvenient, and too remote for a school which all can attend. The subject is again presented to the attention of Congress, with the recommendation that it shall be extended to California and New Mexico, and also to all the other new states and territories containing the public domain."

Acting upon the first of these recommendations, but not carrying them fully into effect, Congress doubled the school-section grants—an advance upon the former system. But, in my judgment, the benefits intended will never be fully realized until four school sections, instead of two, are granted in every township, locating the school section in the centre of every quarter township; thus, by only doubling the school sections, causing every section of the public domain in the new states to adjoin a school section, which would add immensely to the value of the public lands, whilst at the same time, affording an adequate fund not only for the establishment of common schools in every township, but of high schools, normal schools, and free academies, which, together with the five-per-cent. fund and university grant before referred to, would place Kansas in a few years, in point of science and education, in the front rank of the states of the American Union and of the world. This is a subject always regarded by me with intense interest, inasmuch as my highest hope of the perpetuity of our Union, and of the continued success of self-government, is based upon the progressive education and enlightenment of the people, enabling them fully to comprehend their own true interests, the incalculable advantages of our Union, the exemption from the power of demagogues, the control of sectional passions and prejudice, the progress of the arts and sciences, and the accumulation of knowledge, which is every day more and more becoming real power, and which will advance so much the great interests of our whole country.

These noble grants for schools and education in some of the new states have not produced all the advantages designed, for want of adequate checks and guards against improvident legislation; but I trust that the convention, by a distinct constitutional provision, will surround these lands with such guarantees, legislative, executive, judicial, and popular, as to require the combined action of the whole under the authority of the legislature in the administration of a fund so sacred.

It will be observed that these school sections and the five-per-cent. fund, or their equivalent, have always been made good to the new states by Congress, whether the lands were sold in trust, for Indians, or otherwise.

Upon looking at the location of Kansas, equidistant from north to south, and from the Atlantic to the Pacific, I find, that, within reasonable boundaries, she would be the central state of the American Union. On the north lies the Nebraska territory, soon to become a state; on the south the great and fertile Southwestern Indian Territory, soon, I hope, to become a state also. To the boundary of Kansas run nearly all the railroads of Missouri, whilst westward, northward, and southward, these routes continued through Kansas would connect her directly with Puget Sound, the mouth of the Oregon river, and San Francisco. The southern boundary of Kansas is but five hundred miles from the Gulf of Mexico, and the same railroad through the great Southwestern Indian Territory and Texas would connect her with New Orleans, with Galveston, with all the roads of Arkansas, and through Texas to San Francisco, and other points upon the Pacific; northward and eastward our lines would connect with the roads of Iowa, Illinois, Wisconsin, Nebraska, Minnesota, and the lakes of the north.

It is the people of Kansas who, in forming their state constitution, are to declare the terms on which they propose to enter the Union. Congress cannot compel the people of a territory to enter the Union as a state, or change, without their consent, the constitution framed by the people. Congress, it is true, may for constitutional reasons refuse admission, but the state alone, in forming her constitution, can prescribe the terms on which she will enter the Union. This power of the people of a territory in forming a state constitution is one of vital importance, especially in the states carved out of the public domain. Nearly all the lands of Kansas are public lands, and most of them are occupied by Indian tribes. These lands are the property of the federal government, but their right is exclusively that of a proprietor, carrying with it no political power.

Although the states cannot tax the constitutional functions of the federal government, they may assess its real estate within the limits of the state. Thus, although a state cannot tax the federal mint or custom-houses, yet it may tax the ground on which they stand, unless exempted by state authority. Such is the well-settled doctrine of the Supreme Court of the United States. In 1838 Judge McLean, of the Supreme Court of the United States, made the following decision:—

"It is true the United States held the proprietary right under the act of cession, and also the right of sovereignty until the state government was established; but the mere proprietary right, if it exist, gives no right of sovereignty. The United States may own land within a state, but political jurisdiction does not follow this ownership. Where jurisdiction is necessary, as for forts and arsenals, a cession of it is obtained from the state. Even the lands of the United States within the state are exempted from taxation by compact."

By the recent decision of the Supreme Court of the United States, so justly favorable to the rights and interest of the new states, especially those formed out of the territory acquired, like Kansas, since the adoption of the constitution, it is clear that the ownership of the public lands of such territory is viewed by the court exclusively as a proprietary right, carrying with it no political power or right of eminent domain, and affecting in no way the exercise of any of the sovereign attributes of state authority. When Kansas becomes a state, with all the attributes of state sovereignty coextensive with her limits, among these must be the taxing power, which is an inherent element of state authority. I do not dispute the title of the government to the public lands of Kansas, but I do say that this right is that of an owner only, and that, when Kansas becomes a state, the public lands are subject to taxation by state authority, like those of any individual proprietor, unless that power is relinquished by the state in the ordinance, assuming the form of a compact, by which the state is admitted into the Union.

This relinquishment of the taxing power as to the public lands, so important to the general government, and which has heretofore been exacted by Congress on their own terms from all the new states, is deeply injurious to the state, depriving her almost entirely of the principal recourse of a new state by taxation to support her government. Now that this question is conclusively settled by the Supreme Court of the United States, as a consequence of their recent decision, it is proper for the state, in making this relinquishment of the right to tax the public lands, to annex the conditions on which she consents to such exemption. This should be done in the constitution upon terms just to Kansas and to the federal government.

Should Kansas relinquish the right of taxing the public lands for equivalent, she should, in my judgment, although sustained by irresistible conclusions from the decision of the Supreme Court of the United States, and sound constitutional views of state rights, place the question in its strongest form, by asking nothing more than has been granted to the other new states, including the grants for education, railroads, &c. She will thus give the highest proof that she is not governed by sordid views, and that she means to exact nothing from Congress that is unjust or unusual.

I cannot too earnestly impress upon you the necessity of removing the slavery agitation from the halls of Congress and presidential conflicts. It is conceded that Congress has no power to interfere with slavery in the states where it exists; and if it can now be established, as is clearly the doctrine of the constitution, that Congress has no authority to interfere with the people of a territory on this subject, in forming a state constitution, the question must be removed from congressional and presidential elections.

This is the principle affirmed by Congress in the act organizing this territory, ratified by the people of the United States in the recent election, and maintained by the late decision of the Supreme Court of the United States. If this principle can be carried into successful operation in Kansas—that her people shall determine what shall be her social institutions—the slavery question must be withdrawn from the halls of Congress, and from our presidential conflicts, and the safety of the Union be placed beyond all peril; whereas, if the principle should be defeated here, the slavery agitation must be renewed in all elections throughout the country, with increasing bitterness, until it shall eventually overthrow the government.

It is this agitation which, to European powers, presents the only hope of subverting our free institutions, and, as a consequence, destroying the principle of self-government throughout the world. It is this hope that has already inflicted deep injury upon our country, exciting monarchical or despotic interference with our domestic as well as foreign affairs, and inducing their interposition, not only in our elections, but in diplomatic intercourse, to arrest our progress, to limit our influence and power, depriving us of great advantages in peaceful territorial expansion, as well as in trade with the nations of the world.

Indeed, when I reflect upon the hostile position of the European press during the recent election, and their exulting predictions of the dissolution of our Union as a consequence of the triumph of a sectional candidate, I cannot doubt that the peaceful and permanent establishment of these principles, now being subjected to their final test in Kansas, will terminate European opposition to all those measures, which must so much increase our commerce, furnish new markets for our products and fabrics, and by conservative, peaceful progress, carry our flag and the empire of our constitution into new and adjacent regions indispensable as a part of the Union to our welfare and security, adding coffee, sugar, and other articles to our staple exports, whilst greatly reducing their price to the consumer.

Nor is it only in our foreign intercourse that peace will be preserved and our prosperity advanced by the accepted fact of the permanence of our government, based upon the peaceful settlement of this question in Kansas, but at home the same sentiment will awaken renewed confidence in the stability of our institutions, give a new impulse to all our industry, and carry us onward in a career of progress and prosperity exceeding even our most sanguine expectations; a new movement of European capital will flow in upon us for permanent investment, and a new exodus of the European masses, aided by the pre-emption principle, carry westward the advancing column of American states in one unbroken phalanx to the Pacific.

And let me ask you, what possible good has been accomplished by agitating in Congress and in presidential conflicts the slavery question? Has it emancipated a single slave, or improved their condition? Has it made a single state free where slavery otherwise would have existed? Has it accelerated the disappearance of slavery from the more northern of the slaveholding states, or accomplished any practical good whatever? No, my fellow-citizens, nothing but unmitigated evil has already ensued, with disasters still more fearful impending for the future, as a consequence of this agitation.

There is a law more powerful than the legislation of man—more potent than passion or prejudice—that must ultimately determine the location of slavery in this country; it is the isothermal line; it is the law of the thermometer, of latitude or altitude, regulating climate, labor, and productions, and, as a consequence, profit and loss. Thus, even upon the mountain heights of the tropics slavery can no more exist than in northern latitudes, because it is unprofitable, being unsuited to the constitution of that sable race transplanted here from the equatorial heats of Africa. Why is it that in the Union slavery recedes from the north, and progresses south? It is this same great climatic law now operating for or against slavery in Kansas. If, on the elevated plains of Kansas, stretching to the base of our American Alps—the rocky mountains—and including their eastern crest crowned with perpetual snow, from which sweep over her open prairies those chilling blasts, reducing the average range of the thermometer here to a temperature nearly as low as that of New England, should render slavery unprofitable here, because unsuited to the tropical constitution of the negro race, the law above referred to must ultimately determine that question here, and can no more be controlled by the legislation of man than any other moral or physical law of the Almighty. Especially must this law operate with irresistible force in this country, where the number of slaves is limited, and cannot be increased by importation, where many millions of acres of sugar and cotton lands are still uncultivated, and, from the ever-augmenting demand, exceeding the supply, the price of those great staples has nearly doubled, demanding vastly more slave labor for their production.

If, from the operation of these causes, slavery should not

exist here, I trust it by no means follows that Kansas should become a state controlled by the treason and fanaticism of ablition. She has, in any event, certain constitutional duties to perform to her sister states, and especially to her immediate neighbor—the slaveholding state of Missouri. Through that great State, by rivers and railroads, must flow, to a great extent, our trade and intercourse, our imports and exports. Our entire eastern front is upon her border; from Missouri come a great number of her citizens; even the farms of the two states are cut up by the line of state boundary, part in Kansas, part in Missouri; her citizens meet us in daily intercourse; and that Kansas should become hostile to Missouri, an asylum for her fugitive slaves, or a propagandist of abolition treason, would be alike inexpedient and unjust, and fatal to the continuance of the American Union. In any event, then, I trust that the constitution of Kansas will contain such clauses as will forever secure to tho state of Missouri the faithful performance of all constitutional guarantees, not only by federal, but by state authority, and the supremacy within our limits of the authority of the Supreme Court of the United States on all constitutional questions be firmly established.

Upon the south Kansas is bounded by the great southwestern Indian territory. This is one of the most salubrious and fertile portions of this continent. It is a great cotton growing region, admirably adapted by soil and climate for the products of the south, embracing the valleys of the Arkansas and Red rivers, adjoining Texas on the south and west, and Arkansas on the east, and it ought speedily to become a state of the American Union. The Indian treaties will constitute no obstacle any more than precisely similar treaties did in Kansas; for their lands, valueless to them, now for sale, but which, sold with their consent and for their benefit, like the Indian land of Kansas, would make them a most wealthy and prosperous people; and their consent, on these terms, would be most cheerfully given. This territory contains double the area of the state of Indiana, and, if necessary, an adequate portion of the western and more elevated part could be set apart exclusively for these tribes, and the eastern and larger portion be formed into a state, and its lands sold for the benefit of these tribes (like the Indian lands of Kansas), thus greatly promoting all their interests. To the eastern boundary of this region on the state of Arkansas, run the railroads of that state; to her southern limits come the great railroads from

Louisiana and Texas, from New Orleans and Galveston, which will ultimately be joined by railroads from Kansas, leading through this Indian Territory, connecting Kansas with New Orleans, the Gulf of Mexico, and with the Southern Pacific railroad, leading through Texas to San Fransisco.

It is essential to the true interests not only of Kansas, but of Louisiana, Texas, and Arkansas, Iowa and Missouri, and the whole region west of the Mississippi, that this coterminous south-western Indian territory should speedily become a state, not only to supply us with cotton, and receive our products in return, but as occupying the area over which that portion of our railroads should run which connect us with New Orleans and Galveston, and by the southern route with the Pacific. From her central position, through or connected with Kansas, must run the central, northern, and southern routes to the Pacific; and with the latter, as well as with the Gulf, the connection can only be secured by this south-western territory becoming a state, and to this Kansas should direct her earnest attention as essential to her prosperity.

Our country and the world are regarding with profound interest the struggle now impending in Kansas. Whether we are competent to self-government—whether we can decide this controversy peacefully for ourselves by our own votes, without fraud or violence—whether the great principles of self-government and state sovereignty can be carried here into successful operation—are the questions now to be determined, and upon the plains of Kansas may now be fought the last great and decisive battle, involving the fate of the Union, of state sovereignty, of self-government, and the liberties of the world. If, my fellow-citizens, you could, even for a brief period, soften or extinguish sectional passions or prejudice, and lift yourselves to the full realization of the momentous issues intrusted to your decision, you would feel that no greater responsibility was ever devolved upon any people. It is not merely shall slavery exist in or disappear from Kansas; but, shall the great principles of self-government and state sovereignty be maintained or subverted. State sovereignty is mainly a practical principle, in so far as it is illustrated by the great sovereign right of the majority of the people, in forming a state government, to adopt their own social institutions; and this principle is disregarded whenever such decision is subverted by Congress, or overthrown by external intrusion, or by domestic fraud or violence. All those who oppose this principle are the enemies of state rights, of self-government, of the constitution and the Union. Do you love slavery so much, or hate it so intensely, that you would endeavor to establish or exclude it by fraud or violence, against the will of the majority of the people? What is Kansas, with or without slavery, if she should destroy the rights and union of the states? Where would be her schools, her free academies, her colleges and university, her towns and cities, her railroads, farms, and villages, without the Union, and the principles of self-government? Where would be her peace and prosperity, and what the value of her lands and property? Who can decide this question for Kansas, if not the people themselves? And if they cannot, nothing but the sword can become the arbiter.

On the one hand, if you can and will decide peacefully this question yourselves, I see for Kansas an immediate career of power, progress, and prosperity, unsurpassed in the history of the world. I see the peaceful establishment of our state constitution, its ratification by the people, and our immediate admission into the Union, the rapid extinguishment of Indian title, and the occupancy of those lands by settlers and cultivators; the diffusion of universal education; pre-emptions for the actual settlers; the state rapidly intersected by a network of railroads; our churches, schools, colleges, and university carrying westward the progress of law, religion, liberty, and civilization; our towns, cities and villages prosperous and progressing; our farms teeming with abundant products, and greatly appreciated in value; and peace, happiness and prosperity smiling throughout our borders. With proper clauses in our constitution, and the peaceful arbitrament of this question, Kansas may become the model state of the American Union. She may bring down upon us from north to south, from east to west, the praises and blessing of every patriotic American, and of every friend of self-government throughout the world. She may record her name on the proudest page of the history of our country and of the world, and as the youngest and last-born child of the American Union, all will hail and regard her with respect and affection.

On the other hand, if you cannot thus peacefully decide this question, fraud, violence, and injustice will reign supreme throughout our borders, and we will have achieved the undying infamy of having destroyed the liberty of our country and of the world. We will become a byword of reproach and obloquy; and all history will record the fact that Kansas was the grave of the American Union. Never was so momentous a question submitted to the decision of any people; and we cannot avoid the alternatives now placed before us of glory or of shame.

May that overruling Providence who brought our forefathers in safety to Jamestown and Plymouth—who watched over our colonial pupilage—who convened our ancestors in harmonious councils on the birthday of American independence—who gave us Washington, and carried us successfully through the struggles and perils of the revolution—who assembled, in 1787, that noble band of patriots and statesmen from north and south who framed the federal constitution—who has augmented our numbers from three millions to thirty millions, has carried us from the eastern slope of the Alleghanies through the great valleys of the Ohio, Mississippi, and Missouri, and now salutes our standard on the shores of the Pacific—rouse in our hearts a love of the whole Union, and a patriotic devotion to the whole country. May it extinguish or control all sectional passions and prejudice, and enable us to conduct to a successful conclusion the great experiment of self-government now being made within your boundaries.

Is it not infinitely better that slavery should be abolished or established in Kansas, rather than that we should become slaves and not permitted to govern ourselves? Is the absence or existence of slavery in Kansas paramount to the great questions of state sovereignty, of self-government, and of the Union? Is the sable African alone entitled to your sympathy and consideration, even if he were happier as a freeman than as a slave, either here or in St. Domingo, or the British West Indies or Spanish America, where the emancipated slave has receded to barbarism, and approaches the lowest point in the descending scale of moral, physical, and intellectual degradation? Have our white brethren of the great American and European race no claims upon our attention? Have they no rights or interests entitled to regard and protection? Shall the destiny of the African in Kansas exclude all considerations connected with our own happiness and prosperity? And is it for the handful of that race now in Kansas, or that may be hereafter introduced, that we should subvert the Union and the great principles of self-government and state sovereignty, and imbrue our hands in the blood of our countrymen! Important as this African question may be in Kansas, and which it is your solemn right to determine, it sinks into insignificance compared with the perpetuity of the Union and the final successful establishment of the principles of state sovereignty and free government. If patriotism, if devotion to the constitution and love of the Union, should not induce the minority to yield to the majority on this question, let them reflect, that in no event can the minority successfully determine this question permanently, and that in no contingency will Congress admit Kansas as a slave or free state unless a majority of the people of Kansas shall first have fairly and freely decided this question for themselves by a direct vote on the adoption of the constitution, excluding all fraud or violence. The minority, in resisting the will of the majority, may involve Kansas again in civil war; they may bring upon her reproach and obloquy, and destroy her progress and prosperity; they may keep her for years out of the Union, and, in the whirlwind of agitation, sweep away the government itself; but Kansas never can be brought into the Union with or without slavery except by a previous solemn decision, fully, freely, and fairly made by a majority of her people in voting for or against the adoption of her state constitution. Why, then, should this just, peaceful, and constitutional mode of settlement meet with opposition from any quarter? Is Kansas willing to destroy her own hopes of prosperity, merely that she may afford political capital to any party, and perpetuate the agitation of slavery throughout the Union? Is she to become a mere theme for agitators in other states, the theatre on which they shall perform the bloody drama of treason and disunion? Does she want to see the solemn acts of Congress, the decision of the people of the Union in the recent election, the legislative, executive, and judicial authorities of the country all overthrown, and revolution and civil war inaugurated throughout her limits? Does she want to be "bleeding Kansas" for the benefit of political agitators, within or out of her limits; or does she prefer the peaceful and quiet arbitrament of this question for herself? What benefit will the great body of the people of Kansas derive from these agitations? They may, for a brief period, give consequence and power to political leaders and agitators, but it is at the expense of the happiness and welfare of the great body of the people of this territory.

Those who oppose slavery in Kansas do not base their opposition upon any philanthropic principles, or any sympathy for the African race; for in their so-called constitution, framed at Topeka, they deem that entire race so inferior and degraded as to exclude them all for ever from Kansas, whether they be bond or free—thus depriving them of all rights here, and denying even that they can be citizens of the United States; for, if they are citizens, they could not constitutionally be exiled or excluded from Kansas. Yet such a clause, inserted in the Topeka constitution, was submitted by that convention for the vote of the people, and ratified here by an overwhelming majority of the anti-slavery party. This party here, therefore, has, in the most positive manner, affirmed the constitutionality of that portion of the recent decision of the Supreme Court of the United States declaring that Africans are not citizens of the United States.

This is the more important, inasmuch as this Topeka constitution was ratified, with this clause inserted, by the entire Republican party in Congress—thus distinctly affirming the recent decision of the Supreme Court of the Union, that Africans are not citizens of the United States; for if citizens, they may be elected to all offices, state and national, including the presidency itself; they must be placed upon a basis of perfect equality with the whites, serve with them in the militia, on the bench, the legislature, the jury box, vote in all elections, meet us in social intercourse, and intermarry freely with the whites. This doctrine of the perfect equality of the white with the black, in all respects whatsoever, social and political, clearly follows from the position that Africans are citizens of the United States. Nor is the Supreme Court of the Union less clearly vindicated by the position now assumed here by the published creed of this party, that the people of Kansas, in forming their state constitution (and not Congress), must decide this question of slavery for themselves. Having thus sustained the court on both the controverted points decided by that tribunal, it is hoped they will not approve the anarchical and revolutionary proceedings in other states, expunging the Supreme Court from our system by depriving it of the great power for which it was created, of expounding the constitution. If that be done, we can have in fact no unity of government or fundamental law, but just as many ever-varying constitutions as passion, prejudice, and local interests may from time to time prescribe in the thirty-one states of the Union.

I have endeavored heretofore faintly to foreshadow the wonderful prosperity, which would follow at once in Kansas the peaceful and final settlement of this question. But, if it should be in the power of agitators to prevent such a result, nothing but ruin will pervade our territory. Confidence will expire, and law and order will be subverted. Anarchy and civil war will be reinaugurated among us. All property will greatly depreciate in value. Even the best farms will become almost worthless. Our towns and cities will sink into decay. Emigration into our territory will cease. A mournful train of returning settlers, with ruined hopes and blasted fortunes, will leave our borders. All who have purchased property at present prices will be sacrificed, and Kansas will be marked by universal ruin and desolation.

Nor will the mischief be arrested here. It will extend into every other state. Despots will exult over the failure here of the great principles of self-government, and the approaching downfall of our confederacy. The pillars of the Union will rock upon their base, and we may close the next presidential conflict amid the scattered fragments of the constitution of our once happy and united people. The banner of the stars and stripes, the emblem of our country's glory, will be rent by contending factions. We shall no longer have a country. The friends of human liberty in other realms will shrink despairing from the conflict. Despotic power will resume its sway throughout the world, and man will have tried in vain the last experiment of self-government. The architects of our country's ruin, the assassins of her peace and prosperity, will share the same common ruin of all our race. They will meet, whilst living, the bitter curses of a ruined people, whilst history will record as their only epitaph: *These were the destroyers of the American Union, of the liberties of their country and of the world.*

But I do not despair of the republic. My hope is in the patriotism and intelligence of the people; in their love of country, of liberty, and of the Union. Especially is my confidence unbounded in the hardy pioneers and settlers of the west. It was such settlers of a new state devoted to the constitution and the Union, whom I long represented in the Senate of the United States, and whose rights and interests it was my pride and pleasure there, as well as in the treasury department, to protect and advocate. It was men like these whose rifles drove back the invader from the plains of Orleans, and planted the stars and stripes upon the victorious field of Mexico. These are the men whom gold cannot corrupt nor foes intimidate. From their towns and villages, from their farms and cottages, spread over the beautiful prairies of Kansas, they will come forward now in defence of the constitution and the Union. These are the glorious legacy they received from our fathers, and they will transmit to their children the priceless heritage. Before the peaceful power of their suffrage this dangerous sectional agitation will disappear, and peace and prosperity once more reign throughout our borders. In the hearts of this noble band of patriotic settlers the love of their country and of the Union is inextinguishable. It leaves them not in death, but follows them into that higher realm, where, with Washington and Franklin, and their noble compatriots, they look down with undying affection upon their country, and offer up their fervent prayers that the Union and the constitution may be perpetual. For recollect, my fellow-citizens, that it is the constitution that makes the Union, and unless that immortal instrument, bearing the name of the Father of his Country, shall be maintained entire in all its wise provisions and sacred guarantees, our free institutions must perish.

My reliance also is unshaken upon the same overruling Providence which has carried us triumphantly through so many perils and conflicts, which has lifted us to a height of power and prosperity unexampled in history, and, if we shall maintain the constitution and the Union, points us to a future more glorious and sublime than mind can conceive or pen describe. The march of our country's destiny, like that of His first chosen people, is marked by the foot-prints of the steps of God. The constitution and the Union are "the cloud by day, and the pillar of fire by night," which will carry us safely under his guidance, through the wilderness and bitter waters, into the promised and ever-extending fields of our country's glory. It is His hand which beckons us onward in the pathway of peaceful progress and expansion, of power and renown, until our continent, in the distant future, shall be covered by the folds of the American banner, and, instructed by our example, all the nations of the world, through many trials and sacrifices, shall establish the great principles of our constitutional confederacy of free and sovereign states.

R. J. Walker.

THE END.

www.ingramcontent.com/pod-product-compliance
Lightning Source LLC
LaVergne TN
LVHW010202110826
845151LV00002B/582

* 9 7 8 1 4 2 5 5 3 5 2 0 9 *